Storyworlds across Media

Frontiers of Narrative

Storyworlds across Media

Toward a Media-Conscious Narratology

EDITED BY MARIE-LAURE RYAN
AND JAN-NOËL THON

University of Nebraska Press | Lincoln and London

Manufactured in the United States of America.

Publication of this volume was assisted by the Research Unit Media Convergence at the Johannes Gutenberg-University of Mainz, Germany.

Library of Congress Cataloging-in-Publication Data

Storyworlds across media: toward a media-conscious narratology / edited by Marie-Laure Ryan and Jan-Noël Thon.
p. cm.—(Frontiers of narrative)
Includes bibliographical references and index.
ISBN 978-0-8032-4563-1 (pbk.: alk. paper)
ISBN 978-0-8032-5532-6 (pdf)
ISBN 978-0-8032-5533-3 (epub)
ISBN 978-0-8032-5534-0 (mobi) 1. Narration (Rhetoric) 2. Discourse analysis, Narrative. 3. Storytelling in mass media. 4. Mass media and language. I. Ryan, Marie-Laure, 1946– editor of compilation. II. Thon, Jan-Noël, editor of compilation.
P96.N35S86 2014
302.2301'4—dc23
2014003405

Set in Minion Pro by Renni Johnson.
Designed by A. Shahan.

Contents

Illustrations

Acknowledgments

All the contributions collected in this volume are based on papers presented at the international conference *Storyworlds across Media: Mediality—Multimodality—Transmediality*, which took place from June 30 to July 2, 2011, at the Johannes Gutenberg-University of Mainz, Germany. We are greatly indebted to Karl N. Renner and his colleagues from the Research Unit Media Convergence and the Transmedial Narration Work Group for inviting us to stay in Mainz and for co-organizing the conference with us.

Patrick Colm Hogan's contribution to this volume, "Emplotting a Storyworld in Drama: Selection, Time, and Construal in *Hamlet*," first appeared in Hogan's *How Authors' Minds Make Stories* (Cambridge, UK: Cambridge University Press, 2013. Print).

Jesper Juul's contribution to this volume, "On Absent Carrot Sticks: The Level of Abstraction in Video Games," contains portions of his chapter "A Certain Level of Abstraction" in *Situated Play: DiGRA 2007 Conference Proceedings*, ed. Akira Baba (Tokyo: DiGRA Japan, 2007. 510–15. Print).

Storyworlds across Media

Storyworlds across Media

Introduction

Popular culture has accustomed us to narratives that refuse to leave the stage, returning repeatedly for another round of applause and for another pot of gold. For examples, think of the many installments of the novel-based franchises of *The Lord of the Rings* and *A Song of Ice and Fire*, the movie-based franchises of *Star Wars* and *Indiana Jones*, the comics-based franchises of *Batman* and *Spiderman*, or the video game–based franchises of *Tomb Raider* and *Warcraft*. Each of the sequels, prequels, adaptations, transpositions, or modifications that make up the body of these franchises spins a story that provides instant immersion, because the recipient is spared the cognitive effort of building a world and its inhabitants from a largely blank state. The world is already in place when the recipient takes his or her first steps in it, once again.

Following the established custom of the sequel, this book builds upon another book one of us edited in 2004, *Narrative across Media*. We decided to call the present book *Storyworlds across Media* instead of *Narrative across Media II*, though, in order to reflect the new directions that the study of the multiple medial incarnations of narrative has taken in the meantime. The replacement of "narrative" with "storyworld" acknowledges the emergences of the concept of "world" not only in narratology but also on the broader cultural scene. Nowadays we have not only multimodal representations of storyworlds that combine various types of signs and virtual online worlds that wait to be filled with stories by their player citizens but also serial storyworlds that span multiple installments and transmedial storyworlds that are deployed simultaneously across multiple media platforms, resulting in a media landscape in which creators and fans alike constantly expand, revise, and even parody them. Another difference between the present volume and the original *Narrative across Media* is the scope of the term "across." In *Narrative across Media*, it referred to the comparison of the expressive power of different media with respect to the cognitive construct constitutive of narrativity, for stories and their worlds are crucially shaped by the affordances and limitations of the media in which they are realized. Now, however, "across" is taken in both this comparative sense and in an additional sense that refers to the expansion of transmedial storyworlds across multiple media.

Thinking of storyworlds as representations that transcend media not only expands the scope of narratology beyond its "native" territory of language-based narrative (native both because language was among the first media in which stories were told and because classical narratology was developed primarily with literary fiction in mind) but also provides a much-needed center of convergence and point of comparison to media studies. The explosion of new types of media in the twentieth century and their ever-increasing role in our daily life have led to a strong sense that "understanding media" (McLuhan) is key to understanding the dynamics of culture and society. Media are widely credited with the power to shape opinions and to participate in what has been called the "social construction of reality" (Berger and Luckman). But where, might we ask, does this power to construct social reality come from? For narratologists, the evident answer from media's ability to transmit stories that shape our view of the world and affect our behavior. The stories transmitted by media do not have to concern the real world to produce real behaviors. Indeed, one only needs to look at the fan cultures that develop around the sprawling fictional narratives of film and television or at the distinctive social habits of the diverse groups of players who immerse themselves in increasingly complex game worlds to find examples of a much more direct interrelation between "fictional" narrative representation and "real" social interaction.

The proliferation of the term "media convergence" (Jenkins) in the discourses of advertising and academia has created the sense that media are currently entering a new phase of control over culture and over our lives, capturing us in their increasingly thick web. But until we are able to tell what it is that media converge around, the term will remain a buzzword—as it was in the slogan of a 2003 technology exhibit in New Orleans: "Come worship at the altar of convergence" (Jenkins 6). In *Storyworlds across Media,* we take the deliberate step of placing narrative at the center of media convergence. This center can be conceived of in both a concrete and an abstract sense. In a concrete sense, it consists of a specific story or rather, to use the other concept of our title, of a specific storyworld; different media converge around this world by presenting different aspects of it. This form of convergence is illustrated nowadays by the previously mentioned tendency of popular narratives, such as *The Lord of the Rings*, *Star Wars*, *Batman*, or *Tomb Raider*, to migrate from medium to medium in any imaginable order. But while particularly widespread in contemporary culture, this practice is not unique to it, as the multiple medial incarnations of Greek myths or biblical stories demonstrate for Western civilization.

The other way to conceive of the center of convergence is to associate it not with a particular narrative but more generally with the abstract type of content constitutive of "narrativity," a content that we can define as that which all stories share. Here, again, the concept of storyworld plays a prominent role, for it captures the kind of mental representation that a text must evoke in order to qualify as narrative. David Herman describes narratives as "blueprints for a specific mode of world-creation" (105), but it would be more appropriate to say "world imagination," for while the author creates the storyworld through the production of signs, it is the reader, spectator, listener, or player who uses the blueprint of a finished text to construct a mental image of this world. The convergence of media around a common center that we may call "narrativity"—a center that is itself organized around a storyworld—will serve as an opportunity to capture their distinctive narrative resources. In this case it is not convergence per se that we are interested in but the divergences that the common center reveals. To parody the title of an article by Seymour Chatman, the leading question now becomes: what can medium *x* do in terms of storyworld creation (or representation) that medium *y* cannot?

Any attempt to adequately discuss the manifestation of narrative meaning in different media must begin with the assessment of the relations between narratological concepts and media categories. We would like to suggest that these relations cover, at least theoretically, a scale ranging from "medium free" to "medium specific," with various degrees of transmedial validity in the middle. Or to put it another way, the transmedial applicability of narratological concepts ranges from "all media" to "one" or perhaps even to "none." (This case would apply to the narratological description of media that have yet to be invented, such as a medium that would allow users to touch the head of characters in a visual display and see a three-dimensional [3-D] film of their thoughts.) Solid candidates for the *medium-free* pole are the defining components of narrativity: character, events, setting, time, space, and causality. A good example of a *transmedially* valid yet not medium-free concept is interactivity. It is applicable to video games, improvisational theater, hypertext fiction, tabletop role-playing games, and even oral storytelling, if one considers the impact of the audience on the narrative performance, but not to literary narrative, print-based comics, and film. *Medium-specific* concepts, finally, are explicitly developed for a certain medium, but they can occasionally be extended to other media through a metaphoric transfer. For instance, the concepts of gutter, frame, and the arrangement of panels on a page are tailor-made for the medium of comics. But since narratologists hardly ever agree on the definition of any term, the borders between the three types of concepts are relatively fuzzy. As a point in case, some narratologists regard a "narrator" as constitutive of narrativity, which makes it medium free, while others regard it as a transmedial concept applicable only to narratives with a language track. Furthermore, there is usually ample latitude for transferring seemingly medium-specific concepts to other media, just as there is often a need to modify seemingly transmedial concepts with regard to the specific affordances and limitations of a particular medium.

The essays collected in this volume are all concerned with the representation of storyworlds across media and with the further development of a media-conscious narratology, but they can be grouped into three parts according to their specific focus.[1] The first section addresses theoretical problems of mediality and transmediality, the second section deals with issues of multimodality and intermediality, and the third section discusses the relationship between media convergence and transmedial storyworlds. To help readers plan their journey through this book we present a brief sketch of the theoretical background and core arguments of the various chapters.

Part 1: Mediality and Transmediality

The first section, "Mediality and Transmediality," is devoted to the expansion of classical narratology, which has traditionally been concerned with literary narrative, into what we have called a "media-conscious narratology." The particular focus of the section is on the distinction—or, rather, the interrelation—between medium-free, transmedially applicable, and medium-specific terms and concepts. The first chapter, Marie-Laure Ryan's "Story/Worlds/Media: Tuning the Instruments of a Media-Conscious Narratology," provides a common theoretical basis to both the project of a media-conscious narratology and to the chapters to come by proposing definitions of the two leading concepts of the title—*media* and *storyworld*. Aiming to expand media theory beyond the purely technological approach that currently dominates the field in the United States—an approach that, for example, cannot justify regarding comics as an autonomous medium since they rely on the same technological support as print literature—Ryan suggests that *medium* is best understood as an inherently polyvalent term whose meaning involves a technological, semiotic, and cultural dimension. The degree of prominence of these three dimensions differs from medium to medium, but all of them must be taken into consideration in the description of a medium's narrative affordances and limitations. Ryan's discussion of storyworld similarly reveals two different possible conceptions of this notion—the logical and the imaginative. In a *logical* conception, storyworlds admit no contradiction. Thus if a text rewrites an existing narrative, modifying the plot and ascribing different features or destinies to the characters, it creates a new storyworld that overlaps to some extent with the old one. While a given storyworld can be presented through several different texts, these texts must respect the facts of the original text if they are to share its logical storyworld. In an *imaginative* conception, by contrast, a storyworld consists of named existents and perhaps of an invariant setting (though the setting can be expanded), but the properties of these existents and their destinies may vary from text to text. Whether logical or imaginative, however, the concept of storyworld will only earn a legitimate place in the toolbox of narratology if it opens new perspectives on the relations between media and narrative. To demonstrate the theoretical usefulness of the notion, Ryan examines the interplay of world-internal and world-external elements in various media.

Among transmedially valid concepts, few have caused as much controversy as the seemingly intuitive concept of the *narrator*. Debates have been raging about whether it is medium free—that is, constitutive of all narratives, limited to media with a language track, or even optional within these media. Several scholars have spoken of a cinematic narrator, or narrator-*ersatz*, but comparatively few have applied the concept to drama, as does Patrick Colm Hogan in his contribution to this volume, "Emplotting a Storyworld in Drama: Selection, Time, and Construal in the Discourse of *Hamlet*." Hogan believes that his notion of dramatic narrator is not essential to the main point of his chapter, but the reasons that lead him to speak of a narrator, even in the case of discourse spoken by a character, are worth examining for what they tell us about drama. Traditionally, drama is taken to represent dialogue between characters; this dialogue supposedly takes as much time on stage as it does in the storyworld. Against this overly realistic conception, Hogan argues that the speech of the characters is not limited to communicative speech acts and that time does not necessarily pass at the speed required by the dialogue. Soliloquies are a prime example of a noncommunicative use of speech, if one conceives of communication as transmitting information to other people native to the same world. Much of what is said in soliloquies is actually addressed to the audience. Moreover, soliloquies provide far more extensive access to the mind of a character than what one can infer from most spoken discourse. Hogan's reasoning can be reconstructed as follows: if the information provided by Hamlet's speech were offered in a novel, it would be presented as a report of thought, and we would attribute it to an omniscient narrator. By analogy, Hogan proposes to speak of a dramatic narrator who can turn off and on the power to read the mind of characters and to transpose the result of this reading into what looks like speech. As already mentioned, however, we do not have to accept this conception of the narrator to follow Hogan's analysis of the emplotting strategies—that is, the presentation of events that aims at achieving a particular effect on the audience—in *Hamlet*. The concept of storyworld plays a major role in this functional approach insofar as the idea of a large world containing far more facts, thoughts, and events than the play can represent is essential to the notions of selection and construal. These operations represent the work of the playwright (or implied playwright or dramatic narrator) as deciding what to show and what to keep hidden in order to arouse certain affective or purely aesthetic emotions. In reading (or watching) *Hamlet*, then, it is as if William Shakespeare contemplated a complete world in his mind, a world where specific events took place, and out of the many ways to em-plot these events, he chose the one that would generate the greatest interest of the audience.

Not only are narrative representations emplotted by a (real or represented) narrating agent, but also they provide, as one of their most salient prototypical features, what has been described as "experientialities" or "qualia." It comes as no surprise, then, that both classical and contemporary narratology have given the problem of *subjectivity*—or, more precisely, of the various strategies that a narrative representation may employ in order to represent the mind of a character—a considerable amount of attention. Accordingly, Jan-Noël Thon's "Subjectivity across Media: On Transmedial Strategies of Subjective Representation in Contemporary Feature Films, Graphic Novels, and Computer Games" examines what can be described as transmedial strategies of subjective representation. These strategies allow the spectator, reader, or player to assume a specific kind of direct relationship between the narrative representation and a character's consciousness. Arguing against the prolonged use of terms such as "point of view," "perspective," and "focalization," which have become increasingly vague and open to misunderstanding over the past four decades, Thon begins by introducing a heuristic distinction between subjective, intersubjective, and objective modes of representation that allows for a bottom-up analysis of local, as well as global, structures of subjectivity. If *intersubjective* representation can be considered the unmarked case in which storyworld elements are represented as they are perceived by a group of characters, objective representation and subjective representation are both marked cases, albeit on opposing ends of a continuum of subjectivity. While *objective* representation implies that the storyworld elements in question are not perceived or imagined by any characters at all, *subjective* representation implies that the storyworld elements in question are (subjectively) perceived or imagined by only one character. In a second step, Thon identifies and discusses a number of particularly salient pictorial strategies of subjective representation such as "point-of-view sequences," "(quasi-)perceptual point-of-view sequences," "(quasi-)perceptual overlay," and the "representation of internal worlds." Finally he examines the medium-specific realization of these transmedial strategies of subjective representation in the conventionally distinct media of contemporary feature films, graphic novels, and computer games, emphasizing the dual perspective of a narratology that is both transmedial in analytic scope and media conscious in methodological orientation.

Even if one accepts the idea of transmedially valid narratological concepts, then, these concepts usually need to be fine-tuned to the medium to which they are applied. Comparable to Thon's contribution, Frank Zipfel's "Fiction across Media: Toward a Transmedial Concept of Fictionality" examines the medium-specific realization of the transmedial concept of *fictionality* for literature, theater, and film. Zipfel proposes a multilayered approach to fictionality based on three components: a *world criterion*, which stipulates that in order to pass as fictional, the storyworld must comprise invented elements; a *cognitive criterion*, according to which readers or spectators must engage in a game of make-believe; and an *institutional component*, describing the cultural practices and representational conventions that relate to the medium. While the world criterion remains basically identical for the three media, Zipfel shows that make-believe takes on different nuances in theater and film, where the make-believe of the actors induces make-believe in the spectator, as opposed to literature, where it is a unilateral action of the reader responding to the text. When it comes to the institutional component of fictionality, however, medium-specific differences are much more substantial. One of these differences relates to the number of worlds involved. Theater, as a performance art, depends on a tripartite distinction between the fictional world of the invariant text, the production world imagined by the director, and the highly variable world created by the actors in every performance. A second institutional difference concerns the role of the text, which is major in literature and theater, since drama can be read as a form of literature, but minor in film, since scripts are usually not published. A third difference lies in the possibility to present both fictional and nonfictional worlds. This possibility is available in literature and film but not in drama, as even the most historically accurate play departs from the real world through its use of actors to impersonate the characters.

While Thon and Zipfel explore the various manifestations of subjectivity and fictionality in different media, Werner Wolf's "Framings of Narrative in Literature and the Pictorial Arts" investigates the medium-specific clues that lead audiences to apply a narrative frame to the interpretation of a text. *Frame*, in Wolf's terminology, has both a macro-level and a micro-level manifestation. On the macro level, it refers to the global cognitive model that users activate to make sense of a text; this type of frame corresponds, broadly, to the narrative and descriptive text-types, both of which can be realized in either language-based or visual texts. On the micro-level, frame refers to the internal or external clues that activate a certain type of macro-frame. A particularly salient type of clue resides in paratextual devices such as genre labels for literary texts ("novel," "memoir," "biography") or titles for a painting. Yet as Wolf shows, in some contexts the paratextual indicators are either absent or ambiguous. Many paintings lack titles, or their titles may be deceptive; think of Marcel Duchamp's *La Mariée mise à nu par ses célibataires, même* (*The Bride Stripped Bare by Her Bachelors, Even*), an abstract work that mocks the narrativity promised by its title. In literature, while the term "novel" sends the reader on a search for narrative design, this search may be frustrated (as in some postmodern novels), or the generic label may be neutral with respect to narrativity. Such is the case, Wolf argues, with lyric poetry. While Wolf's investigation could select any medium capable of both narrative and descriptive manifestations, his choice of literature and pictorial arts is particularly illuminating, because it pits against each other two media with strongly contrasting features: literature is a temporal art with immense narrative resources, while painting is a spatial art with limited narrative potential. While paintings can suggest stories, either these stories are known to the spectator from other sources, or, as Wolf observes, they correspond to stereotypical scripts, such as the seduction (or rape) of a young woman depicted in a pair of paintings by William Hogarth. Through his choice of media, Wolf situates his analysis in the time-honored tradition of Gotthold Ephraim Lessing's *Laocoön*, whose distinction between temporal and spatial forms of art should be regarded as one of the cornerstones of a media-conscious narratology.

Part 2: Multimodality and Intermediality

Moving beyond the rather fundamental distinction between medium-free, transmedial, and medium-specific narratological concepts, the chapters in the second part of this volume focus on two different kinds of relationships between media that seem particularly relevant for the project of a media-conscious narratology—multimodality and intermediality. Through *multimodality* (a term that is currently replacing multimediality; see, e.g., Kress and van Leeuwen), different types of signs combine within the same media object—for example, moving image, spoken language, music, and sometimes text in film—while through *intermediality,* texts of a given medium send tendrils toward other media (see Rajewsky). These tendrils can include cross-medial adaptation (film to video game), references within the text to other media objects (a painting playing an important role in a novel), imitation by a medium of the resources of another medium (hypertext structure in print), and ekphrasis, or other forms of description of a type of sign through another type (music or visual artifacts described in language).

Multimodality is found on two levels—the level of the medium and the level of genre. The distinction between medium and genre is admittedly difficult to define (for an attempt see Ryan, *Avatars* 27–28), but given this distinction, the two types of multimodality are easy to understand. On the one hand, multimodality is a feature of medium when the specific nature of the latter implies multiple types of signs; for instance, inherent to the medium of film is its inclusion of images, language, and music. On the other hand, multimodality is a feature of genre when both monomodal and multimodal works are possible within the same genre (and of course within the same medium, since medium is a defining feature of genre). In this case, multimodality is an innovation with respect to a standard monomediality that creates a new subgenre. Consider a musical composition that includes narration such as Sergei Prokofieff's *Peter and the Wolf* as compared to a Beethoven symphony or a novel that includes images compared to a traditional text-only novel.

Wolfgang Hallet discusses this generic type of multimodality in "The Rise of the Multimodal Novel: Generic Change and Its Narratological Implications." Hallet observes that, with its combination of text and images, the multimodal novel comes closer to perception and cognition than monomodal novels do, since our "ways of worldmaking" (Goodman) involve all the senses in addition to language. It is indeed interesting to note that the rise of the multimodal novel coincides with developments in cognitive science that put on equal footing visual and language-based thinking—in stark contrast to the structuralist and poststructuralist claim that language is the foundation of all mental life. Hallet's chapter focuses on three recent American novels whose heroes are children with exceptional cognitive abilities: a savant with Asperger's syndrome, a young inventor, and a genius cartographer. All three characters construct the world much more by means of the photos, maps, diagrams, and tables of data shown in each novel than through language, though language remains the principal narrative mode of signification. Take away the pictures and you still have a story, but take away the text and you have only a disparate collection of visual documents that do not cohere into a whole. Yet if the multimodal novel comes closer to perception and cognition than the monomodal novel does, it still cannot be said to offer a simulation of perception, as does the multimodality of film, because the novel's various signs are presented in distinct frames rather than fused into a homogeneous stream. Consequently it takes an interruption of the process of reading or scrutinizing, one that Hallet compares to the hypertextual practice of jumping from lexia to lexia, in order to pass from text to image and vice versa. This breaking up of linear continuity results in a much more acute *meta-semiotic awareness*, or *modal self-referentiality*, than the fluid and perceptively much more natural multimodality of film, drama, or computer games.

In contrast to Hallet, who discusses an occasionally multimodal genre, Jesper Juul's "On Absent Carrot Sticks: The Level of Abstraction in Video Games" deals with an inherently multimodal medium, since most video games involve haptics, visuals, music, spoken language, and written text. For Juul, video games are not stories—at least not stories in the sense that films and novels are—but rather fictional worlds in which a variety of actions can take place. The common notion of a fictional world forms the basis of a comparison that highlights the (medium) specific features of games on the one hand and novels and films on the other. Borrowing Ryan's principle of minimal departure (MD), as expressed in *Possible Worlds* (chapter 3), Juul claims that both players and readers engage in acts of imagination that conceive of the fictional world as fuller than its strictly textual representation. When a novel mentions a knife lying next to carrots in a kitchen, you imagine that it should be possible in this world to cut the carrot into sticks. MD would tell you to make the same assumption for a game that takes place in a visually represented kitchen; yet, and this point is where an important distinction between "interactive" *game worlds* and "traditional" *fictional worlds* kicks in, the player may find out that the knife can only cut carrots, not turnips nor people's heads, and that it can only cut them into slices. While the game depends to some degree on MD (to facilitate the learning process), it resists its full application. Playing a game in a fictional world therefore means learning which aspects of the world have rules attached to them and which ones do not; thus the proportion of world features attached to rules determines a game's level of abstraction. The rules of video games, Juul reminds us, are abstract principles implemented by the computer through calculation; yet unless the rules allow for fascinating gameplay (as in chess), it is the imaginative act of locating oneself in a fictional world that makes many games exciting. While in novels and films immersion in the fictional world is a sufficient source of satisfaction, in games it must be complemented by a sense of achievement that the ability to play the game efficiently provides. In order to develop this ability, the player must be able to detect the abstract structure determined by the rules, a structure that attributes strategic significance to certain aspects of the fictional world and treats others as decorative, immersion-enhancing features.

While Hallet's and Juul's contributions focus on the narrative affordances and limitations of two multimodal media that could hardly be any more different from each other, Jared Gardner's "Film + Comics: A Multimodal Romance in the Age of Transmedial Convergence" examines the relationship between graphic and audiovisual narratives from a more historical perspective. Tracing the history of the intermedial relationship between comics and film from their birth at the end of the nineteenth century and their rise in popular demand throughout the twentieth century to the current situation, where film often appears to be the dominant partner, Gardner combines an encyclopedic knowledge of both film and comics history with an acute awareness of the institutional and economic contexts of convergent media culture in order to paint a precise picture of how the texts of each of these media are shaped, at least partly, by their long-standing intermedial relationship. According to Gardner, certain changes in the ways contemporary Hollywood cinema narrates its stories can be explained by the influence of comics' conventions on both directors and spectators, as the advent of DVDs increasingly taught the latter how to "read" films closely, engagedly, and repeatedly—that is, how to "read" films as comics readers tend to read comics. While comics have proved to be one of the media most resistant to digitalization, they also seem, at least to Gardner, to be the form most capable of teaching us how to explore the multimodal narratives of the twenty-first century. With their looping, elliptical, and multimodal storytelling strategies, comics have always been a medium open to experimentation, but their status as a "gutter form," both in the formal and in the cultural sense, as well as their resistance to being co-opted by film and other media, serves as a reminder of the importance of institutional and cultural contexts for media-conscious narratology.

Jeff Thoss's "Tell It Like a Game: *Scott Pilgrim* and Performative Media Rivalry" also deals with the intermedial relationships between film and comics, but rather than examining these relations from a broad historical perspective, as Gardner does, he focuses on a particular case—namely, Edgar Wright's 2010 film adaptation of Bryan Lee O'Malley's comic book series *Scott Pilgrim* (2004–10). According to Thoss, the comic book and the film version attempt to outdo each other in their imitation of a third medium—in this case, computer games. The comic book series already makes its readers well aware of the ubiquity of the intermedial references through its plot, which revolves around twenty-something Scott Pilgrim's attempt to win over Ramona Flowers in Toronto. While this brief description may sound similar to any other tired boy-meets-girl story, it turns out that in order to "win" Ramona, Scott must defeat her seven evil ex-boyfriends in a number of ever more spectacular fights, evidently inspired by the beat-'em-up genre of video games. Moreover, the film and the comic books present a number of features, such as representational techniques, extra lives, or save points, that clearly originate in the worlds of computer games. Though these intermedial references are all already present in the comic book series, Thoss goes on to show that the film attempts to outdo the comic book series in its emulation of video game features both on the level of the storyworld and on the level of its representation. But as neither of these two works emerges victorious, their so-called rivalry appears less as a real competition than as a way to illuminate the specific narrative affordances and limitations of comics, films, and computer games.

Concluding the section, Marco Caracciolo's "Those Insane Dream Sequences: Experientiality and Distorted Experience in Literature and Video Games" uses a more general comparative approach to capture a fundamental, almost paradoxical feature of narrative: in order to let recipients attribute mental states to the characters, stories must tap into their "experiential background," yet at the same time narrative expands this background so that recipients can share with the characters experiences that they have never had in real life. Caracciolo addresses this paradox through a close reading of two texts that focus on altered states of consciousness—William Burroughs's experimental novel *Naked Lunch* and the video game *Max Payne*. Both of these texts represent distorted experience through textual clues that exploit the particular resources of their respective medium. In *Naked Lunch*, the reader is shuttled back and forth between the world of a character's drug-induced hallucination and the real world through the use of three strategies typical of literary narrative: *metaphor, internal focalization*, and a handling of *dialogue* that brutally brings the hallucinating character (as well as the reader) back to reality. In *Max Payne*, the experience of waking up from a coma is represented through the embedding of visual panels inspired by graphic novels. This borrowing of resources from another medium reminds us that digital technology is not only a medium but also a meta-medium capable of encoding and displaying any type of signs. In addition to static graphic panels, *Max Payne* uses *cut-scenes*, a standard feature of computer games, to represent dream sequences, but it gives them an unusual twist by allowing the player a low grade of agency. Rather than watching the dream sequences as though they were movies, the player guides Max, the dreamer, in a tour of several locations. Since this tour is strictly linear, offering no choice of itinerary, the dream sequences blur the borderline between pre-rendered cut-scenes and genuinely interactive episodes in which the player must display gaming skills. This limited form of interactivity not only reflects the "painful lack of agency" that dreamers may experience but also allegorizes the illusory nature of the player's sense of free will, since the game's developer considerably shapes the course of events in the vast majority of narrative games.

Part 3: Transmedia Storytelling and Transmedial Worlds

In the first section of this volume, the term "transmediality" was used to describe the applicability of a theoretical concept to different media. Here we turn to another kind of transmediality commonly found in the age of "media convergence," the representation of a single storyworld through multiple media. This specific type of transmedial phenomenon has been discussed under a variety of labels, but the terms "transmedia storytelling" (coined by Jenkins) and "transmedial worlds" (coined by Klastrup and Tosca) have proved to be most influential. According to

Jenkins, "[a] transmedia story unfolds across multiple media platforms, with each new text making a distinctive and valuable contribution to the whole" (95–96). While Jenkins tends to emphasize the coherence of the transmedia story, favoring a logical understanding of the concept of storyworld, Lisbeth Klastrup and Susana Tosca propose to understand transmedial worlds as "abstract content systems from which a repertoire of fictional stories and characters can be actualized or derived across a variety of media forms" (n. pag.), favoring an imaginative understanding of the concept of storyworld. Whether we follow Jenkins or Klastrup and Tosca, whose respective concepts may best be thought of as complementary rather than contradictory anyway, the steadily growing phenomenon of the transmedial representation of storyworlds is a highly productive field of study for the project of a media-conscious narratology.

Emphasizing that few kinds of storytelling can match the TV serial for narrative breadth, Jason Mittell's "Strategies of Storytelling on Transmedia Television" examines how television has given rise to innovative narrative forms in the 2000s and beyond. Briefly touching on the history of transmedial representations—from biblical narratives to nineteenth-century transmedial characters such as Frankenstein or Sherlock Holmes, as well as from the comparatively rare forms of transmedial expansion in the early twentieth century to the proliferation of transmedia franchises in today's media culture—Mittell focuses on contemporary forms of transmedial expansions whose functions go beyond merely hyping, promoting, or introducing another text to a larger audience. Acknowledging, at the same time, the challenges presented by the economic and institutional realities of commercial television and the powerful and innovative potential of some of its attempts at transmedia storytelling, Mittell examines two fairly different transmedial strategies as they are realized by the franchises surrounding the television series *Lost* and *Breaking Bad*. Mittell describes *Lost* as being primarily characterized by a *centrifugal*, or storyworld-driven, use of transmedial expansions aiming at a coherent and consistent representation of the storyworld across media. When compared to *Lost*'s focus on consistent storyworld expansion, *Breaking Bad* is primarily characterized by a *centripetal*, or character-driven, use of transmedial extensions aiming not so much at an expansion of the storyworld itself but at providing additional depths to its already well-established characters. Since the centrifugal expansion of *Lost* tends to focus on a logically consistent expansion of the storyworld while the centripetal expansion of *Breaking Bad* more readily offers hypothetical scenarios and alternative story lines to the audience, Mittell concludes by suggesting that the two shows exemplify what can be described as "What Is" versus "What If?" strategies of transmedia television.

Colin B. Harvey's "A Taxonomy of Transmedia Storytelling" engages even more explicitly and comprehensively with the variety of phenomena commonly associated with transmedia storytelling than Mittell does. Building on the well-established notion that consistency—or the lack thereof—is a central feature of transmedia storytelling, Harvey develops a taxonomy based on the legal relationship between elements in a franchise, as well as on the specific forms of collective remembering, misremembering, non-remembering, or forgetting that they engender. Emphasizing that digitalization is not a necessary condition of transmedia storytelling and that the sheer vastness of possible combinations between analogue and digital media renders a medium-based taxonomy problematic, he distinguishes between six particularly salient forms that may play a part in a given transmedia storytelling franchise: *intellectual property, directed transmedia storytelling, devolved transmedia storytelling, detached transmedia storytelling, directed transmedia storytelling with user participation*, and *emergent user-generated transmedia storytelling*. Using the *Doctor Who*, *Highlander*, and *Tron* franchises as his primary examples, Harvey shows that parts of a franchise are "authorized" in different ways and that these parts vary in the requirements they make on both the producers' and the recipients' memories. On the one hand, what parts of a franchise's previous stories should be remembered is subject to negotiations not only between the producers and the recipients but also between the various parties of what one may call the "author collective." On the other hand, legally binding contracts allow the legal owner(s) of a given franchise to control the extent to which their in-house operatives and licensees are allowed to remember, forget, non-remember, and misremember parts of the transmedia story, its characters, and its setting.

Building on their previous works on transmedial worlds, Lisbeth Klastrup and Susana Tosca's "*Game of Thrones*: Transmedial Worlds, Fandom, and Social Gaming" explores the various ways in which fans can be involved with a transmedial world, particularly focusing on the still under-researched area of fan participation and involvement through social media. As we have already mentioned, Klastrup and Tosca understand transmedial worlds as "abstract content systems" that can be identified via a common core of features defining their "worldness": first, the *mythos* of a transmedial world establishes its backstory, key events that give meaning to the current situation of the world; second, the *topos* describes the world's setting in space and time, the changing landscape, and unfolding of events; and, third, the *ethos* of a transmedial world defines its explicit and implicit norms and values, moral codices, and ethical conducts. Taking as their example *The Maester's Path*, an online game experience designed to generate excitement for the launch of *Game of Thrones*, the TV series based on George R. R. Martin's best-selling novel series *A Song of Ice and Fire*, Klastrup and Tosca combine qualitative and quantitative methods to explore both the development and reception of the social game and the surrounding marketing campaign that took place from February 2011 to July 2011. They show in some detail how the recipients—or fans—responded to the specific medial affordances provided by the combination of online game elements and social media in the context of a considerably larger transmedial world. Not only does Klastrup and Tosca's contribution remind us of the importance of detailed case studies for coming to terms with the various forms of transmedial worlds in contemporary media culture, but it also sets out to illustrate how a text-based media analysis can be combined with both an interview-based qualitative and a survey-based quantitative approach to get a clearer picture of the specific patterns of use through which fans participate in transmedial worlds.

Maria Lindgren Leavenworth's "Transmedial Narration and Fan Fiction: The Storyworld of *The Vampire Diaries*" examines the problem of audience participation in transmedia franchises from a slightly different angle, focusing on unauthorized fan contributions to the transmedial storyworld of *The Vampire Diaries*. Leavenworth's case study, however, is different from the other case studies discussed in this section in at least two ways. First, the novel series written by L. J. Smith and the TV series produced by Kevin Williamson and Julie Plec represent fairly different stories with clearly different characters. While these differences seem to establish two distinct storyworlds rather than one, the franchise also establishes some continuities. Second and perhaps more important,

Lindgren-Leavenworth's focus on fan fiction allows her to draw attention to the fact that, even in franchises dominated by what Mittell describes as "What Is" strategies of transmedial representation, there is usually some kind of *fanon* (as opposed to "canon," the term refers to fan-produced, unsanctioned products) that produces hypothetical "What If?" narratives, thereby modifying and challenging the logically consistent storyworld of the canonical texts. This practice leads Lindgren-Leavenworth to propose that transmedia franchises should be regarded as *archontic texts,* thereby suggesting that scholars should grant equal status to unauthorized fan contributions and to the sanctioned creations of copyright holders. Another noteworthy point of Lindgren-Leavenworth's chapter is that unauthorized fan contributions are often used to question the authority of the canonical products regarding not only what is the case in the transmedial storyworld but also the moral or ideological implications of the authorized parts. The fan fiction of *The Vampire Diaries* demonstrates this rebellious spirit by regularly renegotiating and reexamining questions of gender and sexuality in ways that subvert the often rather conservative norms and values implied in many of the more recent entries in the genre of the vampire romance.

In a final extensive case study, Van Leavenworth's "The Developing Storyworld of H. P. Lovecraft" examines the transmedial storyworld that has developed around the writings of American Gothic writer H. P. Lovecraft. The Lovecraft storyworld is truly transmedial, being represented across a wide variety of media and genres such as traditional textual fiction, interactive fiction, short and feature-length films, fan art, comics, music, board games, role-playing games, computer games, and interactive environments in *Second Life.* Accordingly, the resulting storyworld is not defined by a specific story (or collection of stories) but by a common thematic focus—that is, the cosmic fear inspired by the "Old Ones," such as Cthulhu, whose very existence lies beyond the limits of human imagination. Building on Klastrup and Tosca's concept of transmedial worlds as *abstract content systems,* Leavenworth examines the defining features of the Lovecraft storyworld's "worldness" in considerable detail, focusing on three main questions: Wherein lies the appeal of the Lovecraft storyworld? How can works engage with the Lovecraft storyworld's "mythos" in familiar yet medium-specific ways? How has the development of the Lovecraft storyworld contributed to the elevation of the "pulp writer" H. P. Lovecraft into the American literary canon? In pursuing these questions, Leavenworth examines a wide range of media texts that contribute to the Lovecraft storyworld, particularly focusing on the H. P. Lovecraft Historical Society's silent film *The Call of Cthulhu*, Chaosium's role-playing game *Call of Cthulhu*, and Michael S. Gentry's text-based interactive fiction *Anchorhead: An Interactive Gothic*. His contribution, then, not only illustrates the importance of detailed case studies for the understanding of the forms and functions of the transmedial representation of storyworlds but also demonstrates how such case studies can be connected to broader issues of literary, medial, and cultural historiography.

Not all of the work collected in this volume explicitly use the term "storyworld" or refer to the corresponding narratological concept developed in Marie-Laure Ryan's contribution, but they all rely on the notion of *represented worlds* as sites of creative activity in which cultures elaborate their collective social imaginary. Storyworlds hold a greater fascination for the imagination than the plots that take place in them, because plots are self-enclosed, linear arrangements of events that come to an end while storyworlds can always sprout branches to their core plots that further immerse people, thereby providing new pleasures. As a filmmaker told Henry Jenkins: "When I first started, you would pitch a story because without a good story, you didn't really have film. Later, once sequels started to take off, you pitched a character because a good character could support multiple stories. And now, you pitch a world because a world can support multiple characters and multiple stories across multiple media" (116).

Exploring how media old and new give birth to different types of storyworlds and different ways of experiencing them is the purpose of this volume, as well as the general concern of a media-conscious narratology that gives sustained attention to both the similarities of and the differences in the ways in which conventionally distinct media narrate. Our goal, however, is not to suggest a rigid program for a supposedly new brand of narratology but to invite readers to join a theoretical conversation focused on the question of how narratology can achieve media-consciousness.

It is now time to tune our instruments and to let the storyworlds concert begin.

Note

1. It is, of course, evident that what we propose to call "media-conscious narratology" in this volume, in order to emphasize the medium-specific features of storyworlds across media, shares at least some characteristics with what has previously been described as "transmedial narratology." See, for example, Herman; Ryan, *Avatars*; Thon; Wolf.

Works Cited

Berger, Peter L., and Thomas Luckman. *The Social Construction of Reality: A Treatise in the Sociology of Knowledge.* Garden City NY: Anchor Books, 1966. Print.

Chatman, Seymour. "What Novels Can Do That Films Can't (and Vice Versa)." *On Narrative.* Ed. W. J. T. Mitchell. Chicago: University of Chicago Press, 1981. 117–36. Print.

Goodman, Nelson. *Ways of Worldmaking.* Indianapolis IN: Hackett, 1978. Print.

Herman, David. *Basic Elements of Narrative.* Malden MA: Wiley-Blackwell, 2009. Print.

Jenkins, Henry. *Convergence Culture: Where Old and New Media Collide.* New York: New York University Press, 2006. Print.

Klastrup, Lisbeth, and Susana Tosca. "Transmedial Worlds—Rethinking Cyberworld Design." *Proceedings of the 2004 International Conference on Cyberworlds.* Los Alamitos CA: IEEEE Computer Society, 2004. N. pag. PDF file. June 1, 2012.

Kress, Gunther, and Theo van Leeuwen. *Multimodal Discourse: The Modes and Media of Contemporary Communication.* London: Arnold, 2001. Print.

Lessing, Gotthold Ephraim. *Laocoön: An Essay on the Limits of Painting and Poetry.* Trans. Edward Allan McCormick. Baltimore MD: Johns Hopkins University Press, 1984. Print.

McLuhan, Marshall. *Understanding Media: The Extension of Man.* New York: McGraw-Hill, 1964. Print.

Rajewsky, Irina O. "Border Talks: The Problematic Status of Media Borders in the Current Debate about Intermediality." *Media Borders, Multimodality and Intermediality.* Ed. Lars Elleström. New York: Palgrave Macmillan, 2010. 51–68. Print.

Ryan, Marie-Laure. *Avatars of Story.* Minneapolis: University of Minnesota Press, 2006. Print.

———, ed. *Narrative across Media: The Languages of Storytelling.* Lincoln: University of Nebraska Press, 2004. Print.

———. *Possible Worlds, Artificial Intelligence and Narrative Theory.* Bloomington: Indiana University Press, 1991. Print.

Thon, Jan-Noël. "Toward a Transmedial Narratology: On Narrators in Contemporary Graphic Novels, Feature Films, and Computer Games." *Beyond Classical Narration: Transmedial and Unnatural Challenges.* Ed. Jan Alber and Per Krogh Hansen. Berlin: De Gruyter, 2014. 25–56. Print.

Wolf, Werner. "Narratology and Media(lity): The Transmedial Expansion of a Literary Discipline and Possible Consequences." *Current Trends in Narratology.* Ed. Greta Olsen. Berlin: De Gruyter, 2011. 145–80. Print.

PART 1 *Mediality and Transmediality*

1 Story/Worlds/Media

Tuning the Instruments of a Media-Conscious Narratology

MARIE-LAURE RYAN

Both of the two terms that form the title of this book, "storyworlds" and "media," are common in contemporary narratological and critical discourse, but they tend to be used in a very loose way. In this chapter, I explore the difficulties involved in turning them from conveniently vague catchphrases that can be used in many contexts into the sharp analytical tools that will be needed to impart narratology with media consciousness.

Media

Gregory Bateson once described *media* as "a difference that makes a difference" (453). This formula is seductive, but it cannot offer a satisfactory definition of media because it rests on an unanswered question: a difference for what? Media studies would operate in a vacuum if they were not able to name the object of this difference. But if we take a narrative approach to media, the answer becomes obvious: the choice of medium makes a difference as to what stories can be told, how they are told, and why they are told. By shaping narrative, media shape nothing less than human experience.

Narrative is not, admittedly, the only possible answer to the question "a difference for what"; we could say, for instance, "a difference for art" or "a difference for communication" or even "a difference for human relations." The various domains for which media can make a difference mean that the list of all phenomena that have been called "media" by one scholar or another is strangely reminiscent in its heterogeneous character of the Chinese taxonomy of animals that Jorge Luis Borges mentioned in an essay. This taxonomy divides animals into the following categories: "those that belong to the emperor, embalmed ones, those that are trained, suckling pigs, mermaids, fabulous ones, stray dogs, those that are not included in this classification," and so on (Borges 103). The list of phenomena that have been labeled "media" includes: (a) channels of mass communication, such as newspapers, television (TV), radio, and the Internet; (b) technologies of communication, such as printing, the computer, film, TV, photography, and the telephone; (c) specific applications of digital technology, such as computer games, hypertext, blogs, e-mail, Twitter, and Facebook; (d) ways of encoding signs to make them durable and ways of preserving life data, such as writing, books, sound recording, film, and photography; (e) semiotic forms of expression, such as language, image, sound, and movement; (f) forms of art, such as literature, music, painting, dance, sculpture, installations, architecture, drama, the opera, and comics; and (g) the material substance out of which messages are made or in which signs are presented, such as clay, stone, oil, paper, silicon, scrolls, codex books, and the human body. Some scholars even consider air to be a medium (as the substance through which sound waves travel in oral communication), and the term "biomedia" has been floating around to designate manipulations of the DNA code (see Thacker); however, in this present volume we can easily ignore these interpretations because they have no direct narrative relevance.

The confusion that reigns in media studies is epitomized by the occasionally heard term of "multimedia media" (or mixed media media), which describes the vast majority of the categories I have just mentioned. Only the purely semiotic categories of language, image, and sound are single-medium media. (W. J. T. Mitchell goes as far as claiming that all media are mixed media.[1]) If we give the same meaning to both occurrences of "media" in the expression "multimedia media," we get something as difficult to conceive of as a set that is a member of itself, which is a well-known paradox in logic. But people have no trouble understanding the expression "multimedia media" because they spontaneously interpret the two uses of media differently—the first (in multimedia) in a semiotic sense and the second (in media) in a technological or cultural sense. *Multimedia media* are technological or cultural phenomena such as film or theater that use signs of various kinds and speak to various senses. We have become so accustomed to live performances and art installations that mix various types of signs and technologies in an innovative way that multimedia almost becomes a medium in itself.

Like most words in a language, medium or media has multiple meanings. Working out a definition of media that covers all of its particular uses has advantages and disadvantages. The advantage of establishing a unified, global definition is that it could serve as a rallying point for the various disciplines concerned with media and create a convergence, if not of media, then at least of media researchers. In this age of interdisciplinarity, finding common interests is always a welcome event. Without a common definition, the sociologists will continue to mean *p*, the art critics *q*, the philosophers *r*, the historians of culture and technology *s*, and so on, and interdisciplinarity will remain a dialogue of the deaf.

The disadvantage of a unified global definition is that the more phenomena the definition encompasses, the less useful it becomes as an analytical tool. Language is polysemic by nature, but while polysemy is good for poetry it is bad for science and for the discourse of the humanities. It is better to work with a large collection of sharp tools that fulfill precise tasks than with a single blunt one, even if everyone cannot share the tools. It could be that the concept of medium is similar to the concept of game. The philosopher Ludwig Wittgenstein has suggested that the word "game" does not stand for a collection of necessary and sufficient properties that make a given activity a member of the set of all games; rather, it designates a "family-resemblance" notion (sec. 1–32). In a large family, some features are widely distributed, but no trait is shared by all members and there is no prototypical individual. Should we conceive of media based on this model? The idea of family resemblance, if it is appropriate in this case, should not be used as an easy cop-out for giving up the attempt to define medium but as a challenge to identify the features on which the resemblance is based.

A widespread trend in media studies, especially in the United States, consists of associating media with specific technologies of communication, such as writing, film, photography, TV, radio, the telephone, and all the uses of digital technology known as "new media." This conception of media as technologies permeates the newly developing fields of media archaeology (the unearthing of the dead ancestors of contemporary media) and comparative media studies, a project that, so far, has mainly consisted of comparing "the book" with digital forms of writing (Hayles 9–10). While a narrowly technological conception of media presents the advantage of resting on a solid definition, it cannot serve the purpose of this chapter because it excludes many culturally important narrative forms, especially art forms, that do not have their own technology. Comics, for instance, rely on the same printing technology that the press and literature do; the theater and the opera make only optional use of technologies, such as stage machinery, light effects, microphones, or film projection; and oral storytelling does not need any technology at all. It could be argued that as an unmediated form of communication, oral storytelling does not qualify as a medium, but from the point of view of narrative it certainly fulfills the conditions of mediality because the live performance of face-to-face interaction makes a difference as to what kind of stories are told, how they are told, and why they are told. This example demonstrates how problematic it is to establish a basic list of media that transcends disciplines; what is clearly a medium for the narratologist may not be one for the historian of culture or technology.

Another way to avoid the ambiguity of the concept of medium is to focus on what Gunther Kress and Theo van Leeuwen call "modes." The study of multimodal texts—that is, texts that use a variety of signs, such as image, language, and sound—is currently one of the hottest fields of narratology (see Wolfgang Hallet's contribution to the discussion in chapter 6 of this volume). But "mode" is as difficult to define as medium is, and Kress and van Leeuwen's attempt to list and classify modes of signification are similar in their apparent randomness to Borges's Chinese taxonomy. Their list includes "any semiotic resource, in a very broad sense, that produces meaning in a social context; the verbal, the visual, language, image, music, sound, gesture, *narrative*, color, taste, speech, touch, plastic, and so on" (Elleström 14; emphasis added). If narrative is itself a mode, how then can one study the modes of multimodal narrative? In addition, modes of signification do not make the concept of medium dispensable, for there must be a way to distinguish the various cultural forms in which a given mode appears. Comics and illustrated stories, for instance, share the modes of language and image, but they certainly differ in their use of these modes and, hence, meaning in their narrative affordances. In "Reading Images," Kress sketches a theory that includes both modes and media: he regards "text" as a mode and "book" as one of its media, "image" as a mode and "the screen" or "the CDROM" as some of its media, and, conversely, "the teacher's body" as a medium and his or her speech, movements, and gestures as the body's modes. The list of media that this approach produces is not a catalog of culturally recognized forms of communication, as would be film, photography, literature, painting, or music, but rather a catalog of their material supports.

In contrast to the analytical approach, which takes a top-down method to determine media by applying certain criteria (such as asking if written text is a mode and the book one of its media, then what are the media of oral language, of still pictures, or of sound), I propose a bottom-up approach that takes as its point of departure the media categories informally used in Western cultures. These categories, which form a kind of folk taxonomy, rest on three kinds of criteria: semiotic substance, technical dimension, and cultural dimension.

Semiotic substance encompasses categories such as image, sound, language, and movement. These basic types of signs can be further analyzed in terms of spatiotemporal extension, signifying dimensions (that is, line, color, shape, and dimensionality for images or pitch, rhythm, and loudness for sound), sensorial impact (auditive, visual), and mode of signification (iconic, indexical, or symbolic). Examples of semiotically based media categories are mostly art forms: music (sound), painting (two-dimensional image), sculpture (three-dimensional image), and oral verbal art (language).

Technical dimension includes not only media-defining technologies such as film, TV, photography, and so on but also any kind of mode of production and material support. Not all media involve technologies, but all of them have a technical dimension since they cannot exist without a mode of production and a material support. In film, the mode of production involves the technologies of live-action recording or of animation, and the material support apprehended by the user is the silver screen. In certain cases the mode of production cannot be distinguished from the material support; for example, in the theater or in ballet, the human body fulfills both of these functions. In other cases, the mode of production is multilayered. In literature, for instance, it involves the technology of writing (with pen and paper, with a typewriter, or with the computer) and the technology of printing. The material support produced by the second stage of production is the book. The case of multilayered modes of production suggests a distinction between technologies that record and transmit other media (writing for language, books for writing, scripts for video, radio for speech and music, and digital technology for every kind of visual or verbal medium) and technologies that capture life directly (photography, film, and sound recording). The technologies that transmit other media may, however, develop their own idiosyncrasies and evolve from mere channels of transmission into autonomous media of information or artistic expression (e.g., artist books for books, serials and live broadcasting for TV, and computer games and hypertext for digital technology[2]).

Cultural dimension addresses the public recognition of media as forms of communication and the institutions, behaviors, and practices that support them. I regard as culturally based media those means of communication, such as the press, the theater, or comics, that are widely recognized as playing a significant cultural role but that cannot be distinguished on purely semiotic or technological grounds.

Corresponding to these three dimensions of mediality are three approaches for what I call a "media-conscious narratology" (see also figure 1.1 for a map that shows the relationships between media, art forms, and technologies):[3]

- A semiotic approach, which investigates the narrative power of language, image, sound, movement, face-to-face interaction, and the various combinations of these features (Wolf, "Problem der Narrativität"; Wolf, "Narrative").
- A technical approach, which explores such issues as how technologies configure the relationship between sender and receiver—for instance, one to one, few to many, many to many, and close or remote in either space or time—how they affect dissemination, storage, and cognition (Ong); and what affordances certain types of material supports bring to storytelling (for instance, interactivity in the case of digital technology). It is also under this heading that the cognitive impact of material supports, such as the page or the screen, will be investigated in the future.
- A cultural approach, which focuses on the behavior of users and producers, as well as on the institutions that guarantee the existence of media. Applied to narrative, this approach will investigate such topics as fan cultures (Hellekson and Busse; Jenkins; Thomas), the kind of stories one tells in blogs or on Twitter (Page), and the process of production and selection of TV news stories.

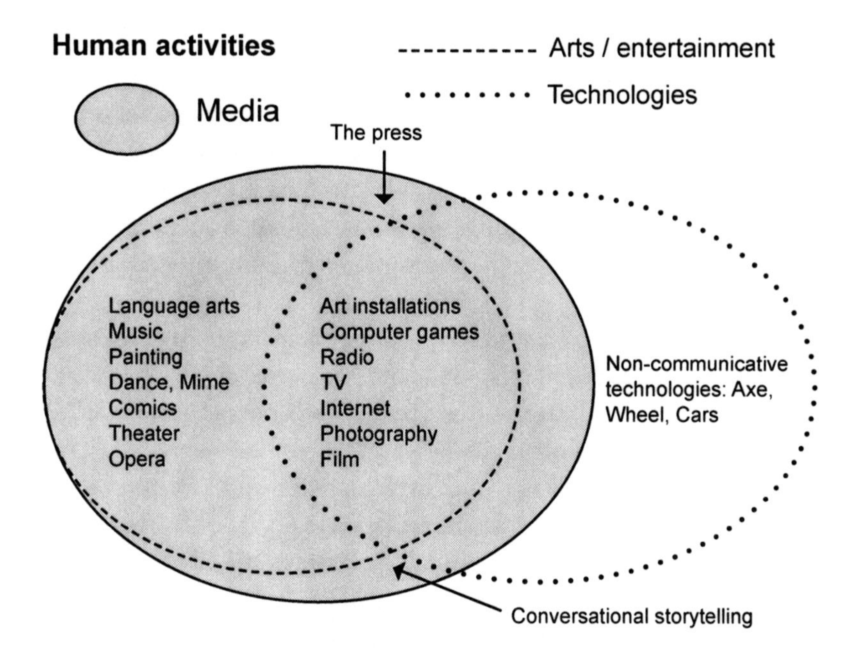

Fig. 1.1. A map of media. Radio, TV, and others, have both artistic and informational manifestations. The press uses a technology—printing—but it is not distinctive. Art categories are either semiotically defined (music, painting, dance, mime) or culturally defined (comics, theater, opera). In this case they do not rely on a distinctive set of signs.

Storyworlds

The other component of our title, *storyworlds*, is only slightly less problematic than the concept of medium. As Jiří Koten (47) has pointed out, its genealogy comprises two lines of ancestry: one is the possible worlds of analytic philosophy, adapted to literary theory by Thomas Pavel, Lubomír Doležel, Umberto Eco, and myself; the other lies in cognitive approaches to literature and linguistics as represented by Richard Gerrig, David Herman, and the British linguist Paul Werth. The possible worlds of analytic philosophy are used in literature to solve such problems as the definition of fiction, the truth value of statements about fictional entities, the ontological status (complete or incomplete?) of these entities, the semantic classification of literary worlds (historical, realistic, fantastic, impossible), the relationships between the worlds of distinct texts (expansion, transposition, modification), the description of the mechanisms of plot in terms of conflicts, and the general organization of the semantic domain of texts as a universe in which an actual world is opposed to a variable number of alternate possible worlds created by the mental activity of characters. As for the worlds of cognitive approaches, they focus the attention of scholars on how they are constructed and "simulated" in the mind of the reader, on what kind of cues trigger this process of simulation, or on the description of the narrative experience as one of immersion.

The concept of storyworld differs from what literary critics (or readers) have in mind when they speak about "the world of Marcel Proust," "the world of Ingmar Bergman," or "the world of Friedrich Hölderlin." In this traditional but informal sense, "world" stands for various ideas: the social and historical setting typical of the author's works (the Proust example), the major themes and recurrent images of this work (Bergman), and the author's general ideas and philosophy of life (Hölderlin)—or what we call, not coincidentally, a "worldview." The narratological concept of storyworld differs from this interpretation of "world" in at least three major ways. First, it is something projected by individual texts, and not by the entire work of an author, so that every story has its own storyworld (except in transmedial projects, where the representation of a world is distributed among many different texts of different media). Second (and this point may seem obvious), it requires narrative content, so the applicability of the concept of storyworld to lyric poetry is questionable. Finally, it cannot be called the "world of the author" because in the case of fiction, authors are located in the real world while the storyworld is a fictional world. If a storyworld is anybody's world, it is the world of the characters.

Narratology and literary criticism have not awaited David Herman to connect the idea of "world" to individual texts. The term "textual world" has long been part of critical vocabulary, and more recently the concept of "text world" has gained currency in linguistics under the influence of Werth (*Text Worlds*). But if we conceive of a world as some kind of container for individual existents, or as a system of relationships between individual existents, not all texts project a world. For instance, a philosophical text that deals with abstract topics and general ideas does not create a world, even though it does speak about the real world. Among the texts that do represent individual objects, some (such as travel guidebooks or ethnographic reports) are purely descriptive while others represent events that unfold in time and create changes of state within their world. The former texts have a world, the latter a storyworld. The recipient's mental construction of a static text world can be represented by something that resembles a classic map. But a storyworld is more than a static container for the objects mentioned in a story; it is a dynamic model of evolving situations, and its representation in the recipient's mind is a simulation of the changes that are caused by the events of the plot.[4] Because of their temporal nature, storyworlds are very difficult to diagram. The famous Russian critic Mikhail Bakhtin captured this inseparability of space and time in narrative thought in his concept of the chronotope.

Narratologists also commonly use the concept of fictional world, which resembles the concept of storyworld but does not completely correspond to it. Storyworld is a broader concept than fictional world because it covers both factual and fictional stories, meaning stories told as true of the real world and stories that create their own imaginary world, respectively.[5] But it could be argued that in the case of nonfictional stories, the notion of storyworld is superfluous. If these stories are told as true of the real world, doesn't reality serve as their referent? In this case we could divide stories into those that project an imaginary storyworld (in which case storyworld would be just a new term for "fictional world") and those whose storyworld is simply the real world. I believe that this interpretation does not work for the simple reason that it would make it impossible for stories to be false. If we conceive of the real world as a domain made of facts that exist independently of the mind and of any attempt to narrate them—as a domain, in other words, whose description is a collection of true propositions—then associating the storyworld of a story with the real world makes this story automatically true. Nonfictional stories are told as true of the real world, but they do not necessarily live up to this ideal. The storyteller can be lying, misinformed, or playing loosely with the facts. It is therefore necessary to distinguish the world as it is presented and shaped by a story from the world as it exists autonomously. The former is the storyworld, the latter the reference world. Assessing the truth of a story means assessing to what extent the storyworld corresponds to the reference world.

Now if we postulate that both fiction and nonfiction create a storyworld, how can we distinguish these two forms of storytelling? The conception of storyworld that I have just outlined goes against the popular (and inaccurate) belief that nonfictional stories are true stories while fictional stories are false. On the contrary, nonfictional stories can be either true or false with respect to their reference world, but fictional ones are automatically true in the world about which they are told. We can account for this difference by invoking the triadic analysis of signs into a *material object* (or signifier), a *meaning* (or signified), and a *referent*. The text of the story is the material object, the storyworld is the meaning, and, in the case of nonfiction, the real world is the referent. Since many different stories can take the real world as referent, there will be mutually incompatible versions of reality, and the recipients must decide for themselves whether the story is true. But in the case of fiction, there is no external referent, because the story creates its own world and normally constitutes the only mode of access to it. (I say "normally" to leave room for the phenomenon of transfictional storytelling, where a given storyworld is represented through many different documents.) The reader (or spectator, player, and so on) of a narrative fiction has consequently no choice but to construct a world image in which the text is true.[6]

Turning to the question of the content of storyworlds, I propose that they are composed of the following components.

- *Existents*: the characters of the story and the objects that have special significance for the plot

In the case of nonfiction, the extent of this inventory poses no problem; every part of reality also belongs, at least implicitly, to the storyworld. But the issue is trickier in the case of fictional storyworlds. According to a radical "textualist" position (a position that proclaims the primacy of the signifier), certain media create storyworlds, and they contain only those entities and those features that are actually shown or referred to by the representing medium. Since media can only show selected aspects of a world, storyworlds would be fundamentally incomplete entities. The alternative to the position of radical textualism is a cognitive and phenomenological approach that focuses on storyworlds as an imaginative experience. In the case of fiction, this experience is a blend of objective knowledge and make-believe; the user who is immersed in a storyworld knows that it is created by the medium, but he or she pretends to believe that it exists autonomously or, in other words, that it is real. The imagination will consequently conceive fictional storyworlds on the model of the real world, and it will import knowledge from the real world to fill out incomplete descriptions. Relying on David Lewis's 1978 article "Truth in Fiction," I have called this idea "the principle of minimal departure" (Ryan, *Possible Worlds*); Kendall Walton calls it "the reality principle" (145). It means that when a text mentions an object that exists in reality, all the real-world properties of this object can be imported into the storyworld unless explicitly contradicted by the text.[7] For instance, when a text refers to a location in the real world, all of the real geography is implicitly part of the storyworld, and when it refers to a historical individual, this individual enters the storyworld with all of his or her biographical data except for those features that the text explicitly overrules.

- *Setting*: a space within which the existents are located

While the vast majority of stories take place in particular locales, in some rare cases the setting is left fully undetermined. For instance, the minimal story proposed by E. M. Forster, "The king died, then the queen died of grief," does not let the reader imagine a setting. But we must still assume that the world in which the events take place has spatial extension since kings and queens have physical bodies.

- *Physical laws*: principles that determine what kind of events can and cannot happen in a given story

These laws are highly dependent on genre. For instance, animals can talk in fairy tales, people can be transformed into animals in fantastic tales, and time travel is possible in science fiction. In realist narratives, physical laws are directly borrowed from the recipient's life experience.

- *Social rules and values*: principles that determine the obligations of characters

This component may be optional (it is, for instance, absent in the Forster plot quoted earlier), but it is a particularly powerful source of narrativity because social rules are opportunities for transgressions and, consequently, a source of conflict. The individual aspirations of characters, for instance, may be incompatible with the laws of the group they belong to, or characters may belong to different groups with competing values, and they may be forced to make a choice between these values. If we define *plot* as a transgression of boundaries (see Lotman), then a plot is made possible by the rules that define boundaries.

- *Events:* the causes of the changes of state that happen in the time span framed by the narrative

This concept of "time span framed by the narrative" can be understood both in a narrow and in a broad sense. In the narrow sense, it consists of the events that form the focus of the story or the events directly brought to life, so to speak, by the narrative medium. In films, plays, and games, this component consists of the action shown on the screen or on the stage as opposed to the events narrated by the characters, but in purely verbal narratives, the two frames are harder to distinguish since there is only one semiotic medium. In the wider sense, the time span framed by the narrative may involve a "backstory" made of events that precede the proper beginning of the story and an afterstory that follows the denouement. An example of a backstory is found in Virginia Woolf's *Mrs Dalloway.* The novel takes place over a single day, but it references many events that precede that day. The use of an afterstory is rarer, but it occurs when a first-person narrator looks at the past from the point of view of the present, stressing the distinction between his or her past and present self: his or her past belongs to the narrow frame, and his present situation belongs to the wide frame.[8]

- *Mental events:* the character's reactions to perceived or actual states of affairs

Physical events cannot be properly understood without linking them to mental events. In the case of actions, these mental events are the motivations of the agents, and in the case of both actions and accidental events, such as earthquakes, they are the emotional reactions of the affected characters. Now if mental events are as much a part of a story as physical ones, then storyworlds are actually narrative universes made of a factual domain—what I call the "textual actual world"—surrounded by a plurality of private worlds: the worlds of the beliefs, wishes, fears, goals, plans, and obligations of the characters (see Ryan, *Possible Worlds*).

Applications

For the concept of storyworld to deserve a place in the toolkit of media-conscious narratology, it must present theoretical applications that lead to a new perspective on narrative or that better bring to light the narrative resources of individual media. The following suggestions, which are far from exhaustive, should give the reader an idea of some of these applications.

1. Storyworld offers a basis for distinguishing two types of narrative elements: *intradiegetic elements*, which exist within the storyworld, and *extradiegetic elements*, which are not literally part of the storyworld but play a crucial role in its presentation. Media differ from each other not only in their ability to focus on certain kinds of intradiegetic elements but, more important, in their repertory of extradiegetic elements. Here is a quick survey of the extradiegetic narrative resources of a number of media.

   Greek drama offers a good example of the narrative use of extradiegetic elements. While the actors and their speech are located within the storyworld, the chorus comments on the events from a perspective that ranges from fully external (when the chorus represents an idealized spectator) to marginal (when the chorus consists of distanced observers). In the latter case the chorus belongs to the wider frame of the storyworld while the characters belong to the narrow frame.

   In language-based narrative fiction, a distinction must be made between the speech of the characters and the discourse of the narrator. The former always belongs to the storyworld while the latter may or may not belong to it. When the narrator is an embodied individual (that is, a first-person narrator) and when the narrative discourse imitates a form of nonfictional communication, such as a letter, a diary, or a written autobiography, then both the narrator and the text belong to the storyworld. In the case of epistolary novels, the text will belong to the narrow temporal frame, because the letters are objects within the storyworld that other characters can read. When a first-person narrator recounts events of the past in a memoir or autobiography or when his or her discourse has no distinct genre, however, the narrating-I is situated in the broader temporal frame of the storyworld while the experiencing-I (the narrator as character) is situated within the inner frame.[9] But when a narrative does not attribute individuating properties to the narrator, does not showcase the act of producing the text, and describes beyond reasonable speculation what no normal human being could know with certainty—namely, what happens inside the minds of other people—we cannot really say that there is an embodied narrating agent who "writes" or "speaks" within the storyworld either in the broad or in the narrow frame.[10] I would locate such narrators at the edge of the outer storyworld: they belong to this world logically because they situate themselves in this world by presenting it as "the real world," but they do not belong to it corporally because they are not individuated members of its population, and their discourse does not exist in either the narrow or the wide frame.[11]

Just as the narration and the narrator may not exist in the world of novels, the camera that records the action does not exist in the storyworld of fiction films unless they thematize the process of their own production. Spectators do not imagine that they are watching a camera recording of certain events; instead, they pretend that they are watching unmediated events. (In a documentary film, by contrast, the spectator remains aware that a camera situated on the scene captured the images; this knowledge is what gives the film its documentary value.) Since the camera does not exist in the storyworld of fiction film, neither do all the effects of camera movement and editing. For instance, in the opening scenes of Steven Spielberg's *Saving Private Ryan*, the shaking of the camera that mimics the sensation of being exposed to relentless gunfire is clearly extradiegetic (the film is not claiming that there was a cameraman on Omaha Beach on June 6, 1944). Meanwhile, the same effect in *The Blair Witch Project* is part of the storyworld because the film is (fictionally) presented as the content of the handheld camera of three students who disappeared in the Maryland woods while producing a documentary about a witch. Another aspect of film that is best explained by the concept of storyworld is the sound track (see Levinson, "Soundtrack"). Film theorists have long been aware of the distinction between diegetic music—music that originates inside the storyworld and that the characters can hear—and extradiegetic music, which controls the expectations and emotions of the spectator but does not exist in the storyworld.

Comics are full of elements that do not belong to the storyworld: for instance, the speech bubbles, the division of the narrative into individual frames, and the so-called gutter that separates them. The story is told through discrete frames, but the reader assumes that the time and space of the storyworld are continuous. The text within the bubbles stands for speech acts or mental acts that take place within the storyworld, but the narrative discourse enclosed in a text box at the top or bottom of the frames does not originate in the same time and space as the picture shown in the fame. It will be a fully extradiegetic element when it belongs to an impersonal narrator, and it will be situated within the larger spatiotemporal frame (as opposed to the pictures, which show scenes located in the narrower frame) when it belongs to a character (as in Marjane Satrapi's *Persepolis*). The same can be said of voice-over narration in film.

Finally, in computer games, the most notorious extradiegetic elements are the menus that offer the player a choice of actions and the statistics that report the player's level of achievement. Playing the game involves a constant movement in and out of the storyworld. This movement is particularly noticeable in online worlds as players can communicate with each other either "in role"—that is, within the storyworld—or "out of role," by addressing real-world players rather than their avatars. Another example of action that takes place outside the storyworld of an online game is the activity of selling objects for real-world money, an activity that designers and many players consider a transgression of the spirit of the game.

2. The distinction between world-internal and world-external features can also be applied to the various semiotic channels of multimodal texts. The distinction between intradiegetic and extradiegetic sound has a correlate in illustrated texts. In some cases illustrations correspond to objects that exist within the storyworld; for instance, the many maps and diagrams that illustrate Reif Larsen's 2009 novel *The Selected Works of T. S. Spivet* (analyzed in chapter 6 of this volume) are intradiegetic because they are presented as drawings created by the narrator. Meanwhile, the maps of Europe that appear in the Neolithic sagas of Jean Auel are clearly extradiegetic because prehistoric man did not have the means to produce maps of large territories.

A distinction can also be made between multimodal-born narratives that use images and text as separate but ontologically equal modes of access to the storyworld and language-born narratives that use illustrations as a kind of paratext. The first case is represented by many children's books—for instance, Maurice Sendak's *Outside Over There* and Lewis Carroll's *Alice in Wonderland* illustrated by Sir John Tenniel. In these books the illustrations relieve the language channel of the task of describing what the characters and setting look like. An example of illustrations functioning as a paratext comes from Salvador Dali's *Don Quixote* illustrations. Miguel de Cervantes's text offers a self-sufficient representation of the storyworlds, and even when Dali's illustrations are published together with the text, the reader remains aware that they are only one of many possible visual interpretations of the novel.

And finally, multimodal texts can problematize the relationship between text and image by introducing pictures that do not relate in obvious ways to the content of the text or that originate in a different world. I am thinking here of the work of W. G. Sebald, who illustrates narratives about fictional characters with (presumably) found photographs that represent unidentified real-world persons. In this case a fictional storyworld integrates real-world documents by redirecting their reference: there was once a boy who posed for a photograph in the real world, and the photograph referred to this boy, but once it is inserted in the novel *Austerlitz*, the image represents an ontologically distinct individual, the fictional Jacques Austerlitz.

3. Another practical application of the notion of storyworld is the distinction between single-storyworld and many-storyworlds texts. While classical narratives are single-storyworld, because they are centered around a unique actual world made of solid facts, the case of multiple storyworlds is illustrated by texts that present many different versions of a basic situation and do not create an opposition among these versions between the actual and the counterfactual.[12] This kind of ontological multiplicity occurs in Robert Coover's short story "The Babysitter," in such films as *The Butterfly Effect* and *Run Lola Run*, or in Michael Joyce's hypertext *afternoon, a story*. Computer games present another type of multi-world narrative. Insofar as they are based on a simulation engine, they generate a different storyworld every time they are played. These different sequences are mutually incompatible because a player who receives a choice of actions cannot take all the branches in the same world. Games should be played several times for the user to experience the different storyworlds that the simulation is capable of generating and to appreciate the extent of the differences, but as most games are too time consuming to be replayed, their potential for variation is often lost on the player.

While texts may project many different storyworlds, a given storyworld may also unfold in many different texts. This situation occurs mostly in oral cultures, when bards tell stories that are familiar to the audience. We also find it in a phenomenon that is currently enjoying great popularity—the phenomenon of "media convergence" or "transmedial storytelling," which Henry Jenkins defines as "the distribution of narrative content across multiple media platforms" (2). As Christy Dena has shown, this phenomenon can be conceived of in two ways: as a spontaneous clustering of texts by various authors, both canonical and apocryphal, that develop the world of a popular film or novel, such as *The Lord of the Rings*, *Harry Potter*, or *Star Wars*; and as the deliberate distribution of narrative content across different media, a process illustrated by the franchise planned by Andy and Larry (now

Lana) Wachowski around *The Matrix* or by the German transmedial universe of *Alpha 0.7* (simultaneously developed as TV series, radio shows, and a variety of websites; see Ryan, "Transmedial Storytelling").[13] The various elements of a transmedial system can either expand a storyworld through processes that respect previous content or create logically distinct, though imaginatively related, storyworlds through modifications and transpositions that alter existing content (see Ryan, "Transmedial Storytelling"). For instance, within the *Star Wars* system, the six movies by George Lucas clearly represent the same world (the later films were planned from the beginning), while the various computer games, online worlds, novels, and texts of fan fictions inspired by the films alter this world in various ways. One of the tasks of media-conscious narratology is to describe the relationships between the worlds of transmedial systems and to provide criteria for deciding in which cases they represent the same world and in which cases they project related but distinct worlds.[14]

4. We may also want to ask how the mental construction of storyworlds is affected by the types of signs that a medium uses. This process of mental construction is highly sensitive to the distinction between language-based and visual media. Language-based narratives require an extensive filling-in work because language speaks to the mind and not directly to the senses. This is why we need a principle such as minimal departure to provide a basis for the import of information. Visual media, by contrast, saturate the senses and leave much less to the imagination. Take a comic book hero like Tintin; the images represent him as flat, and our mind pictures him exactly as he appears in the books. It does not mean, however, that we imagine Tintin living in a two-dimensional world similar to the world depicted in Edwin Abbott's *Flatland: A Romance of Many Dimensions*. On this point I believe that we must make a distinction between *how* we imagine the worlds of visual media and *what* we imagine about them. Cognitive scientists distinguish two modes that we use to store knowledge—as images and as propositions (see Esrock). *How* we imagine Tintin consists of mental images that are determined by the medium, but *what* we imagine about him consists

of internalized propositions, and what propositions hold true of the storyworld is determined by both minimal departure and the logic of the story. In other words we imagine that Tintin is three dimensional (3-D) because he is a human being, but when we run the story of Tintin similar to a film in our head, we visualize him as two dimensional (2-D). This contrast between "imagining how" and "imagining that" holds for all media with a visual channel. For instance, if we watch a film in black and white, we remember the picture in black and white, but we assume that the storyworld has color—unless, of course, this lack of color is thematized, as it is in the film *Pleasantville.*

What, in the end, does the concept of storyworld contribute to narratology? Its usefulness does not lie in adding yet one more technical term to a discipline already overloaded with analytical tools nor in summing up the totality of these tools (for if this were the case, the study of storyworlds would be indistinguishable from narratology as a whole); rather, it resides in signaling a turn within narratology from the mostly formal approach of what Herman has called "classical narratology" ("Introduction," 1) to a phenomenological approach focused on the act of imagination required of the reader, spectator, or player. The concept of storyworld represents a departure from the idea cultivated in literary theory from New Criticism to deconstruction that the experience of literature, whether narrative or not, is essentially an experience of language.[15] By the same reasoning, the experience of film would be the experience of a flux of moving images, the experience of comics would be an experience of pages organized into distinct frames holding image and language combinations, and the experience of computer games would be one of manipulating certain controls to produce transformations in the information displayed on the screen. I am not saying that a focus on storyworlds should make these expressive devices invisible, but if they matter to us, it is because they are able to conjure a certain type of representation. What can be the object of this representation, if not a world in which readers, spectators, and players make themselves imaginatively at home? As the title of Richard Gerrig's book *Experiencing Narrative Worlds* tells us, without the concept of world, one cannot speak of narrative as a lived experience.

Notes

1. "[A]ll media are mixed media, combining different codes, discursive conventions, channels, sensory and cognitive modes" (Mitchell 95).
2. By "hypertext" I mean not only the literary form exemplified by works such as Michael Joyce's *afternoon, a story* but also the principle of organization of the web as a whole, as defined by html code (an organization created by Tim Berners-Lee).
3. Lars Elleström developed a classification of media concepts that comes close to the present proposal, though there is no exact fit between his categories and mine or between our respective purposes. I start with categories that are generally considered media in our culture, and I ask on what criteria these categories are based. Elleström is more interested in analytical than in folk categories, aspects that are present in all media. These aspects are (1) "basic media" (semiotic categories such as "auditory text," "tactile text," "still image," "moving images," "iconic body performance," and "organized nonverbal sound"); (2) "qualified media" (roughly my cultural category) defined in terms of such criteria as origin, delimitation, and use (film, dance, photography, painting, and, I assume, computer games); and (3) "technical media," which "realize" or "display" basic and qualified media. These so-called technical media are more interfaces—for instance, the screen for a TV, a certain kind of paper for photography and another kind for text, and the human body for dance—than technologies. Elleström also proposes to describe every medium in terms of four "modalities" (a term he does not use in the same sense as Kress and van Leeuwen did) that correspond to classes of properties: material modality (human body, paper, clay, silicon and electric pulses, etc.), sensorial modality (sight, hearing, taste, touch, etc.), spatiotemporal modality (extending in space, in time, or in both), and semiotic modality (convention, resemblance, contiguity). I would be inclined to subsume all these modalities under the semiotic category because they all concern the basic properties of signs. (Elleström's semiotic mode could then be renamed "basic principle of signification.")
4. I am talking here about mental simulation, a well-known concept in cognitive psychology, and not about simulation engines such as those we find in computer games.
5. This is the conception of fiction exposed in Lewis, "Truth in Fiction." See also Frank Zipfel's contribution to this volume (chapter 4).
6. Here I am speaking of standard fiction. In some postmodern narratives, however, the text deconstructs itself so perversely that the reader is unable to imagine a world in which all of its assertions are true. See Jan Alber's "Impossible Storyworlds" for suggestions on how readers deal with such texts. Unreliable narration presents another problem for the claim that the truth of fictional

discourse cannot be called into question: in reconstructing the combined storyworld–reference world, the reader cannot take all of the narrator's claims into consideration, though the reader must accept the vast majority of them if he or she is to construct a storyworld out of the text. This suggests that storyworlds as a whole correspond to the vision that (the reader assumes) the author proposes to the reader and not to the interpretation of (fictional) reality intended by the narrator.

7. I am fully aware that minimal departure (MD) has its critics. Proponents of the incompleteness of fictional storyworlds claim that it makes these worlds ontologically complete, while in fact the text that creates them can only specify a limited number of properties. This objection would be legitimate if texts *literally* created worlds, as ontologically autonomous entities, by describing them. But "create" in the case of fictional texts is a metaphor; instead, it would be more appropriate to say that fiction brings a world to the imagination. My claim is that in the user's act of imagination, storyworlds are generally complete. For instance, we don't imagine human characters as lacking some of the properties essential to humans, even if the text does not mention them. (I say generally because I don't want to exclude the possibility of storyworlds lacking some dimensions or presenting logical gaps.)

   Some scholars (Walsh; Wistrand) have objected that MD takes the process of inference too far and fills storyworlds with irrelevant clutter. For instance, do we really need to imagine that Anna Karenina has kidneys? Walsh proposes to replace MD with a "principle of relevance" inspired by Sperber and Wilson, but while MD cannot assess the degree of relevance of an inference, it can tell basically wrong ones from justifiable ones. Thus, no valid interpretation can be based on the premise that Anna Karenina has no kidneys. Furthermore, MD is more a guide to the imagination than a recipe for producing interesting interpretations. MD does not instruct the reader to imagine Anna's kidneys but to imagine that Anna is a normal human being; therefore, she has kidneys.

   I believe that without MD it would often be impossible to draw causal inferences. If a story is told about a character being bitten by a rattlesnake and dying shortly afterward (but without stating why), it is by assuming that fictional rattlesnakes are poisonous, just as real-world ones are, that the reader can infer the snake caused the character's death. No inference can be considered relevant if it violates MD.

   The main problem with MD is that it works best with realistic texts. In the case of fantastic texts, science fiction, fables, or chivalric romances, we cannot assume that everything that exists in the real world also exists in the fictional world. In these cases MD will be superseded by a "generic landscape," or a landscape constructed on the basis of other texts rather than on the basis of life experience.

8. The distinction between a narrow and a wide frame can also be made in the case of setting. The space of a storyworld is always assumed to be larger than the particular locations that form the setting of the events.
9. Here I knowingly depart from Genette's account of extradiegetic narration. Genette would regard first-person narrators telling about their past (such as Humbert Humbert, the narrator of *Lolita*) as extradiegetic. Whereas Genette's model conceives of narrators as either intra- or extradiegetic, my model recognizes three types: *individuated narrators located within the narrow frame* (for Genette, intradiegetic), *individuated narrators located within the wide frame* (for Genette, extradiegetic), and *nonindividuated narrators located outside the storyworld* altogether (for Genette, also extradiegetic). Let's note that Genette's intradiegetic narrators are typically characters, such as Odysseus recounting his adventures in cantos 9–12 of the *Odyssey*. Since the discourse of intradiegetic narrators is embedded within the tale of an extradiegetic narrator, the occurrence of this discourse automatically introduces a higher diegetic level. It should also be noted that Genette's model does not make a distinction between narrators who are embodied individuals and narrators who are impersonal abstractions. Though his concept of *homodiegetic* narrators (narrators who tell about themselves) presuppose individuation and embodiment, his model places in the same extradiegetic category individuated narrators who tell about their life retrospectively (Des Grieux in Abbé Prevost's *Manon Lescaut*), individuated narrators who chronicle the life of others (Dr. Zeitblom in Thomas Mann's *Doctor Faustus*), and impersonal narrators. My three degrees of remoteness do not specify whether narrators tell about themselves or about others, but the possibilities relating to each type are easy to infer: while narrators located within the narrow or the wide frame of the storyworld must be involved to some degree in the story, even if it is only as witnesses, the narrators (or should one call them "narrative instances"?) external to the storyworld cannot tell about themselves since they have neither a self nor a body.
10. Scholars who have denied the presence of a narrator in this case include Ann Banfield, Richard Walsh, and Henrik Skov Nielsen. I personally favor a compromise that makes the impersonal extradiegetic narrator a purely logical placeholder whose purpose is to relieve the author of the responsibility for the textual speech acts. Since this logical placeholder is a disembodied entity, it can look at the storyworld from any perspective.
11. According to David Lewis ("Counterfactuals"), the idea of a "real" or "actual" world is indexical; it refers to the world in which I am situated (184). If impersonal narrators present the fictional world as real, they speak from the logical point of view of members of this world.
12. For another sense in which texts—more precisely, dramatic texts—project many different worlds, see chapter 4 of this volume.

13. The world of *Game of Thrones* described by Lisbeth Klastrup and Susana Tosca (see chapter 13 of this volume) is a hybrid of the two modes of development. It originated in a self-standing literary text, but the second stage of development (in which a game advertised the TV show) was deliberately multimedial.
14. In chapter 11 of this volume, Jason Mittell captures this distinction through the terms "What Is" worlds (worlds that expand another) and "What If?" worlds (worlds that branch out in time from another, outlining a different course of events).
15. Typical of this stance is Roland Barthes's claim that literature should turn its readers into writers who gain access to "the magic of the signifier" (4), a claim that ignores the contribution of the signified—that is, of content—to the pleasure of the text.

Works Cited

Alber, Jan. "Impossible Storyworlds—and What to Do with Them." *Storyworlds* 1 (2009): 79–96. Print.

Bakhtin, Mikhail. "Forms of Time and of the Chronotope in the Novel." *The Dialogic Imagination: Four Essays by M.M. Bakhtin*. Ed. Michael Holquist, trans. Caryl Emerson and Michael Holquist. Austin: University of Texas Press, 1981. 84–258. Print.

Banfield, Ann. *Unspeakable Sentences: Narration and Representation in the Language of Fiction*. Boston: Routledge & Kegan Paul, 1982. Print.

Barthes, Roland. *S/Z*. Trans. Richard Miller. New York: Farrar, Straus and Giroux, 1974. Print.

Bateson, Gregory. *Steps to an Ecology of Mind*. New York: Ballantine 1972. Print.

Borges, Jorge Luis. "The Analytical Language of John Wilkins." *Other Inquisitions, 1937–1952*. By Borges. Trans. Ruth L. C. Simms. Austin: University of Texas Press, 1964. 101–5. Print.

Dena, Christy. *Transmedia Practice: Theorising the Practice of Expressing a Fictional World across Distinct Media and Environments*. Diss. University of Sidney, 2009. PDF file. June 1, 2012.

Doležel, Lubomír. *Heterocosmica: Fiction and Possible Worlds*. Baltimore MD: Johns Hopkins University Press, 1998. Print.

Eco, Umberto. *The Role of the Reader: Explorations in the Semiotics of Texts*. Bloomington: Indiana University Press, 1984. Print.

Elleström, Lars. "The Modalities of Media: A Model for Understanding Intermedial Relations." *Media Borders, Multimodality and Intermediality*. Ed. Lars Elleström. New York: Palgrave Macmillan, 2010. 11–48. Print.

Esrock, Ellen. *The Reader's Eye: Visual Imaging as Reader Response*. Baltimore MD: Johns Hopkins University Press, 1994. Print.

Forster, E. M. *Aspects of the Novel.* New York: Harcourt Brace, 1927. Print.
Genette, Gérard. *Narrative Discourse: An Essay in Method.* Trans. Jane E. Lewin. Ithaca NY: Cornell University Press, 1980. Print.
Gerrig, Richard. *Experiencing Narrative Worlds: On the Psychological Activities of Reading.* New Haven CT: Yale University Press, 1993. Print.
Hayles, N. Katherine. *How We Think: Digital Media and Contemporary Technogenesis.* Chicago: University of Chicago Press, 2012. Print.
Hellekson, Karen, and Kristina Busse, eds. *Fan Fiction and Fan Communities in the Age of the Internet.* Jefferson NC: McFarland, 2006. Print.
Herman, David. *Basic Elements of Narrative.* Malden MA: Wiley-Blackwell, 2009. Print.
———. "Introduction: Narratologies." *Narratologies: New Perspectives on Narrative Analysis.* Ed. David Herman. Columbus: Ohio State University Press, 1999. 1–30. Print.
Jenkins, Henry. *Convergence Culture: Where Old and New Media Collide.* New York: New York University Press, 2006. Print.
Koten, Jiří. "Fictional Worlds and Storyworlds: Forms and Means of Classification." *Four Studies of Narrative.* Ed. Bohumil Fořt, Alice Jedličova, Jiří Koten, and Ondřej Sládek. Prague: Ūstav pro českou literature, 2010. 47–58. Print.
Kress, Gunther. "Reading Images: Multimodality, Representation and New Media." *Expert Forum for Knowledge Presentation: Preparing for the Future of Knowledge Presentation Conference.* Institute of Design, Chicago, 2003. Web. November 6, 2012.
Kress, Gunther, and Theo van Leeuwen. *Multimodal Discourse: The Modes and Media of Contemporary Communication.* London: Arnold, 2001. Print.
Levinson, Jerrold. "Soundtrack." *Routledge Encyclopedia of Narrative Theory.* Ed. David Herman, Manfred Jahn, and Marie-Laure Ryan. London: Routledge, 2005. 550–51. Print.
Lewis, David. "Counterfactuals." *The Possible and the Actual: Readings in the Metaphysics of Modality.* Ed. Michael Loux. Ithaca NY: Cornell University Press, 1979. 182–89. Print.
———. "Truth in Fiction." *American Philosophical Quarterly* 15 (1978): 37–46. Print.
Lotman, Jurij M. *The Structure of the Artistic Text.* Trans. G. Lenhoff and R. Vroon. 1970. Ann Arbor: University of Michigan Press, 1977. Print.
Mitchell, W. J. T. *Picture Theory: Essays on Verbal and Visual Representation.* Chicago: University of Chicago Press, 1994. Print.
Nielsen, Henrik Skov. "Natural Authors, Unnatural Narration." *Postclassical Narratology.* Ed. Jan Alber and Monika Fludernik. Columbus: Ohio State University Press, 2010. 275–301. Print.
Ong, Walter. *Orality and Literacy: The Technologizing of the Word.* London: Methuen, 1982. Print.

Page, Ruth. "Gender and Genre Revisited: Storyworlds in Personal Blogs." *Genre: Forms of Discourse and Culture* 41 (Fall/Winter 2008): 151–77. Print.

Pavel, Thomas. *Fictional Worlds*. Cambridge MA: Harvard University Press, 1986. Print.

Rajewsky, Irina O. "Border Talks: The Problematic Status of Media Borders in the Current Debate about Intermediality." *Media Borders, Multimodality and Intermediality*. Ed. Lars Elleström. New York: Palgrave Macmillan, 2010. 51–68. Print.

Ryan, Marie-Laure. Introduction. *Narrative across Media: The Languages of Storytelling*. Ed. Marie-Laure Ryan. Lincoln: University of Nebraska Press, 2004. 1–40. Print.

———. *Possible Worlds, Artificial Intelligence, and Narrative Theory*. Bloomington: Indiana University Press, 1991. Print.

———. "Transfictionality across Media." *Theorizing Narrativity*. Ed. John Pier and José Angel García Landa. Berlin: De Gruyter, 2008. 385–417. Print.

———. "Transmedial Storytelling and Transfictionality." *Poetics Today* 34.3 (2013): 362–88. Print.

Sperber, Dan, and Deirdre Wilson. *Relevance: Communication and Cognition*. Oxford: Blackwell, 1986. Print.

Thacker, Eugene. *Biomedia*. Minneapolis: University of Minnesota Press, 2004. Print.

Thomas, Bronwen. "What Is Fan Fiction and Why Are People Saying Such Nice Things about It?" *Storyworlds* 3 (2011): 1–24. Print.

Walsh, Richard. *The Rhetoric of Fictionality: Narrative Theory and the Idea of Fiction*. Columbus: Ohio State University Press, 2007. Print.

Walton, Kendall. *Mimesis as Make-Believe: On the Foundations of the Representational Arts*. Cambridge MA: Harvard University Press, 1990. Print.

Werth, Paul. *Text Worlds: Representing Conceptual Space in Discourse*. London: Longman, 1999. Print.

Wistrand, Sten. "Time for Departure? The Principle of Minimal Departure: A Critical Examination." *Disputable Core Concepts of Narrative Theory*. Ed. Göran Rossholm and Christer Johansson. Bern: Peter Lang, 2012. 15–44. Print.

Wittgenstein, Ludwig. *Philosophical Investigations*. Trans. G. E. M. Anscombe. New York: Macmillan, 1968. Print.

Wolf, Werner. "Das Problem der Narrativität in Literatur, bildender Kunst und Musik: Ein Beitrag zu einer intermedialen Erzähltheorie." *Erzähltheorie transgenerisch, intermedial, interdisziplinär*. Ed. Vera Nünning and Ansgar Nünning. Trier: WVT, 2002. 23–104. Print.

———. "Narrative and Narrativity: A Narratological Reconceptualization and Its Applicability to the Visual Arts." *Word & Image* 19.3 (2003): 180–97. Print.

2 Emplotting a Storyworld in Drama

Selection, Time, and Construal in the Discourse of Hamlet

PATRICK COLM HOGAN

There is a common view that drama is "mimetic" rather than "diegetic," or narrated (see Richardson, "Drama" 151). In the sense intended by Plato and Aristotle, this is true. With limited exceptions, drama has no overt narrator, no speaker of the entire piece. However, as several authors have pointed out, given a more complex notion of narration, one may argue that drama does have a narrator.[1] More generally, drama involves not only a storyworld—thus *what* is represented—but also a discourse, or a means of representing the storyworld and thus *how* that storyworld is represented.[2] The point is perhaps more evident when exploring emplotment, one of the two components of discourse (along with narration).

Emplotment comprises selection, organization, and construal.[3] *Selection* is what storyworld information is presented in the narrative. For example, in telling a story about being taken to a room for special security screening at the airport, I may or may not recount how many guards were involved, what they said, and so on. *Organization* is the placement of information: when it is presented (thus timing), what it is presented with (thus collocation), the degree to which it is highlighted (thus foregrounding and backgrounding), and so on. To take an instance of timing, I may begin my airport security story with the phrase, "Fortunately, I got to the airport two hours early, because I needed nearly an hour for security"; or I may wait until the end of the narration, leaving you uncertain as to whether I made my flight. *Construal* is the precise verbal characterization or sensory depiction of the selected story information. For example, roughly the same physical information is given in the following sentences: "Surrounding me, the three guards moved me to a security office," and "The three guards walked with me to a private room." However, the event is characterized, thus construed, differently in the two cases.

The following analyses examine some key discourse features of *Hamlet*. Specifically, this chapter sets out to isolate recurring techniques that transform the storyworld of *Hamlet* into the plot as we encounter it in the play. These techniques are to a certain extent characteristic of the play and of its author. Thus the chapter suggests an analysis of part of Shakespeare's *narrative idiolect*, one treating the set of principles that generated emplotment in his works.[4] At the same time, these principles are presumably not confined to Shakespeare; hence they point to features widely available to dramatists, thereby stressing the importance of discourse operations even in mimetic works. Finally, if successful, the following discussion should illustrate how a careful analysis of emplotment may reveal significant but otherwise ignored aspects of a dramatic work, aspects with both thematic and aesthetic significance, even when that work has been the object of extensive critical scrutiny.[5]

The Emplotment of *Hamlet*: Some General Principles

The emplotment of *Hamlet* is marked by several recurring devices that are characteristic of Shakespeare's narrative idiolect, at least for this play. Two of the most prominent are trajectory interruption and intensified parallelism. *Trajectory interruption* occurs when one emotionally significant causal sequence remains incomplete because another such sequence is initiated. *Intensified parallelism* involves the repetition of more or less isomorphic sequences, or structurally similar complexes of characters, actions, and/or situations.

Intensified parallelism is the more complicated of the two devices. Plot parallels may be spread out across different points of the story (as in the homologies relating Prince Hamlet and King Hamlet to Laertes and Polonius, as well as Prince Fortinbras and King Fortinbras). However, Shakespeare often develops parallels across scenes, which is to say across sets of characters confined to a particular place and time in the storyworld and presented in a single, continuous part of the narrative discourse. (Note that a scene in this technical sense will not always correspond to what is marked as a scene in a play.) This point extends from explicit to implicit scenes—that is, scenes recounted by characters or even scenes that the reader must reconstruct. In some cases, Shakespeare develops the parallel with the same point of view; in other cases, he shifts the point of view. These variables produce sometimes extremely complex cases.

For example, in act 1, scene 4, Hamlet and Horatio are outside the castle awaiting the appearance of the ghost.[6] They hear trumpets and firing of "pieces" (1.4.8). Hamlet explains that the king is drinking. Obviously, we do not see this "rouse" (1.4.8), though we know it occurs by the sounds. In the final scene of the play, Claudius announces that he will drink and have "the battlements their ordnance fire" (5.2.271) if Hamlet does well in his contest with Laertes. Here, we are inside the castle; thus the perspective has changed. Moreover, there is a difference in modality. In the first instance, the rouse actually occurs, but in the second, it is only a possibility. Nonetheless, there is a clear parallel between the two.

Parallelisms and interruptions in *Hamlet* are often guided by what might be called a "selection model." When selecting information for emplotment, an author may draw on a particular model that orients his or her attention to specific aspects of the simulated storyworld. In both productive story generation and discourse selection, writers often rely on models that are salient in the context of writing. These models include the role of an author, who plans out the actions and experiences of his or her characters. In this case, the writer takes authorship as a source domain and uses the idea of authorial creative control as a model for imagining some character. The resulting character is a schemer who tries to script the actions and experiences of other characters, as if he or she were, in effect, an author creating a story with those characters. In the case of plays, the relevant models also include the audience members, who are the unobserved observers of events. The audience-based model fosters spy characters and "overhearers." Both recur cross-culturally.[7]

Shakespeare makes almost obsessive use of these models in both storyworld creation and emplotment. As such, these models have consequences for the work's causal and emotional structures. But some of the key consequences appear to be thematic and to derive from the fact that the schemes and spying, which powerful figures in the government engage in, routinely fail and often with tragic consequences.[8] These models also have important narrational consequences in that the author- and audience-like characters become embedded narrators within the work.[9]

Shakespeare also makes use of complex techniques of construal. In drama, without a general narrator's voice, direct construal—thus the explicit, verbal characterization of events, characters, or scenes—is usually confined to embedded narrators (e.g., a character recounting an event).

However, an author may also use *indirect* or *suggested construals*. One way of indirectly construing events, characters, or situations is through genre categorization. For example, a young woman walking down a street at night is implicitly construed one way in a romantic comedy and a different way in a horror film (a point stressed in Noël Carroll's idea of "criterial prefocusing"). Such genre categorization may occur overtly (e.g., when the genre is named in a work's title) or implicitly (when it is suggested by the ongoing development of the work). In *Hamlet*, changing indirect suggestions of genre may repeatedly shift the spectator's genre evaluations and expectations, thus providing variable indirect construals of events and so on.

More precisely, four genres are at issue in *Hamlet*. The main plot, which involves Hamlet, Claudius, the ghost, and Gertrude, is ambiguous between the heroic and revenge genres. The secondary plot, which involves Hamlet, Ophelia, and Polonius, is ambiguous between the romantic and seduction genres. All four genres are cross-cultural, prototypical kinds of story structure (see chapters 3 and 4 of Hogan, *Affective Narratology*).

Very briefly, the *heroic* prototype includes two story sequences—one bearing on the usurpation of the rightful leader of a group and the other concerning threats to the group from some external enemy, commonly an invading army. The *revenge* genre prototypically concerns the hero's attempt to kill the murderer of a family member. As in *Hamlet*, this attempt often results in the death of innocents and even the death of the revenger himself or herself. The heroic plot most often strongly favors the usurped ruler, presenting his or her restoration as just and even utopian. In contrast, the revenge genre is often highly ambivalent, sympathizing with the hero's grief and anger but condemning his or her violence.

The *romantic* plot features lovers being separated by some social representatives, such as parents, then being reunited in an idealized union. The *seduction* plot incorporates deception and abandonment, often with the woman pregnant. The seduction plot may lead to the deaths of those involved; however, even when it leads to marriage, this genre tends to be highly ambivalent.

Again, *Hamlet* is often ambiguous between being an instance of the heroic or revenge genre (for one part of the play) and the romantic or seduction genre (for another part of the play). At times, these ambiguities serve to intensify the emotional impact of the play. At other times, they seem to have primarily thematic consequences. Note that, in both cases, the genre shifts mean that the play ambiguously moves between more and less ambivalent construals. This shifting greatly increases the emotional and evaluative complexity of the work.

Finally, Shakespeare also takes up discourse features at the intersection of narration and emplotment. The discourse largely confines the depiction of inner psychological states to the title character; however, at certain points Shakespeare strategically violates this restriction, revealing the inner thoughts of other characters. He does this, first of all, to produce an understanding of the main causal sequences. Also, he extends the thematic concerns and enhances the emotional impact of the work, in part through intensifying our empathic response to characters.

In connection with the last point, it is worth briefly considering the varieties of such emotional impacts. The most obvious variety comprises those feelings provoked by the story; however, other sorts of emotional effects occur with discourse manipulation. Somewhat reformulating the valuable analysis of Ed Tan (see 65 and 82), we may distinguish three sorts of affect in narrative: story emotion, plot interest, and artifact emotion. *Story emotion* concerns a response to the events and characters in the storyworld. *Plot interest* is a function of the selection, organization, and construal of the storyworld in emplotment. For example, it includes our curiosity about past, unreported events and our suspense regarding future events (to use Sternberg's terms). *Artifact emotion* bears on the aesthetic features of the narrative as a human creation and includes matters such as style. Commonly, our artifact emotion results from one of two factors. It may derive from our isolation of an unusual patterning, or patterning that goes beyond accident (e.g., the rhythmic variations in meter, which go beyond the patterning of ordinary speech). Alternatively, it may be the result of an unusual prototype approximation. For example, in the case of facial beauty, the most beautiful face is, roughly, the most average face (a prototype is, roughly, an average case, as Langlois and Roggman note).

The Emplotment of *Hamlet*: Acts 1 and 2

Any reader unfamiliar with *Hamlet* may be surprised to find that despite its wealth of story concerns, the play begins with two minor, indeed wholly insignificant characters—Barnardo and Francisco.[10] The opening scene is quite revealing about the nature and function of emplotment. Specifically, Francisco is on watch. Barnardo comes to replace him. He is to be joined by Horatio and Marcellus. In terms of story understanding, there is no clear reason to begin the play here rather than with Horatio, Marcellus, and Barnardo waiting for a ghost to reappear. Note that this point does not concern the story but the plot. In the storyworld, regular changes of the guard would occur; thus a guard would have been on duty before Barnardo reported. The question is, why did Shakespeare select this part of the storyworld for presentation, since it appears irrelevant for understanding the main causal sequences of the play? The reasons seem primarily emotional. The opening presents us with Francisco's isolation and establishes a degree of wariness with the question, "Who's there?" (1.1.1). This setting is significant primarily owing to Hamlet's subsequent isolation. But why connect Francisco with Hamlet? Before leaving, Francisco remarks that he is "sick at heart" (1.1.9). We are never told the reasons for his anxiety, but Francisco's unease is echoed in the final scene of the play when Hamlet remarks to Horatio on "how ill all's here about my heart" (5.2.213–14). The parallelism suggests the pervasiveness of melancholy and foreboding in Denmark, making these feelings more broadly social and less unique to Hamlet. The parallelism also serves to tie the opening scenes more strongly with the end, thus enhancing the pattern of circularity. This pattern is significant because circularity is often an aesthetically consequential artifactual feature of a narrative.

After Francisco leaves, Marcellus introduces the topic of one main story sequence, briefly recounting the appearance of the ghost on two previous nights. The ghost then reappears. In this manipulation of organization we learn about the three appearances of the ghost in quick succession, with the first and second presented in abbreviated form. Clearly, this manipulation serves the function of emotional intensification. In contrast, imagine an emplotment that actually depicted the first watch with the ghost on stage, then had the characters return for the second watch with the ghost, and then reassembled them for the third watch with the ghost. This choice would almost certainly dissipate the audience's response through habituation, perhaps even producing comic effects. At the same time, this tripling of the ghost's appearance (recounted, rather than directly represented) reinforces our sense of his reality (in contrast with a single representation).

The dialogue of the watchers serves to introduce not only the identity of the ghost but also the story of his combat with Fortinbras. This selection of information has a story function in providing us background for a separate story sequence (the conflict with Norway). It also provokes interest (curiosity, in Sternberg's term) regarding the details of this story.

As already noted, a recurring emplotment technique in *Hamlet* is trajectory interruption. Just as a story sequence is moving toward some point of intensity, Shakespeare breaks off and presents us with part of another story sequence. This aspect of emplotment is clearly designed to maintain interest in much the way that cliff-hangers sustain interest in television serials. Often, Shakespeare does so by shifting scenes. (This tack is a version of the "meanwhile, back at the ranch" technique.) Thus, after the meeting with the ghost, the next scene takes us inside the castle, where the relationships among Hamlet, Gertrude, and Claudius are revealed. Before this action, however, the opening scene itself is interrupted.

Specifically, after the ghost has appeared, we are not immediately given his purposes or the consequences of the appearance. Rather, once he leaves, Marcellus speaks of preparations for war, and Horatio proceeds to explain the nature and development of young Fortinbras's actions to regain the lands lost by his father. Realistically speaking, the scene is bizarre. The three men have just seen a ghost. Horatio "tremble[s] and look[s] pale" at the sight (1.1.53). But then they shift to a leisurely conversation about contemporary politics. Evidently, however, audiences do not question the transition, presumably because it so coheres with other aspects of the scene. First, the enhanced watch is due to preparations for war. Second, Horatio's speech elaborates on the story of King Hamlet and Fortinbras that was briefly introduced a moment earlier. Finally, this political situation is used to explain the appearance of the ghost. In short, the political dialogue develops plot interest even as it violates story plausibility. Apparently audiences accept this bizarre interruption because the plot interest outweighs the story's implausibility. We in effect treat this sequence as if it were narrated by someone outside the main action, a narrator who recounts the ghost's appearance and who then unperturbedly shifts to political background.

In keeping with the recurring structure, the interruption is itself interrupted by the ghost's return. Horatio links and justifies the two interruptions by taking up the political theme in relation to the ghostly visitation. Specifically, he asks the ghost about the "country's fate" (1.1.133). But, before the ghost can answer, the cock crows, and he must return to confinement. Here, again, we have an instance of the interruption technique serving to intensify the emotional response.

The crowing of the cock brings up an interesting aspect of the timing of the scene. There is a common, if usually implicit expectation that mimetic works present actual occurrences in (roughly) their actual duration, except in unusual circumstances (e.g., when film speed is altered). In other words, the idea is that plot duration and story duration must be about the same if there is no deletion of story elements in the plot. But this scene suggests something very different. Shortly after Barnardo arrives, he remarks on the time: "'Tis now struck twelve" (1.1.7). A mere thirty-two lines later, when the ghost enters, it is suggested that the time is one o'clock (1.1.36–39). Only about a hundred lines later, it is dawn. Clearly, Shakespeare has drastically reduced the story time in the narration time.[11] This time line may be another reason why we are able to accept the quick transition to ordinary conversation after the ghost's appearance. Perhaps we, as audience members, implicitly sense that the timing in the discourse—that is, what we see and hear—is a radically condensed version of the timing in the storyworld, or of the events themselves.

The scene ends with a plan: Horatio and Marcellus will discuss what they have seen with Hamlet. This decision leads nicely to scene 2, where Hamlet is introduced; however, it does not lead to the colloquy between Hamlet and Horatio. That plan is interrupted, and we are introduced instead to Claudius. Just as Horatio provided the backstory to the appearance of the ghost, Claudius now provides some of the backstory on the death of King Hamlet—thus the backstory to there being a ghost in the first place. This exposition is connected with plot interest in that we are first given the emotionally intense appearance of the ghost. It has led to a range of questions, which Claudius, then, partially answers. But the answers are incomplete, as we still do not know the nature of King Hamlet's death. Nor do we understand the precise relationship between Claudius and Gertrude that led to their quick marriage. Here, we might expect further treatment of the king's demise, but it, too, is interrupted by a reference to Fortinbras—with the movement from the dead King Hamlet to Fortinbras precisely paralleling the sequence in the preceding scene. The danger posed by Fortinbras is, of course, the danger of invasion. This element is, again, a definitive part of the cross-cultural heroic prototype. It tends to give at least some viewers the sense that they are witnessing a heroic plot and orients their expectations accordingly. This topic is then deferred (in another interruption) until there is further communication with the present king of Norway, Fortinbras's uncle.

At this point, one might expect a return to King Hamlet, but now Laertes is introduced. He is given permission to return to France. The point of this plot selection seems to lie merely in contrasting this decision with Claudius's wish that Hamlet not return to his studies at Wittenberg (thus yielding an inverse parallel). Now Prince Hamlet finally enters the play. He does so first in an aside, revealing the nonpersonified, encompassing narrator's internal access that will recur later in the play. Claudius says that Hamlet's departure is "retrograde to our desire" and he wishes Hamlet to remain in "our eye" (1.2.114, 116). Claudius's reasons are putatively a matter of affection; however, insofar as we have hints that this play is a heroic narrative, it is not too difficult to infer that Claudius may worry about an unobserved Hamlet's possibly undertaking subversive actions. Again, it is all a matter of emplotment, a selection from the storyworld. We know from elsewhere in the play that the nonpersonified narrator is not strictly limited to Hamlet's thoughts; rather, Shakespeare is willing to give us access to Claudius's thoughts when needed. He does not do so here, though such access to the storyworld would confirm or disconfirm our suspicions.

Subsequently, we are presented with Hamlet's first soliloquy, again an indication of the narrator's internal access. In this soliloquy, Hamlet explains that Gertrude has married Claudius "within a month" of King Hamlet's death (1.2.145). Today, audience members have become so accustomed to the play that they may hardly even notice this revelation, but it is, indeed, shocking. It strongly suggests a prior relationship between the two that went beyond that of sister-in-law and brother-in-law. In the genre context of the revenge prototype, it may hint at a crime in which the queen was complicit or even active. Put differently, the genre categorization may suggest a particular construal of the relationship between Claudius and Gertrude, as well as their joint responsibility for King Hamlet's death.

At this juncture, with its hints of a revenge narrative, Horatio enters and explains the ghost's appearance to Hamlet. Three points are important for our purposes. First, Hamlet immediately swears Horatio, Marcellus, and Barnardo to silence on this topic. This move suggests his strong mistrust of the other royals and perhaps the beginnings of a strategic plan. Second, this plan may hint at the use of an author model. Finally, Hamlet would not need a plan if he did not already suspect a particular motive for the ghost's appearance. Horatio describes the ghost as expressing "sorrow" rather than "anger" (1.2.232). Nonetheless, Hamlet immediately infers that there has been "foul play" (1.2.256). It seems very unlikely that someone would jump to this conclusion (on the basis of a sorrowful ghost) if he or she did not already have suspicions—a possibility that fosters plot interest. All this discourse information is carefully selected to suggest, but not confirm, the existence of such suspicions. The point is even more striking here than in the case of Claudius, since Shakespeare could easily have had Hamlet spell out these suspicions in an aside or soliloquy.

The next scene again interrupts the development of the King Hamlet story. It begins with Laertes, but the topic is the romantic involvement of Hamlet and Ophelia. This topic introduces a further story—or, rather, two further stories. In the course of the play, Hamlet presents his wooing of Ophelia as part of a romantic narrative; however, Laertes and Polonius both construe it as a seduction narrative. Moreover, they do so by explicitly projecting possibilities for the future "loss" of "honor" (1.3.29) and pregnancy (1.3.109).

The use of plot parallelism is almost obtrusive here. In this scene, Laertes advises Ophelia, then Polonius advises Laertes, then Polonius advises Ophelia. We may also recall that, in the preceding scene, Horatio told Hamlet about the ghost as Barnardo earlier had told Marcellus, Horatio, and us—and as, even before that (we are informed), Marcellus had told Horatio.

The intensified parallelism continues with the next two scenes in which Hamlet, Horatio, and Marcellus wait for and encounter the ghost, just as Horatio, Marcellus, and Barnardo did earlier. Indeed, these scenes end act 1, giving the act a circular formal structure. The link between Hamlet and Francisco is established here initially, for Hamlet introduces the scene by observing that "it is very cold" (1.4.1), echoing Francisco's earlier observation, "'Tis bitter cold" (1.1.8), right before explaining that he is "sick at heart" (1.1.9).

We cannot go through all plot elements in these scenes; however, a few additional points are worth noting. Hamlet's initial worry about the ghost is whether he is real or a demonic impersonator (1.4.40). His concern straightforwardly introduces a question into the minds of the audience, who now can envision two possible outcomes. These results have great consequences for everything that follows, most obviously in suggesting that the ghost is an unreliable (embedded) narrator. The point is elaborated by Horatio, who specifically worries that the ghost will lead Hamlet to suicide (1.4.69). This passage prepares us for Hamlet's subsequent thoughts of suicide. At the same time, it makes those thoughts ambiguous. Is his apparent death wish part of his scheme, a spontaneous emotional tendency, or evidence that the ghost is indeed tempting him? All of these possibilities result from the selection of information presented in the discourse and the construal of that information by the characters (here, Horatio's worry over the ghost's intentions). The answers should be readily available in the storyworld and even to the narrator, who, again, has access to Hamlet's thoughts. These elements of emplotment clearly have emotional consequences, but they also may have thematic resonances relating to questions of satanic temptation.

A scene change occurs when Hamlet follows the ghost to a place where the others cannot observe them. Here, the ghost explains that he has been killed by Claudius and calls for "revenge" (1.5.7). This scene clearly connects the play with the revenge genre, which, subsequently, is probably more salient than the heroic genre is. The play, however, remains ambiguous between the two. No less important, when the ghost explains who committed the murder, Hamlet exclaims, "O my prophetic soul!" (1.5.40), indicating that he did suspect that his uncle had committed murder (or, in terms of the heroic narrative, usurpation). Moreover, the phrasing of the ghost's subsequent speech allows the possibility that Claudius seduced Gertrude before the murder (hence the reference to adultery [1.5.42]).

Finally, Hamlet makes the surprising announcement that he may "put an antic disposition on" (1.5.172). This declaration again suggests the author model, with Hamlet manipulating a story. As he has not had time to formulate a scheme since speaking with the ghost, we must conclude that he had this scheme in mind already. Again, our omniscient narrator could certainly have presented this information to us (e.g., in the form of a soliloquy), but the selection of information is more likely to provoke our interest by eliciting curiosity over what the purpose of the antic disposition could be.[12]

The second act begins as the first did, with something—in this case, a plan rather than a character—that is largely irrelevant to the causal development of the story. It does, however, bear on the audience's attentional orientation and on some thematic concerns of the play. Again, the first act ends with the hint of Hamlet's schemes. The second begins by extending the author model to Polonius. Drawing on the closely related audience model, Polonius has plotted out a scheme of espionage. As a matter of fact, his espionage is not mere eavesdropping but playacting to produce intelligence. Specifically, Polonius explains how Reynaldo can take up a role in order to learn the truth about Laertes's activities in France. This scene calls out for an analysis in terms of emplotment because it is so clearly outside any significant causal sequence in the storyworld. It is entirely superfluous in terms of story information. We therefore infer that it has other functions. Among other things, it enhances our sensitivity to acting and espionage.

This exchange is followed by Ophelia's distressed account of Hamlet's madness. Polonius construes his behavior as the madness of love. Indeed, elements of Hamlet's behavior fit with this aspect of a romantic narrative. Of course, we may recall Hamlet's statement that he will perform the role of madman, especially since strategic playacting has been made salient. At the same time, however, implications of the romantic genre (with its frequently distracted lovers) may lead us to wonder about the degree to which Hamlet is acting and the degree to which Polonius is correct about Hamlet's lovesickness.

Once one becomes aware of patterns in the work's emplotment, the second scene is almost shockingly predictable. In this scene, we learn that the king has brought Rosencrantz and Guildenstern to spy on Hamlet in order to discover the nature of his madness. In short, we have a third instance of playacting to produce intelligence through espionage (the others being the schemes of Hamlet and Polonius). However, it is not simply aesthetic parallelism bearing on the work as an artifact. That Claudius has engaged in this trickery suggests again that he finds Hamlet's behavior worrisome and his intentions potentially dangerous, in the manner of either a heroic or revenge narrative.

Hamlet's idea of acting to produce intelligence is interrupted by Polonius's espionage scheme, which is not developed as we turn to the Rosencrantz and Guildenstern scheme of espionage. This effort is in turn interrupted by Polonius's report that he has discovered the cause of Hamlet's madness. Before this line can be developed, however, yet another interruption occurs, and we return specifically to the invasion sequence of the heroic plot. Just as Fortinbras's threat had interrupted Claudius's speech in the second scene of the first act, it now interrupts his speech in the second scene of the second act. The interest of the audience should be rather intense at this point, given the multiple layering of uncertain futures for the action—all intensified not only by selection and construal but also by the clear manipulation of timing as well. At this point, the Fortinbras issue is supposedly resolved, but the resolution is insane: Denmark is supposed to allow Fortinbras's army free passage through the kingdom to go and fight against Poland. In effect, Norway says, "This army was put together to invade you. If you just let the army enter your territory, however, it won't attack." This situation, too, is likely to provoke plot interest. Claudius does not actually make a decision at this point, leaving that issue also unresolved when we return to Polonius.

As already indicated, Polonius has changed his view and believes that Hamlet's approach to Ophelia is part of a romantic narrative rather than a seduction narrative. (Of course, he would not phrase it this way.) In connection with this change—and in keeping with the romantic prototype—he presumably fears that Claudius and Gertrude will not only reject the marriage to Ophelia as beneath Hamlet but also will be outraged by Polonius's even suggesting the possibility. His apprehensiveness accounts for his nervous attempts to delay introducing the topic. Once he arrives at the point, however, Polonius proposes the one solution that has become obvious in the development of these events—espionage. This spying, as with all other schemes in the play, fails. The thematic suggestion throughout is that intelligence gathering tends to be self-confirming. Polonius, like other spies, finds only what he wants to find.

When Polonius approaches Hamlet, Hamlet indicates that he is aware of Polonius's purposes when he says that Polonius is not "honest" (2.2.176). In this scene, Hamlet's "antic disposition" suggests equivocation, or the play with language that Jesuits used to conceal subversive schemes and actions. This exchange gives us some hint—but only a hint—as to the nature of Hamlet's own scheme, perhaps relating it to the heroic more than the revenge prototype (given the purposes of Jesuitical equivocation). Once again, it is important to stress that it is not simply storyworld simulation but emplotment. Given that Shakespeare tacitly simulated Hamlet as having plans, he could have presented us with those plans. Moreover, he could have given us greater access to Hamlet away from court observation so that we could have a more definitive sense of his madness or sanity. These are all matters of selection and organization. Similarly, Shakespeare could have been less equivocal over the play's genre. Again, it may be a usurpation and restoration plot, aimed at enthroning Hamlet, the rightful heir and a popular leader ("loved of the distracted multitude" [4.3.4]). Alternatively, it may be a revenge plot. At least for the original audience, the former would be likely to provoke less ambivalence, in keeping with the usual operation of these genres.

After Polonius leaves, Hamlet turns to the next set of spies. Here, the suspicions of Claudius are indicated indirectly by Rosencrantz's suggestion that Hamlet's distress is caused by "ambition" (2.2.256). Moreover, "ambition" suggests the heroic usurpation sequence rather than revenge. Hamlet's own knowledge of the espionage comes out when he says, "I know the good King and Queen have sent for you" (2.2.288–89), evidently implying that he has his own spies.

After these multiple instances of acting and espionage, the play introduces real actors. Literalizing the model that has been so fruitful to this point, Hamlet determines to use the real actors for intelligence gathering and specifically to test the ghost's statements about Claudius. Before this point, however, we have another parallel in which the actors recite the story of the murder of a king, a story taken from a heroic narrative. The connections here are so straightforward that they do not require explication.

Shakespeare has elaborated and particularized the emplotment of his story using idiolectal discourse strategies bearing on selection, organization, and construal. By the end of act 2, these strategies are all well established. In the remainder of the play, they are further elaborated and intertwined, but they do not change fundamentally. These strategies include systematic trajectory interruption and intensified parallelism across represented and recounted, actual and hypothetical scenes. They often involve selection models as well. They lead to author-like "plotting," as well as espionage, understood in terms of playacting and audience observation—all of which give rise to embedded narration. Shakespeare also makes tacit use of shifting genre categories, with the different, indirect construals they entail. These strategies serve to develop and complicate the understanding of the story; to sustain interest; to intensify emotional response, both empathic and artifactual; and to elaborate thematic concerns. This particular complex of operations may be characteristic of this play in particular or of Shakespeare's work more generally. Considered individually, however, the operations are undoubtedly found in a wide range of dramas, pointing once again to the importance of discourse manipulation even in mimetic forms.[13]

Notes

1. See, for example, Richardson, "Drama"; Jahn. In *Narrative Discourse*, I argue for conceptually distinguishing an encompassing, nonpersonified narrator as the source of the selected, organized, and construed information defining the plot. Moreover, I discuss the relation of the narrator to the implied author and the relation of the implied author to the real author. Clearly, that discussion cannot be recapitulated here, in an essay on another topic; however, I do not believe anything in the following pages rests on that discussion. Readers who agree with Bordwell in rejecting this idea of a narrator should feel free to follow Bordwell and substitute "narration" for "encompassing nonpersonified narrator." Readers who are simply uncomfortable with the term "narrator" may wish to follow Chatman or Bareis. Given that narrational functions are verbal in the case of prose fiction and partially nonverbal in the case of drama and film, Chatman proposes using the more general term "presenter," rather than "narrator," to cover both cases (115); similarly, Bareis proposes using "mediator."
2. A brief essay can hardly discuss all the discourse elements of drama. For influential discussions of important aspects of discourse and drama, see Fludernik; Nünning and Sommer; Pfister.
3. As Hühn and Sommer write, using somewhat different subdivisions, drama involves "selection, segmentation, combination, and focus."
4. A *narrative idiolect* is a complex of cognitive and affective structures, processes, and contents through which an author produces particular narratives. In an earlier essay ("Narrative Universals"), I considered principles of narrative idiolect that served to generate Shakespearean storyworlds.
5. *Hamlet* has obviously generated a vast amount of criticism. (For a brave attempt to overview this criticism, see Wofford.) However, I have not located a focus on the discourse structure of the play in any of this work.
6. Text references refer to act, scene, and line of the New American Library's 1998 edition of Shakespeare's *The Tragedy of Hamlet, Prince of Denmark*.

7. Schemer characters include Cāṇakya in Viśākhadatta's Sanskrit *Mudrārākṣasa* and Wang Yün in the Chinese Yüan drama *A Stratagem of Interlocking Rings*. Sanskrit works such as Bhāsa's *Svapnavāsavadattam* or Japanese works such as Chikamatsu's *Drum of the Waves of Horikawa* provide examples of the unobserved observer.
8. As would be expected, the representation of espionage in the play points toward some historical considerations that we are not able to explore here. For a discussion of relevant historical context, see Parker.
9. On embedded narration, see Nelles.
10. Ideally, we would go through the entire play, examining the full emplotment; however, constraints of space dictate that we can only consider part of the work. But the same techniques recur in acts 3 through 5. In that sense, a careful analysis of the first and second acts should be sufficient to give a sense of Shakespeare's emplotment of Hamlet's storyworld.
11. This technique recurs elsewhere in Shakespeare's plays and in other works, as Brian Richardson has valuably discussed ("'Time'").
12. In cases such as this one, we see an important, if somewhat obvious, emplotment device not only in Shakespeare's works but almost everywhere else. This selective withholding of information is crucial for understanding the story's main causal sequences. Narratologists refer to a narrator's provision or withholding of information as the narrator's "communicativeness." See, for example, Bordwell 59.
13. I am grateful to Marie-Laure Ryan and Jan-Noël Thon for very helpful comments on earlier versions of this chapter.

Works Cited

Bareis, J. Alexander. *Fiktionales Erzählen: Zur Theorie der literarischen Fiktion als Make-Believe*. Göteborg, Sweden: Acta Universitatis Gothoburgensis, 2008. Print.

Bordwell, David. *Narration in the Fiction Film*. Madison: University of Wisconsin Press, 1985. Print.

Carroll, Noël. "Film, Emotion, and Genre." *Passionate Views: Film, Cognition, and Emotion*. Ed. Carl Plantinga and Greg M. Smith. Baltimore MD: Johns Hopkins University Press, 1999. 21–47. Print.

Chatman, Seymour. *Coming to Terms: The Rhetoric of Narrative and Film*. Ithaca NY: Cornell University Press, 1990. Print.

Fludernik, Monika. "Narrative and Drama." *Theorizing Narrativity*. Ed. John Pier and José Angel García Landa. Berlin: De Gruyter, 2008. 355–83. Print.

Hogan, Patrick Colm. *Affective Narratology: The Emotional Structure of Stories*. Lincoln: University of Nebraska Press, 2011. Print.

———. *Narrative Discourse: Authors and Narrators in Literature, Film, and Art.* Columbus: Ohio State University Press, 2013. Print.

———. "Narrative Universals, Heroic Tragi-Comedy, and Shakespeare's Political Ambivalence." *College Literature* 33.1 (2006): 34–66. Print.

Hühn, Peter, and Roy Sommer. "Narration in Poetry and Drama." *The Living Handbook of Narratology*. Ed. Peter Hühn et al. Hamburg: Hamburg University Press, 2011. Web. June 1, 2011.

Jahn, Manfred. "Narrative Voice and Agency in Drama: Aspects of a Narratology of Drama." *New Literary History* 32 (2001): 659–79. Print.

Langlois, J. H., and L. A. Roggman. "Attractive Faces Are Only Average." *Psychological Science* 1 (1990): 115–21. Print.

Nelles, William. "Embedding." *Routledge Encyclopedia of Narrative Theory*. Ed. David Herman, Manfred Jahn, and Marie-Laure Ryan. New York: Routledge, 2005. 134–35. Print.

Nünning, Ansgar, and Roy Sommer. "Diagetic and Mimetic Narrative: Some Further Steps towards a Transgeneric Narratology of Drama." *Theorizing Narrativity*. Ed. John Pier and José Ángel García Landa. Berlin: De Gruyter, 2008. 331–54. Print.

Parker, Patricia. "*Othello* and *Hamlet*: Dilation, Spying, and the 'Secret Place' of Woman." *Representations* 44 (1993): 60–95. Print.

Pfister, Manfred. *The Theory and Analysis of Drama*. Trans. John Halliday. New York: Cambridge University Press, 1988. Print.

Richardson, Brian. "Drama and Narrative." *The Cambridge Companion to Narrative*. Ed. David Herman. Cambridge, UK: Cambridge University Press, 2007. 142–55. Print.

———. "'Time Is Out of Joint': Narrative Models and the Temporality of the Drama." *Poetics Today* 8.2 (1987): 299–309. Print.

Shakespeare, William. *The Tragedy of Hamlet, Prince of Denmark*. Ed. Sylvan Barnet. New York: New American Library, 1998. Print.

Sternberg, Meir. *Expositional Modes and Temporal Ordering in Fiction*. Baltimore MD: Johns Hopkins University Press, 1978. Print.

Tan, Ed. *Emotion and the Structure of Narrative Film: Film as an Emotion Machine*. Trans. Barbara Fasting. Mahwah NJ: Lawrence Erlbaum Associates, 1996. Print.

Wofford, Susanne. "A Critical History of *Hamlet*." *Hamlet*. Ed. Susanne Wofford. Boston: Bedford Books, 1994. 181–207. Print.

3 Subjectivity across Media

On Transmedial Strategies of Subjective Representation in Contemporary Feature Films, Graphic Novels, and Computer Games

JAN-NOËL THON

Prototypical narrative representations not only represent a storyworld situated in space and time but also populate that storyworld with characters to whom some kind of mental life can be ascribed. Accordingly, narrative representations across media may employ a number of different strategies to represent the consciousness of characters. Providing some kind of "direct access" may be the most obvious option, but it certainly is not the most common. Despite differences with regard to the mediality of conventionally distinct media and the idiosyncrasies of individual narrative representations, however, the *subjective representation* of consciousness can be considered a genuinely transmedial phenomenon in that it is realized across a wide range of media, each with its own specific limitations and affordances.[1] Hence, transmedial strategies of subjective representation appear to be a particularly rewarding area of inquiry for a transmedial narratology that acknowledges both similarities and differences in the ways narrative media narrate.[2]

Since the representation of subjectivity can be considered a salient prototypical feature of narrative, it comes as no surprise that the strategies narratives may employ to represent subjectivity have been at the center of narratological interest for at least the past five decades.[3] Accordingly, there is an impressive amount of research on the narratological problems occurring in the context of representations of subjectivity, but the intense attention toward these problems in both classical and contemporary narratology has also lead to a multitude of competing and often contradictory terms and concepts that does not necessarily further mutual understanding.[4] The lack of consensus becomes particularly apparent in the seemingly endless debates surrounding the three most influential terms that have been proposed to describe the representation of subjectivity in literary texts, feature films, and beyond: "point of view," "perspective," and "focalization."[5] I will also refer to point of view and perspective in a rather technical sense, but it generally seems preferable to use less "charged" expressions such as "the representation of subjectivity" or "subjective representation" to describe the representation of characters' consciousness.

It should be noted, however, that *representing subjectivity* is understood here in a broader sense than subjective representation is. The former includes comparatively indirect modes of representation that allow recipients to infer certain aspects of the represented characters' minds without providing anything amounting to what may roughly be described as "direct access."[6] It is precisely this kind of direct access to a represented character's subjectivity that subjective representation provides. Moreover, while narratologists usually refer to the representation of the mind or the consciousness of a character in this context, I will focus on the subjective representation not of a character's mind or consciousness in general but on what may be described as perceptual or quasi-perceptual aspects of the latter. Thus I will be able to give particular emphasis to the representation of various kinds of mental imagery that occur in the context of characters' perceptions, hallucinations, memories, dreams, and fantasies.[7]

The primary aim of this chapter is to make plausible the notion that, on the one hand, certain strategies of subjective representation of (quasi-) perceptual aspects of characters' consciousness may be treated as transmedial phenomena on a certain level of abstraction, but, on the other hand, a transmedial narratology that remains media conscious also needs to focus on the medium-specific realization of these strategies and on the medium-specific functions they fulfill. Before I take a closer look at the realization of these strategies of subjective representation in feature films such as Bryan Singer's *The Usual Suspects*, Ron Howard's *A Beautiful Mind*, or David Fincher's *Fight Club*; graphic novels such as Alan Moore and Kevin O'Neill's *The League of Extraordinary Gentlemen*, Frank Miller's *Sin City*, or Neil Gaiman's *The Sandman*; and computer games such as Infinity Ward's *Call of Duty*, Rocksteady's *Batman: Arkham Asylum*, or Double Fine's *Psychonauts*, however, I would like to sketch how what I consider to be transmedial strategies of subjective representation relate to transmedial strategies of intersubjective and objective representation, respectively.

Objective, Intersubjective, and Subjective Representation

Narrative representations across media are arguably "best understood as deploying certain global strategies of narration within which the local perturbation, seen in a specified fashion, can be made to fit" (Wilson, *Narration* 3). I would maintain, however, that a bottom-up approach (such as Branigan's in *Narrative Comprehension*) that analyzes local strategies of subjective representation in order to arrive at the global structure of a given narrative representation is methodologically preferable to a top-down approach (such as Genette's in *Narrative Discourse* and *Narrative Discourse Revisited*) that tends to postulate a global structure before analyzing local perturbations from it. Against this background I propose to distinguish between *subjective*, *intersubjective*, and *objective modes of representation* as three particularly salient prototypical relations between a character's consciousness and its narrative representation. As Edward Branigan's examination of what he calls "focalization" makes clear, what is represented by narrative representations across media can often be understood as "diegetically intersubjective, or 'objective,' in the sense that it is reported independently of a narrator, or else appears seemingly without any mediation as a 'fact' of some kind" (*Narrative Comprehension* 161). But, of course, this does not mean that the recipients are unable to infer, at least to a certain extent, how the characters that are intersubjectively represented experience the situation, how they perceive the represented storyworld elements, what is on their minds.

While much of classical narratological research focused on what Alan Palmer calls "the speech category approach" (53) to the representation of characters' consciousness in literary texts, the past decade has seen an increasing interest in these kinds of intersubjective representations of subjectivity. What Lisa Zunshine describes as our "mind-reading skills"—that is, "our ability to explain people's behavior in terms of their thoughts, feelings, beliefs, and desires" (6)—is no longer seen as being limited to the actual world, but "[c]onstructions of fictional minds" appear to be "inextricably bound up with presentations of action. Direct access to inner speech and states of mind is only a small part of the process of building up the sense of a mind in action" (Palmer 210–11).

Similarly, Per Persson examines the role of folk psychology for the construction of characters' minds in feature film, emphasizing that "mental attribution of fictional characters is not solely a question of face and body-cue ability," since these cues are always "placed within a context of mental states" (183).

Even if we leave the more philosophical implications of objectivity, intersubjectivity, and subjectivity aside, however, it seems clear that narrative representations may not only represent storyworld elements, first, as they are (subjectively) represented in the mind of a particular character and, second, as they are (intersubjectively) perceived by a group of characters, but also, third, represent storyworld elements that are not perceived by any character in the storyworld at all. If one keeps in mind that some nonsubjective modes of representation contribute significantly to the recipients' construction not only of the characters' consciousness but also of the less conscious, or "directly accessible," aspects of characters' minds, a heuristic distinction between objective and intersubjective (as well as subjective) modes of representation becomes important for any bottom-up attempt to analyze a narrative representation's global structure of subjectivity as the specific combination of local strategies of more or less subjective representation.[8]

Incidentally, my insistence on drawing such a distinction should not be misunderstood as a claim that subjectivity, intersubjectivity, and objectivity are always clearly delineated. Just as our mental perspective on something can be more or less subjective or objective (see Eder 578), so can the intersubjective representation of storyworld elements, since "objectivity and subjectivity interact in a narrative film [or other kinds of narrative representation—JNT] by being alternated, overlapped, or otherwise mixed, producing complex descriptions of space, time, and causality" (Branigan, *Narrative Comprehension* 160). However, the observation that we are confronted with a scalar distinction between subjectivity and objectivity does not prevent us from identifying certain points on the scale that appear to be particularly salient for narrative representation across media. At least in contemporary feature films, graphic novels, and computer games, intersubjective representation may be considered the unmarked case while objective representation and subjective representation are both marked cases, albeit on opposing ends of a continuum that measures the extent to which a given segment of a narrative representation represents the consciousnesses of characters. While objective representation implies that the storyworld elements in question are not perceived or imagined by any characters at all, subjective representation implies that the storyworld elements in question are perceived or imagined by only one character (and often in a way that is not compatible with an intersubjective version of the storyworld).[9]

Against this background, it becomes clear that the analysis of local strategies of subjective representation needs to be augmented by the analysis of local strategies of intersubjective and objective representation in order to arrive at an appropriate reconstruction of a given narrative representation's global structure. Such an approach also includes distinguishing between different modes of intersubjective representation according to the characters or groups of characters that are represented as being conscious about the represented events. Despite the importance of intersubjective and objective modes of representation of characters' consciousnesses, however, the focus of this chapter remains on strategies of subjective representation—that is, on strategies of representation that provide the recipient with more or less direct access to what is on a character's mind at a given point in storyworld time, including not only his or her perception of the storyworld in which the character is located but also the quasi-perceptual experience of his or her hallucinations, memories, dreams, and fantasies.

Strategies of Subjective Representation in Contemporary Feature Films

While this chapter does not propose an overly simple hierarchy between conventionally distinct narrative media, such as feature films, graphic novels, and computer games, with regard to their narrative affordances and limitations, it still seems evident that audiovisual narrative in general and feature films in particular had an enormous impact on twentieth-century media culture. Accordingly, the pictorial strategies of subjective representation developed within the mediality of the feature film have heavily influenced the pictorial strategies of subjective representation employed by both graphic novels and computer games. Moreover, feature film is by far the most thoroughly researched medium beyond literary texts in contemporary narratology, and both film theory in general and film narratology in particular have examined film's pictorial strategies of subjective representation in considerable detail.[10] Hence, I will draw on Branigan's *Point of View in the Cinema* and George Wilson's "Transparency and Twist in Narrative Fiction Film" to sketch what I consider the most salient pictorial strategies of subjective representation across media.

In his influential study of *Point of View in the Cinema*, Branigan not only provides a description of the "point-of-view [POV] shot" that remains a major benchmark for much of contemporary film studies but also locates it in the broader field of audiovisual strategies of subjective representation, distinguishing between "six major forms of subjectivity: reflection, POV, perception, projection, flashback, and mental process" (79). While "reflection" refers to an intersubjective mode of representation and "flashback" may refer not only to subjective but also to intersubjective and objective modes of representation, the remaining four categories—"POV," "perception," "projection," and "mental process"—refer to what may be considered particularly salient audiovisual strategies of subjective representation in the feature film. Moreover, Branigan not only discusses the narrative functions of these (as well as other) strategies in considerable detail but also examines a range of more or less strongly conventionalized and at least partially medium-specific markers of subjectivity, such as "superimpositions, titles, slow motion, spinning images, intercuts, lighting, or color" (90).

Wilson, in building on Branigan's groundbreaking work and on his own *Narration in Light*, has recently elaborated on these four audiovisual strategies of subjective representation as well, describing them as "point-of-view shots," "subjectively inflected point-of-view shots" (which roughly corresponds to Branigan's "perception shots"), "subjectively inflected impersonal shots" (which roughly corresponds to Branigan's "projection"), and "subjectively saturated shots" (which includes Branigan's "flashback" and "mental process" categories). In fact, Wilson's general discussion of these four strategies—which usually correspond to "a reasonably clear marking of the fact that they are, in one of several different ways, 'subjective'" even though "the nature and functioning of the factors that contextually mark the epistemic status of a movie segment [. . .] can be surprisingly elusive" ("Transparency" 81)—seems to capture an emerging consensus in film studies.[11] Against this background, I would like to illustrate what I take to be the four most salient pictorial strategies of subjective representation across media by briefly examining examples of their realization in contemporary feature films.

First, an example of what is usually called a "point-of-view shot" in film theory can be found in Bryan Singer's *The Usual Suspects* when, during the suspects' attack on the supposed drug dealers' ship, Michael McManus counts the guards while looking through the aim of his sniper rifle. This kind of sequence, where the audiovisual representation shows a character, then shows what that character sees from his or her spatial position, and finally shows the character again, is probably the most common and conventionalized example of subjective representation in feature film. In the context of a transmedial narratology, it may be defined as referring to segments of a narrative representation where the storyworld is pictorially represented from the spatial position of a particular character. While it is obvious that the spatial position of a character heavily influences his or her perception, this pictorial strategy of subjective representation usually still represents an intersubjectively valid version of the storyworld, albeit from the specific spatial position and resulting "visual perspective" of a particular character. Hence, what I propose to call a "spatial point-of-view sequence" (in order to avoid the overly medium-specific notion of "shot"[12]) may be considered the least subjective of the pictorial strategies of subjective representation examined in this chapter.

The situation is different in the special case of what I propose to call "(quasi-)perceptual point-of-view sequence" (and which corresponds to Branigan's "perception shot" and Wilson's "subjectively inflected point-of-view shot"). Here the pictorial representation approximates not only the spatial position of a character but also represents more clearly subjective aspects of his or her perception and/or consciousness, resulting in a representation of storyworld elements that can often not be considered intersubjectively valid anymore. At the beginning of Ron Howard's *A Beautiful Mind*, for example, we find a brief (quasi-)perceptual point-of-view sequence (following an even briefer spatial point-of-view sequence) in which the audiovisual representation simulates how the protagonist, John Nash, perceives his colleague's tie in a rather unusual way, as he compares its geometric pattern to that of slices of lemon and rays of light (see figures 3.1 and 3.2). Incidentally this striking visualization of both Nash's mathematical prowess and his social ineptitude already prepares

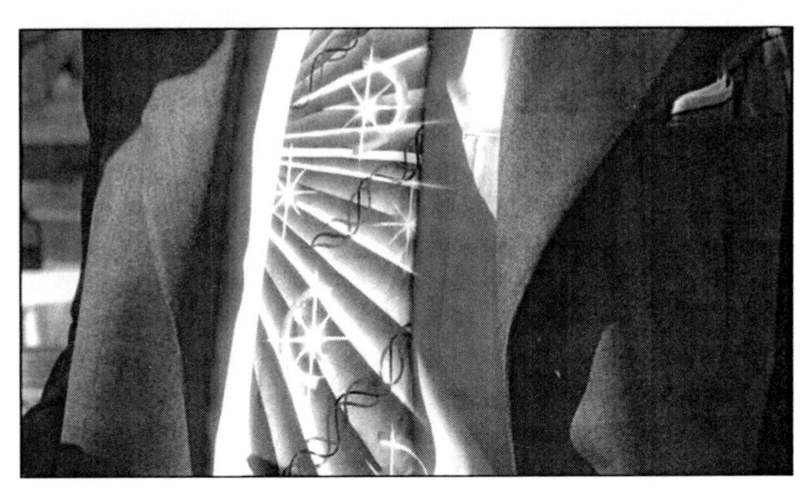

Figs. 3.1 and 3.2. Perceptual point-of-view sequence from *A Beautiful Mind*.

the ground for the film's unreliable narrative representation, which is based on Nash's rather subjective (that is, schizophrenic) perception of the storyworld in which he is located.[13]

While the spatial point-of-view sequence tends to be exclusively marked *contextually* (through the highly conventionalized point-of-view structure that shows a character, then shows what that character perceives from his or her spatial position, and finally shows the character again), the (quasi-)perceptual point-of-view sequence often uses additional *representational markers* such as filters, soft focus, or various (other) kinds of postproduction effects on the filmic image in order to communicate the subjective quality of what is being shown (in addition to the point-of-view structure). Considering that (quasi-)perceptual point-of-view sequences are usually treated as a special case of spatial point-of-view sequences and that the markers of subjectivity that define the former can be rather subtle, however, it might be best to think of these two strategies of subjective representation as opposed points on a continuum of representation that always approximates the spatial position of particular characters but adds additional aspects of their subjective (quasi-)perceptual experience to varying degrees.

Strategies of subjective representation in contemporary feature films do not have to simulate the spatial position of the character in question, though. Accordingly, I propose to call the third mode of subjective representation, in which the pictorial representation simulates (quasi-) perceptual aspects of a character's consciousness without also simulating his or her spatial position, "(quasi-)perceptual overlay." In fact, this mode of representation, which roughly corresponds to Branigan's "projection" and Wilson's "subjectively inflected impersonal shots," has become increasingly conventionalized in the last two decades and is often used in the context of unreliable narrative representation in particular. While *A Beautiful Mind* is itself a good example for a film that uses unmarked (quasi-)perceptual overlay to unreliable effect, David Fincher's *Fight Club* provides an even more striking example. When the unnamed protagonist begins to realize that he has only imagined Tyler Durden, this realization is further emphasized by the contrast between the subjective sequences using (quasi-)perceptual overlay to represent the latter fighting with or talking to the former (see figure 3.3) and the intersubjective sequences that represent the unnamed protagonist beating himself up or talking to himself in a hotel room (see figure 3.4). Just as in the (quasi-)perceptual point-of-view sequence, then, what is represented in cases of (quasi-)perceptual overlay may seem closer to a character's private domain than to the factual domain of the storyworld in which he or she is located, but at the same time it is marked as (at least partly) being that character's perception of the storyworld's factual domain (see Ryan, *Possible Worlds* 109–23).

This last criterion allows us to distinguish (quasi-)perceptual overlay

Fig. 3.3. (*top*) (Quasi-)perceptual overlay from *Fight Club*.

Fig. 3.4. (*bottom*) Intersubjective representation from *Fight Club*.

from, fourth, the full-fledged "representation of internal worlds," where what is represented is contextually and/or representationally marked as being neither the factual domain of the storyworld nor a character's perception of it but rather as consisting "exclusively" of quasi-perceptions such as hallucinations, memories, dreams, and fantasies. These kinds of highly subjective representation—called "mental processes" by Branigan or "subjectively saturated shots" by Wilson—consist, in other words, of a change of diegetic level, or subworld. Thus if the character to whom we can ascribe the represented private domain is located in the primary storyworld, what is represented in the case of a representation of internal worlds would be a secondary storyworld. A particularly interesting example can be found in Terry Gilliam's *Twelve Monkeys*, where a recurring sequence of a boy watching a man being shot at an airport is initially marked as a dream both representationally (through overexpo-

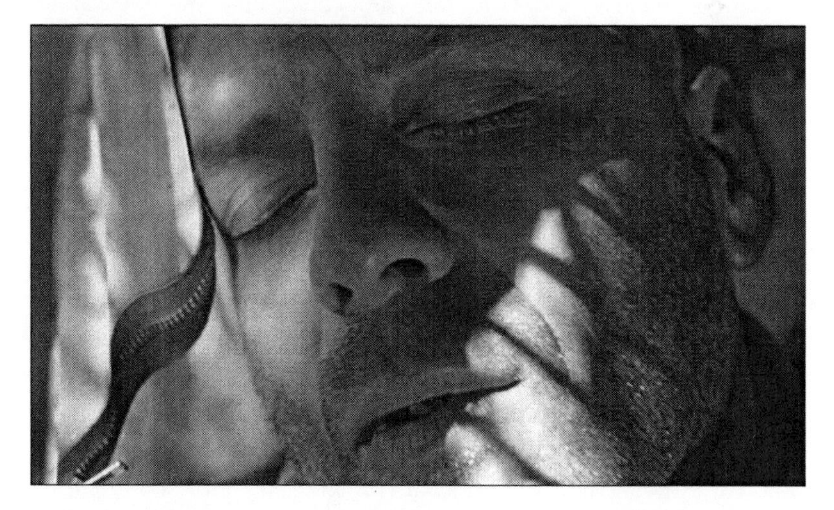

Fig. 3.5. (*top*) Representation of internal worlds from *Twelve Monkeys*.

Fig. 3.6. (*bottom*) Contextual marker of the representation of internal worlds from *Twelve Monkeys*.

sure and slow motion, among other strategies; see figure 3.5) and contextually (through showing the dreamer when he awakes after the dream; see figure 3.6). However, later the represented situation turns out to have been the twisted memory of a time traveler, who then, owing to the causal loops typical for time travel stories, would be both the man being shot and the boy watching the shooting.

While, in contemporary feature films in general and so-called mind-benders in particular, (quasi-)perceptual overlay is increasingly used without transparent representational or contextual markers and, therefore, can require relatively complex processes of inference based on what one could call "content markers" in order to be recognized, the full-fledged representation of internal worlds seems somewhat more strongly conventionalized, or at least seems more often to use both the kind of contextual markers typical for spatial point-of-view sequences and the representational markers (that is, changes in the quality of the image or other elements of the presentation) typical for (quasi-)perceptual point-of-view sequences. However, as the recurring dream/memory sequence from *Twelve Monkeys* impressively illustrates, it may be difficult (if not impossible) to distinguish between the representation of characters' hallucinations, memories, dreams, fantasies, and flashbacks—not least so, since, despite a certain amount of conventionalization, no stable 1:1 relations exists between the (partially medium-specific) representational, contextual, and content markers and the ontological status of the represented storyworld elements.[14]

Strategies of Subjective Representation in Contemporary Graphic Novels

Contemporary graphic novels may be considered a multimodal medium with a strong visual emphasis.[15] Comparable to both feature films and computer games, however, they use not only pictorial but also various verbal elements representing characters' speech and thought in speech or thought bubbles as part of the verbal-pictorial mode of representation that prototypically defines their mediality, as well as representing narratorial voices or the "inner voices" of characters through the use of narration boxes or thought boxes typically located above or below the verbal-pictorial representation in the panel body. While distinguishing between certain kinds of subjective perceptions of spoken language or the "inner voice" of a character and the narratorial voice of a homodiegetic narrator is sometimes difficult, the distinction itself remains useful, since a narrator may subjectively represent aspects of both his or her own consciousness and that of another character, but the representation of a character's "inner voice" will be subjective by definition.[16] Despite the importance of verbal elements for subjective representation, however, once more I will focus primarily on how spatial point-of-view sequences, (quasi-)perceptual point-of-view sequences, (quasi-)perceptual overlay, and the representation of internal worlds are realized in contemporary graphic novels, leaving a discussion of most of the intricate relations between narratorial verbal and non-narratorial verbal-pictorial strategies of subjective representation for another time.

My first example, a page of the first volume of Alan Moore's *The League of Extraordinary Gentlemen* that shows the invisible Mr. Griffin applying white makeup to his face in front of a mirror, already illustrates that subjective representations simulating a character's spatial position do not necessarily have to be marked contextually. Alternatively they can also be marked as subjective by content markers located on the level of what is represented, requiring the reader to draw inferences on the basis of what is being shown, which in this case is mainly the painted face in the mirror and the pot of makeup hovering before it (see figure 3.7). Remarkably, the narration boxes used in this sequence are not attributable to Mr. Griffin but to Ms. Murray, who is located in another room, describing the league's plan of attack in what may be understood as a hypothetical form of anterior narration. Accordingly, Ms. Murray functions as a secondary homodiegetic narrator who allows Moore to combine a narratorial strategy of intersubjective representation and a non-narratorial strategy of subjective representation, with the narratorial voice telling one part of the story and the sequence of panels another. That the pictorial aspects of the representation of the spatial point-of-view sequence to be found in this example indeed simulate only an approximation of the spatial position of the invisible Mr. Griffin and not other, more subjective aspects of his perception or consciousness becomes particularly clear when he puts on sunglasses, but the color and brightness of the supposedly subjective image remain the same.

This is different in my second example, yet another page from the first volume of *The League of Extraordinary Gentlemen*, in which the reader learns that Mr. Hyde has a rather peculiar way of perceiving the world: he can literally "see" temperature (see figure 3.8). Knowledge about this unusual ability is communicated using a fairly conventional form of the (quasi-)perceptual point-of-view sequence, where the second panel shows the perceiving character, Mr. Hyde; the third panel represents

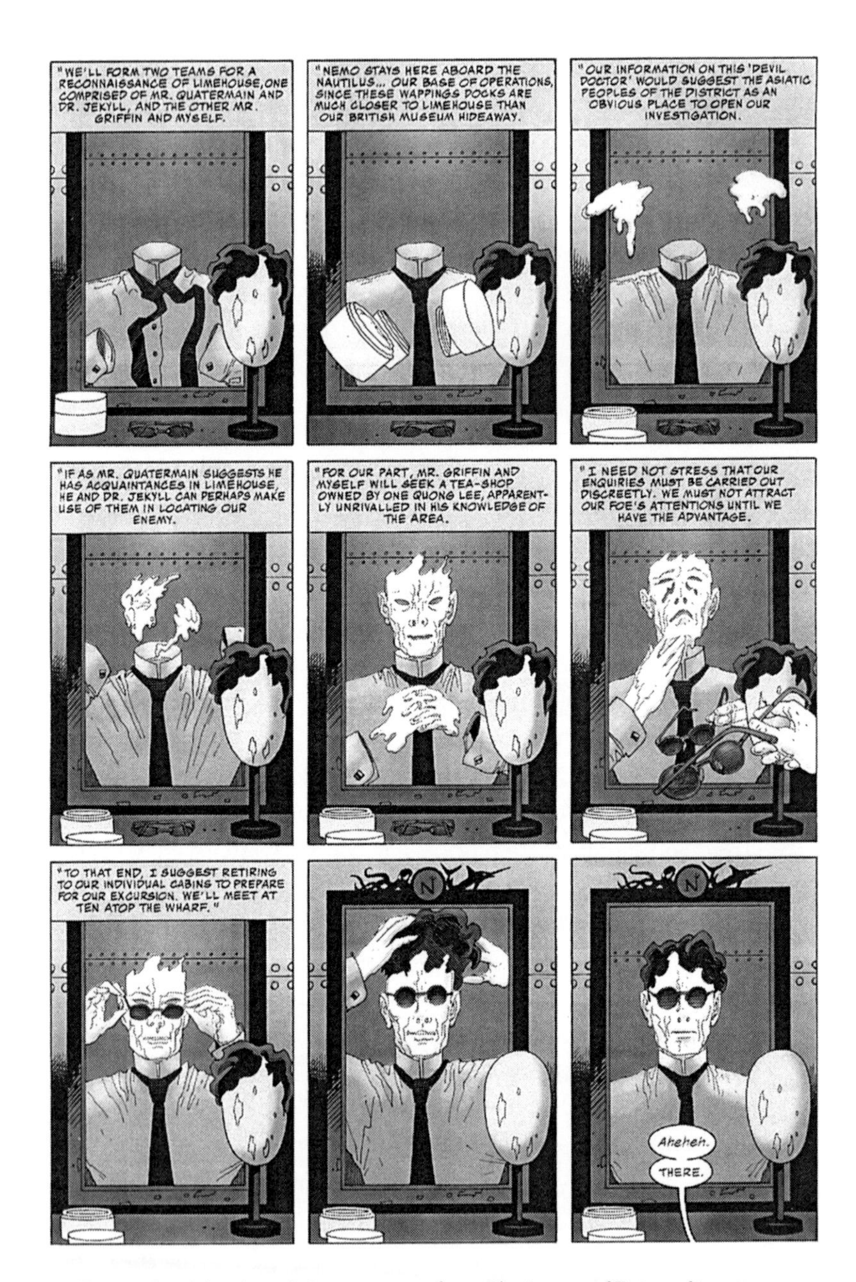

Fig. 3.7. Spatial point-of-view sequence from *The League of Extraordinary Gentlemen*.

Fig. 3.8. (Quasi-)perceptual point-of-view sequence from *The League of Extraordinary Gentlemen.*

what he perceives; and the fourth panel shows Mr. Hyde again. In this case, then, the narrative representation uses a combination of contextual and representational markers to communicate that what is represented in the third panel is not an intersubjective representation of the factual domain of the storyworld but rather a representation of Mr. Hyde's subjective perception of it. Once more, these observations only apply to the pictorial aspects of the representation, as the speech of both Mr. Hyde and Mr. Griffin is represented intersubjectively through the highly conventionalized form of speech bubbles. Incidentally, this (quasi-)perceptual point-of-view sequence helps to create an interesting "knowledge hierarchy" (see Branigan, *Narrative Comprehension* 63–85) and a disparity in "epistemic perspectives" between Mr. Griffin, Mr. Hyde, and the reader (see Eder 565–646). This difference will make an impact later in the second volume of *The League of Extraordinary Gentlemen*, when Mr. Hyde brutally rapes and murders the supposedly invisible Mr. Griffin, whose body heat Mr. Hyde can "see" perfectly well.

My third example, which comes from Frank Miller's *Hell and Back*, the seventh volume of his *Sin City* series, illustrates that, just like feature films, graphic novels are not forced to simulate the spatial position of a character in order to represent (quasi-)perceptual aspects of his or her consciousness. In a rather spectacular case of (quasi-)perceptual overlay during the last third of the story, the former "war hero" Wallace is given some kind of drug—which serves as a contextual marker (see figure 3.9)—and the following pages are devoted to representing his drug-induced hallucinations. Miller, however, combines this contextual marker with various in-panel markers: not only do the represented events fail to follow the rules of the previously established storyworld, but their representation is uncharacteristically colorful as well. Moreover, Wallace comments on the whole experience through thought boxes, providing a prototypical example of how a character's "inner voice" can (temporarily) function as a non-narratorial verbal marker of subjectivity that also reinforces the subjective status of the verbal-pictorial representation (see figure 3.10). It might bear repeating, however, that this kind of (quasi-)perceptual overlay still represents the character's perception of the storyworld in which he is situated. This becomes particularly evident once the drug's effects—as well as the colors used in its representation—fade and Wallace starts to recognize the car he crashed in, even though he is still hallucinating heavily.

Fig. 3.9. (*top*) Contextual marker of (quasi-)perceptual overlay from *Sin City: Hell and Back*.

Fig. 3.10. (*bottom*) (Quasi-)perceptual overlay from *Sin City: Hell and Back*.

Perhaps unsurprisingly, this is different in my fourth and final example of subjective representation in contemporary graphic novels, a case of the representation of a character's internal world where what is represented can no longer be seen as that character's perception of the storyworld in which he or she is located. The example comes from *Season of Mists*, the fourth volume of Neil Gaiman's *The Sandman* series, which is almost entirely focused on dreams, dreamers, and the mysterious Dream (one of the seven godlike entities referred to as "The Endless"). Once more the dream sequence I have chosen is contextually marked, with the character in question, Hob Gadling, shown sleeping next to his lover before the dream sequence (see figure 3.11) and then again when he awakes after the dream sequence (see figure 3.12). Moreover, the sequence is marked by what is represented—a strange combination of elements from different times in history, probably owing to Hob's being more or less immortal—and by the somewhat faded colors and diffuse lines used to represent it. Interestingly, Gaiman uses the slightly fuzzy frame of the panel to representationally mark the different ontological status of its contents as well. As in the memory sequence from *Twelve Monkeys*, then, the combination of contextual, representational, and content markers allows the reader to distinguish the secondary storyworld of Hob's dream from the primary storyworld in which Hob is dreaming.[17]

Strategies of Subjective Representation in Contemporary Computer Games

Just like feature films and graphic novels, computer games may use the four pictorial strategies of subjective representation sketched earlier, but their specific mediality and their "interactive" nature provide an opportunity not only to emphasize the formal differences in how conventionally distinct narrative media realize these strategies but also to focus on their medium-specific functions. As is well-established within game studies, contemporary computer games do not exclusively consist of interactive gameplay but commonly incorporate more clearly narrative elements such as cut-scenes or scripted events. Since computers are currently capable of emulating various kinds of semiotic systems, including cinematic sequences and graphic narrative, the semiotic range of cut-scenes in particular is at least as broad as it is in feature films and graphic novels. In fact, while filmic cut-scenes are still the default case, various

Figs. 3.11 and 3.12. Representation of internal worlds from *The Sandman: Season of Mist*.

games such as *Max Payne* make use of graphic narrative (that is, verbal-pictorial modes of representation) in their "noninteractive" elements (see also Marco Caracciolo's contribution in chapter 10 of this volume). As important as narrative elements are for the overall experience of playing certain kinds of computer games, however, I will primarily focus on how and to what end contemporary computer games may realize transmedial strategies of subjective representation through their interactive gameplay.[18]

In fact, the strategy of subjective representation that I have described as a spatial point-of-view sequence is realized in particularly medium-specific ways in computer games, since the spatial position from which the game spaces are represented is both more static and more flexible than it is in feature films and graphic novels. It is more static because most games use roughly the same kind of spatial perspective over long stretches of time, and it is more flexible because the "virtual camera" adapts to the gameplay and players are often given the opportunity to change its angle and distance. Following Britta Neitzel's discussion of point of view in computer games, one can nevertheless draw some distinctions. Real-time strategy games such as those in the *Warcraft* series typically use what can be described as an "objective point of view," where the position from which the game space is represented is not determined by the position of a character in that space. Adventure games such as those in the *Tomb Raider* series typically use what can be described as a "semi-subjective point of view," where the position from which the game space is represented is determined by the position of the player-controlled character but does not coincide with that position. Finally, first-person shooter games such as those in the *Doom* series typically use what can be described as a "subjective point of view," where the position from which the game spaces are represented coincides with the position of the player-controlled character.[19]

Keeping in mind that the first-person shooter genre typically uses a subjective point of view (that is, the medium-specific form of spatial point-of-view sequences) for the most part of the game, it will come as no surprise that my first example for a computer game that simulates not only the spatial position of the player-controlled avatar but also his or her perception is taken from this genre as well. In the first-person shooter *Call of Duty*, the player controls various soldiers partaking in a number of battles in World War II, and these battles are mainly represented from the spatial position of the player's avatar. If the player's avatar is shot or hit by a grenade, however, the game simulates the avatar's perception by applying a red filter to the image. The ludic function of this rather medium-specific kind of (quasi-)perceptual point-of-view sequence is evident: since preventing the avatar from dying is the primary game goal of *Call of Duty* (and most other first-person shooters), it is important for the player to know if the avatar gets hurt. Incidentally, while *Call of Duty* still uses a "health bar" as part of the head-up display to allow the player to keep track of the avatar's overall health, the second part in the series, *Call of Duty 2*, not only employs more sophisticated effects to simulate the avatar's perception (particularly when he is affected by a grenade) but also replaces the overly explicit health bar with a red filter and the sound effect of a heavily beating heart to signal to the player that the avatar is badly hurt.

An examination of the ways in which contemporary computer games beyond the genre of the first-person shooter use these kinds of by-now highly conventionalized effects would also allow for the observation of a certain continuity not only between spatial and (quasi-)perceptual point-of-view sequences but also between (quasi-)perceptual point-of-view sequences and (quasi-)perceptual overlay. However, I would like to focus on a slightly different case of (quasi-)perceptual overlay that illuminates the saliency of the ludic functions of strategies of subjective representation in contemporary computer games just as clearly. Rocksteady's *Batman: Arkham Asylum*, which usually represents the game spaces from what can be described as a "semi-subjective point of view," allows the player to switch between an intersubjective mode of representation (see figure 3.13) and what is called the "detective mode"—a kind of (quasi-)perceptual overlay that activates a number of enhancements in Batman's cowl in order to help the player solve the game's various puzzles (see figure 3.14). In a game set in an asylum for the criminally insane that has been taken over by Batman's archenemy The Joker, however, it will come as no surprise that this kind of still fairly intersubjective (quasi-)perceptual overlay is not all there is to the game.

On the contrary, in several parts of the game Batman is affected by a gaseous hallucinogen that is the trademark weapon of yet another of his enemies, The Scarecrow, and that causes severe hallucinations. Accordingly, several passages of the game simulate Batman's increasingly hallucinatory (quasi-)perceptual experience by sliding from intensify-

Fig. 3.13. (*top*) Intersubjective representation from *Batman: Arkham Asylum*.

Fig. 3.14. (*bottom*) (Quasi-)perceptual overlay from *Batman: Arkham Asylum*.

Fig. 3.15. (Quasi-)perceptual overlay from *Batman: Arkham Asylum.*

ing forms of (quasi-)perceptual overlay (see figure 3.15) to the full-fledged representation of internal worlds, where the man under the mask has to face his various fears or relives the traumatic childhood experience of witnessing his parents being murdered (see figure 3.16). Interestingly, while the sequences that use (quasi-)perceptual overlay as a transition between the intersubjective representation of the game world's factual domain and the representation of the internal world of Batman's hallucinations employ a fairly reduced and rather unchallenging mode of gameplay, the hallucinations themselves occasionally fulfill more pronounced ludic functions when the game switches to a comparatively unusual mode of gameplay that focuses not so much on Batman's combat abilities but rather on a kind of hide-and-seek against the unrelenting—and rather deadly—gaze of a huge, albeit wholly imaginary, Scarecrow.

What the range of strategies of subjective representation employed in *Batman: Arkham Asylum* also serves to emphasize, then, is that the simulation of (quasi-)perceptual aspects of a character's consciousness in computer games is necessarily connected to the player's actions, foregrounding its ludic function. Accordingly, the representation of a char-

Fig. 3.16. Representation of internal worlds from *Batman: Arkham Asylum.*

acter's internal world through interactive gameplay presupposes that the player—or, rather, his or her avatar—is able, at least to a certain extent, to act in the storyworld as it is perceived by a character, as well as in the more clearly subjective worlds of a character's memories, dreams, or fantasies. A particularly striking example of how this can be realized not only with regard to the avatar's internal world (as it is the case in *Batman: Arkham Asylum*) but also with regard to other characters' internal worlds is Double Fine's adventure game *Psychonauts.* In this game, the player controls an aspiring Psychonaut, the Psycadet Raz, on his quest to prevent Dr. Loboto from extracting the brains of the children taking part in the Whispering Rock Psychic Summer Camp. To this end, Raz—who is usually represented using a semi-subjective point of view—learns not only to use a variety of psychic powers but also to enter the minds of the camp's other inhabitants. Again, the game employs contextual markers—Raz uses tiny doors on the forehead of his fellow camp mates to metaphorically "enter their heads" (see figure 3.17)—as well as representational markers and content markers.[20]

Fig. 3.17. Contextual marker of the representation of internal worlds from *Psychonauts*.

The content markers in particular, however, fulfill primarily ludic functions once again, since Raz is tasked with collecting "figments of imagination," tidying up "emotional baggage," and opening "mental vaults" that contain repressed memories and, somewhat ironically, can be "punched open" by Raz (see figure 3.18). Hence, on the one hand, *Psychonauts* illustrates quite clearly that the foregrounded ludic functionality of strategies of subjective representation in contemporary computer games does not prevent these games from using a full range of transmedial strategies, including strategies that could not be discussed in this chapter, such as metaphorical, metaleptic, and unreliable modes of representation. On the other hand, however, the primarily ludic functions of strategies of subjective representation in contemporary computer games also serve to emphasize that transmedial narratology would do well to focus not only on the transmediality and/or the medium specificity of representational (as well as other kinds of) markers but also on these strategies' medium-specific functions. While these functions may be primarily narrative in feature films and graphic novels, this is not

Fig. 3.18. Representation of internal worlds from *Psychonauts*.

necessarily the case in computer games, where ludic functions tend to be foregrounded instead.

I would like to conclude, then, by once again stressing the dual perspective of a narratology that is transmedial in analytical scope but remains media conscious in methodological orientation, allowing for the examination of strategies of subjective representation on a transmedial level while at the same time acknowledging their medium-specific realization. Despite the limited scope of this chapter, I moreover hope to have at least hinted at the heuristic value and future potential of such a media-conscious transmedial narratology—a narratology that, among other things, provides a theoretical frame within which medium-specific models from literary and film narratology, from comics studies and game studies, and from various other strands of narratological practice may be critically reconsidered, systematically correlated, modified, and complemented to further illuminate the forms and functions of a variety of transmedial strategies of narrative representation, including the transmedial strategies of subjective representation that I have focused on here.

Notes

1. In this chapter, the term "medium" is used to refer to conventionally distinct media *sensu* Rajewsky, emphasizing what Ryan calls "a cultural point of view" (*Avatars* 23). I cannot discuss the complex relation between what may be abbreviated as "medial" and "generic" conventions in any detail here, but while feature films, graphic novels, and the kind of "highly narrative" single-player computer games that I focus on may be more appropriately described as prototypical "media forms" that are realized within the media of film, comics, and computer games, respectively (and, moreover, span a range of different genres), they still exemplify the specific "semiotic," "technological," and "cultural mediality" of these media rather well. See also the discussion in Thon, "Mediality."
2. Current literary and media studies tend to use *transmedial narratology* as an umbrella term for a variety of narratological practices concerned with media other than literary texts. However, it could also be argued that a genuinely transmedial narratology should not merely aspire to be a collection of medium-specific narratological models but should, instead, examine a variety of transmedial phenomena and strategies of narrative representation across a range of conventionally distinct narrative media while at the same time consciously acknowledging the latters' specific narrative limitations and affordances. See Thon, "Transmedial Narratology"; Herman, "Transmedial Narratology"; Ryan, "Theoretical Foundations"; Wolf, "Narratology." The account of subjective representation across media presented here is part of a larger research project that will be further developed in Thon, *Transmedial Narratology*.
3. On "experientiality" and "qualia" as prototypical features of narrative representations across media, see, for example, Fludernik 20–43; Herman, *Basic Elements* 137–60; Wolf, "Narrative."
4. This complaint is common within literary narratology and beyond, even though it seldom leads to an abandonment of the terms. See, for example, Fludernik 343–47; Palmer 48–52; Schmid 89–99, on literary texts; Chatman on audiovisual narrative; Horstkotte and Pedri on graphic narrative; and Thon, "Perspective" on computer games.
5. Genette's introduction of the (then) freshly minted term "focalization" in *Narrative Discourse* (and *Narrative Discourse Revisited*) was considered a major breakthrough among literary narratologists. Bal's critique of Genette and the attempts by Branigan (in *Narrative Comprehension*), Deleyto, Horstkotte and Pedri, Schüwer, Neitzel, or Nitsche to transfer the concept to feature films, graphic novels, or computer games are certainly illuminating, but "focalization" is at least as problematic a term as "point of view" or "perspective" are by now. Readers interested in more extensive surveys of previous research on point of view, perspective, and focalization in literary narratology may consult,

for example, Eder 565–656; Herman and Vervaeck; Jahn; Lorente; Niederhoff, "Focalization"; Niederhoff, "Perspective"; Schmid 89–99; and the contributions in Hühn, Schmid, and Schönert.

6. Speaking of "direct access" to the minds of characters in this context does not call into question the mediated nature of narrative representation; rather, it aims at distinguishing "direct," or subjective, representations from "indirect," or intersubjective, representations of characters' minds. See, for example, Cohn or Palmer on direct access, as well as the following discussion of subjective, intersubjective, and objective modes of representation.
7. While there are examples, particularly narratorial or other verbal strategies of subjective representation, that provide some kind of direct access to other aspects of a represented character's consciousness (or even to non-conscious aspects of a represented character's mind), the more salient prototypical cases of subjective representation—particularly non-narratorial multimodal strategies of subjective representation—seem to be primarily concerned with providing direct access to what may be described as a represented character's perceptual or quasi-perceptual experience (see, for example, Currie and Ravenscroft; Richardson; Thomas). Hence, my discussion of transmedial strategies of subjective representation will focus on perceptual or quasi-perceptual aspects of a character's consciousness, allowing me to include the representation of various kinds of mental imagery that occur in the context of hallucinations, memories, dreams, and fantasies but to exclude (or deemphasize) the—usually less direct or subjective—representation of other aspects of characters' minds, such as knowledge, beliefs, wishes, motivations, or systems of norms and values.
8. I had the fortunate opportunity to test the applicability of this distinction in the context of various undergraduate courses in media analysis that I taught at the University of Hamburg, the University of Mainz, and the University of Tübingen. I would like to express my gratitude to the participants for their intriguing questions, which helped me to eventually draw the distinction the way it is presented here.
9. On this kind of objective representation in literary texts, see, for example, Banfield. The borders between modes of representation can, of course, be drawn differently, but Genette's distinctions between internal, external, and nonfocalization (*Narrative Discourse* 189–94; *Narrative Discourse Revisited* 64–71), as well as Mitry's distinction between the subjective, semi-subjective, and objective image (206–19), remain common points of reference. Moreover, various approaches that seem to adhere to a binary subjective/objective distinction at first glance often allow for further subdivisions within at least one of the categories. See, for example, Branigan, *Narrative Comprehension* 125–91; Deleuze 73–88; Deleyto.
10. Influential works on subjective (as well as intersubjective) representation in the feature film include, for example, Branigan, *Point of View*; Branigan, *Narrative Comprehension*; Kawin; Mitry.

11. Even when different distinctions are drawn and different terms proposed, there still seems to be a common consensus on what aspects of the phenomena in question should be considered particularly salient. Eder (610–13), for example, draws an only slightly different distinction between "POV shots," "subjectivized POV shots," "partially imagined shots," and "fully imagined shots," emphasizing that the latter two are often combined with a "subjectivized external view."
12. While coining entirely new terms would seem to be a textbook case of what Ryan calls "radical media relativism" (*Avatars* 5), I will generally speak of "spatial point-of-view sequences" and "perceptual point-of-view sequences" when discussing pictorial strategies that film theory usually describes as "point-of-view shots" or "perception shots" on a transmedial level, since referring to the realization of these strategies in contemporary graphic novels and computer games as "shots" would render any transmedial concept unnecessarily metaphorical. Then again, one might argue that speaking of "shots" with regard to contemporary digital film (or even with regard to traditional analog film) is not significantly less metaphorical than it is with regard to contemporary graphic novels and computer games. See also Branigan's *Projecting a Camera* for a meta-theoretical discussion of the various notions of "camera" in film studies.
13. In the last few years, unreliable narration or, rather, unreliable narrative representation has gained increasing attention not only within literary narratology but also within film narratology, and the label is currently attached to a large number of loosely interrelated phenomena. However, strategies of unreliable narrative representation are usually attributed to characters in some way—either to the unreliable narration of a narrator or to the unreliable perception of a non-narrating character (see, for example, Hansen; Laass; Thon, "Mind-Bender"; Thon, "Transmedial Narratology").
14. The indeterminacy of markers of subjectivity is well established in film narratology and has, for example, been remarked on by Branigan, *Point of View*; Eder; Reinerth. As important as the previously mentioned pictorial strategies of subjective representation appear in the context of film theory and transmedial narratology alike, however, it needs to be emphasized that not only feature films but also graphic novels and computer games are multimodal media that cannot be reduced to visual or pictorial representation (see, for example, Kress and Leeuwen; and Wolfgang Hallet's contribution to this volume in chapter 6). More specifically, just as the representation of storyworld space can be more or less strongly subjectivized in the spatial point-of-view sequence or the (quasi-) perceptual point-of-view sequence, so can the representation of storyworld sound. Accordingly, one could follow Chion in (cautiously) speaking of a "point-of-audition" from which storyworld sound is represented. As opposed to the representation of storyworld space in the spatial point-of-view sequence, though, representing storyworld sound roughly from the represented charac-

ters' spatial position is very much the default case not only in feature films but also in graphic novels and computer games. Hence, "spatial point-of-audition sequence" may be considered to be even less subjective than spatial point-of-view sequences are. See also Flückiger 362–411, for a comprehensive discussion of subjective sound in the feature film.

15. At least with regard to the multimodal configurations characteristic for contemporary feature films, graphic novels, and computer games, I would argue that distinguishing between verbal and pictorial representation is more helpful than distinguishing between verbal and visual representation since a substantial part of verbal representation in multimodal media is presented visually—that is, in the form of written verbal representation. Further, feature films and computer games may also use sound for forms of spoken verbal representation. For a discussion of subjective representation in contemporary graphic narrative, see, for example, Horstkotte and Pedri; Kukkonen; Schüwer 392–404. For a more general discussion of the medium-specific combination of words and pictures in graphic narrative, see Groensteen; Hatfield; McCloud. For a sample of current research, see also the contributions in Gardner and Herman; or Stein and Thon.
16. Unfortunately, I cannot discuss the various intriguing problems connected to narratorial strategies of subjective representation in this chapter. However, see Cohn on literary-narratorial strategies of subjective representation; Thon, "Who's Telling the Tale?," for a discussion of authors and narrators in graphic narrative; and Thon, "Transmedial Narratology," for a more general discussion of the interplay between narratorial and non-narratorial strategies of narrative representation in contemporary graphic novels, feature films, and computer games.
17. Of course, the whole setup is further complicated by the fact that a character from the primary storyworld, Dream of the Endless, "enters" Hob's dream and that his gift, a bottle of wine, sits on Hob's night table after he wakes, rendering the sequence at least slightly metaleptic despite the fact that the otherworldly nature and the supernatural abilities of Dream distinctly dissolve the apparent paradox. Again, I cannot discuss the problem of metalepsis in any detail here. On the concept of metalepsis, see, for example, Fehrle; Meister; Ryan, *Avatars* 204–30; Thon, "Zur Metalepse"; Wolf, "Metalepsis"; as well as the contributions in Kukkonen and Klimek.
18. For a discussion of the interplay between genuinely narrative elements and simulated gameplay in contemporary computer games, see, for example, Frasca; Jenkins; Juul; Ryan, *Avatars* 181–203; Thon, "Computer Games"; Thon, "Game Studies"; Thon, "Immersion"; Thon, "Unendliche Weiten?"
19. It should be noted that "semi-subjective point of view" and "objective point of view" are not to be conflated with intersubjective representation and objective representation. The distinction between "subjective," "semi-subjective," and "objective point of view" goes back to Neitzel, who mainly builds on Genette's

Narrative Discourse and Mitry. See also the additional discussion in Thon, "Perspective."

20. Pictorial representations of characters' consciousness cannot be "verbatim reproductions," and contemporary feature films, graphic novels, and computer games commonly use metaphorical representations in order to provide their recipients with supposedly "direct access" to the characters' consciousness. See, for example, Fahlenbrach on audiovisual metaphors; Forceville on multimodal metaphors; and the brief remarks in Horstkotte and Pedri on metaphorical representation in graphic novels.

Works Cited

Bal, Mieke. *Narratology: Introduction to the Theory of Narrative.* 2nd ed. Toronto: University of Toronto Press, 1997. Print.

Banfield, Ann. "Describing the Unobserved: Events Grouped around an Empty Centre." *The Linguistics of Writing: Arguments between Language and Literature.* Ed. Nigel Fabb, Derek Attridge, Alan Durant, and Colin MacCabe. Manchester, UK: Manchester University Press, 1987. 265–85. Print.

A Beautiful Mind. Dir. Ron Howard. Universal Pictures, 2001. Film.

Branigan, Edward. *Narrative Comprehension and Film.* London: Routledge, 1992. Print.

———. *Point of View in the Cinema: A Theory of Narration and Subjectivity in Classical Film.* Berlin: Mouton, 1984. Print.

———. *Projecting a Camera: Language-Games in Film Theory.* London: Routledge, 2006. Print.

Chatman, Seymour. "Characters and Narrators: Filter, Center, Slant and Interest-Focus." *Poetics Today* 7.2 (1986): 189–204. Print.

Chion, Michel. *Le son au cinema.* Paris: Editions de l'Etoile, 1985. Print.

Cohn, Dorrit. *Transparent Minds: Narrative Modes for Presenting Consciousness in Fiction.* Princeton NJ: Princeton University Press, 1978. Print.

Currie, Gregory, and Ian Ravenscroft. *Recreative Minds: Imagination in Philosophy and Psychology.* Oxford, UK: Oxford University Press, 2002. Print.

Deleuze, Gilles. *Cinema 1: The Movement-Image.* Trans. Hugh Tomlinson and Barbara Habberjam. London: Athlone Press, 1986. Print.

Deleyto, Celestino. "Focalisation in Film Narrative." *Narratology: An Introduction.* Ed. Susana Onega and José Angel García Landa. London: Longman, 1996. 217–33. Print.

Double Fine Productions. *Psychonauts.* Majesco Entertainment, 2005. Windows.

Eder, Jens. *Die Figur im Film: Grundlagen der Figurenanalyse.* Marburg, Germany: Schüren, 2008. Print.

Fahlenbrach, Kathrin. *Audiovisuelle Metaphern: Zur Körper- und Affektästhetik in Film und Fernsehen.* Marburg, Germany: Schüren, 2010. Print.

Fehrle, Johannes. "Unnatural Worlds and Unnatural Narration in Comics?" *Unnatural Narratives—Unnatural Narratology.* Ed. Jan Alber and Rüdiger Heinze. Berlin: De Gruyter, 2011. 210–45. Print.

Fight Club. Dir. David Fincher. 20th Century Fox, 1999. Film.

Flückiger, Barbara. *Sound Design: Die virtuelle Klangwelt des Films.* Marburg, Germany: Schüren, 2001. Print.

Fludernik, Monika. *Towards a "Natural" Narratology.* London: Routledge, 1996. Print.

Forceville, Charles. "Cognitive Linguistics and Multimodal Metaphor." *Bildwissenschaft zwischen Reflexion und Anwendung.* Ed. Klaus Sachs-Hombach. Cologne, Germany: Herbert von Halem, 2005. 264–85. Print.

Frasca, Gonzalo. "Simulation versus Narrative: Introduction to Ludology." *The Video Game Theory Reader.* Ed. Mark J. P. Wolf and Bernard Perron. London: Routledge, 2003. 221–35. Print.

Gaiman, Neil. *The Sandman.* Vol. 4, *Season of Mists.* 1990–1991. New York: DC Comics, 1992. Print.

Gardner, Jared, and David Herman, eds. *Graphic Narratives and Narrative Theory.* Spec. issue. *SubStance* 40.1 (2011): 3–202. Print.

Genette, Gérard. *Narrative Discourse: An Essay in Method.* Trans. Jane E. Lewin. Ithaca NY: Cornell University Press, 1980. Print.

———. *Narrative Discourse Revisited.* Trans. Jane E. Lewin. Ithaca NY: Cornell University Press, 1988. Print.

Groensteen, Thierry. *The System of Comics.* Trans. Bart Beaty and Nick Nguyen. Jackson: University Press of Mississippi, 2007. Print.

Hansen, Per Krogh. "Unreliable Narration in Cinema: Facing the Cognitive Challenge Arising from Literary Studies." *Amsterdam International Electronic Journal for Cultural Narratology* 5 (2009): n. pag. Web. March 1, 2012.

Hatfield, Charles. *Alternative Comics. An Emerging Literature.* Jackson: University Press of Mississippi, 2005. Print.

Herman, David. *Basic Elements of Narrative.* Malden MA: Wiley-Blackwell, 2009. Print.

———. "Toward a Transmedial Narratology." *Narrative across Media: The Languages of Storytelling.* Ed. Marie-Laure Ryan. Lincoln: University of Nebraska Press, 2004. 47–75. Print.

Herman, Luc, and Bart Vervaeck. "Focalization between Classical and Postclassical Narratology." *The Dynamics of Narrative Form: Studies in Anglo-American Narratology.* Ed. John Pier. Berlin: De Gruyter, 2004. 115–38. Print.

Horstkotte, Silke, and Nancy Pedri. "Focalization in Graphic Narrative." *Narrative* 19.3 (2011): 330–57. Print.

Hühn, Peter, Wolf Schmid, and Jörg Schönert, eds. *Point of View, Perspective, and Focalization: Modeling Mediation in Narration.* Berlin: De Gruyter, 2009. Print.

Infinity Ward. *Call of Duty*. Activision, 2003. Windows.
———. *Call of Duty 2*. Activision, 2005. Windows.
Jahn, Manfred. "Focalization." *The Cambridge Companion to Narrative*. Ed. David Herman. Cambridge, UK: Cambridge University Press, 2007. 94–108. Print.
Jenkins, Henry. "Game Design as Narrative Architecture." *FirstPerson: New Media as Story, Performance, and Game*. Ed. Noah Wardrip-Fruin and Pat Harrigan. Cambridge MA: MIT Press, 2004. 118–30. Print.
Juul, Jesper. *Half-Real: Video Games between Real Rules and Fictional Worlds*. Cambridge MA: MIT Press, 2005. Print.
Kawin, Bruce. *Mindscreen: Bergman, Godard, and First-Person Film*. Princeton NJ: Princeton University Press, 1979. Print.
Kress, Gunther, and Theo van Leeuwen. *Multimodal Discourse: The Modes and Media of Contemporary Communication*. London: Arnold, 2001. Print.
Kukkonen, Karin. "Comics as a Test Case for Transmedial Narratology." *SubStance* 40.1 (2011): 34–52. Print.
Kukkonen, Karin, and Sonja Klimek, eds. *Metalepsis in Popular Culture*. Berlin: De Gruyter, 2011. Print.
Laass, Eva. *Broken Taboos, Subjective Truths: Forms and Functions of Unreliable Narration in Contemporary American Cinema*. Trier, Germany: Wissenschaftlicher Verlag, 2008. Print.
Lorente, Joaquín Martínez. "Blurring Focalization: Psychological Expansion of Point of View and Modality." *Revista Alicantina de Estudios Ingleses* 9 (1996): 63–90. Print.
McCloud, Scott. *Understanding Comics: The Invisible Art*. Northhampton MA: Tundra, 1993. Print.
Meister, Jan Christoph. "The Metalepticon: A Computational Approach to Metalepsis." *NarrPort* 2003. Web. March 1, 2012.
Miller, Frank. *Sin City*. Vol. 7, *Hell and Back*. 1999–2000. 2nd ed. Milwaukee: Dark Horse, 2005. Print.
Mitry, Jean. *The Aesthetics and Psychology of the Cinema*. Bloomington: Indiana University Press, 1997. Print.
Moore, Alan. *The League of Extraordinary Gentlemen*. Vol. 1. Illus. Kevin O'Neill. 1999–2000. London: Titan Books, 2002. Print.
———. *The League of Extraordinary Gentlemen*. Vol. 2. Illus. Kevin O'Neill. 2002–2003. London: Titan Books, 2004. Print.
Neitzel, Britta. "Point of View und Point of Action: Eine Perspektive auf die Perspektive in Computerspielen." *Computer/Spiel/Räume: Materialien zur Einführung in die Computer Game Studies*. Ed. Klaus Bartels and Jan-Noël Thon. Hamburg: Department of Media and Communication, University of Hamburg, 2007. 8–28. Print.
Niederhoff, Burkhard. "Focalization." *Handbook of Narratology*. Ed. Peter Hühn,

John Pier, Wolf Schmid, and Jörg Schönert. Berlin: De Gruyter, 2009. 115–23. Print.

———. "Perspective/Point of View." *Handbook of Narratology*. Ed. Peter Hühn, John Pier, Wolf Schmid, and Jörg Schönert. Berlin: De Gruyter, 2009. 384–97. Print.

Nitsche, Michael. *Video Game Spaces: Image, Play, and Structure in 3D Worlds*. Cambridge MA: MIT Press, 2008. Print.

Palmer, Alan. *Fictional Minds*. Lincoln: University of Nebraska Press, 2004. Print.

Persson, Per. *Understanding Cinema: A Psychological Theory of Moving Imagery*. Cambridge UK: Cambridge University Press, 2003. Print.

Rajewsky, Irina O. "Border Talks: The Problematic Status of Media Borders in the Current Debate about Intermediality." *Media Borders, Multimodality and Intermediality*. Ed. Lars Elleström. New York: Palgrave Macmillan, 2010. 51–68. Print.

Reinerth, Maike Sarah. "Spulen, Speichern, Überspielen: Zur Darstellung von Erinnerung im Spielfilm." *Probleme filmischen Erzählens*. Ed. Hannah Birr, Maike Sarah Reinerth, and Jan-Noël Thon. Münster, Germany: LIT, 2009. 33–58. Print.

Richardson, Alan. *Mental Imagery*. London: Routledge & Kegan Paul, 1969. Print.

Rocksteady Studios. *Batman: Arkham Asylum*. Eidos Interactive, 2009. Windows.

Ryan, Marie-Laure. *Avatars of Story*. Minneapolis: University of Minnesota Press, 2006. Print.

———. "On the Theoretical Foundations of Transmedial Narratology." *Narratology beyond Literary Criticism: Mediality, Disciplinarity*. Ed. Jan Christoph Meister. Berlin: De Gruyter, 2005. 1–23. Print.

———. *Possible Worlds, Artificial Intelligence, and Narrative Theory*. Bloomington: University of Indiana Press, 1991. Print.

Schmid, Wolf. *Narratology: An Introduction*. Berlin: De Gruyter, 2010. Print.

Schüwer, Martin. *Wie Comics erzählen: Grundriss einer intermedialen Erzähltheorie der grafischen Literatur*. Trier, Germany: Wissenschaftlicher Verlag, 2008. Print.

Stein, Daniel, and Jan-Noël Thon, eds. *From Comic Strips to Graphic Novels: Contributions to the Theory and History of Graphic Narrative*. Berlin: De Gruyter, 2013. Print.

Thomas, Nigel J. T. "Mental Imagery." *Stanford Encyclopedia of Philosophy*. Ed. Edward N. Zalta, 2010. Web. July 1, 2011.

Thon, Jan-Noël. "Computer Games, Fictional Worlds and Transmedial Storytelling: A Narratological Perspective." *Proceedings of the Philosophy of Computer Games Conference 2009*. Ed. John R. Sageng. Oslo: Department of Philosophy, History of Art and Ideas, University of Oslo, 2009. 1–6. PDF File. July 1, 2011.

———. "Game Studies und Narratologie." *Game Studies: Aktuelle Ansätze der Computerspielforschung*. Ed. Klaus Sachs-Hombach and Jan-Noël Thon. Cologne, Germany: Herbert von Halem, forthcoming. Print.

———. "Immersion Revisited: On the Value of a Contested Concept." *Extending Experiences: Structure, Analysis and Design of Computer Game Player Experience*. Ed. Olli Leino, Hanna Wirman, and Amyris Fernandez. Rovaniemi: Lapland University Press, 2008. 29–43. Print.

———. "Mediality." *Johns Hopkins Guide to Digital Media*. Ed. Lori Emerson, Benjamin Robertson, and Marie-Laure Ryan. Baltimore MD: Johns Hopkins University Press, 2014. 334–37. Print.

———. "Mind-Bender: Zur Popularisierung komplexer narrativer Strukturen im amerikanischen Kino der 1990er Jahre." *Post-Coca-Colanization: Zurück zur Vielfalt?* Ed. Sophia Komor and Rebekka Rohleder. Frankfurt am Main: Peter Lang, 2009. 171–88. Print.

———. "Perspective in Contemporary Computer Games." *Point of View, Perspective, and Focalization: Modeling Mediation in Narration*. Ed. Peter Hühn, Wolf Schmid, and Jörg Schönert. Berlin: De Gruyter, 2009. 279–99. Print.

———. "Toward a Transmedial Narratology: On Narrators in Contemporary Graphic Novels, Feature Films, and Computer Games." *Beyond Classical Narration: Transmedial and Unnatural Challenges*. Ed. Jan Alber and Per Krogh Hansen. Berlin: De Gruyter, 2014. 25–56. Print.

———. *Transmedial Narratology*. 2015/forthcoming. Print.

———. "Unendliche Weiten? Schauplätze, fiktionale Welten und soziale Räume heutiger Computerspiele." *Computer/Spiel/Räume: Materialien zur Einführung in die Computer Game Studies*. Ed. Klaus Bartels and Jan-Noël Thon. Hamburg: Department of Media and Communication, University of Hamburg, 2007. 29–60. Print.

———. "Who's Telling the Tale? Authors and Narrators in Graphic Narrative." *From Comic Strips to Graphic Novels: Contributions to the Theory and History of Graphic Narrative*. Ed. Stein and Thon 67–99. Print.

———. "Zur Metalepse im Film." *Probleme filmischen Erzählens*. Ed. Hannah Birr, Maike Sarah Reinerth, and Jan-Noël Thon. Münster, Germany: LIT, 2009. 85–110. Print.

The Usual Suspects. Dir. Bryan Singer. MGM, 1995. Film.

Twelve Monkeys. Dir. Terry Gilliam. Universal Pictures, 1996. Film.

Wilson, George. *Narration in Light: Studies in Cinematic Point of View*. Baltimore MD: Johns Hopkins University Press, 1986. Print.

———. "Transparency and Twist in Narrative Fiction Film." *Journal of Aesthetics and Art Criticism* 64.1 (2006): 81–95. Print.

Wolf, Werner. "Metalepsis as a Transgeneric and Transmedial Phenomenon: A Case Study of the Possibilities of 'Exporting' Narratological Concepts." *Narratology beyond Literary Criticism: Mediality, Disciplinarity*. Ed. Jan Christoph Meister. Berlin: De Gruyter, 2005. 83–107. Print.

———. "Narrative and Narrativity: A Narratological Reconceptualization and Its Applicability to the Visual Arts." *Word & Image* 19.3 (2003): 180–97. Print.

———. "Narratology and Media(lity): The Transmedial Expansion of a Literary Discipline and Possible Consequences." *Current Trends in Narratology*. Ed. Greta Olsen. Berlin: De Gruyter, 2011. 145–80. Print.
Zunshine, Lisa. *Why We Read Fiction: Theory of Mind and the Novel*. Columbus: Ohio State University Press, 2006. Print.

4 Fiction across Media

Toward a Transmedial Concept of Fictionality

FRANK ZIPFEL

During the past forty years, the questions of the nature of fiction or fictionality and of the importance of this concept for the theory of art have been hotly debated. A huge part of this discussion has been and still is focused on narrative literature. But by now fictionality has become an important notion not only in literary theory but also in other disciplines, such as film studies, theater studies, computer games studies, and more generally the philosophy of art. The theoretical question of whether and how the concept of fictionality can be applied to nonliterary art forms and to nonverbal or not exclusively verbal phenomena in different media has become more and more pressing. Against this background, the essential questions underlying this chapter could be phrased as follows: Is there a transmedial concept of fiction or fictionality? And if so, to what end do we try to establish such a concept?[1] Since this chapter concerns the nature of fiction, not of media, I will avoid the problem of defining media, and I will take the word "medium" in a rather intuitive and broad sense, passing over such controversial questions as whether theater is an art form or a medium and what it means to perceive theater as one or the other.[2]

It is rather obvious that we speak about fictionality with reference to different art forms or media: literary narratives, film, comics, and theater performances. Moreover, there have been investigations of the fictionality of painting, photography, computer games, or even music, though the usefulness of some of these investigations has been questioned.[3] We nonetheless can say that *fictionality* is often used as a transmedial concept in the philosophy of art and in less theoretical contexts; however, attempts to investigate this transmedial understanding of fictionality have been few up to this point.[4]

One of the most influential attempts to conceive of fiction or fictionality as a transmedial concept is the theory proposed by Kendall Walton in his seminal *Mimesis as Make-Believe*. Walton investigates what works of representational art "are made of and how they work, the purpose they serve and the means by which they do so, the various ways in which people understand and appreciate them" (2). The list of items that Walton regards as instances of representational art is more or less conventional: novels, paintings, films, drama, opera, sculptures, photography, and so on. Much less conventional is his conception of what makes a work representational, with the common feature of the types of works listed being that they all function as what he calls "props in games of make-believe" (69). Moreover, for Walton the fact that representations function as props in games of make-believe means that they mandate imaginings according to certain principles of generation. These principles are to be understood as the conventions of the game of make-believe. Walton's definition of the characteristics of *representational arts*—that is, "function[ing] as a prop in a make-believe game" or "prescrib[ing] imaginings" (see 35–43)—seems better suited to a definition of fictionality than to one of representation. But this issue is not a problem for Walton, as he stipulates that the concepts of fiction, mimesis, and representation are all but one: works of representational arts are works of fiction, and "only fiction will qualify as 'representational'" (3). Walton is very consistent in excluding works of nonfiction from representation. However, his stipulations entail the slightly odd consequence that nonfictional works such as biography, news reports, or historiography are explicitly banished from the realm of representations, whereas painting and photography are fictional arts by definition. These far-from-obvious stipulations may indeed be the reason why "few theorists have followed Walton in his effort to locate and explain the phenomenon of fiction across all the representational arts" (Gorman 165). Much more could be said about Walton's theory, but most of it is beyond the scope of this chapter.[5] I will, however, come back to some of Walton's insights while presenting my own different approach to a transmedial concept of fictionality.

Elements of a Transmedial Concept of Fictionality: Fictional Worlds, Make-Believe, and Institutional Practice

In the following section I argue that fiction or, rather, fictionality is a concept that designates phenomena that in some way deal with fictional worlds, that the way these fictional worlds are dealt with involves a game of make-believe, and that this game is embedded in an institutional practice.[6] The three components of this multilayered approach to a transmedial concept of fictionality—namely, fictional worlds, make-believe games, and institutional practice—can benefit from further development; therefore, I elaborate briefly on each of them.

Fictional Worlds

In contrast to quite a large number of theoretical approaches, I would say rather bluntly that in order to be *fictional*, a world must present some degree of deviation when compared to the real world or, more precisely, when compared to what we usually regard as the real world.[7] To put it another way, for a world to be fictional it has to comprise invented elements—that is, elements that do not occur in the real world. I know that theorists of fiction have a strong tendency to do away with invention or non-reality.[8] But I can hardly conceive of a full-fledged theory of fiction that omits the fact that calling a world "fictional" basically means that it contains individuals who do not exist or events that did not occur in the real world. As Jean-Marie Schaeffer writes, "Invented entities and actions are the common stuff of fiction, and for this reason the idea of the non-referential status of the universe portrayed is part of our standard understanding of fiction" ("Fictional" 105–6).[9] Hence I would like to argue that as a general rule fictional worlds contain unreal, purely imaginary elements. For most fictional works these imaginary elements consist of invented characters, by which I mean either actually invented characters or significantly altered versions of real persons.[10] But for those to whom the notion of invented characters or of fictional objects seems too pedestrian or too prone to lead into a semantic, ontological, or metaphysical morass, I am willing to accept other ways of talking about fictional content, be it by calling fictional texts "non-referential" (see Cohn, *Distinction* 9–15) or by saying that in fictional representations the rule of reference is irrelevant (see Gibson).[11]

Of course, not everything in a fictional world is invented. Fictional worlds are, as Umberto Eco puts it, "parasitic" upon the real world (83). There would be a lot to say about the relationship between fictional worlds and the actual world, for example, by elaborating on Marie-Laure Ryan's "principle of minimal departure" ("Fiction, Non-Factuals") or on Walton's "mutual belief principle" (*Mimesis* 150–61), but the interesting problem of how fictional worlds are related to and relying on the real world is beyond the scope of this chapter.[12] I will therefore limit myself to stressing that in order to talk about "minimal departure" there must be some kind of difference between what is true in a fictional world and what is true in the real world.

Games of Make-Believe

I have already mentioned that Walton introduced the concept of make-believe into the theory of fiction. *Make-believe* for Walton is the attitude an audience adopts toward fictional works. Walton actually gives two different explanations of make-believe as a "fictional stance." First, he develops an analogy between children's games and fiction. Just as children in a game of cowboys and Indians believe for the duration of the game that some of them are cowboys while others are Indians, or that a wooden stick is a rifle with which an enemy can be shot, the audience of fictional works engage in a similar game of make-believe concerning what they are reading, hearing, or seeing for the time of their engagement with the work. Fictional works can thus be conceived as "props in games of make-believe," to quote, once again, one of Walton's favorite phrases. At this point it is important to notice that Walton introduces not only the notion of make-believe but also the notion of games into the theory of fiction. One characteristic feature of games that is especially important for theories of fiction is a "double attitude." On the one hand, they require people to engage in the game—that is, take the game world seriously and behave according to its rules—and, on the other hand, the people must retain an awareness that the world of the game is a game world and not the actual or real world.[13]

Walton's second explanation of make-believe as characteristic of the fictional stance is that fictions mandate imaginings. Unfortunately, Walton refuses to give an explicit account of what he means by "imaginings." We can get an idea of the kind of imagining he has in mind when he claims that the imagining in question is an imagining *de se*, or imagining about oneself, thus stressing the similarity with the pretense of children's games. Walton believes that audiences enter the world of a fictional work imaginatively, and he uses this view to explain emotional reactions to these works.

Here is how Thomas Pavel elaborates on Walton's argument:

> We are moved by the fate of fictional characters, since, as Kendall Walton argues, when caught up in a story, we participate in fictional happenings by projecting a fictional ego who attends the imaginary events as a kind of nonvoting member. [. . .] We send our fictional egos as scouts into the territory, with orders to report back; *they* are moved, not us, they fear Godzilla and cry with Juliet, we only lend our bodies and emotions for a while to these fictional egos, just as in participatory rites the faithful lend their bodies to the possessing spirits. (85, original emphasis)

The question to which Pavel alludes in this passage is central to Walton's interest—that is, to the question of how and why fictional works generate emotions. Other theorists, however, have expressed doubts about whether audiences really engage in make-believe when they respond to fictional works.[14] It has been argued that explaining the fictional stance in terms of make-believe overstates the attitude toward fictional works on the believe side. John Gibson, for instance, contests the claim "that we make-believe these sentences and descriptions *to be true*, that we *imagine* they are descriptive of something *real*" (165, original emphases). Most of the scholars who take a critical attitude toward the concept of make-believe stick to the notion of imagination, but they give it a meaning that differs from the one Walton implicitly favors. They rather revert to concepts of imagination inspired by the one that Roger Scruton or Noël Carroll have proposed when they speak of "suppositional imagination" (Carroll, "Fiction" 184), or a form of mental activity that they describe as holding something before the mind, as "entertaining the proposition that *p* unasserted" (Scruton 88), or as "entertaining a thought non-assertively" (Carroll, *Philosophy* 88).[15]

I think that both of the interpretations of the game we play with fictional works—the stronger one relating to make-believe and the weaker one of contemplating propositional content as unasserted—have their advantages and disadvantages; therefore, I will not try to argue in favor of one or the other. To conclude the discussion of make-believe, I would simply like to stress that both of Walton's interpretations of the attitude toward fictional works imply that the world of the works is fictional in the sense of "not real" because it would be preposterous to assume that audiences make-believe or contemplate as unasserted what they actually do believe and would therefore be willing to assert (see New 72).

Institutional Practice

For an explanation of what *institutional practice* means in the context of theories of fictionality I rely on the explication given by Peter Lamarque and Stein Haugom Olsen in their seminal book *Truth, Fiction, and Literature*: "An institutional practice [. . .] is *constituted* by a set of conventions and concepts which both regulate and *define* the actions and products involved in the practice. [. . .] An institution, in the relevant sense, is a rule-governed practice which makes possible certain (institutional) actions which are defined by the rules of the practice and which could not exist as such without those rules" (256, original emphases). Lamarque and Olsen also argue that "any attempt to explain how fictive stories are told and enjoyed in a community, without deceit, without mistaken inference, and without inappropriate response, seems inevitably to require reference to co-operative, mutually recognized, conventions" (37). This institutional concept of fiction highlights the fact that fictionality can be explained neither solely by means of the intention of the author (as Searle would have it) nor exculsively in terms of reader response (as Walton advocates). For a "fictional transaction" to take place, both authorial intent and reader response must come into play (Gorman 163). Dealing with fictional works thus involves some kind of mutual agreement between producers and audiences. Or to put it more precisely, the specific attitude of audiences is triggered because they recognize the intentions of the producers that the audience should adopt a fiction-specific attitude, that is, the attitude that has been outlined in what has been said about games of make-believe.[16] Moreover, the general make-believe conventions that define the institutional practice of fiction in a transmedial understanding can be considered as a frame that allows for fiction-specific representational conventions—that is, conventions that regard the particular ways in which fictional worlds can be presented in a specific art form or medium. These conventions, however, can differ considerably from one art form or medium to another.[17]

I would like to conclude this brief survey of the three different components of my transmedial approach to fiction with a rather general remark about the basic concern of theories of fiction. In my opinion this basic concern is to explain the relationship between fiction and reality or, to put it differently, to explain how it is that fictions play such an important role in our lives. This explanation involves both of the two communicational aspects of fictional works—namely, production and response. I think that the principal aim of theories of fiction regarding production is to distinguish the presentation of fictional worlds from other ways of representing the unreal or invented, especially deceitful ones. More specifically, the purpose of these theories is to refute, in one way or another, the old Platonian allegation that all poets (or artists or producers of fictional worlds) are liars. As far as response is concerned, theories of fiction mostly try to explain why audiences bother with the unreal. Why is it that people spend time, energy, or emotions on fictions when they could engage in activities that have a more practical impact on their lives and a more direct influence on their survival? This question may be the reason why explanations of fictionality based on make-believe and imaginative activity have become so important. They prepare the ground for a deeper understanding of such topics as the value of imaginings, the nature of aesthetic illusion, the phenomenon of immersion, and more generally the cognitive benefits offered by fictional works.[18]

In the following sections I use the three elements of my multilayered approach to a transmedial concept of fictionality to discuss the relevance of the notion of fictionality in three artistic media. I hope to show not only that these three elements can be used to capture the fictionality of different kinds of works but also that for each art form specific qualifications are needed in order to describe their particular form of fictionality.

Fictionality and Literature

In a first approach I would like to concentrate on the most obvious genre of literary fiction, the narrative. When we talk about fictionality with regard to literary texts we usually focus on novels, novellas, short stories, and so forth. Applying the multilayered account of fictionality to textual narration does not raise any problems; the production of and the response to textual fictional narration can easily be explained in terms of fictional worlds, make-believe, and institutional practice. A general explanation could run as follows: A *text-based fictional narration* is a narration that is produced and read according to the conventions of the institutional practice of literary fiction. These conventions stipulate that the author has composed the text with the specific intent that readers adopt the make-believe stance to the fictional story, and readers will actually adopt this stance toward the narration because they recognize this intent.[19] That text-based fictional narration can be easily described by means of the multilayered account should not come as a surprise, since this account is largely inspired by the theoretical discussion of fictionality of the last fifty years, a discussion that was predominantly concerned with literary narratives.[20]

In the discussion of narrative literary fiction, an additional interpretation of make-believe has been proposed. This interpretation can be linked to the way the concept is used by Gregory Currie, a scholar who has bridged the gap between analytic philosophy and narratology. In Currie's opinion our make-believe regarding fictional narrations is "not merely that the events described in the text occurred, but that we are being told about those events by someone with knowledge of them" (*Nature* 73). Thus Currie opens the path for a narratological understanding of fictionality as the audience's act of make-believe. Many narratologists—especially those who have become part of the classic canon, such as Gérard Genette or Dorrit Cohn—anchor their distinction between fictional and factual narrative on the distinction between the real author and the fictional narrator, as well as the fictional narratee and the real readers. This explanation of fiction by means of the introduction of fictional entities in the communicative transaction has been questioned by those scholars who reject the assumption that every fictional narration has a narrator.[21] The question of whether it is correct to assume that there is a fictional narrator in every fictional narration or whether there are narratorless narrations is indeed an intriguing one, and there do not seem to be any clear-cut answers to it. Maybe it all depends on how the concept of narrator is understood—that is, whether one adheres to a narrow definition of *narrator* as a personalized teller or to a wider definition of narrator as a narratorial function, as a narrative instance, or simply as a story-presentation device.[22] In spite of this controversy, the dissociation between real author and some kind of substitute speaker has often been considered—and not without good reasons—as a defining feature of fictional narration. This definition is fully compatible with Currie's concept of make-believe.

As for the specific conventions the institution of fiction allows for regarding textual narrations, they are of course manifold. The most important of these conventions are without any doubt the special features of fictional narratives that (at least since Käte Hamburger) have been discussed as narratorial specificities of textual fictions (e.g., internal focalization or omniscient narration).[23]

Although literary narrative undoubtedly represents the most important manifestation of literary fiction, the multilayered account allows for radically non-narrative forms of fictionality—a fictionality that cannot be understood as narrative even under the broadest conception of narration as the presentation of a story.[24] Not all fictional worlds are necessarily storyworlds, thus there can be fictional texts without a story. A literary text can consist of a pure description of an invented or non-real object—for example, a description of a fictional character or of an invented place, be it some paradisiacal garden or a planet in a far-off galaxy.[25] This kind of description can certainly be regarded as a text transmitted with the intention that the reader shall adopt the attitude of make-believe toward its content. If we accept descriptive texts as fiction, we should also accept versified descriptions. This argument demonstrates the potential applicability of the concept of fiction to poetry.[26] Moreover, if there can be fictionality without narrativity, this opens the door for a discussion of fictionality within painting.

Fictionality and Theater

It has often been said that the art form of the theater is invested with a double fictionality—*dramatic fiction* on the one hand and *theatrical fiction* on the other (see Birkenhauer 107). The concept of *dramatic fiction* points to the fictionality of the semantic content of the written play and highlights that the presented story or storyworld is fictional. It usually means that the drama does not depict events that occurred in the real world or—if we want to emphasize the existence of genres such as chronicle play or historical play—that the drama does not depict events *as* they occurred in the real world. Moreover, the readers of a written play are invited to play a game of make-believe with the text they are reading. The interpretation of the kind of make-believe involved in this case depends on the general illocutionary status that is assigned to written drama. It will depend on whether we conceive dramatic texts as "a set of instructions for how to do something, namely, how to perform a play" (Searle, "Logical" 329) or whether we equate the stage directions with the utterances of a narrator and thus treat the written drama as a kind of literary narrative.

Let us now turn to the concept of *theatrical fiction*, or the fact that the representation of a story on the stage produces a specific performance world. For a closer investigation of the concept's meaning, I want to briefly elaborate on the particular conditions, possibilities, and conventions of theater as an art form. My point of departure will be the minimal definition of theater proposed by Eric Bentley in his book *The Life of Drama*: "A impersonates B while C looks on" (50).[27] This short sentence expresses the two major defining features of theater: the co-presence of the producing agents (or part of the producing agents) and of the audience while the work of art is presented and the fact that theater is based on an activity that can in general terms be called role-playing.[28] Thus when David Osipovich explores the sine qua non of theatrical performance in 2006, he doesn't do much more than elaborate on the aspects already contained in Bentley's short definition from 1964. Osipovich lists three necessary conditions for theatrical performance: "1) at least one performer and at least one observer in the same space and at the same time, 2) a pretense on the part of the performer that the interaction between performer and observer is somehow other than it actually is, and 3) an awareness on the part of the observer that the pretense is occurring" (465). I will briefly elaborate on the second aspect of Osipovich's definition, because the performer's pretense can easily be related to concepts of fictionality.

While of course much can be said about the performer's pretense or about what an actor's impersonation of a character on stage means, I concentrate on the conceptual relations between acting and fictionality. In Osipovich's definition, an actor's playing a character involves some kind of pretense. Nicholas Wolterstorff argues that an actor does not pretend to be a character but rather plays a character by pretending to be an example of that character (251). He thereby wants to highlight that although different productions of the same play present the fictional world of the written drama, every single production presents its own production world. The various choices that have to be made in order to stage a play—that is, determining the cast, costumes, setting, lighting, and so on—characterize its production world.[29] Moreover, in the aftermath of Searle's influential article on the logical status of fictional discourse in which he defends the thesis that authors of narrative fiction do not perform illocutionary acts but only pretend to perform these acts, theorists of theatrical performance—for example, Carroll, David Saltz, and James

Hamilton—have had great discussions about whether actors on stage also pretend to perform illocutionary acts and more generally about whether acting is related to some kind of pretense. It is beyond the scope of this chapter, however, to retrace this rather complex discussion.[30]

As a matter of fact what actors do in a performance can be explained not only in terms of pretense but also in terms of make-believe. As children do, actors engage in a game of make-believe in which they pretend to be somebody else, but there are obvious differences between children's games and acting in a play. While children invent their games and characters as they go along, actors usually enact scripted stories. Moreover, children usually impersonate character types (an Indian, a cowboy, a gangster, a chief, a sheriff, a crime boss), and actors usually impersonate individuals. (Even characters such as Alceste in Molière's *Le Misanthrope* are individuals, although they are meant to represent a type.) Despite these differences, the fact that actors engage in a game of make-believe is certainly a major component of the institutional practice known as *theater.*

However, when the performance of actors is described as make-believe, the term means something slightly different than when it is applied to the description of the institutional practice of fiction. To impersonate a character it is essential that the actor perform certain actions, such as uttering the lines and pretending to make the assertions that the character is supposed to make with these utterances. In contrast to the make-believe that explains the fictional stance, this kind of make-believe cannot be described as simply imagining. While imagining may be an important component of acting, actors also have to perform actual actions (see Meskin 55–56). Moreover, the make-believe of actors involves not only themselves but also the other members of the cast and the audience. As Jorge Luis Borges puts it in his short story "Everything and Nothing": "[The actor] on a stage plays at being another before a gathering of people who play at taking him for that other person" (76).

At this point we can ask about the audience in the theater. Following Borges, one can say that a theater audience is invited to make-believe what is represented on stage. Moreover, the different ways of understanding make-believe as constitutive of the fictional stance that have been discussed so far can easily be applied to theater audiences. Walton would say that the make-believe of the theatrical audience is also an imagining de se. Currie, by contrast, argues rather convincingly that there is no imagining de se, because we do not pretend that we see Othello; rather, we see an actor on stage and are invited to pretend that he is Othello ("Visual Fictions" 138–39). Moreover the audience's attitude in theater can be described in terms of "suppositional imagination." Of course, the difference between theater and literary narrative lies in the fact that when reading texts, audiences engage imaginatively with what they read, whereas in theater audiences engage imaginatively with what is enacted and thus is presented to them visually and acoustically. In spite of this difference, the explanation of "imagination" as holding something before the mind unasserted can also be applied to theater audiences. They imaginatively take what is shown on the stage for what it is supposed to show, usually the enactment of a specific story. Through an act of imagination the audience engages with the performed story or with the performance world of the production. Furthermore, the concept of a theatrical narrator has been defended, although much more rarely than the concept of a cinematic narrator. If a theater performance can be taken as a theatrical discourse (similar to a literary or filmic discourse), then it is possible to assume a theatrical narrator or a theatrical composition device, and this narrator or device is understood as the fictional authority of story presentation in theater (see Alber and Fludernik 185).[31]

To summarize, one can say that in the theater the active make-believe of the actors induces a passive make-believe by the audience, with the audience pretending that they are told a story as known fact by means of the conventions of the medium. Saltz captures the essence of theatrical fictionality when he writes that in theater performances "the object the audience uses as a prop in *its* game of make-believe is *itself* a game of make-believe" ("Infiction" 212, original emphases). Theatrical fiction can thus be explained by means of a specific realization of the three components of our multilayered approach to fictionality: it displays non-real worlds, it is an institutional practice, and the conventions of this practice involve games of make-believe on both the production and the reception sides.

The specific representational conventions that the institution of theatrical fiction allows for are again manifold. Moreover, they can vary from one production to another. As Hamilton points out, it depends upon the style of a production as to what counts as a salient feature of the theatrical representation. Depending on the style of production, for example, not all of an actor's features may count as features of the character he enacts (see ch. 6).

Fictionality and Film

As a last example of an art form for which fictionality is a relevant category, I now turn to film. It is interesting to note that in contrast to the theater but in agreement with literature, an established distinction exists between a fictional and a nonfictional, or factual, genre of filmmaking. This distinction is corroborated by the fact that film schools, film festivals, and film awards usually have different classes and categories for feature film and documentary film. This division raises the question of what it means to call feature film "fictional" and, although this issue is not central to the topic of this chapter, of whether documentary is the factual "other" of feature film.

For a start I briefly look at the factual side in order to clarify the medium-specific background of my investigation. Carroll calls attention to the fact that in film history the term "documentary" is not tantamount to "nonfictional film" but has acquired a specific meaning that goes beyond the denial of fictionality. He asserts that *documentary,* in the tradition established by such filmmakers as Robert J. Flaherty or John Grierson, represented "creative treatment of actuality" ("Fiction" 173). This understanding of documentary film highlights the artistic dimension of nonfictional filmmaking and makes the term "documentary" equivocal when used to designate nonfiction film as such or to distinguish nonfictional from fictional film. Carroll therefore proposes the label "film of presumptive assertion" or even "film of putative fact" (175) for nonfictional film. Factual film as film of presumptive assertion is defined by the fact that the filmmaker intends the audience to believe or to entertain as asserted truth the propositional content conveyed by the film. With the label "film of presumptive assertion," Carroll wants to highlight that the concept of nonfictional film is not linked to a specific form of filmic representation. Films of presumptive assertions do not have to include any kind of documentary footage; they can be made entirely of computer animations or even of enacted scenes.

"Documentary film" corresponds to a subclass of Carroll's films of presumptive assertion—that is, the "film of the presumptive trace." This subclass is defined by the fact that "the relevant structure of sense-bearing signs is such that the film-maker intends that the audience regards the images in the films as historic traces" (188). The concept of "trace" alludes to the idea that photographic images are mechanically caused representations. As such they are to some extent independent of the photographer's intentions or beliefs. According to Currie, being a trace is what differentiates photographic images from painted images, which he describes as "testimonies," or representations that express the maker's beliefs or intentions ("Visual Fictions" 65–66). Walton similarly holds the view that in contrast to drawings and paintings, photographic images are to a certain extent transparent with respect to what they represent ("Transparent Pictures").[32] That photographic images are traces leads to the view that one can distinguish between "representation by origin" and "representation by use" with regard to filmic representation (Currie, *Narratives* 19). Traditional documentary presumes a harmony between the two (20), whereas in fictional film there is an obvious distinction between what is represented by *origin* (an actor like Cary Grant, for example) and what is represented by *use* (Grant's character, Roger Thornhill, in *North by Northwest*).

As a result of these rather sketchy remarks about factual film as the "other" of fiction film, I want to emphasize two aspects of the discussion. First, *nonfictional film* can be seen as an institutional practice that is not limited to the representational conventions of films of presumptive trace; rather, it is defined by the agreement between the makers and the audience that the film is meant to convey in some way a truthful representation of a given reality. Second, one of the specificities of filmmaking is that it involves the photographic medium, which in turn can be characterized by the concept of representational traces.

We can now explicate the fictionality of feature films with the help of our multilayered account of fictionality. Feature films share some characteristics with theater performances, especially in that the presentation of the fictional world relies in large part on role-playing by actors, so most of what has been said about role-playing and fictional worlds in theater applies to film as well.[33] But there are also major medium-specific differences. For one, the filmic production process consists of recording scenes and leads to a fixed work, whereas a theater production is a non-recorded work that needs to be performed anew every night. Consequently, there is no distinction between the performance world and the production world for film fiction. Moreover, when feature films are not adaptations of literary works, there is no difference between the production world and the fictional world of the work because the film script is usually not published; and even if it is published, it is normally not regarded as an authoritative text that defines a fictional world independently of the actual film.

Turning to the question of make-believe, most of what has been said about theatrical fiction again applies also to filmic fiction. One of the major medium-specific differences—that is, the co-presence of actors and viewers—has vanished, but the fact that the audience does not perceive real persons on a stage but images on a screen is of no importance here. Significantly, however, in both film and theater, make-believe is involved not only on the audience's side but also on the production side. Moreover, the make-believe that the audiences of films are invited to witness can be interpreted in the ways already outlined in our general definition and applied in the sections on literature and theater. One last remark about the interpretation of make-believe as suppositional imagination may be appropriate at this point. When the term "imagination" is used to explain the fictional stance, it does not necessarily entail mental visualization; this point is important since it precludes the argument that imagination cannot be part of a definition of fictionality of film because one cannot imagine what one already sees.[34]

The narratological (i.e., narrator-based) interpretation of make-believe encounters the same difficulties with film as with literature and theater. The question of whether the concept of a cinematographic narrator or filmic composition device is essential for an understanding of filmic communication has been the object of rather acrimonious discussions in film studies. On the one hand, the fact that what is shown in a film is always presented from a specific point of view or perspective, or that a film establishes a specific relationship between story time and discourse time, has led semiotically oriented critics such as Seymour Chatman, André Gaudreault, François Jost, or Tom Gunning to claim that every film has a cinematic narrator.[35] On the other hand, Currie (*Image* 265–70), David Bordwell, and other critics who adopt a more cognitivist approach argue that filmic communication should be understood as a direct unmediated presentation of a story that makes the postulation of a narrator superfluous and misleading.[36] Further discussion, however, is beyond the scope of this chapter and irrelevant to its main thesis, since the multilayered account of fictionality works equally well with or without a narrator.

Looking more closely at the institutional aspect of filmic fiction, one can say that the institutional practice of fictional film is to a certain extent similar to the one established for narration or the theater. With fictional film the audience is invited to adopt the attitude of make-believe toward the represented story by imagining what is represented by origin as showing what it is intended to be represented by use. The make-believe attitude can be seen as a passive play, which again is partly based on the actors' active game of make-believe. Moreover, there are film-specific conventions of representation that establish what a specific film sequence is supposed to represent.

Again, the specific representational conventions of fictional film are manifold, especially because all the different means of filmic representation come into play. The fictional world of a film is constituted by aspects of mise-en-scène such as setting, costumes, makeup, lighting, or music. Further, the spectator's apprehension of the fictional world is dependent on features that are specific to film art, especially framing and editing.[37] To give only one example, a shot showing a person from behind and from a diagonal angle with an object obstructing the visual field of the camera is conventionally interpreted as meaning that another person is observing the character. The film may also give clues (e.g., via acoustic signals) as to whether the observer has good or bad intentions. Going more deeply into the conventions specific to fictional films is beyond the scope of this chapter, and it suffices to note the existence of conventions regarding how fictional worlds are to be conceived or how audiences indulge in make-believe in relation to films.

To summarize the preceding discussion, we can say that the usefulness of the multilayered account of fictionality presented in this chapter lies in its power to explain how fictionality can be seen as a common feature of phenomena belonging to different art forms or media. Moreover, this account makes it possible to spell out the medium-specific differences of these various kinds of fictional artworks. Future investigations will have to show whether and how the present analysis of fictionality can be applied to art forms or media—for example, paintings, computer games, photography, and music—that are not discussed in this chapter. An important part of these future investigations will be to determine what makes the concept of fictionality useful for a given medium.

Notes

1. The second question highlights the fact that investigations into more or less philosophical concepts such as "fictionality" do not actually answer questions about what there is; rather they answer questions about how we can understand and/or regroup specific cultural phenomena. Therefore, I understand concepts of fictionality, be they transmedial or not, as heuristic devices that help us to grasp complex cultural interactions and provide us with tools to analyze these cultural interactions in their complexity.
2. See Ryan, "Introduction" 15–20; Ryan, "Theoretical Foundations" 14–21.
3. See, for example, Walton, *Mimesis*; Walton, "Listening"; Rabinowitz; Ryan, *Avatars*.
4. See Ryan, *Avatars* 31–58; Ryan, "Fiction, Cognition."
5. For a clear distinction between fictionality and representation, see, for example, Schaeffer, "Fictional" 103–18. For arguments against Walton's terminology, see, for example, Zipfel, *Fiktion* 23–24.
6. In this chapter I use the term "fictionality" rather than "fiction." The notion of fiction in English is very much associated with literary narration, whereas fictionality can be used to designate works of art in different art forms or media.
7. What counts as real or what is considered as fact may be relative to a specific "truth program" (Schaeffer, "Fictional" 99).
8. Again, one of the most ardent proponents of a theory of fiction that omits reference to fictional content is Kendall Walton, who alleges that "there is no reason why a work of fiction could not be exclusively about people and things (particulars) that actually exist" (*Mimesis* 74). Similar assertions can be found in many other theoretical approaches: for example, Bareis 55–63; Bunia 138; Davies 44–48; Gertken and Köppe 234–36; Gibson 160.
9. For a similar approach, see New, for whom "the notion of invention is part of the notion of fiction" (48); Lamarque and Olsen 51; Schmid 27.
10. For a more detailed account, see Zipfel, *Fiktion* 76–106. I have to pass over the long-standing debate about the status of fictional characters. For a brief survey, see, for example, Jannidis.
11. Maybe one of the most elegant ways to talk about fictional content as differing from reality is to say that "content is fictional just in case what is true of those objects, events etc. is dependent on the fictive descriptions which characterize them in the first place" (Lamarque and Olsen 51). See also Köppe 51.
12. See Zipfel, "Fictional Truth."
13. See Duflo 239–46; Zipfel, "Zeichen." For a critical view regarding the explanatory force of "game" or "play" in theories of fiction, see Gibson 165; and for a more positive view see Köppe.

14. Here, I especially refer to the ongoing debate about the so-called paradox of fiction. Compare, for example, Yanal; Zipfel, "Emotion."
15. For similar explanations, see Lamarque; Yanal. For the complex question of the meaning of "imagination," see Stevenson; Sutrop.
16. See Currie, *Nature*, ch. 1; Lamarque and Olsen ch. 2. Evidentially an institutional concept of fictionality does not preclude misunderstandings or misreadings. There is always the possibility that an audience will disregard the intention of the producer or, for example, read a fictional text as if it were factual, but that is not an argument against a conception of fiction as institutional practice. As for Walton's examples of authorless texts, such as the ones that are generated by cracks in rocks, yes, we can read those authorless texts as fiction, but to discuss this kind of authorless texts is to engage in a rather spurious and not very enlightening thought experiment. To put it differently, if somebody will at some time stumble upon such a text and read it as fiction, the right explanation would be that the crack-in-rock text is then treated as if it was produced with the fiction intention.
17. The distinction between the defining conventions of the institutional practice and the representational conventions of fiction in a specific art form can roughly be mapped on the distinction between constitutive and regulative rules in Searle's theory of institutions (*Construction* 27–29, 43–48). For an application to a theory of fiction, see Sutrop 83–87.
18. For a similar understanding of theories of fiction, see Ryan's claim: "A truly meaningful theory of fiction should be more than an instrument by which to sort out all texts into fiction and non-fiction: it should also tell us something about how we experience these texts, what we do with them, why we consume them, and why it is important to make a distinction between fiction and non-fiction. It should, in other words, have a phenomenological and a cognitive dimension" ("Fiction, Cognition" 8).
19. For a more elaborate version of this kind of explanation of textual fictional narration, see, for example, Lamarque and Olsen; Zipfel, *Fiktion*.
20. Disagreeing with Walton and following Ryan, I do not think it is a bad idea to draw upon results stemming from the discussion about verbal fiction when we try to elaborate on a transmedial concept of fictionality (see Ryan, "Fiction, Cognition").
21. See, for example, Banfield; Brooke-Rose; Weber; Weimar; or more recently Köppe and Stühring; Walsh.
22. See, for example, Thon; Wilson.
23. See, for example, Martínez and Scheffel.
24. I distinguish between narration in a broad sense of story presentation and narration in a narrow sense of the presentation of a story that is mediated by a narrator or narrative function. For a differentiated account of the different meanings of narration, see, for example, Ryan, "Theoretical Foundations."

25. Some short stories by J. L. Borges come to mind—for example, "Tlön, Uqbar, Orbis Tertius" or "Pierre Menard, Author of Quixote."
26. Note, however, that while multilayered analysis of fiction allows for fictional poetry, it does not answer the question whether all poetry is fictional (see Zipfel, "Lyrik").
27. See also Fischer-Lichte 16.
28. A theater production is an artwork that is created by producing agents with differing functions who all take part in the creation process but who are not all present during the performance (e.g., director and stage and costume designers).
29. It could also be argued that every single performance creates its own performance world.
30. See Alward for a detailed account.
31. See also Patrick Colm Hogan's chapter 2 in this volume.
32. See also Ryan, "Fiction, Cognition" 16–18.
33. I leave aside cartoon film, which would need an investigation of its own.
34. This remark could, of course, have been made already in the discussion of theatrical fiction. But although the remark is equally true when made about theater as it is when made about film, it is perhaps more pertinent for the realm of cinematographic images, as the latter are traditionally more closely linked to visual representational realism than is the case with theatrical performances.
35. For a recent version of this approach, see Kuhn 72–103.
36. See also Branigan; Ryan, "Fiction, Cognition" 18; Stam, Burgoyne, and Flitterman-Lewis 103–18; Thomson-Jones; Thon.
37. See, for example, part 4 in Bordwell and Thompson.

Works Cited

Alber, Jan, and Monika Fuldernik. "Mediacy and Narrative Mediation." *Handbook of Narratology*. Ed. Peter Hühn, John Pier, Wolf Schmid, and Jörg Schönert. Berlin: De Gruyter, 2009. 174–89. Print.

Alward, Peter. "Onstage Illocution." *Journal of Aesthetics and Art Criticism* 67 (2009): 321–31. Print.

Banfield, Ann. *Unspeakable Sentences: Narration and Representation in the Language of Fiction.* Boston: Routledge & Kegan Paul, 1982. Print.

Bareis, Alexander. *Fiktionales Erzählen: Zur Theorie der literarischen Fiktion als Make-Believe.* Göteborg, Sweden: Acta Universitatis Gothoburgensis, 2008. Print.

Bentley, Eric. *The Life of Drama*. New York: Atheneum, 1964. Print.

Birkenhauer, Theresia. "Fiktion." *Metzler Lexikon Theatertheorie.* Ed. Erika Fischer-Lichte, Doris Kolesch, and Matthias Warstat. Stuttgart: Metzler, 2005. 107–9. Print.

Bordwell, David, and Kristin Thompson. *Film Art: An Introduction*. 7th ed. Boston: McGraw-Hill, 2004. Print.

Borges, Jorge Luis. "Everything and Nothing." *Everything and Nothing*. New York: New Directions, 1999. 76–78. Print.

Branigan, Edward. *Narrative Comprehension and Film*. London: Routledge, 1992. Print.

Brooke-Rose, Christine. "Ill Locutions." *Narrative in Culture: The Uses of Storytelling in the Sciences, Philosophy, and Literature*. Ed. Cristopher Nash. London: Routledge, 1990. 154–71. Print.

Bunia, Remigius. *Faltungen: Fiktion, Erzählen, Medien*. Berlin: Erich Schmidt, 2007. Print.

Carroll, Noël. "Fiction, Non-Fiction, and the Film of Presumptive Assertion: A Conceptual Analysis." *Film Theory and Philosophy*. Ed. Richard Allen and Murray Smith. Oxford, UK: Clarendon, 1997. 173–202. Print.

———. *The Philosophy of Horror or Paradoxes of the Heart*. New York: Routledge, 1990. Print.

Cohn, Dorrit. *The Distinction of Fiction*. Baltimore MD: Johns Hopkins University Press, 1999. Print.

———. "Signposts of Fictionality: A Narratological Perspective." *Poetics Today* 11 (1990): 775–804. Print.

Currie, Gregory. *Arts and Minds*. Oxford, UK: Clarendon, 2004. Print.

———. *Image and Mind: Film, Philosophy, and Cognitive Science*. Cambridge, UK: Cambridge University Press, 1995. Print.

———. *Narratives and Narrators: A Philosophy of Stories*. Oxford, UK: Oxford University Press, 2010. Print.

———. *The Nature of Fiction*. Cambridge, UK: Cambridge University Press, 1990. Print.

———. "Visual Fictions." *The Philosophical Quarterly* 41.163 (1991): 129–43. Print.

Davies, David. *Aesthetics & Literature*. London: Continuum, 2007. Print.

Duflo, Colas. *Jouer et philosopher*. Paris: Presses Universitaires de France, 1997. Print.

Eco, Umberto. *Six Walks in the Fictional Woods*. Cambridge MA: Harvard University Press, 1994. Print.

Fischer-Lichte, Erika. *Semiotik des Theaters: 1, Das System der theatralischen Zeichen*. Tübingen, Germany: Narr, 1983. Print.

Genette, Gérard. *Fiction et diction*. Paris: Seuil, 1991. Print.

Gertken, Jan, and Tilmann Köppe. "Fiktionalität." *Grenzen der Literatur: Zu Begriff und Phänomen des Literarischen*. Ed. Simone Winko, Fotis Jannidis, and Gerhard Lauer. Berlin: De Gruyter, 2009. 228–66. Print.

Gibson, John. *Fiction and the Weave of Life*. Oxford, UK: Oxford University Press, 2007. Print.

Gorman, David. "Theories of Fiction." *Routledge Encyclopedia of Narrative Theory*. Ed. David Herman, Manfred Jahn, and Marie-Laure Ryan. London: Routledge, 2005. 163–67. Print.

Hamburger, Käte: *Die Logik der Dichtung*. 3rd ed. Stuttgart: Klett-Cotta, 1977. Print.

Hamilton, James R. *The Art of Theater*. Malden MA: Wiley-Blackwell, 2007. Print.

Jannidis, Fotis. "Character." *Handbook of Narratology*. Ed. Peter Hühn, John Pier, Wolf Schmid, and Jörg Schönert. Berlin: De Gruyter, 2009. 14–29. Print.

Köppe, Tilmann. "Fiktion, Praxis, Spiel: Was leistet der Spielbegriff bei der Klärung des Fiktionalitätsbegriffs?" *Literatur als Spiel: Evolutionsbiologische, ästhetische und pädagogische Konzepte*. Ed. Thomas Anz and Heinrich Klauen. Berlin: De Gruyter, 2009. 39–56. Print.

Köppe, Tilmann, and Stühring, Jan. "Against Pan-Narrator Theories." *Journal of Literary Semantics* 40.1 (2011): 59–80. Print.

Kuhn, Markus. *Filmnarratologie: Ein erzähltheoretisches Analysemodell*. Berlin: De Gruyter, 2011. Print.

Lamarque, Peter. "How Can We Fear and Pity Fictions?" *British Journal of Aesthetics* 21 (1981): 291–304. Print.

Lamarque, Peter, and Stein Haugom Olsen. *Truth, Fiction, and Literature: A Philosophical Perspective*. Oxford, UK: Clarendon, 1994. Print.

Martínez, Matías, and Michael Scheffel. "Narratology and Theory of Fiction: Remarks on a Complex Relationship." *What Is Narratology? Questions and Answers Regarding the Status of a Theory*. Ed. Tom Kindt and Hans-Harald Müller. Berlin: De Gruyter, 2003. 221–37. Print.

Meskin, Aaron. "Scrutinizing the Art of Theater." *The Journal of Aesthetic Education* 43 (2009): 51–66. Print.

New, Christopher. *Philosophy of Literature: An Introduction*. London: Routledge, 1999. Print.

Osipovich, David. "What Is a Theatrical Performance?" *Journal of Aesthetics and Art Criticism* 64.4 (2006): 461–70. Print.

Pavel, Thomas. *Fictional Worlds*. Cambridge MA: Harvard University Press, 1986. Print.

Ponesch, Trevor. "What Is Non-fiction Cinema?" *Film Theory and Philosophy*. Ed. Richard Allen and Murray Smith. Oxford, UK: Clarendon, 1997. 203–20. Print.

Rabinowitz, Peter J. "Music, Genre, and Narrative Theory." *Narrative across Media: The Languages of Storytelling*. Ed. Marie-Laure Ryan. Lincoln: University of Nebraska Press, 2004. 305–28. Print.

Ryan, Marie-Laure. *Avatars of Story*. Minneapolis: Minnesota University Press, 2006. Print.

———. "Fiction, Cognition and Non-Verbal Media." *Intermediality and Storytelling*. Ed. Marina Grishakova and Marie-Laure Ryan. Berlin: De Gruyter, 2010. 8–26. Print.

———. "Fiction, Non-Factuals, and the Principal of Minimal Departure." *Poetics* 9 (1980): 403–22. Print.

———. Introduction. *Narrative across Media: The Languages of Storytelling*. Ed. Marie-Laure Ryan. Lincoln: University of Nebraska Press, 2004. 1–40. Print.

———. "On the Theoretical Foundations of Transmedial Narratology." *Narratology beyond Literary Criticism: Mediality, Disciplinarity*. Ed. Jan Christoph Meister. Berlin: De Gruyter, 2005. 1–23. Print.

———. *Possible Worlds, Artificial Intelligence, and Narrative Theory*. Bloomington: Indiana University Press, 1991. Print.

Saltz, David Z. "How to Do Things on Stage." *Journal of Aesthetics and Art Criticism* 49.1 (1991): 31–45. Print.

———. "Infiction and Outfiction: The Role of Fiction in Theatrical Performance." *Staging Philosophy: Intersections of Theater, Performance, and Philosophy*. Ed. David Krasner and David Z. Saltz. Ann Arbor: University of Michigan Press, 2006. 203–18. Print.

Schaeffer, Jean-Marie. *Pourquoi la fiction?* Paris: Seuil, 1999. Print.

———. "Fictional vs. Factual Narration." *Handbook of Narratology*. Ed. Peter Hühn, John Pier, Wolf Schmid, and Jörg Schönert. Berlin: De Gruyter, 2009. 98–114. Print.

Schmid, Wolf. *Elemente der Narratologie*. 2nd ed. Berlin: De Gruyter, 2008. Print.

Scruton, Roger. *Art and Imagination: A Study in the Philosophy of Mind*. London: Methuen, 1974. Print.

Searle, John R. *The Construction of Social Reality*. London: Penguin, 1995. Print.

———. "The Logical Status of Fictional Discourse." *New Literary History* 6 (1974–75): 319–32. Print.

Stam, Robert, Robert Burgoyne, and Sandra Flitterman-Lewis. *New Vocabularies in Film Semiotics: Structuralism, Post-Structuralism, and Beyond*. New York: Routledge, 1992. Print.

Stevenson, Leslie. "Twelve Conceptions of Imagination." *British Journal of Aesthetics* 43.3 (2003): 238–59. Print.

Sutrop, Margit. *Fiction and Imagination: The Anthropological Function of Literature*. Paderborn, Germany: Mentis, 2000. Print.

Thomson-Jones, Katherine. "The Literary Origins of the Cinematic Narrator." *British Journal of Aesthetics* 47.1 (2007): 76–94. Print.

Thon, Jan-Noël. "Toward a Transmedial Narratology: On Narrators in Contemporary Graphic Novels, Feature Films, and Computer Games." *Beyond Classical Narration: Transmedial and Unnatural Challenges*. Ed. Jan Alber and Per Krogh Hansen. Berlin: De Gruyter, 2014. 25–56. Print.

Walsh, Richard. *The Rhetoric of Fictionality: Narrative Theory and the Idea of Fiction*. Columbus: Ohio State University Press, 2007. Print.

Walton, Kendall L. "Listening with Imagination: Is Music Representational?" *Journal of Aesthetics and Art Criticism* 52.1 (1994): 47–61. Print.

———. *Mimesis as Make-Believe: On the Foundations of the Representational Arts.* Cambridge MA: Harvard University Press, 1990. Print.

———. "Transparent Pictures: On the Nature of Photographic Realism." *Critical Inquiry* 11.2 (1984): 246–77. Print.

Weber, Dietrich. *Erzählliteratur: Schriftwerk, Kunstwerk, Erzählwerk.* Göttingen, Germany: Vandenhoeck & Ruprecht, 1998. Print.

Weimar, Klaus. "Wo und was ist der Erzähler?" *Modern Language Notes* 109 (1994): 495–506. Print.

Wilson, George M. "Elusive Narrators in Literature and Film." *Philosophical Studies* 135.1 (2007): 73–88. Print.

Wolterstorff, Nicholas. *Works and Worlds of Art.* Oxford, UK: Clarendon, 1980. Print.

Yanal, Robert J. *Paradoxes of Emotion and Fiction.* University Park: Pennsylvania State University Press, 1999. Print.

Zipfel, Frank. "Emotion und Fiktion: Zur Relevanz des Fiktions-Paradoxes für eine Theorie der Emotionalisierung in Literatur und Film." *Emotionen in Literatur und Film.* Ed. Sandra Poppe. Würzburg, Germany: Königshausen & Neumann, 2012. 127–53. Print.

———. "Fictional Truth and Unreliable Narration." *Journal of Literary Theory* 5.1 (2011): 109–30. Print.

———. *Fiktion, Fiktivität, Fiktionalität: Analysen zur Fiktion in der Literatur und zum Fiktionsbegriff in der Literaturwissenschaft.* Berlin: Erich Schmidt, 2001. Print.

———. "Lyrik und Fiktion." *Handbuch Lyrik.* Ed. Dieter Lamping. Stuttgart: Metzler, 2011. 162–66. Print.

———. "Zeichen, Phantasie und Spiel als poetogene Strukturen literarischer Fiktion." *Anthropologie der Literatur: Poetogene Strukturen und ästhetisch-soziale Handlungsfelder.* Ed. Rüdiger Zymner and Manfred Engel. Paderborn, Germany: Mentis, 2004. 51–80. Print.

5 Framings of Narrative in Literature and the Pictorial Arts

WERNER WOLF

It is well-known that we humans are story-telling animals and that our stories can be transmitted by more media than verbal texts. Therefore, further belabouring these and similar facts is no longer necessary in narratology. Yet what has not been researched sufficiently, if at all, is this question: how do we know in the first place that a text, an artifact, or, more precisely, a particular represented world (be it of a verbal, visual, or acoustic nature) is a *story*world?

In an essay titled "Toward a Definition of Narrative," Marie-Laure Ryan claimed with reference to "verbal or visual information" that "[a]ssessing the narrative status of a text is not a cognitive question that we must consciously answer for proper understanding" (32–33). This assertion is true enough from the perspective of the general "user" of narratives. Yet from a *narratological* perspective finding out which mechanisms and clues actually encourage us to perceive a given artifact within a narrative framework rather than, for example, a descriptive one is a cognitive question that merits further attention.

My ensuing reflections aim at finding answers to this question on the basis of the frame-theoretical idea that *narrative* is a major cognitive frame whose application is elicited by certain clues, "keys," or "framings," typically and preferably at the outset of a reception process. As for the media involved in this process, we must remember, following Ryan, that media are not neutral conduits without any impact on what is transmitted by them; rather, they "make [. . .] a difference as to what kind of [. . .] content can be evoked" ("Media and Narrative" 290). If so, it should also apply to their different potentials to trigger certain cognitive frames, including the frame narrative. This is what I intend to discuss in the following. More precisely, I inquire into the framings of narrative that operate at the beginning of reception processes and elicit narrative readings. In doing so, my aim is not to present an exhaustive survey of all possible devices and conditions triggering the frame narrative in individual arts and media. Rather, my focus is on the main means of framing narratives from a media-comparative, transmedial perspective with reference to only two fields—namely, verbal art (literature) and the pictorial arts.

Preliminary Theoretical Reflections: Types of Cognitive "Framings" and of Narrativity

Before engaging in a discussion of framings of narrative, some remarks on framings in general and on different types of framings (see Wolf, "Introduction"), as well as on basic qualities of narrative, may not be amiss. In my 2006 book on *Framing Borders* I distinguished between cognitive *frames* and cognitive *framings* as codings or "keyings" (see Goffman) of such frames and thus as triggers of certain expectations. In art, which loves to play with expectations, such codings or framings can assume a playful, defamiliarized, or even deceptive form (see Wolf, "Defamiliarized"). We therefore should reformulate our main question concerning the framing of narratives. Rather than asking whether a given represented world is a *story*world, we should perhaps say, how are we induced to *think* that a represented world is a storyworld?

Framings come in many typological forms and may be combined with each other (in the following I will draw on Wolf, "Introduction"). A first typological distinction refers to the constituents of communicative processes and thus to different framing agencies; that is, they may be sender, message, context, or recipient based (15–17). The recipient as the subject of narrativization is a particularly important factor in producing a narrative reception, all the more so as narrative is a favorite frame for humans to make sense of experience, time, change, and identity. However, the narrative-friendly predispositions of individuals and perhaps most recipients notwithstanding, we may safely say that not all artifacts elicit narrativization or, if they do, not to the same degree. Obviously, the work or message in question also plays a crucial role in triggering the frame narrative, and this factor is therefore privileged in the following discussion. My focus is thus on textual, or message-based, framings with occasional glances at contextual (extracompositional) framings, including generic framings, since, generally speaking, framing results first and foremost from a combination of what we know and what we perceive.

With the message-based variant, framings can be located on the level of the paratexts or on the (intra)textual level, and both sub-forms can include formal and content aspects. All of these intracompositional facets are relevant to the following inquiry, provided we accept a wide definition of "text" that also includes nonverbal signs and thus avoids terminological complications (19–21).

The second major typological distinction refers to the extension of framings. Although given artifacts can require the activation of more than one frame simultaneously or in individual parts, for simplicity's sake I concentrate on total rather than partial framings—that is, on framings that refer to the entire artifact in question and provide a dominant frame for its understanding (18–19).

The third distinction concerns the possibility that framings can use the same medium as the framed message or, alternatively, other media. In other words, framings can be homomedial or heteromedial (18).

A fourth distinction refers to the location of framings in the process of reception. In principle, given artifacts can locate framings at any moment in a prescribed or suggested reception process. However, as already noted, the initial position is cognitively of particular relevance, since it is at the beginning of a reading, viewing, or listening process that expectations are created and then are applied to the entire artifact under scrutiny, at least as a default option. Obviously, one could object to the temporal terms "initial," "internal," or "terminal" framings (21) if used for the visual arts as nontemporal media. Thus I would like to reaccentuate "initial framings" for our transmedial inquiry and use this category to refer to the first few moments of the first reception of both verbal and visual artifacts.

As a fifth typological differentiation, one may distinguish between framings that refer directly to the framed artifact and those that do so indirectly. Again, both forms are relevant to our purpose. Direct framings are most clearly seen in overtly metareferential mentions (e.g., "this is a narrative"), while indirect framings address the cognitive frames in question via a "detour."[1] Thus, when we read that a given title of a television (TV) program is a horror film, it is first and foremost a direct and overtly metareferential framing of a filmic genre. However, according to our cultural expertise, we also know that this genre denotes films that are typically narrative; therefore, this direct generic framing is at the same time also an indirect framing indicating narrativity.

As for the functions of framings, they always include metareferential ones, since, semiotically speaking, framings are signs controlling the use and meaning of other signs and are thus located on a logically higher level than are the framed signs. In our case, the framings in question amount to the aforementioned metareferential statement: "The artifact referred to is a narrative." However, clearly not all framings contain only metareferential messages, nor do all of them convey such messages in an overt or explicit way. Rather, as far as the saliency of framings—the sixth differentiation—is concerned, there is a whole range of gradations between overt and covert framings that at first glance may even seem to be no framings at all but simply parts of the artifact in question (19).

Concerning the framing of narrative, all the prototypical features of narratives, or "narratemes" (see Prince 46; Wolf, "Narrative" 183), may function as such covert framings. Most notably, this refers to the representation of settings, characters, and events, implying a chronological, causal, and teleological order. Yet such covert framing may also extend to one feature of typical narratives that has hardly found attention in research—that is, our assumption that stories, including their ending, have happened (in reality or imagination) before they are told, performed, or otherwise represented and that they elicit the "sense of the precedence of event[s]" or of a pastness of the story in question (see Abbott 535; Wolf, "'Sense'"). Thus, in verbal artifacts, the past tense can also function as one "key" to narrativity. However, assessing a complex phenomenon such as the frame narrative according to prototypical features may take some time; therefore, not all narratemes may be equally relevant for initial framing.

Finally, a crucial distinction concerning the narrative quality of given works must be introduced. Besides the well-known fact that narrative is a prototypical phenomenon and thus gradable, many representations do appear to possess genuine narrativity to a considerable extent in themselves, whereas other representations, while not actually narrative as such, may yet encourage a narrativization based on intertextual or intermedial references to clearly narrative representations. In literature, the distinction between such genuinely or directly narrative works and texts with "borrowed or indirect narrativity" may be illustrated by the obvious difference between the actual narrativity of Homer's *Iliad* and the predominant descriptivity rather than narrativity of Edgar Allan Poe's poem "To Helen," which only refers to a narrative character in Homer's epic:

TO HELEN

Helen, thy beauty is to me
Like those Nicéan barks of yore,
That gently, o'er a perfumed sea,
The weary, way-worn wanderer bore
To his own native shore.

On desperate seas, long wont to roam,
Thy hyacinth hair, thy classic face,
Thy Naiad airs have brought me home
To the glory that was Greece
And the grandeur that was Rome.

Lo! In yon brilliant window-niche
How statue-like I see thee stand,
The agate lamp within thy hand!
Ah! Psyche, from the regions which
Are Holy Land!
(quoted from Ferguson, Salter, and Stallworthy 975–76)

In the pictorial arts, the same difference may be seen at work when comparing the descriptive, portrait-like painting *Helen of Troy* by Pre-Raphaelite painter Frederick Sandys (1829–1904) (figure 5.1) and the painting *The Abduction of Helen of Troy* by the Italian Baroque painter Cesare Dandini (1596–1657) (figure 5.2). Over and above its reference to Homer's epic, Dandini's painting contains strong narrative clues in its suggestion of a chronology and causality of events. They are revealed when reading the picture's three scenes: Paris's abduction of Helen in the center, causing the persecutors to rush in from the left side and toward the ship on the right-hand side that is waiting to take the couple to Troy.

In the following discussion, I focus on "genuinely" narrative artifacts

Fig. 5.1. Frederick Sandys (1829–1904), *Helen of Troy*.

as illustrated by Dandini. Before analyzing pictorial clues of narrative, however, I start with initial framings of narrativity in literature.

Initial Framings of Narrative in Literature

"Literature," as we understand the term today, comprises mostly fictional texts, which are relatively independent of pragmatic contexts. In all of its typical traditional variants, such as epic, drama, and lyric, literature

Fig. 5.2. Cesare Dandini (1596–1657), *The Abduction of Helen of Troy.*

can be realized in two ways—as performance and as printed text. For simplicity's sake and since the printed form is arguably most important, at least today, I concentrate on the latter variant.

Literature as printed text—as a rule and in spite of the growing importance of e-books and discounting special cases, such as loose manuscripts found in odd places or photocopies for educational purposes—still comes in traditional book form. Usually, readers do not simply happen to come across books but purposely borrow them from libraries or buy them in traditional or online bookshops before reading them. In all of these cases, contextual framings of individual books in the form of more or less consistent text type and generic classifications will occur; that is, contextual framings in conjunction with the readers' knowledge of cultural conventions will furnish indirect information on the applicability of the frame "narrative" to the item in question. Thus, Amazon's fiction section or the fiction and drama departments in a large bookshop or library will inform a potential recipient with some reliability right from the start that the books found there will in all probability be narratives.

If such contextual, extracompositional framings are unavailable for some reason, intracompositional framings directly connected with the book in question may be used as a supplement to yield clues of narrativity as well. First in the reception process among the intracompositional framings are the paratexts, which have become a regular feature of printed texts at least since the Renaissance. These more or less elaborate paratexts render the identification of literature as such relatively easy and may also function as initial framings of narrative. Such framing may occur in the indirect variant—for example, through macro-generic subtitles that refer to genres known to be narrative ("A Tragedy")—or even in a direct way by titles and subtitles denoting narrativity, such as *The History of Tom Jones.*

In addition, in printed literature, the general textual form as a variant of "form-based" intratextual framing—always in conjunction with the necessary cultural knowledge on the part of the recipient—may also immediately indicate narrativity: books containing fiction, drama, and poetry are characteristically different in the layout of the main text's pages, and this layout may thus contribute to framing the narrative. For instance, while fiction is usually printed with both left- and right-justified margins, poetry typically is set with left-justified margins only, is often divided into stanzas, and is usually printed with more margin space surrounding the individual text than texts of novels or short stories. Finally, drama is also easily recognizable by its layout, which distinguishes between speech tags, stage directions, and text spoken by characters.

Where contextual and paratextual framings indicate the text type literature and, in addition or in conjunction with general textual form, also bespeak fiction or drama, the informed recipient's default setting will certainly be "narrative" even before he or she has read the first line of the respective main texts. Poetry, in this context, is a more difficult case, since the markers of "lyricalness" do not necessarily also function as reliable indirect framings of narrativity. On the contrary, and in spite of recent attempts on the part of scholars such as Peter Hühn to extend narrativity to poetry in a general way, poetry is not typically narrative (see Wolf, "The Lyric" 30) or at least prototypically contains only low degrees of narrativity. Genuinely narrative poetic genres such as the ballad are an exception here. In order to direct readers' expectations toward narrativity, paratexts that inform the reader about the ballad genre may be helpful, yet Samuel Taylor Coleridge's "The Rime of the Ancient Mariner," one of the most famous ballads in English literature, does not give this clue. It is true that this poem is part of a collection generally known as *Lyrical Ballads*, yet as the assembled texts are a mixture of narrative and non-narrative poems (as the 1798 edition covertly indicates in the full title *Lyrical Ballads with a Few Other Poems*), the paratextual framing of the title is inconclusive with respect to narrativity.

It is thus with reference to poetry in particular that intratextual framings become necessary for triggering the frame narrative. In "The Rime of the Ancient Mariner," such intratextual framing functions quickly, owing to the general text form of the ballad stanza. Yet for anyone unable to make the connection between this metrical form and a probable narrative content, the opening frame with the lyrical persona meeting the eponymous mariner is as yet ambiguous. It starts:

> It is an ancient Mariner,
> And he stoppeth one of three.

Yet with line 10, and still relatively early in the reception process, we read:

> "There was a ship," quoth he.
> (quoted from Ferguson, Salter, and Stallworthy 812)

In this past-tense beginning of the embedded text, a first strong, form-based narrative framing is given. This is confirmed shortly afterward when the tense of the diegetic embedding text changes to past tense, too, and the mariner starts with his hypodiegetic story of a sea voyage, initiating a potentially eventful and therefore eminently narrative script:

> The wedding guest sate on a stone:
> He cannot choose but hear;
> And thus spake on that ancient man.
> The bright-eyed Mariner.
>
> "The Ship was cheered, the harbor cleared,
> Merrily did we drop
> Below the kirk, below the hill,
> Below the light-house top.
> (quoted from Ferguson, Salter, and Stallworthy 813)

As noted earlier, the past tense as the typical narrative tense may contribute to the signaling of narrativity and thus function as a form-based intratextual framing in poetry and in fiction. Yet fiction in particular has other form-based initial framings at its disposal. Among them, the opening formula "Once upon a time there was . . ." combines the introduction of the narrative past tense with an indirect framing of narrative by means of the generic marking of the "fairy tale."

However, such formulaic framings can also be deceptive, as the opening of James Joyce's *A Portrait of the Artist as a Young Man* shows: "Once upon a time and a very good time it was there was a moocow coming down along the road and this moocow that was coming down on the road met a nicens little boy named baby tuckooo. . . . His father told him that story: his father looked at him through a glass: he had a hairy face" (3).

Owing to the device of the "missing opening frame" (see Wolf, "Defamiliarized" 315) used here in the form of missing quotation marks, the opening formula "Once upon a time" may at first be misread (by an uninformed reader) as a total framing of the text as a whole and is only belatedly revealed as possessing a restricted relevance. Yet even if its function as the direct generic framing of a fairy tale is restricted to a few lines, the function of this phrase as an indirect framing of narrative holds true for the entire novel.

The narrative past tense, which is used in both the hypodiegetic and the diegetic opening sentences of Joyce's novel, may be absent in other narrative texts, including their openings. The narrativity of the text in question, however, may become clear even when one disregards contextual and paratextual framings. The opening paragraph of *Only Joking* (2010), a recent novel of contemporary author Gabriel Josipovici, is a case in point: "When the Baron, as he likes to be called, wants to talk, he always sits in the front. Felix, at the wheel, knows better than to initiate a conversation. He busies himself manoeuvring the large silent car through the congested streets of Henley" (1). Here, we find typical literary devices such as the introduction of proper names without apposition or other explanation and the in medias res beginning of the action after only two sentences outlining habitual states of affairs. These devices function as direct framings of literature but not necessarily of narrative. Yet, in combination with the layout, which is typical of fiction, an indirect framing of narrative also emerges right at the outset of the text.

All of the initial framings of narrative discussed here trigger a trial-and-error process of unconscious categorization and require confirmation so that the default option of "narrative" elicited at the beginning is corroborated. It is, however, a curious fact emerging from the discussion that in literature, a first framing of narrative does not require much time, and even occasionally no time at all, spent in reading the text proper. Indeed, in most cases the contextual and paratextual framings in combination with formal intratextual markers, which can all be quickly taken in and unconsciously assessed, suffice to elicit the frame "narrative" as a default option and to maintain it as long as the text does not give contrary signals. It is also remarkable that among these framings of narrative, directly metareferential framings that mark a story quality are not necessary and that much framing functions through an interaction of covert signals with a corresponding cultural knowledge on the part of the recipient.

In our examples, this cultural knowledge is, of course, the knowledge of contemporary, twenty-first-century readers. Clearly, framing also has a historical dimension and was realized differently in former times—as can be seen in the intratextual incipit formulas of medieval texts—but that discussion would be the matter of a further inquiry. At present we should look at the ways in which the pictorial arts can produce framings of narrative.

Initial Framings of Narrative in the Pictorial Arts

Like books, pictures are rarely perceived without contextual, including generic, framings, and frequently such framings are perceptible right at the beginning of the reception process. However, in the case of the pictorial arts, these framings often prove to be far less helpful than in literature when it comes to signaling narrativity.

From the Middle Ages until well into the Renaissance, the pictorial arts, such as painting, tapestry, mosaic, or stained glass, used to be firmly linked to religious and aristocratic spheres and were restricted to a limited number of genres, in particular to religious, mythological, or history pictures and portraits. Among these genres, portraits were and are the least narrative, whereas history painting contains a narrative element in that it refers to more or less well-known historical events, which in turn tend to be known in forms of narratives. A relatively recent case in point, which happens to combine action-loaded historicity with a portrait, is Jacques-Louis David's *Napoleon at the Saint-Bernard Pass* (figure 5.3), recalling Napoleon's memorable crossing of the Alps in 1800 in order to reconquer Italian territory that the Austrians had pre-

Fig. 5.3. Jacques-Louis David (1748–1825), *Napoleon at the Saint-Bernard Pass*.

viously occupied. If one focuses on the historical component, the painting is at least indirectly narrative (by referring to historiography, which in turn—*pace* Fludernik—may be conceived of as a variant of narrative); but if one concentrates on the portrait component, its non-narrative, descriptive quality becomes apparent.

In contrast to portraits and history paintings, religious images, which for a long time formed the most important pictorial genre, are ambivalent when it comes to their generic power of signaling narrativity. On the one hand, many religious pictures and picture series (for instance, in the

Fig. 5.4. Christ in the Mandorla with Saints from Ratisbone (ca. 1100).

form of stained glass), in particular those illustrations serving as a *biblia pauperum* in ecclesiastic contexts, acquire a certain degree of narrativity indirectly—that is, from intermedial references to biblical stories. On the other hand, religious pictures could also be mere descriptions or at any rate non-narrative (iconographic) re-presentations of religious persons and phenomena such as the Holy Trinity, Mary as nursing mother, or Christ Pantocrator in the Mandorla, as depicted in the apsis of the

Fig. 5.5. Jan Steen (1626–79), *The Merry Family*.

cathedrals of Grado or Monreale (Sicily) and in book illuminations (figure 5.4). So, at least in religious images, a clear indirect framing of narrative through the connotations of contextual framings (churches and other religious spaces) and generic framings (as in the case of the rubrics of libraries and bookshops) is impossible.

From the seventeenth century onward, pictorial artifacts steadily liberated themselves from the framings of religious and aristocratic architectures; however, their gradual invasion of middle-class homes and curiosity cabinets (*Kunstkammern*) was again not always helpful in terms of keying narrativity. At the same time painterly genres multiplied or rose to a degree of respectability that they had not previously possessed, as was the case with Dutch landscape and genre painting, as well as with still lifes. With some of these new genres, an indirect, genre-based—positive or negative—relevance for the framing of narrative may be assumed. Thus, still lifes and landscape painting tend to be non-narrative, whereas genre painting, like religious painting, is per se ambiguous. It can be predominantly descriptive and narrative, as a comparison between Jan Steen's mostly descriptive *The Merry Family* and his much more narra-

Fig. 5.6. Jan Steen, *The Saint Nicholas Feast.*

tive *The Saint Nicholas Feast* may show (compare figure 5.5 and figure 5.6). (For more on the narrativity of the latter painting see the discussion in Wolf, "Narrative" 190–92).

In many cases of the pictorial arts, contextual, including generic, framings of narrative thus prove to be less reliable than they are in literature. Interestingly, painterly paratexts, in particular heteromedial picture titles and captions, do not appear to be more helpful either. For much of pictorial history, however, such paratexts, at least in written form, were absent to a large extent. While religious pictures in ecclesiastic contexts sometimes (yet not always) had written captions or inserted texts for the learned, viewers of many other pictures who required explanations, titles, and generic indications could at best hope for oral comments. This also remained true for the curiosity cabinets of the Renaissance and Baroque age, and even middle-class picture collectors often displayed their treasures untitled.[2] Even from the eighteenth century on when public art galleries were established and paratexts that accompanied the pictures on exhibition appeared more frequently, the titles were often in small print or not easily attributable to individual paintings (which were often hung in several rows).

As a result, within our context one can say that in the face of the unreliability of many pictorial contextual and paratextual framings, intratextual, or rather intrapictorial, clues obtain an increased importance in the pictorial arts. William Hogarth's dyptich of engravings entitled *Before* and *After* (1736) is a case in point (figure 5.7 and figure 5.8). Without viewing the pictures in question, the titles are obscure and thus hardly indicative of narrativity. At best they are indicative of two points in time and something—missing—in between. That we have a rudimentary picture series is, of course, per se a strong formal incentive for a narrative reception, since juxtaposition is frequently read as a temporal sequence, and a temporal sequence is in turn often viewed as a causal relationship.

Yet even if by some mischance only the first of the two engravings (or the first corresponding painting in oil) had survived, some intrapictorial framings of narrative—all of which are content rather than form based—would nevertheless be discernible. Let us take a first quick look at *Before*. It becomes immediately clear that this picture follows a well-known script, namely that of a quasi-rape: a young lady tries forcefully to disentangle herself from the grip of a man, who powerfully wants to draw her onto a bed; indeed, his desire is so impetuous that his wig has become dislocated (as a sign of the violence of his passion). This representation of a disruptive event conforms in many respects to a typically narrative and at the same time eminently "tellable" event (compare with Pratt 136).[3] Moreover, the action forms a Lessingian "pregnant moment" par excellence (in more than one respect), capturing the split second in which the dressing table tilts before crashing to the floor. It is a moment that temporally points to, and makes us infer, a preceding state in which the lady was as yet unmolested, as well as a potentially disas-

Fig. 5.7. William Hogarth (1697–1764), *Before*.

trous sexual event in the future. Intrapictorial elements triggering a narrative script thus clue us to consider what we see as implicated in a temporal and causal flow, thereby providing crucial narratemes and, hence, a covert framing of narrative.

Taking a closer look, details of this narrative script come to the fore. The man's passion is mirrored in the lower animal realm in a leaping dog, as well as in a picture *mise en abyme* showing a "cupid lighting the fuse of a rocket" (Hallett and Riding 79). In addition, the tension between

Fig. 5.8. William Hogarth, *After*.

two texts displayed in the picture emphasize what, after all, is represented as a moral problem: the gaping drawer of the lady's tilting and falling dressing table contains a book whose spine shows the generic framing "novel" and another one partly displaying the title of a pious treatise *The Practice of Piety: Directing a Christian How to Walk, that He May Please God* (1602) (Hallett and Riding 79). This detail alone shows both the past religious commitment of the lady and her inclination to what in the eighteenth century was still widely held as a dangerous and morally corrupting pastime—namely, reading novels. On top of the dressing table, an even more dubious text is implicated in the "fall"—a book displaying the name of the notorious Restoration rake and poet of explicit sexual texts, the Earl of Rochester. The pursuer presumably used the book as a means of seduction and corruption.

As we could see, as opposed to my previous discussion of literary framings of narrative, in order to reveal triggers of the frame narrative in the visual arts, I had to dwell much more on intratextual and content-based clues, some of which were so covert as not to be discernible at first glance. To what extent the narrative reading of these triggers is nevertheless justified in our example becomes clear once we include the second engraving, *After,* into our interpretation. It represents the emotional consequences of what Hogarth did not actually show, thus creating a classic *Leerstelle sensu* Iser (that is, a gap in a meaningful sequence)—namely, the sexual intercourse and its circumstances. (Was it really rape, as may be surmised from various allusions to violence in *Before*, or, at least to a certain extent, sex by mutual consent?) At any rate, the consequences are sad, and overtly so, for the young man, who thus exemplifies what is also hinted at on a sheet of paper lying on the floor that reads, "Omne animal post coitum triste." Sad consequences are also suggested concerning the lady, for she has lost her honor, as is indirectly suggested by the symbolically broken mirror and immediately discernible by her gaze. This look may only be ambiguous from a very modern point of view, for in this perspective she may be asking for more sex, as Hallett and Riding indicate as one possible interpretation; or—and that is historically more probable in the moralizing context of the two pictures—it may well be that she, by this means, implores the young man to make good her broken honor through marriage. The rest of the story is silence, thus illustrating the limits and the lack of precision of pictorial narratives without the sustained help of words. After all, we are dealing with a medium that materially presents static, spatial depictions rather than moving temporal representations and is therefore able to represent time only by way of hints for readerly inferences.

As was to be expected, we have seen that framings of narrative are possible in both literature and in the pictorial arts, since both media are capable of narrativity. However, it appears that in literature, the frame narrative can be elicited more quickly and more reliably than it is in pictures. The reason for this difference is arguably that narrativity in the pictorial arts, to the extent that it relies on temporality and causality as narratemes, can only be inferred. Because it cannot be represented directly, as in the temporal medium of literature, the pictorial arts' narrativity thus takes longer to understand.

A second difference should also be noted: in literature, contextual, paratextual, and intratextual form-based frames are frequently sufficient to trigger narrativity, perhaps because narrativity is more intimately linked to verbal than to pictorial representations. In the pictorial arts, when it comes to frames of narrative, considerable weight is shifted to intrapictorial clues and content-based ones in particular (notably scripts with culturally acquired narrative connotations). In many cases these intrapictorial keyings take a much longer time to decipher than the extratextual and formal framings of narrative in literature and thus could be classified as "initial framings" only with difficulty. Indeed, the pictorial arts have no form-based framing of narrative that may be compared with the simple literary formula "Once upon a time . . ." in its immediate efficiency.

Our foregoing reflections have shown that Ryan is indeed right with her evaluation of media not as harmless conduits but as agencies that shape what they transmit (see "Media and Narrative"). This observation is true not only of individual storyworld contents (the *Iliad* as a verbal text will differ from an *Iliad* as a picture series or comic) but also of semiotic macro-frames such as narrative and the descriptive (see Wolf and Bernhart, *Description*), as well as of such referential forms as factuality, fictionality, and metareferentiality. Further, as the foregoing discussion also demonstrated, this at least partial media specificity equally applies to what is important at the outset of the process of perceiving representations—namely, the framings, including the framings of narrative.

The transmedial approach, which was used here and is best for highlighting such media specificities, could be applied to other media, of course. It seems to me that, for the question of how storyworlds are marked as such, a particularly fruitful area is TV and the various filmic genres that this technical medium transmits. Owing to the technical device of the remote control and the zapping activity it encourages, we seem to have been trained to make sometimes remarkably quick, if unconscious, assessments and classifications of programs we like or dislike.

Narrative classifications are arguably part of this framing process. Yet investigating TV along the lines of what I just have adumbrated with reference to literature and the pictorial arts is the subject of another inquiry.

Notes

1. I did not discuss this typological differentiation between "direct" and "indirect" framing in Wolf, "Introduction." For *metareference* as an umbrella term for medial meta-phenomena, see Wolf, *Metareference across Media*.
2. See, for instance, the picture cabinet of Johann Wolfgang von Goethe's father as preserved in the Frankfurt Goethe Haus.
3. Interestingly, Herman classifies "tellable" disruptions of the canonical or expected order of events as forming per se a signal of narrativity (135).

Works Cited

Abbott, H. Porter. "The Future of All Narrative Futures." *A Companion to Narrative Theory*. Ed. James Phelan and Peter J. Rabinowitz. Blackwell Companions to Literature and Culture. Oxford, UK: Blackwell, 2005. 529–41. Print.

Coleridge, Samuel Taylor. "The Rime of the Ancyent Marinere." 1798. *Lyrical Ballads, 1798*. By William Wordsworth and Samuel Taylor Coleridge. Ed. W. J. B. Owen. Oxford, UK: Oxford University Press, 1969. 7–32. Print.

Ferguson, Margaret, Mary Jo Salter, and Jon Stallworthy, eds. *The Norton Anthology of Poetry*. 5th ed. New York: Norton, 2005. Print.

Fludernik, Monika. *Towards a "Natural" Narratology*. London: Routledge, 1996. Print.

Goffman, Erving. *Frame Analysis: An Essay on the Organization of Experience*. Cambridge MA: Cambridge University Press, 1974. Print.

Hallett, Mark, and Christine Riding. *Hogarth*. London: Tate Publishing, 2006. Print.

Herman, David. *Basic Elements of Narrative*. Oxford, UK: Blackwell, 2009. Print.

Hühn, Peter. "Plotting the Lyric: Forms of Narration in Poetry." *Theory into Poetry: New Approaches to the Lyric*. Ed. Eva Müller-Zettelmann and Margarete Rubik. Amsterdam: Rodopi, 2005. 142–72. Print.

Josipovici, Gabriel. *Only Joking*. London: CB editions, 2010. Print.

Joyce, James. *A Portrait of the Artist as a Young Man*. 1916. Ed. Hans Walter Gabler with Walter Hettche. New York: Vintage, 1993. Print.

Lessing, Gotthold Ephraim. *Laocoön: An Essay on the Limits of Painting and Poetry*. Trans. Edward Allen McCormick. Baltimore MD: Johns Hopkins University Press, 1984. Print.

Poe, E. A. "To Helen." 1845. Ferguson, Salter, and Stallworthy 1975. Print.

Pratt, Mary Louise. *Toward a Speech Act Theory of Literary Discourse*. Bloomington: Indiana University Press, 1977. Print.

Prince, Gerald. "Revisiting Narrativity." *Grenzüberschreitungen: Narratologie im Kontext/ Transcending Boundaries: Narratology in Context*. Ed. Walter Grünzweig and Andreas Solbach. Tübingen, Germany: Narr, 1999. 43–51. Print.

Ryan, Marie-Laure. "Media and Narrative." *Routledge Encyclopedia of Narrative Theory*. Ed. David Herman, Manfred Jahn, and Marie-Laure Ryan. London: Routledge, 2005. 288–92. Print.

———. "Toward a Definition of Narrative." *The Cambridge Companion to Narrative*. Ed. David Herman. Cambridge, UK: Cambridge University Press, 2007. 22–35. Print.

Wolf, Werner. "Defamiliarized Initial Framings in Fiction." *Description in Literature and Other Media*. Ed. Wolf and Bernhart 295–328. Print.

———. "Introduction: Frames, Framings and Framing Borders in Literature and Other Media." *Description in Literature and Other Media*. Ed. Wolf and Bernhart 1–40. Print.

———. "The Lyric: Problems of Definition and a Proposal for Reconceptualization." *Theory into Poetry: New Approaches to the Lyric*. Ed. Eva Müller-Zettelmann and Margarete Rubik. Amsterdam: Rodopi, 2005. 21–56. Print.

———, ed. *Metareference across Media: Theory and Case Studies—Dedicated to Walter Bernhart on the Occasion of his Retirement*. With Katharina Bantleon and Jeff Thoss. Amsterdam: Rodopi, 2009. Print.

———."Narrative and Narrativity: A Narratological Reconceptualization and Its Applicability to the Visual Arts." *Word & Image* 19.3 (2003): 180–97. Print.

———. "'The Sense of the Precedence of [. . .] Event[s]'—'a Defining Condition of Narrative' across Media?" *Germanisch-Romanische Monatsschrift* 63 (2013): 245–59. Print.

Wolf, Werner, and Walter Bernhart, eds. *Description in Literature and Other Media*. Amsterdam: Rodopi, 2007. Print.

———. *Framing Borders in Literature and Other Media*. Amsterdam: Rodopi, 2006. Print.

PART 2 *Multimodality and Intermediality*

6 The Rise of the Multimodal Novel

Generic Change and Its Narratological Implications

WOLFGANG HALLET

Since the 1990s an ever-growing number of novels have not merely consisted of verbal text but have also incorporated a wide range of visual representations and modes such as (the reproduction of) photographs, hand-drawn sketches, maps and diagrams, and all sorts of other graphic and symbolic elements in the narrative discourse. Apart from such conspicuous visual elements, other generic and mostly typographically distinct modes such as typed, handwritten, or electronic letters; film scripts; websites; pieces of academic writing; and many other generic forms can be identified in an increasing number of novels. This chapter argues that this multiplication of semiotic modes changes the notion of "narrative discourse" in the traditionally word-based genre of the novel and turns reading into a multiliterate act.

The Integration of Nonverbal Semiotic Modes in the Novel

Multimodality is an obvious and conspicuous feature of the type of novel addressed in this chapter, visible at a glance and represented in the layout of the book page that is totally different from the traditional printed page. Some of the most popular and much acclaimed exemplars of this type of novel—such as Mark Z. Danielewski's *House of Leaves*, Mark Haddon's *The Curious Incident of the Dog in the Night-Time*, Jonathan Safran Foer's *Extremely Loud & Incredibly Close*, or W. G. Sebald's *Austerlitz* (see Hallet, "*Fictions*"; Hallet, "Visual Images")—do not just occasionally insert a photograph or some other graphic element; rather, they combine a wide range of different semiotic modes and integrate large numbers of all these other, nonverbal elements into the otherwise language-based novelistic narrative.

At this stage, before examples from different novels are introduced to characterize the range of semiotic modes displayed in these narratives and the kind of composition of the novel with which this chapter is concerned, it is advisable to briefly outline the concepts of "mode" and "multimodality" as developed in recent theories of social semiotics (Kress; Kress and van Leeuwen; van Leeuwen). In these theoretical frameworks of contemporary signifying practices and communication, *modes* are regarded as *semiotic resources*—that is, as "signifiers, observable actions and objects that have been drawn into the domain of social communication and that have a *theoretical* semiotic potential constituted by all their past uses and all their potential uses and an *actual* semiotic potential constituted by those past uses that are known to and considered relevant by the users of the resource, and by such potential uses as might be uncovered by the users on the basis of their specific needs and interests" (van Leeuwen 4, original emphasis).

Thus, family photographs and snapshots, maps and hand-drawn sketches, typography and layout, and even color, graphic frames and margins are semiotic resources as much as written language and speech are, since all of these modes can be drawn into processes of meaning making and communication.[1] As opposed to the multiplicity of semiotic modes in various communicative contexts, the traditional novel exclusively relies on the written word in printed form, with black letters on the white page in a paper-bound book. In light of all the other potential modes of communication and signification, this limitation to solely linguistic communication and the medium of the printed book comes into view as a cultural (and historical) mode of communication that is closely connected with the historical emergence of reading as a particular type of social (individualized) practice, with the constitution of markets and practices of distribution, and, of course, with traditional book production, whose print and media technologies are currently substantially challenged by all kinds of digital media and electronic communication technologies. Therefore, in terms of the multimodality concept in social semiotics, the traditional novel is basically *monomodal* (although, strictly speaking, layout, black letters, paper, and margins on the page are also different modes and meaningful semiotic resources).

A few examples from *multimodal* novels may demonstrate the substantial changes caused when other semiotic modes are introduced in the genre of the novel. In Haddon's novel *The Curious Incident of the Dog in the Night-Time*, Christopher, the autodiegetic narrator, employs a whole range of different semiotic modes. He regularly inserts artifacts in his narration that he has mostly created by himself. Among them are astronomic diagrams to represent the Milky Way that he observes or to illustrate the speed of light (10, 15); street plans of his neighborhood or ground plans and all sorts of maps (35, 87, 92, 188–89); drawings of all sorts of objects, even of cow patterns or seat patterns "that looked like this" (a phrase that he often uses to introduce his drawings; 13); lists of all sorts, including a list of "some of my Behavioral Problems" and timetables (46, 155–56); mathematical problems, such as "The Monty Hall Problem" and his own algorithm to solve it (64–65); a historical photograph (88); a population growth graph and formula (101); long handwritten letters, set off typographically in italics from Christopher's own narration (104–12); individual constructions of star constellations (125); and many other symbolic forms of representation.

Since the narrator is characterized by deviant forms of world apprehension and shows signs of autism, it is obvious that all of these nonverbal forms of representation not only serve to communicate his experiences and actions to the reader or to replace further detailed descriptions but also to show Christopher's individual, possibly solipsistic ways of understanding and constructing the world. In this way, these different semiotic forms—every single one of them and all of them combined in the act of multimodal novelistic narration—not only are a constitutive part of the fictional world of the novel but also represent Christopher's thoughts, cognitive strategies, and consciousness, or his "ways of worldmaking" (see Goodman). This point is important to note here since it emphasizes that the introduction of nonverbal symbolic forms in the novel changes the ways in which the novel communicates the fictional world to the reader—for example, by adding a few illustrative elements—and offers the reader access to dimensions of the fictional world that cannot be rendered in verbal form. Christopher's often-repeated formula of "It looked like this" is, therefore, also an indication of the specific affordances of nonverbal semiotic forms, a semantic, cognitive, or epistemological surplus that multiplies aspects and dimensions of the storyworld that are accessible to the reader. Therefore, the multimodality of the novel also raises a number of narratological questions that are related to the narrative status, functions, and affordances of these other semiotic modes.

Another novel that has attracted a great deal of academic interest because of its conspicuous multimodality is Foer's 9/11 novel, *Extremely Loud & Incredibly Close.*[2] A closer examination of this novel emphasizes how the integration of nonverbal modes of signification and communication is intrinsically connected with the constitution of the narrative and the construction of its storyworld in terms of the individual and social symbolic practices that are displayed. Paradigmatically, the novel incorporates four different functions of visual images and graphic forms. The first one concerns the narration of motion. The quest for traces of his father, who died in the 9/11 attack, and of the lock to a key that he has "inherited" takes Oskar, the young autodiegetic narrator, right across New York. However, his routes and itineraries are not exclusively narrated in verbal form. Imitating mimetically Oskar's habit of collecting in his scrapbook all the "important evidence and litter" (Foer 87) that he finds along the way—"maps and drawings, pictures from magazines and newspapers and the Internet, pictures I'd taken with Grandpa's camera" (325)—the visual images in the novel are a representation not only of artifacts but also of the narrator's perceptions, memory practice, and archive. This way, the novel itself takes on the character of the scrapbook, which is, simultaneously, a part of the storyworld that it sets up narratively.

The second function is an epistemological one. Since he suspects that his father is one of the men that jumped from the collapsing towers, Oskar is obsessed with the fall of objects and creatures (birds, cats, human beings) and develops a scientific interest in gravity. Thus the book is crowded with photographs of "a flock of birds [. . .] by the window, extremely fast and incredibly close" (265), or cats that can fall from great heights without hurting themselves, and with reflections on how "falling" actually feels when it is physically experienced. On the occasion of a roller coaster ride, Oskar wonders, "If what I was feeling was at all like falling. In my head, I tried to calculate all of the forces that kept the car on the tracks and me in the car. There was gravity, obviously. And centrifugal force. And momentum. And the friction between the wheels and the tracks. And wind resistance, I think, or something. Dad used to teach me physics with crayons on paper tablecloths while we waited for our pancakes. He would have been able to explain everything" (147). Therefore, visualizations, like the photograph of the roller coaster (89, 148), are also epistemological tools and serve as one of the narrator's ways of apprehending and reflecting upon the natural laws and physical constitution of the world, his own actual world.

The third function refers to the creation of a textual possible world, a visionary sequence of images that transforms the cultural icon of the falling man into a moving image of a "rising man." Oskar rearranges a series of stills of the falling man in reverse order, so when one flips through them, "it looked like the falling man was floating up through the sky. And if I'd had more pictures, he would've flown through a window, back into the building, and the smoke would've poured into the hole that the plane was about to come out of. Dad would've left his messages backward, until the machine was empty, and the plane would've flown backward away from him, all the way to Boston" (325). This visual symbolization and vision of his father's "resurrection," as well as the specific visual technique of the flipbook, are also psychological tools that help Oskar come to terms with the 9/11 attacks and overcome the trauma of his father's death (see Gibbons, *Multimodality* 157–65). In the novel, this imaginary rise of a man is, at least to a large extent, image based, whereas the verbal text tells the story of the making of this part of the book. In the narrative discourse, the verbal and the visual modes are employed each according to their specific affordance; but they are also directly interrelated and complemented by the reader's haptic activities of traditional page turning (verbal narration) and page flipping (visual narration) so that the multimodality of the novel even comprises the physical mode and the motor senses that are involved in using the book (see Gibbons, "Narrative Worlds" 303–11).

The fourth function concerns exactly this performative role of the reader and the act of reading itself. As in the case of the flipbook and other instances of evoking readers' physical activities, the introduction of other modes of representation and narration in the novel has a performative side to it, since the multimodal novel directs the readers to explore the book page and interrelate its different semiotic elements. It urges them to engage in the physical activities of "moving" on the page and between pages (see Gibbons, "Narrative Worlds" 293–303; Hallet, "Visual Images" 233–34) and even of flipping the pages. The flipbook "is an invitation to the readers, making a call to them for traumatic cowitness and coparticipation to which reader-response is constituted in physical engagement with the flipbook. Finally, the flipbook works to direct readers to perform curative procedures for post-traumatic stress, enabling them to deal with the unforgettable image of the falling man so central to the trauma of 9/11" (Gibbons, *Multimodality* 157). Thus, not only does the multimodality of this novel represent the narrator's "symbolical re-appropriation of the control over the visual images" (Grolig n. pag.) that circulate in the media and evoke the reader's active role in overcoming the 9/11 trauma, but also, at the level of genre, the reader's physical act of flipping the pages transforms the novel into a flipbook and thus constitutes a complete shift of the generic form (and mode). This convergence of linguistic narration and the filmic mode of storytelling indicates that extreme cultural and individual experiences such as the 9/11 attack, or traumatic experiences of death and complete loss, cannot be rendered and overcome adequately and solely in verbal form.

At this point, and before entering into a more detailed case study in the next section, it can already be stated that the status of nonverbal elements in the multimodal novel is substantially different from that of additional illustrations or other paratexts. Nonverbal elements are part of the narrative discourse since they are at the narrator's disposal and displayed as the narrative unfolds, and they are artifacts that are produced and located in the fictional world of the novel. Therefore, it is appropriate to categorize this type of multisemiotic narrative as a literary subgenre and designate it as the multimodal novel.[3] Multimodality, as a literary practice of producing and reading novels and as a social semiotic theory, seems to challenge the historical predominant role of language in literature and in literary studies and of the written word in printed form in particular.

The Functions of Semiotic Modes in Reif Larsen's Novel *The Selected Works of T. S. Spivet*

In Reif Larsen's novel, titled after the twelve-year-old main character, Tecumseh Sparrow Spivet, the narrator develops an almost incredible, ingenious skill in and obsession with drawing almost everything that he comes across in the immediate surroundings of his home in Montana. One day, after mistaking Spivet for an adult artist, the Smithsonian

Institution awards the gifted protagonist a major scientific prize and invites him to Washington DC. The novel is the fictional autobiography of this young artist's life on his parents' Coppertop Ranch in Montana (chapter 1, "The West"), the story of his adventurous passage (chapter 2, "This Crossing") to "The East" (chapter 3), and his initiation into the scientific community of the Smithsonian (an experiment that finally fails). Although the main corpus of the novel is narrated in traditional verbal form, even a brief glance at the novel reveals that visualization is an integral dimension of the novel's narrative discourse. The verbal text and a whole range of different types of visual representations—mostly Spivet's hand-drawn maps and itineraries; scientific biological, geological, or topographical drawings; charts and statistical diagrams of all sorts; and the reproduction of diary pages or other documents—are directly and closely interwoven (see fig. 6.1). Often, dotted arrows direct the reader from written discourse to visual elements in the margins of the page and urge them to interrelate the different semiotic elements, thus breaking up the linear continuity of the verbal text and transforming the act of reading into a hypertextual activity. Since visual representations of the world, and cartography in particular, are also major themes of the novel and constant objects of the narrator's reflections, it soon becomes clear that the visual mode is an important part of the narrator's way of apprehending the world and an everyday practice of expressing himself and of presenting his story—a whole way of life, as it were.

In the following sections, I demonstrate the ways in which this specific texture of the novel affects different levels of the narration and constitutes the true multimodality of this narrative, as being distinct from the traditional monomodality of the novel. The examination of the multimodal quality of this narrative is bound to question the general assumption that signification in literary narratives exclusively relies on linguistic signs ("symbols" in Charles S. Peirce's terminology). For instance, in an essay on the relation between cartography and literature in the twentieth century, Robert Stockhammer contends that "literary texts do not directly participate in the cartographic power of localization but instead reflect it in narrative form" (323). However, this purely philological approach to literary texts and novels is at stake as soon as indexical signs, as used in maps (see Stockhammer 320–25), come into play in a traditionally word-based genre. A merely philological reading of Larsen's book, as

Fig. 6.1. A typical multimodal page from Reif Larsen's *The Selected Works of T. S. Spivet*, displaying verbal discourse, a map of the narrator's hometown Divide, a plan of his bedroom, a marginal note on his bedroom, and the sketch of a sparrow skeleton, alluding to the narrator's second name "Sparrow" (Larsen 3).

much as of other multimodal novels, is not suited to grasp the different types of signification in photographs, drawings, diagrams, ground plans, or maps and their substantial contribution to the narrative discourse.

Plot Development and Narrative Structure

As the title of the second chapter and the topological chapter structure of the novel suggest, spaces, distances, and boundaries are major concerns of the novel and the narrator. The book cover and the two-page spread that precedes the first chapter show Spivet's map of "Montana as

Rivers" in which the Continental Divide is the only prominent feature. It is complemented by other maps and drawings showing that his family's hometown and his parents' Coppertop Ranch are situated precisely on that geological demarcation and borderline. This is the reason why "the divide" is an existential experience; why, in a sense, it can be equated with the narrator's whole life; and why exploring this mysterious, invisible boundary of paramount historical and cultural importance is a driving force in the young man's mind: "The divide, oh, the divide. I had grown up with this great border at my back, and its quiet, unerring existence had penetrated deep into my bones and brain. The divide was a massive, sprawling boundary not determined by politics, religion, or war but by tectonics, granite, and gravity. How remarkable that no U.S. president had signed this border into law, and yet its delineation had affected the expansion and formation of America's frontier in a million untold ways. This jagged sentinel sliced the nation's watersheds into east and west, the Atlantic and the Pacific" (Larsen 6).

This divide is a paradigmatic experience and concept in many ways. The child grows up with an awareness of being indissolubly articulated with the history and shape of the nation to which he belongs. It incorporates the historical frontier notion and westward movement, the nation's almost notorious east-west (or Atlantic-Pacific) division, and even the gold rush as a founding myth, since the narrator goes on to explain that "out west, water was gold, and where the water went, people followed" (6). Therefore, it comes as no surprise that the middle chapter of the novel, "The Crossing," is the story of the narrator's reenactment both of the American westward movement and of his family's migration but in reverse direction. Spivet thus appropriates and experiences the collective historical route subjectively, and the cross-continental journey is also a trip into history. Thus, throughout the book, cartography is not only a spatial but also always a temporal-historical way of structuring and ordering observations and perceptions, and events in this novel consistently take on a topological form. Therefore, although "a novel is a tricky thing to map" (36), it is clear from the first chapter that the map as a semiotic mode is also a narrative tool, representing and structuring events in time as much as in spaces. The narrator's blue notebook contains "maps covering nearly every action that had been performed on this farm over the last four years," from "diverting the irrigation ditches" and "mending the fences" to "picking and shucking the sweet corn, mowing, sweeping, cleaning the tack" to "punching the goats' heads out of the fences to keep 'em from the coyotes." Spivet notes, "I had been meticulously mapping all of these activities since I was eight" (32). In the same vein, the map of the North American continent and the events that constitute the plot are one, a hobo's journey on freight trains from east to west (and back again). The adventurous crossing of space that is represented as a continent's topography is thus transformed into a narrative (subjective) topology.

That such a journey is always also a *rite de passage* is emphasized by the incident that triggers the plot: the phone call (the first three words of the novel) from the Smithsonian Institution and the decision whether to accept the award and travel to Washington or to be honest, admit that he is a child, and stay in Montana. This alternative is perceived as a "great divide" in the young narrator's life, and he describes and maps it in the form of a T-junction: "I saw myself coming to a great T-junction. *To the left lay the plains.* [. . .] *To the right, the mountains*" (27, italics original). Spivet's subsequent decision to accept the invitation to Washington results in the twelve-year-old's initiation into the scientific-academic realm so distinct from the rural, restricted world of his ranch in Montana. Hence, the territorial crossing is simultaneously the crossing of social and cultural borderlines through the introduction to an adult and academic world that is normally off-limits to a boy of Spivet's age and origin.

Last but not least, cartographic thinking is also plot constitutive regarding an important detail that finally leads to the boy's deep epistemological skepticism in terms of a sudden questioning and absence of familiar geographical categories. During the train ride, Spivet experiences an estranging, deeply disturbing experience in a dissociation of the train's physical movement from the universal categories of time and space and the experience of an absolute temporal-spatial vacuum (called the "Lorentzian wormholes") in which there was "no Middle. No West. No East. No nothing" (229). After his arrival in Washington, this subplot is further developed after Spivet learns that an entire secret society is concerned with this physical mystery that shakes the fundamentum of all laws of nature and the validity of the claims that the sciences make.

The importance of cartographic representation in terms of narration in this novel, as a way of structuring events, and the prominent role of boundaries can be regarded as a convincing instance of Jurij M. Lotman's theory of the literary text (Lotman; see Frank 65–68). In his theory, the crossing of simultaneously geographical, cultural, and epistemological borderlines by fictional agents is crucial to the constitution of the literariness—the aesthetic quality and tellability—of a story. "The transgression of fundamental topological boundaries in the spatial structure" of a text constitutes its "sjuzhet" since "the crossing of a semantic borderline" causes the "unfolding of an event" (Lotman 338, 339).[4] The underlying assumption is that something is perceived as an event only if a move of some sort is displayed that is either impossible or exceptional in a given (nontextual) culture (see Hühn 35–41). According to Lotman, cultural conditions define whether something constitutes an event or a nonevent: "Within one and the same cultural schema, the same episode may become an event or not, depending on the structural level on which it is located" (Lotman 333). It seems obvious that this fundamental role of the crossing of boundaries applies particularly to an epic genre like the novel. Therefore, it comes as no surprise that a novel such as Larsen's, whose major concern is of a topographical nature—with the protagonist's breaking away from familiar, restricted (closed) grounds into unknown (open) territories and to distant places—mapping is not only a plot-constitutive and narrative activity but also the dominant mode of representation and thinking. After all, according to the narrator's own words, this reasoning is the deeper psychological (and, in Lotman's terms, "cultural") rationale behind "mapping": "I firmly believed that drafting maps erased many of the unwarranted beliefs of a child. Something about measuring the distance between *here* and *there* cast off the mystery of what lay between, and since I was a child with limited empirical evidence, the unknown of what might just lie between *here* and *there* could be terrifying. I, like most children, had never been *there*. I had barely even been *here*" (Larsen 32, original emphasis). Hence, in part 2 of the novel, the maps and geographical vertical lines in the margins with the names of towns and geographical places on them do not only visualize the young protagonist's train ride that is narrated on that page. In Lotman's sense, they are much more: the fictional topology represents a cultural topography, fictional itineraries are also cultural routes, and the narrator's individual acts of mapping are deeply rooted in cultural cartographic and semiotic practices (also see Böhme xviii–xx).

Character and Identity Constitution

As has meanwhile become evident, mapping is the narrator's nearly all-encompassing, everyday way of looking at the world and expressing himself to such an extent that he defines himself through the art of mapping and develops the self-image and identity of a cartographer. As is always the case with the use of signs, the functions of the cartographic practice of signifying are manifold. First, drawing and mapping allow the child access to a world, or to some of its aspects, that would otherwise remain hidden: geological formations, the structure of railway hubs, patterns of actions and behaviour, insects' interior organs, seismographic representations of tremors, body and facial languages, and many more. In the beginning, the boy is deeply fascinated with and, like his mother and great-great-grandmother, completely devoted to the sciences. He considers them a "life force that bound my mother to unsquirreling the natural world, the discipline that housed her unexhaustible searching, and the method of inquiry that put all of my longing and curiosity to use crafting my little maps instead of mailing bombs to prominent capitalists" (Larsen 49–50). This fascination with symbolic representation as a tool of scientific analysis and apprehension is the beginning of the boy's deeper epistemological reflections on the human mind's ability to understand and describe the world.

Second, there is a very individual, self-reflexive side to Spivet's occupation (and obsession) with cartography, since he does not simply apply culturally and scientifically standardized ways and tools of mapping but also individualizes and subjectivizes them. Such maps as the "Location of eight North American boys, age twelve, pinching Honey Nut Cheerios at the same exact moment in time" (203) or a map of "personal interest levels" based on "A Log of the Secretary's Very Boring Speech" (305) are idiosyncratic and of a rather limited cultural significance. Instead, this personalized type of mapping serves to explore and demarcate Spivet's own immediate surroundings and experiences and to determine his own place and position in the world: "There was a deep impulse ingrained in us to take these directions, coordinates, declarations out of the mush of our heads and actualize them in the real world. Since making my first maps of how to shake hands with God, I had learned that the representation was not the real thing, but in a way this dissonance was what made it so good: the distance between the map and the territory allowed us breathing room to figure out where we stood" (56–57). Therefore, Spivet's mapping of his own small world and the world at large is also a metaphor for the need to navigate through one's own life and seek orientation. Spivet's desire and ambition to map "the" world cognitively is comprehensive, is universal in the literal sense since ultimately all of his cartographic work is determined by the question of whether there was "some invisible map of the land buried inside my head" (201), and is driven by a "longing for this hidden map to be true, for all of us have the atlas of the universe preloaded into our synapses, because somehow this would confirm the feeling I had had my entire mapping life, since I first charted how one could walk up the side of Mr. Humbug and shake hands with God" (201–2). In a sense, this more or less "genetic" cartographic disposition as part of the narrator's identity is emphasized when Spivet discovers that his own scientific interest and way of thinking is preceded by a long genealogical line that can be traced back to his great-great-grandmother, "one of the first female geologists in the country" (143), and to his mother's work as a coleopterist. This way, Spivet is able to "localize" himself in "The Spivet Genealogy," a history that he, once again, has mapped on a placemat for his father (175).

Third, by representing and symbolizing important events and experiences in his life in visual form, the narrator is able to express himself and to communicate with the reader in a manner that is most adequate to his ways of thinking and feeling. Since the reader is able to study a whole range of artifacts produced or collected by a character from the fictional world, the narrator is thus "naturalized" as a cultural agent who, like the reader, engages in a large variety of modes of signification and communication (and not just in the linguistic mode of verbal storytelling, as in the traditional novel). Thus, multimodal narration is also a way of approximating the reader's nontextual experiences with a person's expression and communication and the same processes in the fictional world: "There are inevitable losses entailed by 'telling' nonverbal resources in words rather than 'showing' them directly" (Page 9) because "multimodality is an everyday reality. It is the experience of living; we experience everyday life in multimodal terms through sight, sound, movement" (Gibbons, *Multimodality* 8; also Hallet, "Multimodality").

The Epistemological and Meta-Cultural Dimension

As previously adumbrated, the boy's journey from the West to the East also represents the crossing of an epistemological borderline. At the beginning of the novel, while in Montana, Spivet is completely convinced of the universal epistemological potential of maps. This confidence is shattered when, during the train ride, he experiences a physical and orientational vacuum (the "Lorentzian wormholes"), the absence of all physical laws and geographical direction in which he used to believe. His scientific confidence subsides completely when, visiting the Smithsonian in Washington, he is invited into the secret society of scientists called the "Megatherium Club," which resembles a religious sect (Larsen 354–74). Thus, the novel questions the core axioms of the sciences—the belief that time and space can be calculated in physical and mathematical formulae—and skeptically regards the epistemological power that the sciences claim to possess. Since Spivet is also familiar with historical mapping practices, such as those of George Washington, whom he accuses of "imagining all sorts of false geographies" (33), Spivet's skepticism also applies to his own art of mapping and questions the representational power of maps. What has been said about the representational inadequacy of language must be generalized and finally results in a general skepticism that applies to all semiotic modes that are used to represent, make meaning, and create reliable knowledge. Ironically enough, the boy's scientific and cartographic enthusiasm is shattered by those who appeared to be committed "to the rigorous standards of modern science and [. . .] advancing the collective knowledge of the human project" (236), as Spivet's great-great-grandmother Emma once put it in her address to the National Academy of Sciences.

Apart from and in addition to this epistemological critique, the novel also reflects on the political and economic role of cartography. Spivet's own practices of mapping give evidence to the fact that maps can virtually produce realities and "make" the world they claim to represent—that is, produce "physical and perceptual world-versions [. . .] with words, numerals, pictures, sounds, or other symbols of any kind," as Nelson Goodman puts it (93–94). Thus, historically, cartographers have opened up "blank" spaces to economic and political exploitation, and cartography has participated in the conquest of the land that it mapped. As Spivet contends: "[T]hese early cartographers of the Corps of Topographical Engineers [. . .] were conquerors in the most basic sense of the word, for over the course of the nineteenth century, they slowly transferred the vast unknown continent piece by piece into the great machine of the known, of the mapped, of the witnessed—out of the mythological realm of empirical science. For me, *this* transfer was the Old West: the inevitable growth of knowledge, the resolute gridding of the great Trans-Mississippi territory into a chart that could be placed alongside others" (16, original emphasis).

In such passages, the novel also narrates the history of cartography as a discipline and critiques its political alliances and strategies. This way, the cartographic mode not only is displayed as an individual and cultural epistemological tool and signifying practice but also is reflected on and critiqued in the verbal mode. As with so many other multimodal novels, *The Selected Works of T. S. Spivet* is also a *meta-semiotic* and *meta-cultural narrative* that reflects on the semiotic practices in which it engages and employs semiotic modes according to their specific affordances. It displays maps and plans that are culturally and scientifically valued as best suited to represent and create spaces and topographies; simultaneously, language and verbal discourse in the novel are used to name, reflect on, and critique the semiotic and epistemological potential and limits of the cartographic and other nonverbal signifying modes. Therefore, in this novel and in others briefly introduced earlier in the chapter, multimodality is a method not only of representation and storytelling but also of epistemological and meta-semiotic reflection and critique.

The Multimodal Constitution of the Fictional World, Generic Change, and the Role of the Reader

Larsen's novel is particularly suited to demonstrate and illustrate, in the literal sense, the specific capacities and affordances of different modes and their interplay since both its story and narrative discourse rely heavily on perceptions and experiences that are not primarily linguistically shaped. Fictions of space, which focus on the individual and cultural perception, signification, and construction of spaces and motion (see Hallet, "*Fictions*"), make us particularly aware of the fact that literary texts, to a large extent, render basically physical bodily and sensory experiences.[5] In the traditional novel, for more than two hundred years, all of these sensations and ways of meaning making were translated into and (re-) presented in linguistic form, privileging written language over all other modes of signification and communication. The construction of the fictional world was based on words and a linear "sequence of signs," or a linguistic realm, "made of names, definite descriptions, sentences, and propositions."[6] Thus, in the traditional novel, the only material manifestations and artifacts from the fictional world that were accessible to the reader were words, sentences, and verbal discourse. In dialogues exchanged between fictional characters, letters or e-mail written by them, and the story told by the narrator, a whole world was made from words and diegesis as a linguistic act.

The multimodal novel is about to revise and rework this fictional way of world making. Its narrative discourse breaks up the discursive linearity and textual coherence of the novel and transforms it into a hypertextual ensemble of different types of symbolic representations that the reader must interrelate (see Hallet, "Medialisierung"). It relativizes the role of language in the processes of meaning making and communication; it destroys the (philological) illusion and simplification that stories, knowledge, and epistemologies exist in verbal form only. Reading the multimodal novel, the reader does not have to rely on the written word alone. Rather readers are now able to access the fictional world via other sensory channels and symbolic pathways, to study artifacts produced in the textual world by fictional characters, and to recognize a multitude of semiotic practices with which they are familiar from their own "lifeworlds" (see fig. 6.2). Some of these artifacts do not even have to be explicitly contextualized or addressed in the narrative discourse; they can be presented in unmediated and uncommented form. As in the reader's experiential world, they can simply "exist"—that is, be existents in the fictional world and simply "be there"—similar to objects in the reader's world, contributing to a more holistic construction of the storyworld, or being related or relevant to one of the characters in the story in ways to be construed by the reader.

The multimodal novel also reminds the reader that the same phenomenon—a room, a journey, a bodily movement, and, as Spivet demonstrates, even a sequence of actions or events—can be conceptualized and represented in different ways ("world versions" in Goodman's terminology). For example, Spivet's bedroom as represented in a floor plan is different from a (more subjective and selective) verbal description or

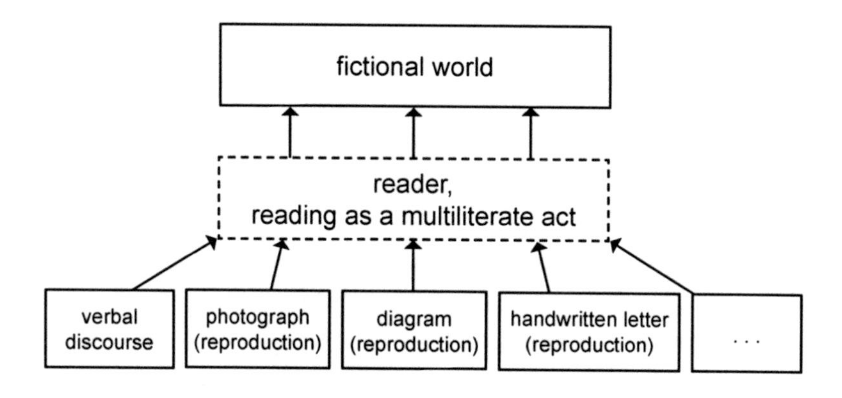

Fig. 6.2. The multimodal (multisemiotic) constitution of the fictional world.

from a certain graphic (or photographic) frame and perspective. The multiplicity of semiotic modes that the multimodal novel deploys is obviously better suited than the linguistic mode to express and communicate different "world versions," or ways of experiencing and looking at the world, including very individual versus very intersubjective and scientific ones. In the multimodal novel, it is even possible to present the specific capacity that cartographic and other visualizations supposedly have to represent and express the physicality and sensuality of space and motion and simultaneously to question and critique it on a meta-semiotic level.

When, as readers, we feel that other types of representation and signification are "better suited," this insight, of course, stems from the fact that in everyday life we always engage in multiple ways of making sense of perceptions and making meaning, and when in the mental act of creating the fictional world, we rely on familiar ways of apprehending and making sense of the world. For instance, in order to "orient themselves on the map of the fictional world" and to "picture in imagination the changing landscape along the routes followed by the characters" (Ryan, *Narrative* 123), readers have to construct mental models of the spaces represented in a novel and in fictions of space in particular (see Hallet, "*Fictions*").

However, it is evident that the multimodal novel offers the reader a broader range of modes as a basis for their construction of the fictional world. Since these textual worlds are of a more or less holistic nature, comprising a "connected set of objects and individuals; habitable environment; reasonably intelligible totality for external observers, [and] field of activity for its members" (Ryan, *Narrative* 91), readers will intuitively draw upon their real-world experiences, including the use of various sensory channels; different types of signs (e.g., in Peirce's terminology, "indexical," "iconic," and "symbolic") to understand and make meaning; and different symbolic languages to express themselves and communicate. Regarding the multimodality of cognition and of all meaning making, the reader's construction of the fictional world therefore imitates the multiplicity of modes that are involved in everyday cognitive processes and is therefore becomes part of the experientiality of reading narrative texts (for details, see Hallet, "Multimodality").

Since the reader of the multimodal novel must be able to understand all of the "languages" of which the narrative discourse consists, to integrate them in the construction of the storyworld, and to synthesize them into a coherent novelistic meaning, reading becomes a multi-literate act. In this act of multisemiotic reading, on the one hand, the reader must decode and comprehend each of the semiotic modes utilized and displayed in the novel in its own right. A map or a photograph or a diagram each employs its own codes and grammars and unfolds a meaning of its own. On the other hand, the reader must be able to understand the semiotic interplay of all these modes and often of visual modes and verbal discourse in particular, so that reading becomes a multi-literate act based on the capacity to integrate a range of single literacies (e.g., linguistic, visual, topographical, mathematical, and so forth) in an act of making meaning out of the narration.

All of this effort also applies to the professional reader who approaches the multimodal novel more systematically from the perspective of literary studies and narratology. Against the backdrop of the philological approach of the past that is so closely connected with the monomodal, linguistic form of the traditional novel, the multimodal novel makes them aware that meaning is never produced in a single mode, not even in the case of the monomodal literary text. Since the construction of the storyworld is an experiential act, the reader, when assigning meaning to the words on a page, will always also draw upon other sensory perceptions, other forms of knowledge, and other symbolic languages they have acquired (see Hallet, "Multimodality"). Thus even theories of a single semiotic mode—for example, picture theory—must be conceptualized as multimodal, as W. J. T. Mitchell explains in an early multimodal approach *avant la lettre*: "The image/text problem is not just something constructed 'between' the arts, the media, or different forms of representation, but an unavoidable issue *within* the individual arts and media. In short, all arts are 'composite' arts (both text and image); all media are mixed media, combining different codes, discursive conventions, channels, sensory and cognitive modes" (94–95, original emphasis). The multimodality of reader cognition is only one of the aspects that a new, multimodal narratology needs to consider and theorize. The multisemiotic composition of the narrative discourse is another, with "discourse" no longer being defined as word based and merely linguistic but as a complex interplay of modes that needs to be analyzed and synthesized at the same time. Drawing on the expertise in various related disciplines—for example, picture theory, film studies, art history, geography—a multimodal narratology needs to develop a methodology that is able to analyze and theorize the "dynamic interplay of semiotic resources as they contribute to narrative meaning" (Page 8).

From a more general disciplinary point of view, the study of the multimodal novel and, in Mitchell's sense, possibly of literature in general requires the self-critical reassessment of the role of language and its relationship to other types of semiosis or other symbolic languages (see Herman and Page 218; Ryan, "Fiction"). The philologies need to reflect on their own practices of privileging the written word and of neglecting the other forms of signification and communication that have been copresent in the production of literary texts at any given historical time (see, e.g., Dünne). Therefore, the "introduction of the concepts of *mode* and *multimodality* produces a challenge to hitherto settled notions of language" (Kress 79, original emphases) in more than one respect. As Kress points out, "If all modes are used to make meaning [. . .], then 'language' has to be seen in a different light: no longer as central and dominant, fully capable of expressing all meanings, but as one means among others for meaning making, each of them specific" (79). In this case, in order to fully comprehend the meaning of any literary text, be it multimodal or monomodal, its interplay with other modes of signification and communication has to be analyzed. The full meaning of the written word can never be grasped by studying its linguistic form alone; rather, it must be studied in connection with other semiotic modes that co-determine its meaning.

Note

1. See Kress 79–88; Kress and van Leeuwen 49–56; Nørgaard, "Multimodality" 116–19.
2. See, for example, Gibbons, *Multimodality* 127–66; Grolig; Hallet, "Multimodal Novel"; Hallet, "Visual Images"; Hoth; Nørgaard, "Multimodality"; Nørgaard, "Modality" 70–78.
3. See Hallet, "Multimodal Novel"; Hallet, "Visual Images"; Hallet, "Medialisierung"; Gibbons, "'I Contain'" 99; Gibbons, "Narrative Worlds" 287.
4. Translations from German sources by the author.
5. See Böhme xv; Hallet, "Multimodality"; Gibbons, "'I Contain Multitudes'"; Gibbons, *Multimodality* 39–45.
6. See Ryan, *Narrative*, 91. Also see Grabes; Hallet, "Multimodality"; Gibbons, *Multimodality* 34–39.

Works Cited

Böhme, Hartmut. "Einleitung: Raum—Bewegung—Topographie." *Topographien der Literatur: Deutsche Literatur im transnationalen Kontext.* Ed. Hartmut Böhme. Weimar, Germany: Metzler, 2005. ix–xxiii. Print.

Danielewski, Mark Z. *House of Leaves.* New York: Pantheon Books, 2000. Print.

Dünne, Jörg. "Die Karte als imaginierter Ursprung: Zur frühneuzeitlichen Konkurrenz von textueller und kartographischer Raumkonstitution in den Amerika-Reisen Theodor de Brys." *Topographien der Literatur: Deutsche Literatur im transnationalen Kontext.* Ed. Hartmut Böhme. Weimar, Germany: Metzler, 2005. 73–99. Print.

Foer, Jonathan Safran. *Extremely Loud & Incredibly Close.* London: Penguin, 2005. Print.

Frank, Michael C. "Die Literaturwissenschaften und der *spatial turn*: Ansätze bei Jurij Lotman und Michail Bachtin." *Raum und Bewegung in der Literatur: Die Literaturwissenschaften und der Spatial Turn.* Ed. Wolfgang Hallet and Birgit Neumann. Bielefeld, Germany: Transcript, 2009. 53–80. Print.

Gibbons, Alison. "'I Contain Multitudes': Narrative Multimodality and the Book that Bleeds." *New Perspectives on Narrative and Multimodality.* Ed. Ruth Page. 99–114. Print.

———. *Multimodality, Cognition, and Experimental Literature.* London: Routledge, 2012. Print.

———. "The Narrative Worlds and Multimodal Figures of *House of Leaves*: '—find your own words; I have no more.'" *Intermediality and Storytelling.* Ed. Marina Grishakova and Marie-Laure Ryan. Berlin: De Gruyter, 2010. 285–311. Print.

Goodman, Nelson. *Ways of Worldmaking.* Indianapolis IN: Hackett, 1978. Print.

Grabes, Herbert. "Turning Words on the Page into 'Real' People." *Style* 38.2 (2004): 221–35. Print.

Grolig, Lorenz. "Narrative Konstruktion, Bild und Photographie in Jonathan Safran Foers *Extremely Loud & Incredibly Close.*" *Komparatistik Online* 2 (2007): n. pag. Web. March 15, 2012.

Haddon, Mark. *The Curious Incident of the Dog in the Night-Time*. London: Vintage, 2004. Print.

Hallet, Wolfgang. "*Fictions of Space:* Zeitgenössische Romane als fiktionale Modelle semiotischer Raumkonstitution." *Raum und Bewegung in der Literatur: Die Literaturwissenschaften und der Spatial Turn*. Ed. Wolfgang Hallet and Birgit Neumann. Bielefeld: Transcript, 2009. 81–113. Print.

———. "Medialisierung von Genres am Beispiel des Blogs und des multimodalen Romans: Von der Schrift-Kunst zum multimodalen Design." *Medialisierung des Erzählens im englischsprachigen Roman der Gegenwart: Theoretischer Bezugsrahmen, Genres und Modellinterpretationen*. Ed. Ansgar Nünning and Jan Rupp. Trier, Germany: WVT, 2011. 85–116. Print.

———. "The Multimodal Novel: The Integration of Modes and Media in Novelistic Narration." *Narratology in the Age of Cross-Disciplinary Narrative Research*. Ed. Sandra Heinen and Roy Sommer. Berlin: De Gruyter, 2009. 129–53. Print.

———. "The Multimodality of Cultural Experience and Mental Model Constructions of Textual Worlds." *Yearbook of Research in English and American Literature*. Vol. 24, *The Literary Mind*. Ed. Jürgen Schlaeger. Tübingen, Germany: Narr, 2008. 233–50. Print.

———. "Visual Images of Space, Movement and Mobility in the Multimodal Novel." *Moving Images—Mobile Viewers: 20th Century Visuality*. Ed. Renate Brosch. Berlin: LIT Verlag, 2011. 227–48. Print.

Herman, David, and Ruth Page. "Coda/Prelude: Eighteen Questions for the Study of Narrative and Multimodality." *New Perspectives on Narrative and Multimodality*. Ed. Ruth Page. 217–20. Print.

Hoth, Stefanie. "From Individual Experience to Historical Event and Back Again: '9/11' in Jonathan Safran Foer's Extremely Loud & Incredibly Close." *Kulturelles Wissen und Intertextualität: Theoriekonzeptionen und Fallstudien zu Kontextualisierung von Literatur*. Ed. Marion Gymnich, Birgit Neumann, and Ansgar Nünning. Trier, Germany: WVT, 2006. 283–300. Print.

Hühn, Peter. "Event and Eventfulness." *The Living Handbook of Narratology*. Ed. Peter Hühn et al. Hamburg: Hamburg University Press, 2011. Web. March 18, 2012.

Kress, Gunther. *Multimodality: A Social Semiotic Approach to Contemporary Communication*. London: Routledge, 2010. Print.

Kress, Gunther, and Theo van Leeuwen. *Multimodal Discourse: The Modes and Media of Contemporary Communication*. London: Arnold, 2001. Print.

Larsen, Reif. *The Selected Works of T. S. Spivet*. London: Harvill Secker, 2009. Print.

Lotman, Jurij M. *Die Struktur literarischer Texte*. Munich: Fink, 1972. Print.

Mitchell, W. J. T. *Picture Theory: Essays on Verbal and Visual Representation.* Chicago: University of Chicago Press, 1994. Print.

Nørgaard, Nina. "Multimodality and the Literary Text: Making Sense of Safran Foer's *Extremely Loud and Incredibly Close.*" *New Perspectives on Narrative and Multimodality.* Ed. Ruth Page. 115–26. Print.

———. "Modality: Commitment, Truth Value and Reality Claims across Modes in Multimodal Novels." *Journal for Literary Theory* 4.1 (2010): 63–80. Print.

Page, Ruth. Introduction. *New Perspectives on Narrative and Multimodality.* Ed. Ruth Page. London: Routledge, 2010. 1–13. Print.

Ryan, Marie-Laure. "Cognitive Maps and the Construction of Narrative Space." *Narrative Theory and the Cognitive Sciences.* Ed. David Herman. Stanford CA: CSLI, 2003. 214–42. Print.

———. "Fiction, Cognition and Non-Verbal Media." *Intermediality and Storytelling.* Ed. Marina Grishakova and Marie-Laure Ryan. Berlin: De Gruyter, 2010. 8–26. Print.

———. *Narrative as Virtual Reality: Immersion and Interactivity in Literature and Electronic Media.* Baltimore MD: Johns Hopkins University Press, 2001. Print.

Sebald, W. G. *Austerlitz.* London: Penguin, 2001. Print.

Stockhammer, Robert. "Verortung: Die Macht der Kartographie und die Literatur." *TopoGraphien der Moderne: Medien zur Repräsentation und Konstruktion von Räumen.* Ed. Robert Stockhammer. Munich: Fink, 2005. 319–40. Print.

Van Leeuwen, Theo. *Introducing Social Semiotics.* London: Routledge, 2005. Print.

7 On Absent Carrot Sticks

The Level of Abstraction in Video Games

JESPER JUUL

Here is a naïve question: why am I not allowed to cut a carrot into sticks? Figure 7.1 shows the action of chopping carrots in *Cooking Mama* (Office Create). In this game, the player is tasked with preparing, heating, and arranging ingredients according to the recipes that the game provides. While we expect to perform all of these actions in a kitchen, we can also list an infinite number of other actions that are possible in a regular kitchen but not here. *Cooking Mama* lets us slice the carrots, for instance, but not make them into sticks. In a regular kitchen, moreover, we can decide that we do not want to cook after all and order takeout instead. At first, these may seem like mere technological limitations, but I argue that they derive from the fact that we are dealing with *a game*. Finally, *Cooking Mama* offers us something that we do not regularly experience—namely, an infinite supply of replacement ingredients whenever the player burns or otherwise spoils the food (see figure 7.2).

Fiction plays a different role in different video games. Some games are abstract (e.g., *Tetris* [Pajitnov and Gerasimov]), others have a thin veneer of fiction (e.g., *Angry Birds* [Roviio Entertainment]), and others feature elaborate fictional worlds with character development and plotlines (e.g., *Mass Effect 2* [BioWare]). Given that games by definition allow players to influence the course of events, thus contradicting many definitions of "narratives," I find that it is preferable to discuss video games using the broader concept of "fictional worlds." Since a *fictional world* may or may not contain a fixed sequence of events, the concept of fiction is a more precise tool for examining video games than is narrative. This concept also lets us see that video games are *half real*, meaning that they are an intersection of two quite different things—real rule-based activities that we perform in the actual world and fictional worlds that

Fig. 7.1. Slicing carrots in *Cooking Mama* (Office Create 2006).

Fig. 7.2. Burning all the cutlets but receiving infinite replacement ingredients in *Cooking Mama* (Office Create 2006).

we imagine when playing (Juul). All content in a representational game will therefore fall into one of three categories.

1. *Fiction implemented in rules*: The most straightforward situation, where the game rules are motivated by the game's fiction. We expect to be able to chop a carrot, and the game lets us do it. Other examples would include cars that can drive, birds that can fly, and so on.
2. *Fiction not implemented in game rules*: When fiction suggests a possibility that is not accessible to players. We generally expect to be able to leave a kitchen and to cut a carrot in any way we like, but the game *Cooking Mama* prevents us from doing so.
3. *Rules not explained by fiction*: When rules are difficult to explain by referring to the game's fiction—for example, the way *Cooking Mama* gives the player unlimited replacement ingredients or the multiple lives characters experience in arcade games.[1]

Figure 7.3 illustrates these categories in a Venn diagram, with some game elements only represented in the game rules, some only represented in the fiction, and some being represented as both rules and fiction. The left side of the diagram covers amusing examples of video game rules that are not explained by fiction, such as *Cooking Mama*'s infinite supply of ingredients, the three lives of Mario in the traditional arcade game,

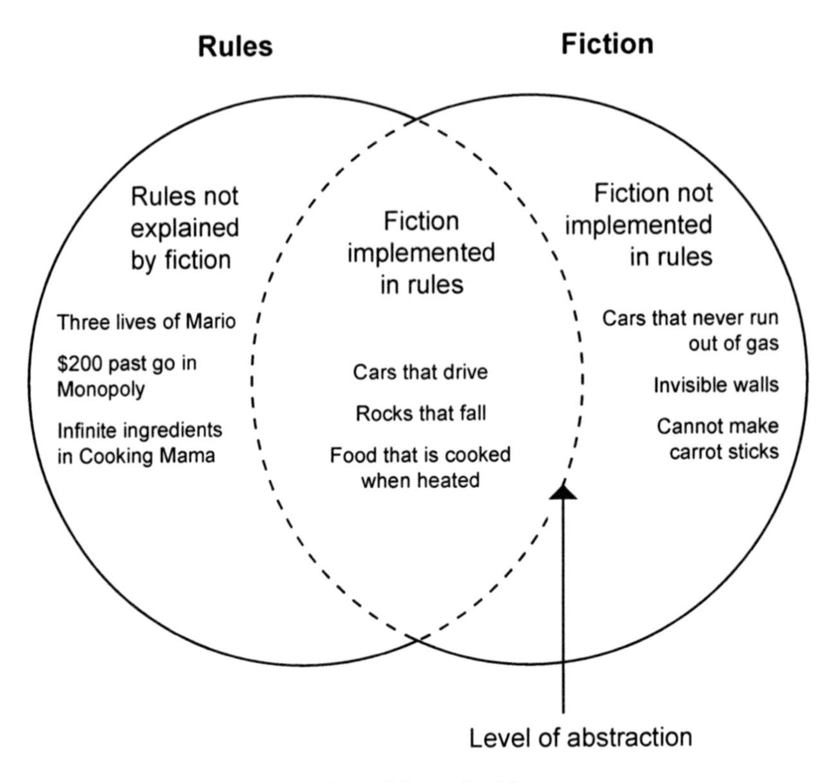

Fig. 7.3. Three variations on rules and fiction in video games.

or even the source of the money given to players when they pass Go in *Monopoly*. I have discussed such examples elsewhere (Juul 5).

In the following discussion I focus on the game elements on the right—that is, on the level of abstraction that distinguishes between the aspects of the game fiction that are implemented in the game rules (middle overlapping section of the diagram) and the aspects that are not (right side of the diagram). Like all nonabstract games, *Cooking Mama* has such a level of abstraction. The game presents a fictional world, but the game rules only give players access to certain parts of this world and only allow players to act on a certain level.

Game design *abstraction* can be illustrated through a language metaphor, since language can describe actions with different levels of detail. Going to work can be described as exactly that, "going to work," or it can be listed as a number of individual steps—such as "open front door, walk to subway, take subway, leave subway, walk to work"—and it can be as detailed as offering a description of the concrete path to walk or even of the individual muscles to activate. In a way, a level of abstraction is a general trait of how we perceive actions, since any action that we take will always entail muscle movements or other biological processes to which we have no conscious access.

The question of abstraction is parallel to (but different from) a general issue in representational art: descriptions of fictional worlds are always incomplete (Pavel 50). Since a description of a fictional world is of finite size, while any world contains an infinite number of facts, it will also omit an infinite number of facts that we cannot determine simply by looking at the artwork itself. As an example, it is impossible to determine how many children Lady Macbeth had (see Ryan, "Possible Worlds"). Any representational art will describe its subject matter in smaller or greater detail, and especially in verbal narrative, we find that this level of detail has changed over time and between genres. For example, the rise of the realist novel shifted the level of description compared to earlier literary forms by recounting mundane actions and objects that had otherwise been absent in narration. The level of abstraction that I discuss here rather refers to whether game rules implement the imagined fictional world of a game (regardless of the detail by which it was presented).

To illustrate the difference between the level of abstraction as it concerns game rules and the level of detail in a description, consider this passage from the 1983 text adventure game *Witness* (Infocom). The lines preceded by > are actions taken by the player; the remaining lines are responses by the game.

```
>wait
The rain is falling heavily now.

>drink rain
(Sorry, but the program doesn't recognize the word "rain.")
```

As can be seen, on the one hand, the description of the game world is sufficiently detailed to include notes about the weather (and the particular quality of the rain). On the other hand, the game rules do not grant the player access to the same weather elements. An element of the fictional world of a game (such as rain in *Witness* or the tablecloth in *Cooking Mama*) may or may not be implemented in the programming and rules of a video game. However, the relationship between the

Fig. 7.4. *Diner Dash: Flo on the Go* (PlayFirst 2006).

world's description and the level of abstraction is rather subtle: given that users fill in the blanks about any fictional world using real-world or fictional expectations (see Ryan, *Possible Worlds*), a player can make as detailed assumptions about a cursorily described world as about one described in excruciating detail. The gap of abstraction between what appears to be possible in the fictional game world and what is actually possible in the game rules is therefore logically the same regardless of how the world is presented to a player. Yet, in actuality, a player approaching a new game does not go through the process of identifying the game's level of abstraction from scratch but builds on the fact that each game genre has its own particular level of abstraction. For example, a racing game always lets players control the steering wheel of a car, but a city simulation generally keeps the act of driving a car beyond the player's control.

Abstraction as Design

In the cooking example, any level of detail from selecting the dish to controlling the muscles of the hand holding the knife can be imagined;

however, changing the level of abstraction would make *Cooking Mama* a different game. For example, PlayFirst's game *Diner Dash: Flo on the Go* (see figure 7.4) is about running a restaurant. Plausibly, the chef in the game is cooking food, as is the player's character in *Cooking Mama*, but that action is not available to the player. Though the two games could be conceived as being part of the same fictional world, they are completely different games due to their differing levels of abstraction.

In effect, a game genre *is* a level of abstraction; a game genre is a way of distilling a fictional world into a set of actions that the player can perform. Thus larger franchises, such as *Star Wars* or *Harry Potter*, can lead to the creation of numerous different video games, each in their own genre and each selecting a particular set of actions from their respective fictional universes.

Decoding Abstraction

This discussion of abstraction in *Cooking Mama* and *Diner Dash: Flo on the Go* is a view of the two games in retrospect, from the vantage point of having played these games for a while. But playing games is actually a process of exploring abstraction. As players, we come to new games and especially new game genres not knowing their level of abstraction. Consider two classic real-time strategy games—*StarCraft* (Blizzard Entertainment) and *Age of Empires II: The Age of Kings* (Ensemble Studios) (see figure 7.5). The initial impression of these two games is very different depending on the player's experience with real-time strategy games.

The novice game player will try to make assumptions about the game based on the game's fiction. *Age of Empires II: The Age of Kings* has units and a setting that the player can recognize from other media: the knights presumably have some sort of battle function, the catapult is probably used for attacking castles, and the people on the fields probably gather food in some way. From the setting, the player has the possibility of making assumptions about the game's rule structure. But to a player unfamiliar with real-time strategy games, *StarCraft* (and especially the Zergs pictured here) yields little information about the rules of the game. What are the blue crystals? What do the critters do? Thus because they can use the fiction to make inferences about the rules, new players will generally find *Age of Empires II: The Age of Kings* more accessible.

Fig. 7.5. *StarCraft* (Blizzard Entertainment 1998) and *Age of Empires II* (Ensemble Studios 1999).

The experienced game player, meanwhile, can identify the genre of the previously mentioned games on the basis of the number of units, the placement of resources, the bird's-eye view, and the general interface layout. That is, the experienced player identifies the game as belonging to the real-time strategy genre and uses this genre identification to make assumptions about the rule structure of the game and the general limits within which the interaction takes place: for example, telling units where to go but not directly controlling the path finding of the individual unit, dealing with battles but not with making food, and accepting that human units can be "built" in a few minutes. However, even the experienced game player does not know precisely where the level of abstraction lies in this specific game. Perhaps this game adds political or social structure as a new component to the real-time strategy genre. Or perhaps, in this game, resource-gathering units become fatigued.

Abstraction of What?

In the example of *Cooking Mama*, I discussed to what extent its kitchen setting is reflected in the game rules. Discussing this aspect relies on being able to compare a set of assumptions about the represented world (a kitchen) with the possibilities that the game offers. In other words, the experience that a game is an abstraction depends on the player's identification of the particular setting of which the game is an abstraction.

Consider the game shown in figure 7.6, which features a number of geometrical objects in different colors. Rod Humble's experimental game *The Marriage* is meant to illustrate the tensions and developments in a marriage, with the two squares representing the partners and the circles representing the external influences upon the relationship. As Humble notes, this portrayal is not something that players can generally intuit from seeing the game: "This is a game that requires explanation. That statement is already an admission of failure. But when working with new art forms one has to start somewhere and it's unfair to an audience to leave a piece of work (even if it's not successful) without some justification. It's probably some kind of record to have such a small game give hundreds of words of explanation" (n. pag.).

The Marriage can only be perceived as a radical abstraction of the workings of a relationship if the player understands that the game represents a marriage at all. An element of communication is integral to rep-

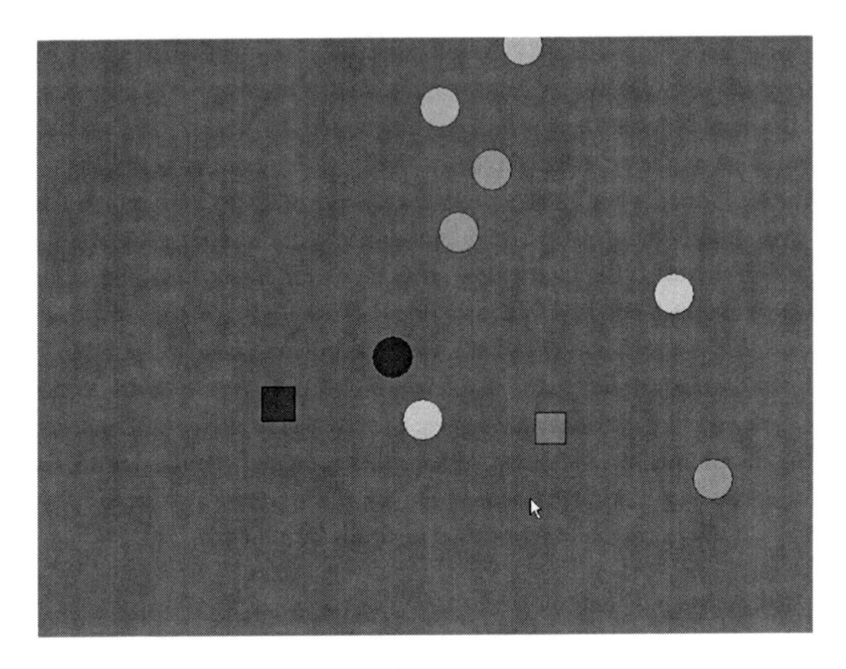

Fig. 7.6. *The Marriage* (Humble 2006).

resentational games; that is, the player must in some way be convinced to see the game as a representation of something. The player can then consider the difference between his or her assumptions about the fictional world and the actions that the game actually allows.

Virtual Reality: The Dream of Removing the Level of Abstraction

Given that video games have changed quite drastically along with improvements in computing and graphics technology, it could be tempting to assume that the level of abstraction is simply due to technological limitations. Perhaps, given the right technology and sufficient amount of resources, we can make a game that both photorealistically represents a kitchen and simulates it to an arbitrary level of detail. This goal was the 1990s' dream of virtual reality or of the holodeck from *Star Trek* (Murray): to have a game-like experience without a level of abstraction, or a game where anything was possible and everything was simulated to arbitrary detail. In a hypothetical virtual reality game of *Cooking Mama*, we would finally be able to make carrots sticks or even order takeout, as we would in a real kitchen.

This idea of a hypothetical, perfect simulation resurfaces at regular intervals, but critical voices remain. As game designer Frank Lantz has put it:

> I think there is a widespread and largely unexamined belief in this community that computer games are evolving towards an infinitely detailed and utterly seamless simulation. That this is their destiny. To evolve to a Star Trek Holodeck, a seamless simulation indistinguishable from real experience. [. . .]
>
> Even if you could by some magic create this impossible perfect simulation world, where would you be? You'd need to stick a game in there. You'd need to make chess out of the simulation rocks in your world. It's like going back to square one. I don't want to play chess again. I want to play a game that has the dense simulation and chess combined. This requires a light touch. This requires respect for the gap. The gap is part of your toolset. (n. pag.)

Furthermore, the role of abstraction is not simply to make the game different from what it represents but also to make it different for specific purposes. Chaim Gingold has compared game development to the aesthetics of Japanese gardens: "A miniature garden, like a snow globe, model train set, or fish tank, is complete; nothing is missing, and nothing can be taken away. Clear boundaries (spatial and non-spatial), overviews, and a consistent level of abstraction work hand in hand to make the miniature world believable, complete, and tractable for both the author and player" (6–7).

Gingold's view presents abstraction as a way of both making a world and of making that world readable. Indeed, abstraction can be seen as the process by which any given subject matter is transformed into game form. Consider fighting games. When the genre began with games such as *Street Fighter* (Capcom) or *Karate Champ* (Data East) (see figure 7.7), fighting games were predominantly two dimensional. At the time, this limitation was out of technological necessity since the hardware was not capable of representing three-dimensional worlds.

What happened once technology progressed to the point where three-dimensional worlds could easily be created? Compare *Karate Champ* to *Super Street Fighter IV* (Dimps/Capcom) shown in figure 7.8.

Even in this lavish three-dimensional game world, the fighting is

Fig. 7.7. *Karate Champ* (Data East 1984): 2-D game in a 2-D world.

placed on a single axis, where the players are always facing directly toward or away from each other.[2] This design can be motivated in several ways: the amount of possible actions is more manageable when players can only attack each other from the front or the back, it makes the game easier to learn, and it allows the visuals to be more elaborate without making the gameplay too complex.

This example represents an abstraction that remains part of a genre even when technological advances would allow games to remove an abstraction, in this case the absence of the third dimension. It proves that the history of video games is not simply driven by technological advances. Rather, a genre that is well understood by game players and game de-

Fig. 7.8. *Super Street Fighter IV* (Dimps/Capcom 2010): a 2-D game in a 3-D world.

signers can remain stable over time regardless of changing technological affordances.

Abstraction as Player Optimization

To play a game is to learn and to examine that game's level of abstraction. Additionally, games tend to push the player toward optimizing his or her strategy and influences the way players perceive a game. As in the previous discussion of real-time strategy players, an experienced player may understand the game as a variation on a genre, but a player not used to the genre may use the fiction to understand what type of actions are possible in the game. A study of first-person shooter players (Retaux and Rouchier) found that acquiring proficiency in a game was often accompanied with decreasing the level of detail of the graphics. It would be possible to make the argument that this change constitutes a shift of the player's focus away from the subject matter of the game—the game as fiction—to the rules of the game (Juul 139). In certain types of games, this player's focus probably is the standard: the novice player begins playing with a focus on the game fiction and ends up thinking only about the game as an opportunity for optimizing strategies. However, for psychological reasons there is great variation between different games.

One of the theories of skill acquisition examines how users learn to separate task-relevant from task-redundant information: "[W]e argue that people learn, over the course of practice, to separate task-relevant from task-redundant information and to limit their processing to relevant aspects of the task. Thus, the information processed early in skill acquisition may be qualitatively different from the information processed late in skill acquisition. [Performance improvement] may at least partially reflect systematic reductions in the amount of information that is processed, rather than changes in the efficiency with which task components can be performed" (Haider and Frensch 306).

Any game that enforces its goals strongly or is highly competitive, pressuring the player to improve his or her performance, will push the player toward information reduction, or to thinking only about what is relevant for the present task. If the fiction is not relevant for the player's task, it becomes possible for the player to play the game as if it were an abstract game.

To shift the focus away from the fiction means that when thinking about the game, we can plan strategies by considering the abstract rules of the game exclusively and without using the knowledge that we have from the game fiction. On the one hand, in a game like chess, it is straightforwardly true that we can play chess without considering the societal roles of the pieces, because thinking about the societal roles of the pieces is unlikely to be of any help when playing the game. On the other hand, while *The Sims 2* (Maxis), shown in figure 7.9, could theoretically be played as an abstract game containing a number of entities with parameters that had to be optimized, it is hard to imagine playing the game without thinking about it as consisting of virtual people with emotions.[3]

Incidentally, the way we play *The Sims* is explained by philosopher Daniel Dennett's concept of the *intentional stance*. Dennett argues that it is not as much that objects (humans included) have intentionality but that it simply is more efficient to predict other people's behavior by considering their possible intentions than by thinking of them as physical systems or designed objects (16–18). And surely, even though we know that *The Sims 2* contains no actual people but only simplistic simulations thereof, it is much easier to play *The Sims 2* by thinking of the on-screen characters as having genuine intentions and desires than by thinking of the game as a mathematical problem.

The other interesting aspect of *The Sims* is the game's focus on quotidian actions such as taking out garbage. Before the launch of *The Sims*, it

Fig. 7.9. *The Sims 2* (Maxis 2004).

was generally assumed that household chores were too dull a subject to become a central part of a video game. In a historical perspective, *The Sims* game mirrors the appearance of the realistic novel in the later part of the nineteenth century where, broadly speaking, novels began to describe everyday life rather than heroes and dramatic events. In the case of video games, the change reflects not only a change of description detail (describing hitherto unmentioned aspects of human existence) but also that the game implements everyday life in game rules such that the player can make mundane decisions about what furniture to buy, what food to cook, and when to take a nap. The executives at software company Maxis were famously skeptical of the concept when designer Will Wright proposed it, but *The Sims* went on to become the best-selling personal computer (PC) game of all time (Donovan 25).

Finally, the player's attitude toward a game cannot simply be reduced to one of optimization; the player may possess a will to fiction, or a desire to engage in make-believe. For example, Jonas Linderoth has documented the struggles of a guild in *World of Warcraft* (Blizzard Entertainment) whose players had decided to actively avoid any reference to their game

Fig. 7.10. *SSX* (EA Canada 2012): Fictional space.

playing as a rule-based game. Instead, they preferred to explain every interface element or out-of-game action (both the left and right sides of the model in figure 7.3) by way of elaborate fictional argumentations (see Linderoth). For example, players who had to temporarily step away from their computers would refrain from employing the standard AFK (away from keyboard) expression, choosing rather to say that they were adjusting their armor, and so on.

Space: The Unabstractable

Although figure 7.10 may appear to show otherwise, there is no space inside the snowboarding game *SSX* (EA Canada). It has no snow, no snowboarder, no mountain, and no space. All of these elements are fictions, but some of them—the spatial layout of the mountain, the snow, a somewhat abstracted version of normal laws of physics—happen to be partially implemented in the rules of the game. Rune Klevjer has argued that concerning the issue of space, the rules-fiction distinction outlined earlier "is dangerously close to the breaking point" (61). He has a case: analytically, we can explain why the space is a fiction, but at the same time it is hardly possible to play the game without *perceiving* it as space. Space in video games is special because most video games take place in a space, because the space usually is part of the fiction of the game, and because space is at least partially implemented in the rules (belonging to the overlapping middle of the diagram in figure 7.3). In the same way that *The Sims 2* could theoretically be played as an abstract game of numbers, so could SSX. This model would involve a long series of calculations determining which different variables were close to each other in value and so on. In practice, this version would be a very challenging game that could certainly not be played in real time.

Humans are not general-purpose calculators. We have limited overall processing power but specialties in certain areas. It is comparatively straightforward to make a computer program perform long series of complex mathematical calculations but much more difficult to program a character to navigate a complex landscape in a way that appears intelligent to a human observer. Compared to computers, humans come with amazing spatial skills. Thus problems that can be solved in a spatial way tend to be solved spatially by humans; therefore, it is hard for a player to abstract from and, hence, to disregard the space in a game.

The Game in There

The level of abstraction determines how we can reason about the world as players. In a story about a hungry person in a kitchen, we would reason that he or she would have other ways to acquire food than by cooking in the kitchen according to fixed recipes. In a cooking game, we accept that cooking provides the only source of food. Here, we can see the difference between regular stories and games: In a story, the limit of a character's possible actions is our understanding of the fictional world, by whatever logic it follows. For a game, the limit of a character's possible action is the level of abstraction; that is, the available actions are always a subset of the actions that would be available with hypothetical full access to a fictional world.

This factor is not as strange as it would first appear but pertains to the fact that video games are *games*. In a well-known formulation, Bernard Suits defines games as being about attaining a goal using the "less efficient means" available. For example, the high jump would be easier if we could use a ladder, a race would be easier if we could cut across the tracks, and soccer would be easier if we could pick up the ball. "To stick a game in there," as Lantz was quoted saying, is fundamentally about reducing the number of possibilities available to the player in order to make a game (n. pag.).[4] From this perspective, the level of abstraction comes from the root of video games in non-digital games. The rules that decide what actions are or are not allowed on a soccer or baseball field can be considered a type of abstraction, one that makes certain parts of the physical world off-limits in a game. The soccer ball, for instance, can only be handled in certain ways; the baseball player actually runs on a one-dimensional line with a few discrete bases. The *magic circle* of games (Huizinga) that delineates what is inside from what is outside the game, then, not only is a visible spatial boundary but also can be seen as dividing every single object, action, and player into components that are either part of the game or not part of the game.

Just as real-world soccer removes the ability of field players to touch the ball with their hands, *Super Street Fighter IV* removes many of the details of actual fighting. Furthermore, though a video game version of soccer is an abstraction of the physical game of soccer, players of video game soccer rarely complain about the inability of field players to capture the ball with their hands. Since soccer identifies this contact as an off-limit action, we do not expect to find it implemented in video game form. This previous argument also explains why we do not find it strange that *Cooking Mama* prevents us from ordering takeout. In a game about cooking, we accept that our actions are limited to those directly relevant to cooking. Likewise, we accept that we are not free to cut carrots any way we want, since this subsection of the game is specifically about slicing carrots as fast as we can.

We interpret game events through the lens of game conventions. When we experience a game event that is not explained by the game fiction, we always have two other strategies available: we can explain the event as stemming from the necessities of the rules of the game (see left side of figure 7.3), or we can assume that some fictionally reasonable action is not available to us owing to the level of abstraction (see right side of figure 7.3).[5]

The seemingly strange limitations that prevent video game players from making perfectly logical actions, such as cutting carrots into sticks or ordering takeout, are exactly the limitations that make video games part of the field of games. The level of abstraction at first may seem a by-product of technological limitations, but it is in actuality a central component of game genres and player expectations. Video games are a double movement—giving us access to new fictional worlds but then giving us only limited options in those worlds in order to make a game.

Notes

An earlier version of this article was presented as "A Certain Level of Abstraction" at the DiGRA conference, Tokyo, September 2007. Thanks to Marie-Laure Ryan, Jan-Noël Thon, and Nanna Debois Buhl for comments.

1. It is of course possible to create a fictional motivation for any game rule, but the point is that we often do not. Players do not explain the three lives of Mario in *Donkey Kong* (Nintendo) by claiming Mario was reincarnated but by referring to the rules; otherwise, the game would be too hard (Juul 4).
2. It can be argued that three-dimensional (3-D) fighting games lack certain types of ranged attacks, such as fireballs, because they would have appeared incongruous given that 3-D games often rotate the two-dimensional axes that the opponents play on and ranged attacks would have to move magically with this rotating axis (otherwise it would be possible to sidestep such an attack). I am indebted to Charles Pratt for this observation.
3. A player with autism would perceive *The Sims* as a different type of game, since the player would lack an existing set of skills for processing people interaction and emotional issues.
4. A similar argument is made by Salen and Zimmerman (138).
5. This argument that games allow for interpretation strategies that refer to the medium itself has many parallels in the theory of narrative. For example, Monika Fludernik's concept of narrativization describes "a reading strategy that naturalizes texts by recourse to narrative schemata" (25).

Works Cited

BioWare. *Mass Effect* 2. Electronic Arts, 2010. Xbox 360.

Blizzard Entertainment. *StarCraft*. Blizzard Entertainment, 1998. Windows.

———. *World of Warcraft*. Blizzard Entertainment, 2004. Windows.

Capcom. *Street Fighter*. Capcom, 1987. Arcade.

Data East. *Karate Champ*. Data East, 1984. Arcade.

Dennett, Daniel C. *The Intentional Stance*. Cambridge MA: MIT Press, 1989. Print.

Dimps/Capcom. *Super Street Fighter IV*. Capcom, 2010. Xbox 360.

Donovan, Tristan. *Replay: The History of Video Games*. Sussex, UK: Yellow Ant Media, 2010. Print.

EA Canada. *SSX*. EA Sports, 2012. Xbox 360.

Ensemble Studios. *Age of Empires II: The Age of Kings*. Microsoft, 1999. Windows.

Fludernik, Monika. *Towards a "Natural" Narratology*. London: Routledge, 1996. Print.

Gingold, Chaim. "Miniature Gardens & Magic Crayons: Games, Spaces, & Worlds." MS thesis Georgia Institute of Technology, 2003. Web. May 2, 2012.

Haider, Hilde, and Peter A. Frensch. "The Role of Information Reduction in Skill Acquisition." *Cognitive Psychology* 30.3 (1996): 304–37. Print.

Huizinga, Johan. *Homo Ludens: A Study of the Play Element in Culture*. Boston: Roy Publishers, 1950. Print.

Humble, Rod. *The Marriage*. Rod Humble, 2006. Windows.

Infocom. *Witness*. Infocom, 1983. DOS.

Juul, Jesper. *Half-Real: Video Games between Real Rules and Fictional Worlds*. Cambridge MA: MIT Press, 2005. Print.

Klevjer, Rune. "What Is the Avatar? Fiction and Embodiment in Avatar-based Singleplayer Computer Games." Diss. University of Bergen, 2006. Web. May 2, 2012.

Lantz, Frank. "Game Developers Rant II." San Jose CA, 2006. Web. May 2, 2012.

Linderoth, Jonas. "The Struggle for Immersion: Narrative Re-Framing in World of Warcraft." *Proceedings of the [Player] Conference*. Ed. Olli Leino, Gordon Calleja, and Sarah Mosberg Iversen. IT University of Copenhagen, Denmark, 2008. 242–74. Print.

Maxis. *The Sims 2*. Electronic Arts, 2004. Windows.

Murray, Janet H. *Hamlet on the Holodeck: The Future of Narrative in Cyberspace*. Cambridge MA: MIT Press, 1998. Print.

Nintendo. *Donkey Kong*. Nintendo, 1981. Arcade.

Office Create. *Cooking Mama*. Taito, 2006. Nintendo DS.

Pajitnov, Alexey, and Vadim Gerasimov. *Tetris*. 1985. DOS.

Pavel, Thomas G. *Fictional Worlds*. Cambridge MA: Harvard University Press, 1986. Print.

PlayFirst. *Diner Dash: Flo on the Go*. PlayFirst, 2006. Windows.

Retaux, Xavier, and Juliette Rouchier. "Realism vs Surprise and Coherence: Different Aspect of Playability in Computer Games." *Playing with the Future Conference*. Manchester, UK, April 5–7, 2002. Web. May 1, 2012.

Rovio Entertainment. *Angry Birds*. Chillingo, 2009. iOS.

Ryan, Marie-Laure. *Possible Worlds, Artificial Intelligence, and Narrative Theory*. Bloomington: Indiana University Press, 1991. Print.

———. "Possible Worlds in Recent Literary Theory." *Style* 26.4 (1992): 528–53. Print.

Salen, Katie, and Eric Zimmerman. *Rules of Play: Game Design Fundamentals*. Cambridge MA: MIT Press, 2004. Print.

Suits, Bernard Herbert. *The Grasshopper: Games, Life, and Utopia*. Toronto: University of Toronto Press, 1978. Print.

8 Film + Comics

A Multimodal Romance in the Age of Transmedial Convergence

JARED GARDNER

Born together at the end of the nineteenth century, comics and film were both multimodal narrative forms from the start, telling stories using multiple, interdependent semiotic chains of text and image. Together, comics and film became the first two new narrative media of the twentieth century, and in developing their conventions they borrowed heavily from each other even as they also explored their own unique affordances (see Gardner ch. 1). The significance of this development in the history of narrative media in the last century cannot be overestimated. After all, while narrative, in one sense at least, has *always* been multimodal (see Grishakova and Ryan 4), it is hard to find sustained or culturally significant examples in the West that do not inevitably make one semiotic chain subservient to the other. An illustrated book is not multimodal, after all, in the same way that a sequential comic is; the pictures almost always serve to illustrate the text, which is primarily responsible for the work of telling the story. While our reading experience of *Oliver Twist* would certainly be different without the twenty-four illustrations that accompanied the original serialization of the novel, that they are not essential is evidenced by the fact that few modern editions include all of the original illustrations and many include none at all. And although increasingly we see examples in the twenty-first century of what Wolfgang Hallet has usefully described as the "multimodal novel" (129)—a novel in which "it is the systematic and recurrent integration of non-verbal and non-narrative elements in novelistic narration that makes the difference" (130)—this phenomenon has largely developed in the last twenty years in response to a dramatically changing media ecology. Thus I would argue that we risk misreading both the significance of the phenomenon of the multimodal novel of the twenty-first century *and* the new multimodal narrative forms of the twentieth century—film and comics—if, as Ruth Page recently called for, we start "reconceptualiz[ing] *all* narrative communication as multimodal" (5).

Of course, multimodal narratives existed long before comics and film, with opera and theater being the most obvious predecessors for those encountering film and comics for the first time in the late nineteenth century. But here, too, the differences are worth considering. Theater and opera were experienced "live"—that is, with performers enacting the story in the narrative "present" and "live" in the sense of happening in real time. And neither opera nor theater were available yet for mechanical reproduction—for interactions such as looping, rewinding, and rereading that would be opened up by translating the experience of the multimodal *performance* out of the live space of the theater into a multimodal *text*.

1890–1910: Birth of Modern Multimodal Media

An important part of what defined the unique experience of the twentieth century's new multimodal media is that early comics and film both told their multimodal narratives in complex *transmedial* environments—newspapers, illustrated magazines, vaudeville houses, and nickelodeons—where paratexts multiplied in profusion, creating almost infinitely varied and unruly encounters with the text. From the early Kinetoscope through the heyday of the nickelodeon, early film was experienced in environments that included vaudeville routines, live music, narration, and sound effects, not to mention the lively commentary of the audience itself. As the saying goes, silent film was never silent, but it was also never simply *film*, just as the early sequential comics were never simply comics.

The early narrative strips were experienced across the serial disruptions of the weekly (and later daily) newspaper, with its own cacophony of tragic headlines, advertisements, and data. And as was the case with early film, the audience itself contributed vitally to the transmedial experience of the early comic, with people often reading and commenting upon the comics in public spaces and collaborative environments. With the rise of the daily continuity strip in the late 1910s and 1920s, comics' creators began inviting readers to collaborate on the stories, offering contests and often deliberately blurring the boundaries between front-page news and graphic narrative.

In both cases, at least initially, multimodal narrative was inseparable from transmedial reading experiences and environments; so it is not surprising that within a very short time both film and comics began to discover possibilities for complex transmedial storytelling. They began with the first adaptations of comics by film in 1903 and continued through the rise of the serials of the early teens. They told their stories across both newspaper and film and actively invited audiences to participate in shaping the story and, in so doing, to literally become part of the story (see Stamp 102–53).

These first multimodal narrative forms were inherently interactive in ways we often imagine are unique to new media forms of the twenty-first century, being not only inviting but often responding to active participation from readers. In addition, these narratives placed heavy demands on readers to cross the inevitably contentious relationship between the semiotic systems of text and image—to which, in the case of comics, we must also add the cognitive demands inherent to the elliptical form, requiring the reader to actively fill in the missing "action" from one panel to the next.

Of course this last formal feature of comics would prove significant in the different developments of these first modern multimodal narrative forms in the United States. Even as early film was exploring the transmedial possibilities for the future development of the form with the early serial dramas, the film moguls, recently settling in their new base in Hollywood, were largely consolidating their approach to narrative with the codification of what we now refer to as the "classical Hollywood system." As David Bordwell, Janet Staiger, and Kristin Thompson have effectively demonstrated, the style-less style of the classical Hollywood cinema worked to obscure the mechanics of film. A generation of filmgoers accustomed to playing with their own moving-picture devices or turning the crank on a Kinestoscope at the local arcade was, through the disciplines of the classical narrative system, effectively replaced by passive spectators fixed to their privileged "knot-hole in the fence" (Bordwell, Staiger, and Thompson 215). New guidelines handed down from the industry explicitly worked to diminish many of the features of the earliest cinema that defined it as an *explicitly* multimodal form, erasing the sense of the film as a text to be actively engaged, played with, looped, and edited in favor of, as one screenwriting manual from 1919 put it, making the audience "forget the mechanical end of picture production" (Lescarboura 110).

Whereas the early films up through the rise of the serial queen films of the early teens relished in the materiality of film—and in the spaces for interaction opened up by this new media—classical Hollywood would devote itself after 1916 to obscuring the apparatus and creating an illusion of events unfolding before the viewer in "real time." Now, however, the audience no longer viewed the real time of the theatrical performance (where the fact that it *is* a performance is always rendered visible by the proscenium arch) but what the new screenwriting manuals termed the "illusion of reality"—a cinematic "realism" whose preservation came to trump all other considerations in the production of classical Hollywood cinema. New spectatorial disciplines—including the rise of the picture palace in the 1920s with new disciplines of promptness, silence, and darkness—also were enforced to preserve this illusion of reality and the transformation of the cacophony of the "nickelodeon party" into an "evening's entertainment."

Leaving aside the twenty-first-century failed experiment of "motion comics" (which I touch on later), comics never had the possibility of developing the tools and techniques that would allow them (as Hollywood cinema would do after 1920) to efface the gaps inherent in the form or to obscure the mechanics of its own making. Such acts of "suture" have never been available to comics; so as film became more committed to obscuring its status as a multimodal text (a goal aided by the addition of a new mode—synchronous sound—after 1927), comics remained bound to its formal gutters and its status as a marked text, one whose materiality does not magically dissolve in the experience of reading. If we often experience a film or novel as a kind of virtual reality in which we forget that we were, in fact, watching a movie or reading a book, such forgetting is never truly possible when reading a comic.

All of which is to say that when film began pursuing this path—exploiting certain of its affordances the better to discipline consumers and rationalize production—these two multimodal narrative media began to pursue dramatically different directions that would largely define their history during the remainder of the century. In the twenty-first century, however, this pattern has begun to change. Comics and film are seemingly engaging each other as they have not in a century, and as both media are seeking out creative and financial futures in new digital platforms, there is reason to believe that this collaboration is much more than a passing Hollywood trend. Of course, where a century ago comics and film went their separate ways largely as relative equals, this renewed engagement takes place on very unequal terms with regard to corporate structure, audience, and cultural prominence. Therefore, while there are reasons to see the potential for a new investment in multimodal storytelling and the active and unpredictable readership it encourages, there is also good reason to question what it is Hollywood really wants from comics and their readers this time around.

1997–2013: Hollywood and the DVD

In the digital age Hollywood undeniably has been coming to terms with an audience that increasingly seeks out precisely that which the classical system had long worked to make invisible: the mechanics of film and the seams through which active readers might grab hold of a film text and make of it something other than the platonic ideal of the theatrical screening that remains, even today, what most in the industry and the academy have in mind when they refer to a film. Cinema is now in the final stages of its most significant transformation in almost a century, as it enters the final chapter of the digitization of every aspect of its production, distribution, and exhibition. For some time now theatrical ticket sales have accounted for a fraction of the overall revenue generated by "films," which are increasingly consumed on small screens and in digital (DVD and streaming) formats. Nonetheless, both the mainstream media and academic film criticism continue to speak of "film" and "theaters," even as film and theaters have increasingly little to do with the experience or business of cinema.

At least insofar as the press is concerned, the decision to ignore the changing realities of film production and exhibition in favor of an anachronistic fantasy of the theatrical spectator is no simple case of nostalgia or institutional laziness. For the industry and its attendant media, as Edward Jay Epstein has argued, the relentless attention to theatrical box office receipts obscures the byzantine economy of digital cinema for which the theatrical run largely serves as a loss leader. More important for our purposes, this continued privileging of the theatrical audience allows for the preservation of the ideal of the passive, focused spectator in the dark and distracts attention from the far messier realities of narrative film increasingly being consumed on mobile screens and with controls that allow the spectator to rewind, slow, remix, and break the film down frame by frame as never before.

Paradoxically, even as Hollywood continued to trumpet box office records as if they were meaningful data regarding audience preferences or behaviors, the same industry began exploiting what would prove its most important profit center in the last decade: the DVD. And here, in addition to affording a means through which audiences could explore the unprecedented power accorded them by the remote control in the digital age, many DVDs come loaded with paratexts claiming to provide behind-the-scenes insights into the mechanics of the film, including director's commentaries, deleted scenes, bloopers, and "making of" featurettes (see Gray). Studios created official fan websites for fans to discuss and debate aspects of both the film and its viral marketing, held contests, planted "Easter eggs" in DVDs, and even in some cases provided clues to hidden meanings outside the film itself on websites and other digital environments. All of these efforts make film in the first decade of the twenty-first century look similar to film a century ago when the serial dramas of 1912 were playing out in newspapers and magazines, as well as on the screen, and when audiences were invited to contribute solutions to the mysteries and rescues from the perils that awaited the heroines at every turn.

When we couple the new tools film viewers have at their disposal through the DVD player with the explosion of paratexts that seem to push against the very dictates that the industry began enforcing a century ago in its drive to discipline an active and unruly audience and mystify the mode of production itself, it might appear that in the digital age film is finally, belatedly, returning to that fork in the road to meet an increasingly engaged, interactive, and media-savvy audience. Certainly many academic critics greeted the early years of the new century in these terms. Writing in 2000, for example, Catherine Russell envisioned "a construction of spectatorship that challenges the unitary, transcendental spectator position of the classical period," returning us to the possibilities of early cinema when spectatorship was "more fluid, unstable, and heterogeneous" (553). And a few years later, Graeme Harper saw in the DVD "the culmination of thirty years of change in styles of film production and consumption" originating with "the immediate new punk technologies of videotape and CD-ROM" (100).

Today, however, it is harder to find scholars who see in DVD technology and its attendant paratexts the kind of "punk" or "utopian" possibilities for a transformed and liberated spectator that Russell and Harper quite rightly imaged as possible a decade earlier. More typical is the cautious skepticism that Jo T. Smith articulated in a 2008 essay, "DVD Technologies and the Art of Control," in which she argues that "the promise of greater consumer control and interactivity [. . .] contributes to an ever-expanding regime of capture and immersion that paradoxically enables the media producer to assert a firmer control over the audiovisual market" (141). More recently, Jonathan Gray has convincingly argued that far from destabilizing traditional notions of authority and the "master text, [. . .] new media such as webpages, DVDs, and podcasts surround texts with a paratextual veneer of artistry, aura, and authority" that seeks to reclaim the authority and value of the auteur for media texts that never had access to such cultural capital before the advent of digital media (115).

The growing skepticism on the part of film critics and historians about the more utopian possibilities of film in the digital age is fairly easy to understand. A technology that transformed completely the ways in which we teach and study the medium has, in the course of the last decade, become intimately familiar, making it impossible not to attend to the ways in which the new freedoms of the medium came hand in glove with new restrictions and a *loss* of freedoms enjoyed for a generation on VHS—for example, regional codes and encryption and the inability to skip past trailers or warnings from the Federal Bureau of Investigation (FBI) and Interpol about the consequences of violating those codes. Further, the growing sameness (and smallness) of the paratexts over recent years in particular has made more visible how little is truly being given away and how carefully circumscribed are the freedoms active viewers are being invited to explore. What results is a growing sense of malaise on the part of film scholars regarding a technology once perceived as potentially democratizing and liberating.

It is a malaise felt equally, if not more so, by consumers, whose appetite for DVDs has diminished in the last couple of years after an unprecedented saturation during the first decade of the new millennium. Since

2010 DVD sales have dropped precipitously as audiences have moved to streaming and digital downloads for their films, choosing the convenience, portability, and often reduced pricing of renting or "owning" film content through their PC and mobile devices.

Publicly, Hollywood is wringing its hands over this sudden change of fortunes in what was, briefly, its life raft in the face of declining theatrical attendance. But there is good reason to believe that the rapidly declining appetite for DVDs is not a coincidence. One need only compare the kinds of DVD extras, Easter eggs, and other interactive features available on early DVD films such as *Memento* (2000) and *Se7en* (1995) to what is found on the average release in 2012 to see that the studios of their own volition have been quietly and deliberately killing the golden goose. After trading the VHS for the DVD a little more than a decade ago—a trade most willingly made both for increased picture and sound quality and for the improved freedoms to zoom, rewind, remix, and rewatch—audiences are now "voluntarily" trading the DVD for streaming video services. Not only do these services severely limit most of the freedoms and powers of the DVD but also, in the vast majority of cases, they completely eliminate the paratexts—from Easter eggs to deleted scenes—that promised to make the cinematic experience a more interactive one.

I pause at length over this story of the media transformation unfolding as I write in early 2012 because it gets to the heart of a larger issue that should be central to any attempts to theorize the future of multimodal storytelling in a media ecology dominated by a handful of horizontally integrated multinational media conglomerates. Too often in transmedial narratology we are inclined to theorize a future independent of capital and its controls, but the story of the DVD and its imminent demise should have taught us an important lesson: fostering the kinds of futures for texts or their readers we like to imagine might arise organically with the emergence of new technologies is not in Hollywood's long-term interest. Even the word "Hollywood" is an obfuscation—like the fetishization of box office receipts and, now, DVD sales—one that conjures up images of palm-lined streets, bustling bungalows, and movie sets in Los Angeles. Hollywood in the twenty-first century, of course, is Viacom (Paramount), TimeWarner (Warner Bros.), News Corp. (20th Century Fox), Disney (Disney, Pixar), and GE (Universal). The "Big Five" major studios of classical Hollywood are still there, but each is now one entity in a larger multinational corporation that also owns cable networks, newspapers, publishing houses, Internet service providers, sports teams, and theme parks. The vertical integration of the classical Hollywood system, whereby the five major studios controlled all aspects of production, distribution, and exhibition, has been replaced by the horizontal integration of the twenty-first-century media conglomerates. Now the "Big Six" (which includes CBS, the only one without major film holdings) have an almost monopolistic control (roughly 90 percent by most calculations) over the commercial content that is supplied to our increasingly mobile screens (Epstein, *Big Picture* 82; Campbell, Martin, and Fabos 213). The culture of convergence with all of its utopian possibilities is ultimately inseparable from the economics of transmedial corporate integration. Any fantasies we might have about the possibilities of multimodal storytelling in the twenty-first century must always be attenuated by the realities of transmedial corporations that are determined to shape storytelling environments to serve their horizontal monopolies.

Film + Comics in the Twenty-First Century: A Spectacular Reunion

Returning to the recent re-convergence of comics and film since 1997 and the birth of digital cinema only, the most starry-eyed observers still believe that cinema as we know it is over, that Hollywood producers will now be sharing power with an increasingly savvy and engaged audience, that new voices outside of the Big Six will gain meaningful access to the means of production and distribution, or, to put it more bluntly, that digital cinema will increase in quality or the diversity of the films being commercially distributed. Remarkably little, however, has changed. The vast majority of Hollywood productions are still targeting the same young adult audience with safe, modular products designed primarily to optimize the possibilities for merchandizing, franchising, and synergizing across the media company's television networks, publishing houses, and theme parks. As we have seen, the explosion of transmedial storytelling is intimately related to the horizontal monopolies that seek to maximize the profitability of a "property" by exploiting it via multiple media producers within the corporation.

Of course, if the majority of the ways in which the digital revolution has impacted filmmaking have been in areas that remain largely invisible to audiences (and increasingly so as digital cameras catch up with the quality of the best traditional equipment), one major exception to such claims comes in the area loosely defined as "special" or "visual effects." After all, one of the most important reasons why comics and "live-action" film went in separate directions a century ago was because comics, in addition to engaging an active and unpredictable reader, increasingly came to feature unruly and plastic bodies in dynamic flights of fancy that were impossible to duplicate on film in 1910 or even 1980. While animation developed as a viable narrative form in its own right after 1910 (and it is telling that the cartoonist Winsor McCay served as a pioneer in the new field of animation as well), photographic film began to focus more strenuously on cinematic "realism," leaving to comics and cartoons what Scott Bukatman has recently termed the "poetics of slumberland" (*Poetics*).

In the twenty-first century this long-standing distinction between animation and live-action cinema has increasingly eroded. Digital compositing allows animation and photography to blend seamlessly in a digital environment, such that in both special effects–dependent films (such as *Transformers*) and "indie" films (such as *A Scanner Darkly*) the distinction between "live action" and "animation" often feels as anachronistic as the obsession with "box office." Similar technologies allow actors' bodies to be digitally augmented, transformed, or disguised behind layers of digital animation (*Sin City*, *300*); and advanced motion-capture technology now complicates the category of "actor" itself, as in the digital performances of Andy Serkis in the *Lord of the Rings* trilogy or *Rise of the Planet of the Apes*.

It is not a coincidence that several of the films I have mentioned are based on comics. The digital environment that makes it possible for photographic and animated elements seamlessly to share the frame has brought Hollywood back to the plastic, fantastic possibilities of the comic book body that initially proved impossible to imitate with twentieth-century cinematic technologies. As Bukatman points out, superhero comics were the ideal subject matter for the new digital effects: "The cinematic superhero is a function of special effects, effects of programming[. . .]. [T]he terrain of special effects is a human body that will become uncontainable, a body that not only expresses emotion and physical power (not to mention emotion and physical *trauma*), but also the more-human-than-human capabilities of digital imaging" ("Secret Identity

Politics" 115, original emphasis). Like Shilo T. McClean and Angela Ndalianis, Bukatman is challenging the critical assumption that special effects solely serve to foreground the wonders of the cinematic technology and not any narrative function. But as his previous point suggests, in the end the turn of Hollywood to the comic book superhero has less to do with inherent interest in comics or their readers than in the superhero as the ideal vehicle to display the industrial and technical powers of twenty-first-century digital effects. There is no reason to reinvent the wheel, when the "studio" already owns the superhero.

After all, as we consider the future for comics in the digital age, we must remember that the two major comic book companies in the United States are now wholly owned subsidiaries of two of the Big Six: Marvel Comics is owned by Disney, DC by TimeWarner. And these comic book companies, which have long served as the Big Two within "mainstream comics," are now relatively minor entities within larger media corporations. Making the relationship between comics and film still more unequal, the readership of comics is shrinking markedly in the twenty-first century even as comics-related stories and characters are visible on screen as never before. A best-selling comic book today might hope to sell 100,000 issues, while a movie such as *Spider-Man* (2002) sold more than five million tickets in Germany alone. Despite the flattering attentions bestowed on once-marginal events such as the annual Comic-Con in San Diego, Hollywood is not counting on comic book readers. Instead, Hollywood now understands that comic book readers' *ways* of reading—ways of reading that the film industry had worked to foreclose a century ago—are increasingly vital to multimodal storytelling in the twenty-first century and to Hollywood's economic vitality in a horizontally integrated transmedial corporate environment. Comic book readers had been exploring the pleasures of multimodal serial storytelling for generations, following their favorite characters and narratives across installments, media, and industries. If Hollywood could translate those investments from a relatively small community of active comic book readers to a mass audience, then its success in the twenty-first century was guaranteed. So what better place to start, especially now that movies can finally convincingly make superheroes fly, transform, hurl cars, and catch airplanes?

Yet in 2012, we can confidently say that Hollywood's love affair with Comic-Con's heavily invested and critically engaged fans is cooling fast.

At the convention in 2011, Big Hollywood, which had dominated the convention floor and the largest ballrooms for most of the previous decade, was a greatly diminished presence (Barnes and Cieply). This shift occurred not because comics-related movies are no longer part of the studios' long-term plans; in fact, 2013–14 will likely see the largest number of comics-related films yet. Instead, what the declining interest in comic book readers suggests is that, as with the imminent demise of the DVD, Hollywood's period of bending knee to the active reader (whether film geek or comic geek) is coming to an end. The comic book communities and reading practices that appeared so promising a laboratory for big media to learn about the appetites and demands of twenty-first-century readers now increasingly seem an unnecessary expense as new and more tightly controlled networks of digital distribution and exhibition begin to take shape. If the comic book readers in 2000 represented the ideal transmedial consumers that the horizontally integrated conglomerates desperately desire (inclined to seek out collectibles, merchandizing, and extensions of the narrative world across various media), then their reading *practices* (as with those encouraged by the first wave of DVDs) have proved precisely what Hollywood does *not* wish to encourage. In the very short time since I wrote the conclusion for *Projections* (in 2011), where I described an ongoing interest by Hollywood in the kind of multimodal reading practices that comics have long encouraged, Hollywood has apparently begun to move on.

As Frederic Wertham pointed out with considerable anxiety in 1954, comic book readers are *deliberate and even obsessive* readers, despite the assumption on the part of many that comics are ephemeral works that are quickly consumed and just as easily discarded. For Wertham, of course, this obsessiveness was a very real cause for concern. He saw comics and the reading practices they encouraged—rereading and hoarding treasured comics, plus the medium's demand for the reader to fill in the action between the panels—as inherently corrupting, leading the reader away from healthy, orderly reading practices. Thus, Wertham's comic book readers in *Seduction of the Innocent* are "inveterate" (26, 54, 87), "rabid" (8), "experienced" (81)—and in profound danger.

While media history has largely expunged Wertham from its pages for his association with the anti-comics hysteria that swept through the United States in the late 1940s and early 1950s, in many ways he deserves more respect than we have traditionally accorded him—if only for being among the first to recognize how very serious and engaging was the work of comics reading. In his last published book, almost two decades after *Seduction*, Wertham turned his attention to *fanzines*, or amateur publications by active and engaged readers of comics and science fiction. And here his assessment was almost entirely positive, acknowledging, as he did not in his earlier work, the ways in which the active, "rabid" reading practices that such multimodal forms as comic books and science fiction pulps encouraged might lead to other outcomes than those that he had feared most in *Seduction*.

The outcome Wertham celebrated in *The World of Fanzines* was one in which readers created their own networks and their own publications while repurposing the materials of mass culture that he, as well as his fellow German expatriate Theodor Adorno, had long regarded with deep suspicion. The fanzines, Wertham noted admiringly in 1973, "function outside the market and outside the profit motive. Publishing them is not a business but an avocation" (74). The thin line between the "avocation" he celebrated in one book and the "extreme avidity" (*Seduction* 50) he worried over in the other notwithstanding, clearly Wertham recognized early on that there was something unique about comics reading and the investments it generated, for better and for worse. And these investments did not work in neat consort with the efficiencies and demands of the consumer marketplace. Comic book readers were "slow" readers and compulsive rereaders, and the form had from its earliest days encouraged active agents who were inclined to become producers themselves.

DVDs and the "cinema of complexity" that was produced to engage active film readers eager for a more participatory, interactive, and multimodal storyworld exploration emerged simultaneously with Hollywood's newfound interest in readers of comics (and comics properties). The ultimate convergence of DVD and comics storytelling in cinema might be epitomized by the 2009 adaptation of Alan Moore and Dave Gibbon's 1986 comic *Watchmen*. Directed by Zach Snyder with art design by Alex McDowell (one of the most influential digital designers of the present generation), the film successfully adapted what was long thought to be an unadaptable story due to the previously unrealizable effects required to tell the complex tale. In the theaters, the film was only moderately successful in terms of box office, but Snyder and his collaborators clearly saw the DVD viewer as their intended audience. As McDowell said, "I think if this film works it will be because you have to see it ten times to really get all of that layering" ("Alex McDowell" n. pag.). Several DVD editions offered to the viewer different archives through which to engage in this rigorous archeology, remote control in hand. The feature film on the five-disc *The Ultimate Cut* alone runs more than three and a half hours. Watched ten times, as McDowell insisted that it was meant to be if all the clues and details were to be uncovered, and for the price of one (admittedly pricey) DVD purchase, fans had enough material to keep them occupied for days or weeks (see Gardner 188–89).

However, *Watchmen* and its *Ultimate Cut* DVD will likely serve as objects of film history to which we turn to mark the end of Hollywood's flirtation with comic book readers and their reading practices. After all, if the DVD of *Memento* invited viewers to rewatch the film in "chronological order" and the original website supporting the film offered dossiers and files that promised new insights into the film's unanswered questions, in the end all that the studios would have accomplished was to encourage an engaged, "avid" reader to rewatch the film compulsively in search of clues or Easter eggs they might have missed the first time. In educating audiences in how to be close and engaged readers and rereaders of film texts—how to be, that is, like *comics* readers—Hollywood realized that instead of golden eggs, this goose was laying only endless Easter eggs that led readers to find new pleasures in rewatching the DVD they had already purchased. The "cinema of complexity" requires a spectator with skills at breaking down films frame by frame, and to acquire these skills takes discipline and time—time that might otherwise be spent watching (and buying) new films.

These lessons aren't new. But for a little more than a decade, visions of synergy made the new horizontally integrated media monopolies forget the lessons their vertically integrated predecessors learned in the early years of the industry. Thus the DVD gives way to streaming, and Hollywood no longer goes courting the approval and insights of comic book readers at Comic-Con. After all, the industry never needed the readers, and now it seems determined to leave those reading practices in the margins of the cultural and academic ghettoes, where close reading, rereading, and avid reading are valued and rewarded.

Comics in the Digital Age

Finally we turn to the fate of comics as they follow film and other media forms across the digital rubicon. In many ways comics have remained the narrative medium most resistant to digitization, and in 2013 it remains unclear what form comics will take on our screens in the years to come even as other media are developing complex and relatively stable digital formats and economies. There are, of course, many reasons for this resistance to digital translation. First, comics are always a marked and opaque text in a way that, for example, a novel or a classical Hollywood film is not; the comic page always bears the evidence of the physical labor of what Philippe Marion calls the "graphiateur" on the page (Baetens 149). Further, being a profoundly elliptical form whose parts never hide the spaces and gaps in between, comics are also, as Hillary Chute puts it, a profoundly "site specific" narrative form in a way very different from novels and films (10).

And so we have something of a paradox: the form that is best positioned to teach us how to explore the multimodal narratives of the twenty-first century is also the most resistant to the media convergence within which twenty-first-century storytelling will take place. Moreover, the vast majority of attempts to wrestle with the problem have thus far assumed the problem lies with comics and that the solution, therefore, is to make comics more like film or video games.

That the Hollywood corporations who own the most popular comic book properties have sponsored many of these wrong steps is not surprising. For example, in the buildup to the release of the *Watchman* movie, in 2008 Warner Bros. released a "motion comics" version of the original comic series, and Marvel Entertainment has developed a whole motion comics department, primarily dedicated to tie-ins to its motion picture productions. The idea behind *motion comics* is to set into movement the still figures, to provide voices, and to fill in the action between the frames. What results, inevitably, looks highly similar to early animation and very little like comics.

The other early model for the translation of comics into digital formats also came from Marvel and has since been adopted by other digital platforms with an eye toward making the comics translate to the smaller screens of iPhones, PlayStation®Portables (PSPs), and netbooks—that is, a "guided view" in which the reading program essentially breaks down the comics page into a series of sequential slides, directing the viewer's eye in precisely the disciplined way that the traditional comic page by its nature resists. Stripped of our Dr. Manhattan–like power to see past, present, and future in a single glance, we are also denied our ability to let the eye move across panels—back and forth in time—and to focus on the layout of the two-page spread, the page unit, and the single panel according to our own choosing.

In both of these examples, the shift to digital platforms reduces rather than augments the readers' agency and avenues for interaction with the form. Even leaving aside issues of digital rights management and the lack of cross-platform mobility in all of the early commercial digital comics experiments, there is already reason enough to be wary of the fate of comics in an age of digital convergence. Henry Jenkins's ideal of "convergence culture" envisions "a move from medium-specific content toward content that flows across multiple media channels, toward the increased interdependence of communications systems, toward multiple ways of accessing content, and toward ever more complex relationships between top-down corporate media and bottom-up participatory culture" (243). But as we have seen when the media converging are controlled by the Big Six, there is also the very real likelihood that old corporate structures will continue to dictate terms to those at the "bottom" who might have the best possibility of exploiting the affordances of digital media.

That comics have always remained a gutter form, both formally and culturally, arguably makes them best suited to help map out the narrative possibilities for the new century. But it will require a fairly dramatic change in attitude from their creators, who have long been wedded to the printed page and, especially in the last two generations, to the codex—the graphic novel.

Without more creators and readers exploring the ways in which new media convergence can expand rather than reduce the multimodal potentialities for comics, the example of comics provides a cautionary tale to more utopian visions of the future of new media convergence. Media matter, but so does the institutional history of those media. If we see multimodality everywhere, we miss how rare and important the unique century-long experimentation with multimodal narrative by comic book creators and readers truly is. And if we assume new media convergence is necessarily a force for the emancipation of narrative and its readers, we have only to look to the story of film and comics in the early years of new media convergence to see good reason for a more skeptical and cautious approach.

Works Cited

"Alex McDowell Talks *Watchmen*." *WatchmenComicMovie.Com*. February 19, 2009. Web. May 26, 2012.

Baetens, Jan. "Revealing Traces: A New Theory of Graphic Enunciation." *The Language of Comics: Word and Image*. Ed. Robin Varnum and Christina T. Gibbons. Jackson: University Press of Mississippi, 2001. 145–55. Print.

Barnes, Brooks, and Michael Cieply. "Movie Studios Reassess Comic-Con." *New York Times* June 12, 2011. Print.

Bordwell, David, Janet Staiger, and Kristin Thompson. *The Classical Hollywood Cinema: Film Style & Mode of Production to 1960*. New York: Columbia University Press, 1985. Print.

Bukatman, Scott. *The Poetics of Slumberland: Animated Spirits and the Animating Spirit*. Berkeley: University of California Press, 2012. Print.

———. "Secret Identity Politics." *The Contemporary Comic Book Superhero*. Ed. Angela Ndalianis. New York: Routledge, 2009. 109–25. Print.

Campbell, Richard, Christopher R. Martin, and Bettina Fabos. *Media and Culture: An Introduction to Mass Communication*. Boston: Bedford/St. Martin's, 2012. Print.

Chute, Hillary L. *Graphic Women: Life Narrative and Contemporary Comics*. New York: Columbia University Press, 2010. Print.

Epstein, Edward Jay. *The Big Picture: Money and Power in Hollywood*. New York: Random House, 2006. Print.

———. *The Hollywood Economist 2.0: The Hidden Financial Reality behind the Movies*. New York: Melville House, 2012. Print.

Gardner, Jared. *Projections: Comics and the History of 21st-Century Storytelling*. Palo Alto CA: Stanford University Press, 2012. Print.

Gray, Jonathan Alan. *Show Sold Separately: Promos, Spoilers, and Other Media Paratexts*. New York: New York University Press, 2010. Print.

Grishakova, Marina, and Marie-Laure Ryan. Editors' Preface. *Intermediality and Storytelling*. Ed. Marina Grishakova and Marie-Laure Ryan. Berlin: De Gruyter, 2010. 1–7. Print.

Hallet, Wolfgang. "The Multimodal Novel: The Integration of Modes and Media in Novelistic Narration." *Narratology in the Age of Cross-Disciplinary Narrative Research*. Ed. Sandra Heinen and Roy Sommer. Berlin: De Gruyter, 2009. 129–53. Print.

Harper, Graeme. "DVD and the New Cinema of Complexity." *New Punk Cinema.* Ed. Nicholas Rombes. Edinburgh: Edinburgh University Press, 2005. 89–101. Print.

Jenkins, Henry. *Convergence Culture: Where Old and New Media Collide.* New York: New York University Press, 2006. Print.

Lescarboura, Austin Celestin. *Behind the Motion-Picture Screen.* New York: Scientific American, 1919. Print.

McClean, Shilo T. *Digital Storytelling: The Narrative Power of Visual Effects in Film.* Cambridge MA: MIT Press, 2008. Print.

Ndalianis, Angela. *Neo-Baroque Aesthetics and Contemporary Entertainment.* Cambridge MA: MIT Press, 2004. Print.

Page, Ruth. Introduction. *New Perspectives on Narrative and Multimodality.* Ed. Ruth Page. New York: Routledge, 2010. 1–13. Print.

Rise of the Planet of the Apes. Dir. Rupert Wyatt. 20th Century Fox, 2011. Film.

Russell, Catherine. "Parallax Historiography: The Flâneuse as Cyberfeminist." *A Feminist Reader in Early Cinema.* Ed. Jennifer M. Bean and Diane Negra. Durham NC: Duke University Press, 2002. 552–70. Print.

A Scanner Darkly. Dir. Richard Linklater. Warner Bros., 2006. Film.

Smith, Jo T. "DVD Technologies and the Art of Control." *Film and Television after DVD.* Ed. James Bennett and Tom Brown. New York: Routledge, 2008. 129–48. Print.

Stamp, Shelley. *Movie-Struck Girls: Women and Motion Picture Culture after the Nickelodeon.* Princeton NJ: Princeton University Press, 2000. Print.

300. Dir. Zach Snyder. Warner Bros., 2007. Film.

Transformers. Dir. Michael Bay. DreamWorks SKG, 2007. Film.

Watchmen. Dir. Zach Snyder. Warner Bros., 2009. Film.

Wertham, Frederic. *Seduction of the Innocent.* New York: Rinehart, 1954. Print.

———. *The World of Fanzines: A Special Form of Communication.* Carbondale: Southern Illinois University Press, 1973. Print.

9 Tell It Like a Game

Scott Pilgrim *and Performative Media Rivalry*

JEFF THOSS

Today's media landscape, perhaps more than any past one, is marked by a fierce rivalry among media. In their classic study *Remediation: Understanding New Media*, Jay David Bolter and Richard Grusin argue that "[o]ur culture conceives of each medium or constellation of media as it responds to, redeploys, competes with, and reforms other media" (55). For them, changes to the media landscape are the result of an ongoing process of media refashioning and revising—in short, remediating one another. Coming from a different angle, Uta Degner and Norbert Christian Wolf observe that the current rise of intermedial artistic practices does not reflect a culture of media equality but is rather a "sign of an accelerated dynamics of competition" (*Indiz für eine akzelerierte Konkurrenzdynamik*; 11).[1] The title of their book, *Der neue Wettstreit der Künste: Legitimation und Dominanz im Zeichen der Intermedialität*, hence proclaims a "new *paragone*," one that takes place "under the banner of intermediality." This chapter, too, explores the relationship between remediation or intermediality and media rivalry.[2] My case study, Edgar Wright's screen adaptation of Bryan Lee O'Malley's *Scott Pilgrim* comic books, promises ample material in this regard. Adaptations from one narrative medium to another arguably constitute a privileged site of competition, seeing that different media are charged with telling the same story and representing the same storyworld. Even though, as Linda Hutcheon remarks, our culture harbors a disdain for adaptations, deeming them inferior because they are derivative (2–4), no adaptation aims at inferiority; rather, any adaptation vies with the work it adapts, tacitly claiming that it is at least equal if not superior to its source material. Yet in addition to adaptation, a further dimension to media rivalry enters the equation in the case of *Scott Pilgrim*: O'Malley's comic book contains numerous references to video games, and these mentions are carried over—and, as we shall see, amplified—in the film. This crossover is where a type of media rivalry, or at least a perspective on media rivalry, emerges that has hitherto been neglected in media studies.

One might ask, what motivates media to compete with other media? For Bolter and Grusin, remediation has a double logic as media tend toward both *immediacy* (eradicating the signs of mediation) and *hypermediacy* (foregrounding the signs of mediation) in their attempts to appropriate each other's techniques and forms, to improve upon them, and to outdo one another. However, the pole of immediacy is clearly preferred: remediation is acted out "in the name of transparency" (49), while hypermediacy is relegated to "an awareness of mediation whose repression almost guarantee[s] its repeated return" (37). The two scholars here seem to allude to a way of thinking about media that is deeply embedded in Western culture: where media compete, they primarily do so based on their ability to efface themselves and purely serve that which they represent. One only needs to think of the Renaissance's *paragone*, in which painters pointed to the greater illusionistic quality of their art while sculptors highlighted the haptic and three-dimensional property of theirs, or Gotthold Ephraim Lessing's strict division of verbal and visual art in his treatise "Laokoon." According to Lessing, *literature* is a temporal art form suited to the representation of actions, while *painting* and *sculpture* are spatial art forms suited to the representation of objects (it being understood that the poet who tries to represent objects will always fall short of the painter). In a similar vein, albeit on a less theoretical note, the notorious discussions of whether particular novels are better than their film adaptations frequently involve generalized assertions about medial adequacy—for instance, that narrative fiction is more apt to relate characters' thoughts than film, which must resort to the "unfilmic" technique of voice-over for this purpose. In all these cases media are evaluated according to their mimetic potential, and media rivalry hence takes place in the name of mimesis.

Media rivalry as it is present between the comic book and film versions of *Scott Pilgrim* does not fit into this pattern. In order to characterize it, I use the distinction between mimesis and performance as it has notably been elaborated by Wolfgang Iser. For Iser, representation, while understood as mimesis, always already contains a performative (that is, productive) element, but a "blank" remains for as long as what is represented is considered to exist independently of the representation or, in other words, for as long as the representation is thought of purely in terms of an imitation of something that is already there (284). However, the more the actual process of mimesis comes under scrutiny, the more questionable it becomes as to whether one is really dealing with the "imitation of an object" and not with "producing the illusion of an object" (287). As the focus shifts from the former to the latter, representation reveals its performative nature. An example is found in Andreas Mahler's discussion of Parnassianism and its practice of *transposition d'art*, or "transposition into another medium." In Parnassian poems about art objects, Mahler states, mimesis turns into performance in the course of being "raised to a higher power" (*potenziert*; 36). Literature imitates sculpture or painting not to achieve a "better *effet de réel*" (*besseren effet de réel*) but to achieve a "media-conscious production of art out of art" (*medienbewusste Produktion von Kunst aus Kunst*; 37). Art no longer revolves around "the representation of something (apparently) extant" (*die Repräsentation von [vermeintlich] Existentem*) but around a "presentation that creates this 'extant something' in the first place" (*eine dieses 'Existente' allererst erschaffende Präsentation*; 37). This fact opens up the possibility for a different media rivalry, one where, unlike in the cases described in the previous paragraph, media do not dispute which one of them can best imitate a given object and efface itself in the process of doing so; instead, they contest which one can best produce the illusion of an object and in the process draw attention to its creative processes. In other words, such a performative media rivalry centers on discursive acts of presentation rather than the quality of the representation. In the case of *Scott Pilgrim*, the comic book and film vie with one another not over which medium can tell the story best (render the storyworld in a more detailed, immersive, and plausible fashion) but over which medium can best tell it like a video game. The two media do not claim to be the more adequate, transparent medium for the particular story at hand, but both try to put forward a more opaque, more "inadequate" use of their respective medium in their attempts to create the illusion and simulate the presence of a third medium. In the following paragraphs, I trace this rivalry between comics and film via video games first on the level of story and then on the level of discourse.

Scott Pilgrim the comic book was published in six volumes between 2004 and 2010. It contains a storyworld that could initially be identified as realistic. The setting is contemporary Toronto, and the characters are a group of friends in their early twenties, foremost among them slacker Scott Pilgrim. Much of the narrative's beginning focuses on Scott's relationship with other people and his rock band. Up to this point, *Scott Pilgrim* could pass for a typical slice-of-life indie comic book in the tradition of Daniel Clowes's *Ghost World* (1993–97) or Peter Bagge's *Hate* (1990–98). Yet the narrative shifts with the introduction of Scott's new love interest Ramona Flowers. As Scott soon finds out, he must defeat Ramona's seven evil ex-boyfriends one by one to win her heart. From that moment, the story is propelled forward by Scott's battles against the evil exes, some of whom are surrounded by henchmen and each of whom he faces in hand-to-hand combat. The plot here resembles, and arguably draws upon, that of two video game genres—the beat-'em-up game (best exemplified through the *Double Dragon* or *Final Fight* series) and the fighting game (best exemplified through the *Street Fighter* or *Mortal Kombat* series). In the *beat-'em-up genre*, player characters fight against waves of enemies, who are typically gang members and their leaders, in so-called boss battles. Common objectives include the rescue of a kidnapped girlfriend. In the *fighting game*, player characters confront a series of opponents one-on-one in elaborate melee combat. If it were only for this semblance in their overall structure, one could doubt whether the comic book really simulates video games here and does not rather follow an archetypal narrative pattern—a hero overcomes a series of obstacles to win his beloved's heart—that is not bound to any particular medium. However, in the context of the numerous other elements that O'Malley's comic appropriates from video games, the beat-'em-up and fighting game plot structure is a first indication that *Scott Pilgrim*'s storyworld is a video game storyworld. Using Irina Rajewsky's model of intermedial relations, we could say that the medium of comics is "contaminated" (*kontaminiert*) by that of video games here and that *Scott Pilgrim*'s narrative "continually constitutes itself [. . .] in relation to [a different medial] system" (*konstituiert sich [. . .] durchgehend in Relation zu* [*einem fremdmedialen*] *Bezugssystem*; *Intermedialität* 161–62). When reading the comic book, readers are persistently made aware of its video game characteristics and, in a way, receive a second medium within the first one; yet, as

Fig. 9.1. Scott collects an extra life that pops up in the storyworld (from *Scott Pilgrim & the Infinite Sadness*).

is always the case with such intermedial references, it exists as "a conceptual rather than physical presence" (Wolf 254).[3]

If we turn from the macro level to the micro level of the narrative, we discover a myriad of storyworld details "borrowed" from video games that link O'Malley's book to this medium in general and the genres of beat-'em-up and fighting games in particular. As in those games, characters in *Scott Pilgrim* perform special moves or combos and have designated "weak points" (to use the appropriate jargon). Whenever Scott defeats one of his foes, they drop coins or other video game items. Of particular note is the "1-up" (the extra life) that the protagonist picks up in the course of his adventure (see figure 9.1). In the concluding battle against the last evil ex-boyfriend, Scott is killed, but with the 1-up he has collected, he is revived and able to continue the fight. Purest video game logic is at work here, just as it is when the hero discovers a "save point" in the storyworld earlier on and decides to save his progress before entering the next fight. Similar to a character in a role-playing game, Scott also gains "experience" points (EXP) and once in a while moves up a level. Through the use of such video game conventions and tropes, the game-like nature of the comic book's storyworld is exhibited and underlined time and again. Although *Scott Pilgrim* contains numerous references to specific—and occasionally obscure—titles, many of the video game references possess a generic quality or make use of well-known clichés so that these intermedial references should be obvious to anyone with even a passing knowledge of games. Although we conventionally conceive of storyworlds as being divorced from media—that is, as a represented that exists independently of the representation—the video game references turn *Scott Pilgrim*'s storyworld into a medially marked one. Elements such as extra lives and save points stand out in the storyworld because they typically do not appear and probably also do not make much sense in comic books or, for that matter, any media other than games. As with the case of the beat-'em-up and fighting game narrative pattern, these details make readers aware of their origin in a different medium and contaminate the comic book storyworld.

As with the Parnassian *transpositions d'art*, in imitating video games the comic is calling attention to and exhibiting its own creative means rather than striving for a more perfect mimesis. Each video game reference foregrounds the "intermedial gap" (Rajewsky, *Intermedialität* 70) between comics and video games and thus the media themselves, distracting from a straightforward immersion into the storyworld rather than enhancing it. For Sean Ahern, cartoonist O'Malley "use[s] video game culture as a way to tell a story of romance and self-realization" (n. pag.), yet I would argue that it is the other way around: the relatively trite and uninspired story of romance and self-realization is used as a mere foil for O'Malley to demonstrate his arguably novel and ingenious skills in impersonating games. *Scott Pilgrim* turns its storyworld into a video game storyworld in order to show how comics can performatively simulate the presence of a different medium.

On the surface, *Scott Pilgrim* the film (officially titled *Scott Pilgrim vs. the World*), whose release in 2010 coincided with that of the comic's final volume, does what nearly every screen adaptation does with its source material: it condenses it. O'Malley's comic contains numerous flashbacks, side plots, and secondary characters, but Edgar Wright's film all but does away with them. What it retains and almost exclusively focuses on are Scott's battles against the evil exes. This streamlining of the story, however, cannot simply be explained by the fact that a six-volume comic book is transformed into a two-hour film. Even more so than the book, the film is about a series of fights, which intensify the video game quality of the narrative. Neither the beat-'em-up nor the fighting game is a story-driven genre; at best, the battles might be bookended by cut-scenes containing bits of dialogue or narration, with whatever minimal plot is there serving as but a frame for the game's actual raison d'être, the fights. The film tightens up the story and becomes more similar to this type of game, thus outdoing the comic book.

This process is where performative media rivalry comes into play, for the condensation is obviously not made at the service of the storyworld; on the contrary, there is considerably less of it in the film. If readers are looking for a richer, more lifelike storyworld where characters have some psychological depth and human interactions are portrayed in a somewhat realistic fashion, then they are better served by the comic book. In other words, if one evaluates the screen adaptation from a mimetic point of view, its cuts to the narrative only serve to devaluate its appeal. It is only when one adopts a performative perspective and accepts that what the film tries to do is to present a better simulation of video games that the decision to reduce the comic book's slice-of-life passages to a minimum makes sense. The strategy of condensing the narrative and focusing on the battles is, then, not a necessary by-product of transposing a narrative from one medium into another but a means of heightening the illusion that we are dealing with a different medium altogether.

Attempts on behalf of *Scott Pilgrim* the film to surpass the game-like quality of *Scott Pilgrim* the comic book can also be found on what I previously called the micro level of the storyworld. On the whole, Wright includes most of the elements present in the source material, such as the video game items and the fighting mechanics. While he drops some storyworld details—the save point, for instance—he adds others, such as making the characters flash when they are hurt. The extra life Scott collects is of note, though, since it is put to a rather different use in the film. In the book, Scott is immediately brought back to life after using the 1-up and continues the final battle where he was interrupted. In the film, however, the 1-up takes Scott back to an earlier point and allows him to relive the last part of the story and to correct his previous mistakes. This different use of the 1-up can be viewed as a further claim on the film's behalf to provide a better simulation of video games and perfectly illustrates how the film emulates—*emulation* in its double sense of both imitating and improving—the comic book. O'Malley maintains a linear narrative that is medially inconspicuous and, if one ignores experimental cases, perhaps also medium appropriate. Wright's film, meanwhile, embraces the ergodic nature (to use Espen Aarseth's term) of games and tries to incorporate the trial-and-error procedure and the act of replaying that are ubiquitous in this medium. The 1-up is turned from an object that merely allows two aspects of video games—that is, the existence of collectible items and the ability of the player character to be revived and continue the game—to contaminate the storyworld into an object that transfers additional video game characteristics, such as the ability to replay (parts of) the game, to the storyworld. Thus it has a much more profound effect on the storyworld, effectively creating a completely new section of the story.

Both the comic book and the film version of *Scott Pilgrim* manage to weave a great many video game references into their respective plot structures and storyworlds. However, as has already been hinted at, the story may not actually be *Scott Pilgrim*'s main point of interest but serves rather as a pretext for the comic and the film to display their performative prowess in simulating games. To better characterize this state of affairs, I draw upon Rainer Warning's theory of comedy. For Warning, this genre contains a *syntagmatic axis* on which the plot is located and a *paradigmatic axis* on which the various comic situations are located. Comedies privilege the paradigmatic over the syntagmatic axis insofar as the plot (the Fryean move from order to disorder and back) is secondary and is merely an "enabling structure" (*Ermöglichungsstruktur*; 291) that allows for comic situations to occur. Simply put, we do not see or read comedies because we are interested in the development and outcome of the story; instead, we are interested in the repeated staging of comic situations. In the case of *Scott Pilgrim*, the story could also be described as just an enabling structure for something else, albeit for intermedial references instead of comic situations. *Scott Pilgrim*'s syntagmatic axis of its romantic-comedy plot—boy meets girl, boy encounters obstacles, boy overcomes obstacles, boy gets girl—can hardly be deemed the reason of its success. Yet it is a perfect foil for the exploitation of video game references on the paradigmatic axis, where the performative rivalry between book and film, then, also takes place. Because the course of the narrative is already clear and perhaps even irrelevant, the creators and the audience can focus their attention on the repeated simulation of games and on which medium can do it better. This point becomes even more evident when we turn our attention from the level of story to the level of discourse. After all, the more common way to simulate another medium is not content based but consists in trying to borrow its formal features, or its means of representation and narration that set it apart from other media, and results in what Andreas Böhn terms "intermedial quotations of forms" (*intermediale Formzitat*[*e*]; 7).

In terms of the overall presentation of the narrative, the comic book's six volumes easily correspond to six video game levels, at the end of which player characters typically engage in a boss battle. In each of the volumes 1 through 5, Scott faces one of the evil exes; in volume 6, he faces two. While the film is not divided into distinct units, it nevertheless achieves a similar effect of presenting itself as a game by displaying the words "Level 7" across the screen, in a clear visual nod to the (head-up) displays of video games, when Scott is on his way to meet the final evil ex-boyfriend. As a matter of fact, text and graphic displays styled after games abound in both the comic book and film version of *Scott Pilgrim*. Thus Bryan Lee O'Malley uses a heavily pixelated font reminiscent of the ones used on 8-bit game systems such as the Nintendo Entertainment System (NES) or Sega Master System for numerous captions. Since the video game genres that *Scott Pilgrim*'s storyworld is modeled on are mostly associated with the 8-bit and 16-bit eras—that is, roughly the mid-1980s to the mid-1990s—it follows that the comic book also adopts the look of this period. Text and graphic displays range from relatively inconspicuous indications of time and place in which only the distinctive font points to a different medium to game-specific displays when Scott gains experience points—"+500 EXP" (vol. 4, 62)—or levels up: "Level up!

Guts +2, Hearts + 3, Smarts +1, Will +1. Scott earned the Power of Love" (vol. 4, 180–81). The books also use "Game Over" and "Continue?" displays (vol. 5, 152, 167) and a variety of status bars, most notably a "pee bar" that depletes when Scott visits the bathroom (vol. 4, 79; see figure 9.2), just as health bars do in fighting games when characters are wounded. Anyone who has ever played an (older) video game—and certainly members of *Scott Pilgrim*'s target audience have—likely has encountered such elements, though, again, they possess such a highly generic and clichéd quality that their medial origin should be immediately recognizable. As with the extra life or coins appearing in its storyworld, the comic book here is trying to pass itself off as a video game.

Of course, one could read mimetically the displays, which are obviously not part of the storyworld, and argue that the level-up display exists to trace character development or that the "Game Over" and "Continue?" displays and status bars exist to metaphorically comment upon or reflect the internal state of a character. Yet why would the comic book have recourse to another medium and not use its own medium's affordances in that case? Is *Scott Pilgrim* the tale of someone who has played too many games and as a result experiences life as a game, hence prompting this unusual manner of presentation? It certainly does not read as though it were this kind of narrative, with the protagonist having little psychological depth and there being no indication that he is in some way delusional. Rather than attempt to look through these discursive elements and search for some mimetic (re)solution, readers are perhaps asked to look at them, stay on the medial surface, and rejoice in the ways that the comic book is producing the illusion of a different medium for them.

Edgar Wright's film emulates—once again, in both senses of the word—the discursive intermedial references (or intermedial quotations of forms) present in its source material.[4] In a way, it is better suited to a simulation of games than comics are in terms of its media affordances. Simply put, comic books share the elements of image and text with video games, but film also shares moving images and sound with them. In Rajewsky's terms (*Intermedialität* 161), film can "actualize"—that is, directly use—the medium of video games where their resources are congruent (play the exact same sound effect, for instance), whereas comic books must more often translate that medium and evoke video games' resources through their own methods when they do not have the same

Fig. 9.2. A "pee bar" is displayed as Scott visits the bathroom (from *Scott Pilgrim Gets It Together*).

means at their disposal (for example, by rendering the animated depletion of a status bar through a sequence of still images). This difference might raise the suspicion that the rivalry between the two versions of *Scott Pilgrim* has already been decided in advance, with the comic book never being able to catch up with film's more advanced technological possibilities; however, it is not so. Wright's film claims to surpass O'Malley's book regardless of media affordances. To begin with, discursive intermedial references occur at a much higher frequency in the film version. This higher frequency may be linked to the condensation of the narrative, but as Erin Hollis remarks, the film "go[es] out of [its] way to include video game references" (n. pag.), even adding them to scenes in which the comic book refrains from doing so. Elsewhere, the film version initially seems to behave as expected. It makes use of sound effects and music suggestive of those used in 8- or 16-bit games, some of which are actually directly lifted from well-known game franchises such as *The Legend of Zelda* or *Sonic the Hedgehog*. It also offers many of the comic book's textual and graphic displays—a level-up display, a score counter, a status bar, and a continue countdown—in fully animated versions.

Fig. 9.3. The film emulates the comic book's use of the "pee bar" (from *Scott Pilgrim vs. the World*).

One might get the impression that the screen adaptation faces no competition and simulates video games better simply because it is closer to them as a medium. Yet the film continually exaggerates, doing more than necessary if it were after a straightforward transposition of the book's intermedial references. The beeps and blips on the soundtrack, for example, are omnipresent. For the "continue" display, Edgar Wright chooses to update the comic's blocky low-resolution font to a glossier high-definition type, evoking a later, more technologically advanced stage in video game history. Occasionally, it appears as if the film were out to prove that it can not only do games better than comics can but also do games better than games do themselves. The film's pee bar (see figure 9.3) is not simply animated, it is hyperanimated, containing three-dimensional movement and radiant lighting effects that, owing to hardware constraints, are unlikely to be found in its 8- or 16-bit models. These surplus flourishes demonstrate the film's intent to outdo the book, notwithstanding medial resources; further, they are evidently not motivated by a mimetic desire. If one chose to read the comic as the tale of a delusional gamer, one might be inclined to argue that the film ups the ante on the discursive video game elements to make us experience Scott's affliction in a more visceral, more immediate fashion; yet I have already pointed out the implausibility of such an interpretation (Scott is, in fact, an even shallower character in the film). If O'Malley invites

Fig. 9.4. A panel is designed to resemble a frame from a fighting game (from *Scott Pilgrim's Precious Little Life*).

us to marvel at his simulation of video games, then Wright invites us to marvel even more so at his.

In some passages in the *Scott Pilgrim* books, rather than introducing a foreign medial element into what could otherwise pass for a regular comic book panel, the whole panel is designed to resemble a video game screen. In panels from Scott's first and third encounter with one of the evil ex-boyfriends, the composition of the image, as well as the placement of the characters and the text, recalls that of fighting games.[5] In the first example, Scott is seen standing in the center of the panel with his right arm outstretched after punching his opponent, who is flying head over heels through the air. A text display in the lower right-hand corner indicates that the hero has performed a "reversal," the term for a type of counterattack in fighting games (see figure 9.4). The whole image resembles a freeze frame from *Street Fighter II* (1991) or a similar game. In the second example, Scott and his enemy face each other, with Scott on the left-hand side of the panel and his enemy on the right, while a large text display between the two musicians reads "Bass Battle: Fight!" The text is both a pun on the ubiquitous boss battles in video games and a reference to using such displays to cue players in fighting games. Again, the panel looks as if a player had pressed pause on the gamepad.

If one examines the corresponding scenes in Wright's film, one can discern that the adaptation pursues its familiar strategy of emulation, improving upon the video game aspects not only through its use of sound

Fig. 9.5. The film emulating the comic book's fighting-game panel (from *Scott Pilgrim vs. the World*).

and moving images but crucially also through exaggeration and multiplication. The film meticulously re-creates the panel from Scott's first fight (see figure 9.5), yet its visual opulence—the flickering lights and colors, the extreme but smooth slow motion—far exceeds the jerky movements and reduced color palette of such 16-bit titles as *Street Fighter II*. Once again the film rivals both the comic book and video games themselves. The panel from the third battle appears in slightly modified form, with Scott and his opponent facing each other but with the letters *v* and *s* placed between them (another common text display in fighting games). In fact, all seven battles in the film feature this "versus shot," which goes to show how Wright increases video game references on the discourse level. The fight against ex number 4 arguably even contains the filmic equivalent of a prefight screen, a further fighting-game convention where portraits of the two opponents are shown side by side before the fight proper begins. What I have said previously about the discursive devices also applies to the ones mentioned here, and perhaps even more so, since it is no longer a single video game element that intrudes upon an otherwise medially inconspicuous panel or shot. In basing the design of whole shots or panels on game screens, both versions of *Scott Pilgrim* demonstrate an even less transparent use of their respective medium, one that seems bent on obfuscating or denying the medium that is materially present while conversely engaging in the most exhaustive simulation of video games yet.

Still, the most complete disguise of one medium as another can probably be found at the close of *Scott Pilgrim* the film in a sequence that basically has no parallel in the book. Here the film combines all of the previously encountered discursive elements and adds some more to create a visual and aural video game overkill. Specifically, it models parts of Scott's fight against the final boss, the seventh evil ex-boyfriend, on a fictitious game called *Ninja Ninja Revolution* that Scott and his then-girlfriend Chau played in an arcade at the beginning of the film. *Ninja Ninja Revolution* (the title alludes to the popular *Dance Dance Revolution* series) is a hybrid dancing-fighting game where Scott and Chau have to perform coordinated dance-fight moves on a platform that controls the action on-screen. In the sequence where they play the game, the film alternates between shots of them on the platform and close-ups of the screen, which features such salient display elements as health bars and different texts: "Get Ready!!" "Here We Go!" "Good" and "Combo." A voice also announces these lines, and the game's sound effects—various blips, punches, and groans—are heard on the soundtrack. The closing battle could be said to take place in the mode of *Ninja Ninja Revolution*. While the characters act out a choreographed fight scene, the film appropriates the game's presentation style for its own discourse level, copying the health bar, text displays, announcer, and sound effects (see figure 9.6). Where the earlier scene is about a video game, this one tries to be a video game. And since the game has been prominently featured in the storyworld, no viewer will miss that *Scott Pilgrim vs. the World* has now morphed into *Ninja Ninja Revolution*. Slightly before the climactic battle, a text display even reads "2 Player Mode," creating an additional link to the fictional game and suggesting an interactivity that is otherwise largely absent from both the film and the comic book.

This whole sequence represents the most blatant violation of the concepts of medial transparency and adequacy. If one tries to read it mimetically, one will not gather much from it for just as Scott has battled and defeated the other evil exes, he battles and defeats the seventh evil ex-boyfriend. At times, it is even difficult to know what exactly is going on in the storyworld given the abundant display elements that, so to speak, obstruct our view. The segment embodies the privileging of the paradigmatic over the syntagmatic axis and the triumph of discourse over story, or of style over substance, if you will. Spectators do not watch *Scott*

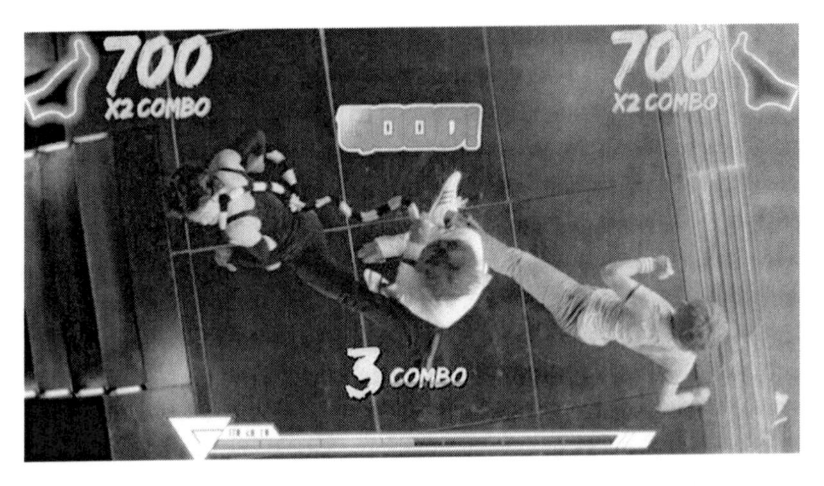

Fig. 9.6. Video game–style displays swamp the frame during Scott's final battle (from *Scott Pilgrim vs. the World*).

Pilgrim's ending because they are interested in the details and outcome of Scott's fight, but this fight is a pretext for the film to find as many ways as it can of styling itself as a game and for viewers to enjoy the resulting discursive spectacle. Even though this specific sequence exists in the film version only, the same strategy is also followed by the comic book version. Both media try continually to come up with new variations on intermedial, discourse- and story-based references to video games in their attempts to outdo one another. This realm is where they compete, where their rivalry takes place.

In the end, one might wonder if one medium emerges victorious from this battle. Since I have discussed in detail the film's claims to surpass the comic book and since its over-the-top finale is unparalleled in the source material, one might be tempted to declare the film the winner. Yet the film does not have the final word. In the same manner that old media are rarely rendered extinct by new ones, it is not as if the comic book were rendered obsolete through the film's alleged better simulation of video games. After centuries of predominantly mimetic media rivalry, we have not arrived at a situation where there are fewer media than, let us say, in the Renaissance. On the contrary, there are many more. If the desire for immediacy, for a better mimesis, has led to a proliferation of media rather than the consolidation of one definitive medium, then there is no reason to assume that the desire for hypermediacy, or a better performative use of media, should lead to opposite results. Instead of creating a better simulation of video games, the film has perhaps merely generated a different one. In any case, it has created a new one. Thus the rivalry between comic book and film is not a game played to be won but a game played for its own sake. Its purpose is to probe media for their potential and to explore and proliferate new medial and narrative possibilities—possibilities that are, crucially, not tied to a mimetic imperative. Rather than finding novel ways to create a storyworld so convincingly that it will let recipients forget all about mediation, the idea is to find novel ways of violating the principle of *ars est celare artem* ("art is to conceal art") by building a storyworld that is already medially contaminated and thus continually reflects recipients' attention back to its medial constitution. Rather than discovering methods of using one's discursive means in an innovative yet unobtrusive fashion, the idea is to discover innovative methods of making them appear to be another media's discursive means. To some, this quest to have media tell stories in the guise of other media may appear as a futile or even decadent endeavor, yet in a media-saturated and media-savvy age, it might also be seen as an instrumental and appropriate update to the traditional concept of *paragone*.

Notes

I would like to thank Judith Brand, Andreas Mahler, Marie-Laure Ryan, and Jan-Noël Thon for their helpful comments on earlier versions of this chapter.

1. All translations are mine.
2. In "Intermedialität und *remediation*," Irina O. Rajewsky duly distinguishes *remediation* as a category that describes the relations between media in general from intermediality as a narrower category denoting aesthetic phenomena involving more than one medium in specific texts, films, and so forth. However, both terms are frequently used in both senses.
3. It is also known as the "'as if' quality" (*"als ob"-Charakter*) of intermedial references, or their way of behaving as though a different medium were materially present (Rajewsky, *Intermedialität*, 39–40).
4. The film also contains discursive intermedial references to comics, first and foremost onomatopoeias, albeit to a smaller extent. These references could be

seen as another way in which the film version tries to establish its supremacy, demonstrating that it can emulate not only the comics' video game references but also the comics themselves. However, this point takes us on to a different level of rivalry, where the book cannot offer anything in reply to the film; it has never tried to simulate this medium.

5. Both panels occur toward the end of their respective volumes (1 and 3), yet as only the last three volumes of *Scott Pilgrim* are paginated, I cannot offer a more precise reference here.

Works Cited

Aarseth, Espen. *Cybertext: Perspectives on Ergodic Literature*. Baltimore MD: Johns Hopkins University Press, 1997. Print.

Ahern, Sean. "'Oh Check It Out! I Learned the Bass Line from *Final Fantasy II*': Scott Pilgrim vs. Geek Culture." *Ol3Media* 10 (2011): n. pag. Web. May 1, 2012.

Böhn, Andreas. "Einleitung: Formzitat und Intermedialität." *Formzitat und Intermedialität*. Ed. Andreas Böhn. St. Ingbert, Germany: Röhrig, 2003. 7–12. Print.

Bolter, Jay David, and Richard Grusin. *Remediation: Understanding New Media*. Cambridge MA: MIT Press, 1999. Print.

Degner, Uta, and Norbert Christian Wolf. "Intermedialität und mediale Dominanz: Einleitung." *Der neue Wettstreit der Künste: Legitimation und Dominanz im Zeichen der Intermedialität*. Ed. Uta Degner and Norbert Christian Wolf. Bielefeld, Germany: Transcript, 2010. 7–17. Print.

Hollis, Erin. "*Scott Pilgrim vs. the World* as Postmodern Parody of Parody: Allusion, Exclusion, and Consumption in the Film Adaptation." *Ol3Media* 10 (2011): n. pag. Web. May 1, 2012.

Hutcheon, Linda. *A Theory of Adaptation*. New York: Routledge, 2006. Print.

Iser, Wolfgang. *The Fictive and the Imaginary: Charting Literary Anthropology*. Baltimore MD: Johns Hopkins University Press, 1993.

Lessing, Gotthold Ephraim. "Laokoon: Oder über die Grenzen der Malerei und Poesie." *Werke VI: Kunsttheoretische und kunsthistorische Schriften*. Ed. Herbert G. Göpfert and Albert von Schirnding. Munich: Hanser, 1974. 7–187. Print.

Mahler, Andreas. "Sprache—Mimesis—Diskurs: Die Vexiertexte des Parnasse als Paradigma anti-mimetischer Sprachrevolution." *Zeitschrift für Französische Sprache und Literatur* 116 (2006): 34–47. Print.

O'Malley, Bryan Lee. *Scott Pilgrim & the Infinite Sadness*. Vol. 3, *Scott Pilgrim*. Portland OR: Oni, 2006. N. pag. Print.

———. *Scott Pilgrim Gets It Together*. Vol. 4, *Scott Pilgrim*. Portland OR: Oni, 2007. Print.

———. *Scott Pilgrim's Finest Hour*. Vol. 6, *Scott Pilgrim*. Portland OR: Oni, 2010. Print.

———. *Scott Pilgrim's Precious Little Life*. Vol. 1, *Scott Pilgrim*. Portland OR: Oni, 2004. N. pag. Print.
———. *Scott Pilgrim vs. the Universe*. Vol. 5, *Scott Pilgrim*. Portland OR: Oni, 2009. Print.
———. *Scott Pilgrim vs. the World*. Vol. 2, *Scott Pilgrim*. Portland OR: Oni, 2005. N. pag. Print.
Rajewsky, Irina O. *Intermedialität*. Tübingen, Germany: A. Francke, 2002. Print.
———. "Intermedialität und *remediation*: Überlegungen zu einigen Problemfeldern der jüngeren Intermedialitätsforschung." *Intermedialität analog/digital: Theorien, Methoden, Analysen*. Ed. Joachim Paech and Jens Schröter. Munich: Fink, 2008. 47–60. Print.
Scott Pilgrim vs. the World. Dir. Edgar Wright. Universal, 2010. DVD.
Warning, Rainer. "Elemente einer Pragmasemiotik der Komödie." *Das Komische*. Ed. Wolfgang Preisendanz and Rainer Warning. Munich: Fink, 1976. 279–333. Print.
Wolf, Werner. "Intermediality." *Routledge Encyclopedia of Narrative Theory*. Ed. David Herman, Manfred Jahn, and Marie-Laure Ryan. London: Routledge, 2005. 252–56. Print.

10 Those Insane Dream Sequences

Experientiality and Distorted Experience in Literature and Video Games

MARCO CARACCIOLO

In the years since the publication of Monika Fludernik's *Towards a "Natural" Narratology*, her key concept of *experientiality* has established an impressive citation record. Defined as the "quasi-mimetic evocation of real-life experience" (Fludernik 12), experientiality provides a tight conceptual link between classical narratological research on the representation of conscious experience in fiction and post-classical, cognitivist approaches. However, Fludernik's central claim that experientiality is the defining feature of narrative has not withstood closer scrutiny. Starting with Meir Sternberg (122) and Jan Alber, scholars have argued that experientiality cannot be straightforwardly equated with narrativity (see Wolf 181; Ryan, "Theoretical Foundations" 4; Herman, *Basic Elements* 211). And yet, this conclusion does not imply that experientiality holds no narratological interest. Theorists such as Werner Wolf and David Herman ("Cognition"; *Basic Elements*) have taken a more prudent course than Fludernik's by including experientiality among their "narratemes" or "basic elements of narrative" without equating it with narrativity. For example, Herman has defined experientiality as "the impact of narrated situations and events on an experiencing consciousness" ("Cognition" 256).

What remains unclear, however, is the level at which we should investigate this impact. Indeed, in fictional narratives there is a significant—and obvious—difference between characters' consciousnesses and the real consciousnesses involved in the act of narrative presentation, or that of the story producers and the recipients. Is experientiality, as in Fludernik's model, a representation of the experiences undergone by a character—usually, the protagonist (see Fludernik 30)? Or should it rather be understood as a measure of the impact a story has on its flesh-and-blood recipients?

In this chapter I attempt to show why it is important—and to some extent necessary—to tie up these aspects of experientiality. In short, my suggestion is that characters' experiences can be represented only because stories tap into the experiential reservoir shared by the recipients, cueing them into attributing experiences to fictional beings. Conversely, a story can have an impact on its recipients because it plays on this experiential repertoire in order to bring the characters' experiences to life. Experientiality becomes, then, the tension that arises between the recipients' experiential background and the experiences that they attribute to characters on the basis of textual cues.[1] An important caveat here is that this tension is not always foregrounded by stories; in many cases, the recipients react to the situations and events in which the characters are involved as if from the outside, without engaging with characters' experiences in any meaningful way. Even when the recipients' reactions are directed toward the experiences of a character, they may take the form of a sympathetic feeling for the character (we may feel hatred for a villain or compassion for someone who has suffered a tragic loss, for instance). Only rarely—and as an effect of specific textual strategies—does the recipients' engagement with characters involve the empathetic perspective taking that I explore in the following pages.

Indeed, both of my case studies invite recipients to imaginatively engage with a character whose experience is distorted by hallucinations or dreams. Martin Heidegger remarks in a passage of his *Being and Time* (sec. 32) that we become aware of the structure of our experience only when something disrupts the flow of our interaction with the world. Likewise, examining two texts that present a character's non-ordinary experience will yield important insights into our experiential engagement with characters and more in general with stories. I analyze a passage from William S. Burroughs's experimental novel *Naked Lunch* (1959) and a few dream sequences from the video game *Max Payne 2: The Fall of Max Payne* (2003) developed by Remedy Entertainment. In the first, a character has drug-induced visions during an interrogation. This text addresses the Burroughsian theme of language as an instrument of control via the reader's empathetic engagement with the character. For its part, *Max Payne 2* is an interesting test bed for transmedial narratology because of the way it implements multimodal techniques and intermedial references to tinge the game world with the dream-like quality of the protagonist's experience. In considering these texts, I describe the medium-specific techniques through which literature and video games generate a tension between the recipients' and the characters' experiences.

At the same time, I would also like to stress the continuity between my case studies by arguing that they fall into the same basic pattern of experientiality. On the one hand, recipients are cued into attributing to a character an experience that is distorted at the perceptual and emotional level. On the other hand, the recipients' imaginative engagement with the character feeds back into their experiential background at a higher, culturally mediated level, since it produces a specific meaning effect (language as an instrument of control in *Naked Lunch*, free will as an illusion in *Max Payne 2*). The distortion in the character's experience in each case is thus used to channel meanings that have a disruptive potential for the recipient's own experiential background. Importantly, this effect is achieved by breaking with the conventions surrounding the medium-specific strategies for narrative presentation. In *Naked Lunch*, the reader's expectations regarding the novelistic form are continually frustrated by the lack of narrative coherence, whereas the dream sequences of *Max Payne 2* defy the traditional distinction between the game proper and narrative-advancing cut-scenes, since they neither offer a significant challenge to the player nor further the story. We have, therefore, a close connection between the character's distorted experience, the innovative solutions through which it is presented, and its unsettling reflection on the recipient's own experience.

The Experiential Background and Its Traces: Imagining Characters' Experiences

To begin, I would like to clarify the idea that stories draw on interpreters' *experiential background* in order to represent the experiences of characters. The term "background" comes from John Searle's theory of intentionality, where it stands for "a set of nonrepresentational mental capacities that enable all representing to take place" (143). Searle distinguishes between a *deep* and a *local* background: the first is constituted by the capacities that are "common to all human beings in virtue of their biological makeup," such as perceiving, running, grasping, and so on; and the second is shaped by social interaction and includes all sorts of sociocultural practices—for example, the "stance we take towards [. . .] cars, re-

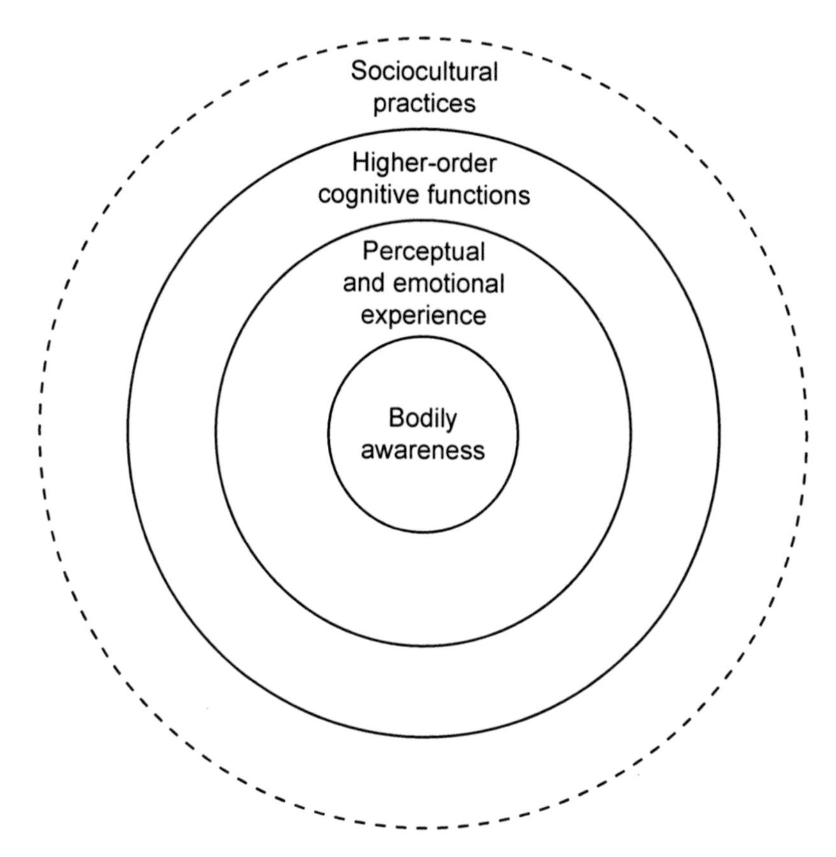

Fig. 10.1. A sketch of the experiential background.

frigerators, money and cocktail parties" (143–44). What I would like to do here is expand Searle's definition in order to provide a somewhat more detailed mapping of this background.

Figure 10.1 is a first attempt at charting out this terrain; it spans from the basic modes of embodied consciousness to the complexity of culturally and linguistically mediated experience. In proposing this model, I follow the embodied and interactionist account of social cognition developed by scholars working in the new wave in cognitive science known as "enactivism" (see Di Paolo, Rohde, and De Jaegher). In the neo-phenomenological framework of this approach, our sense of self (see Gallagher and Zahavi 49–51) is closely bound up with our proprioceptive awareness of our own body. Perceptual and emotional experience includes the sensorimotor patterns that structure our interaction with the world (O'Regan and Noë) and our embodied, precognitive interpretation of what is at stake in situations (Colombetti). Experience at these levels possesses a distinctive, qualitative "feel": humans are conscious of what it is like to have a body, to smell the sea air, or to be angry with someone. Higher-order cognitive functions are abilities such as long-term memory, imagination, conceptual thought, and language. Finally, the last circle contains the sociocultural scaffolding of our encounters with the world, people, and artifacts: beliefs, values, social structures, cultural conventions, and so on.

It is worth emphasizing here that I conceive of the background as a constantly evolving repertoire, with new experiences taking on meanings in the light of past ones and at the same time potentially leaving a mark on the background itself. Moreover, the levels of figure 10.1 are tightly intertwined. To return to Searle's distinction, the "deeper" levels are partly shaped by our "local" cultural background: perception and emotion always exist in, and are influenced by, a network of cultural meanings and sociocultural interactions. Conversely, conceptual thought and cultural practices are structured by our physical makeup and capabilities, as cognitive linguists and theorists of embodiment have repeatedly pointed out (see Gibbs; Evans and Green).

The first proposition that I would like to advance in this section is a version of Marie-Laure Ryan's principle of minimal departure (*Possible Worlds* 51): recipients understand characters' experiences by drawing on regions of their own experiential background. This process involves the activation of what psycholinguists such as Rolf A. Zwaan have called "experiential traces"—that is, the sensations, memories, or knowledge structures that may fall at any point in the continuum represented in figure 10.1.[2] Here are some illustrative passages taken from Ian McEwan's *On Chesil Beach* (2007), from a section that describes the apprehensions and expectations of Florence and Edward, a newly wed couple, as they slowly slide toward their first physical contact.

- *Perceptual experience*: "His napkin clung to his waist for a moment, hanging absurdly, like a loincloth, and then wafted to the floor in slow motion" (27).
- *Emotional experience*: "Even in his exalted, jittery condition he thought he understood her customary reticence" (28).

- *Higher-order cognitive functions*: "She made herself remember how much she loved this man" (28).
- *Sociocultural practices*: "And the thrilling fact remained that it was Florence who had suggested lying on the bed. Her changed status had set her free" (28).

In order to understand these sentences, readers must piece together traces of their past interactions with the world. For example, they must be familiar with the motion of an object that falls gently to the ground, with the mixture of anxiety and excitement that precedes and accompanies Edward's first sexual contact, and with the practices regulating relationships between genders in twentieth-century Western society.

But, of course, stories can invite interpreters to imagine characters' experiences with various degrees of "closeness," in Jens Eder's term. Building on philosophical theories about our imaginative, empathetic responses to fictional characters (Coplan; Currie and Ravenscroft; Gaut), I have argued elsewhere (see "Fictional Consciousnesses") that our engagement with the experiential dimension of characters' mental lives oscillates between two poles: at one pole, recipients limit themselves to attributing an experience to a character without sharing it—a strategy that I call "consciousness-attribution"—and at the other pole, in acts of "consciousness-enactment," recipients simulate, or "try on," the experience that they attribute to a character. In both consciousness-attribution and consciousness-enactment the recipients draw on their experiential backgrounds to understand the characters' experiences. However, in consciousness-enactment the recipients' engagement with a character also has a first-person aspect in that they *simulate* the character's experiences by reutilizing traces stored in their background.

The possibility of consciousness-enactment explains why some stories do more than activate regions of our experiential background. By involving us in the characters' experiences, they can provide us with a full-fledged imaginative experience and therefore bring about a "feedback" effect at various levels of our background. For example, a text can evoke vivid imagery by focusing on a character's perceptions. I have never visited a coal mine, but after reading the internally focalized descriptions of Émile Zola's *Germinal* I think I know what one must be like. However, it is on the plane of our emotional engagement that the impact of stories becomes clearly evident. In broad terms, an *emotion* is a precognitive evaluation of a situation (see Colombetti). Stories can trigger emotional reactions by bringing into play values and evaluations that are part of recipients' experiential background. In one of the last scenes of *Germinal* an explosion traps the protagonist, Étienne, in a mine tunnel. Knowing that being trapped in a mine entails a major risk for one's well-being, I can imagine how I would feel if I found myself in that situation without reading Zola's novel. However, by entangling Étienne's life project (and narrative) in that situation and by implementing strategies that invite readers to put themselves in the character's shoes, Zola is able to convey that emotional experience in a powerfully effective way.

Finally, engaging with the experiences represented by stories can provide what Eileen John has called "cognitive stimulation," which invites us to restructure our background at the level of higher-order knowledge, thus expanding our worldview and changing our cultural beliefs. Part of Zola's agenda was to bring the appalling conditions of the coal miners in northern France to the attention of his bourgeois audience as he attempted to warn his readers that it was not "too late for social changes that could placate the working class" (Aliaga-Buchenau 20). In other cases, stories may offer us a radically different perspective on situations we are already familiar with, bringing about an unsettling effect that has much in common with the Russian formalist notion of "defamiliarization" (Shklovsky).

In sum, there is a two-way exchange between stories and our experiential background: in temporarily adopting the characters' perspectives, we afford them a chance for interacting with—and leaving a mark on—our broader outlook on the world. This dynamic tension between the experiences that recipients attribute to characters and their own experience is, in my view, constitutive of experientiality. In the next sections I home in on this dynamic by concentrating on two cases in which recipients' imaginative engagement with a character's perceptual and emotional experience bears directly upon their sociocultural background. As announced in the introduction, I look at the ways in which two media—literature and video games—can challenge recipients' sociocultural meanings through their empathizing with the distorted experience of a character.

Experientiality through a Distortion Lens: Case Studies

Burroughs's Naked Lunch *and Mind Control*

The first of my case studies is a section from William S. Burroughs's novel *Naked Lunch*. It is one of the few relatively stable narrative sequences in a text that is well known for its assault on narrative sense making (see Murphy, "Intersection Points" 90). And yet, as we will see, the threat this passage presents to its readers is no less serious for its apparent readability. This section, titled "The Examination," is about halfway through *Naked Lunch*. The protagonist, Carl, is hastily summoned for an interview at the Ministry of Mental Hygiene and Prophylaxis, where Doctor Benway—an old acquaintance of Burroughs's readers—makes veiled insinuations about Carl's homosexuality. Carl firmly denies everything, but during the interview he experiences some visions. Perhaps they are signs that Doctor Benway has drugged him in order to extract a confession from him.

The first hint of these visions comes after Doctor Benway's ominous warning: "We'd like to go light on you . . . If you could help us in some way" (*Naked Lunch* 163, ellipsis in the original). Suddenly, these "words open out into a desolate waste of cafeterias and street corners and lunch rooms. Junkies look the other way munching pound cake" (*Naked Lunch* 163). By this point, the readers of *Naked Lunch* will have grown accustomed to this kind of disruption in the narrative texture of the novel. This time, however, we are asked to make the further move of attributing this sudden change of scenery not to the whims of the author/narrator but to the hallucinatory experience of a fictional character. Indeed, as soon as the scene returns to the examination room, Carl has another, unambiguous vision:

> A green flare exploded in Carl's brain. He saw Hans' lean brown body twisting towards him, quick breath on his shoulder. The flare went out. Some huge insect was squirming in his hand. His whole being jerked away in an electric spasm of revulsion.
>
> Carl got to his feet shaking with rage.
>
> "What are you writing there?" he demanded.
>
> "Do you often doze off like that? in the middle of a conversation . . . ?"

"I wasn't asleep—that is . . ."

"You weren't?"

"It's just that the *whole thing* is unreal . . . I'm going now. I don't care. You can't force me to stay."

(*Naked Lunch* 165, ellipses and emphasis in the original)

Carl's first vision (we will never know if it is the recovered memory of a homosexual encounter or a drug-induced hallucination) is framed by the metaphor of a green flare exploding in his brain. This metaphor marks the transition from the shared, public world of perception to Carl's hallucination and seeks to capture the felt quality of the character's experience, its suddenness and incongruity. The same applies to the image of the insect squirming in his hand. Readers imagine both visions on the basis of their own experiential background, particularly their familiarity with explosions and insects and squirming things.[3] At the same time, interpreters are encouraged to engage with the character's perceptual perspective by imaginatively "trying it on" through three stylistic and narrative strategies. The first is the use of what I call a "phenomenological metaphor," one that attempts to render the phenomenological quality of the character's sensation in the same way as he experiences it "from the inside."[4] The second is "internal focalization," which grants readers a more direct access to the character's consciousness than would be possible for an observer on the scene. Since we assume that Carl's hallucinations are not accessible to anyone but himself, recipients are primed to read these lines—and possibly through a recency effect (see Jahn 157), the whole section—by empathizing with him.

The third textual trigger of readers' empathy for the character has to do with Burroughs's handling of dialogue. Indeed, what is really surprising about this passage is the way we learn that the character was asleep while he had his visions. This revelation comes, after the fact, from Doctor Benway's question, and it is likely to reinforce the empathetic bond between readers and Carl. Since both Carl and the readers did not know that he was sleeping before Doctor Benway's words, readers become more acutely conscious that they have been experiencing *with* the character all along and that they have been enacting his consciousness or imagining his experiences from the inside. In this case, the imaginative experience readers undergo falls in the perceptual-emotional zone of figure 10.1. And yet an even more complex identification process seems to play out here. When Carl says that "the *whole thing* is unreal," he is in a sense echoing the reaction of all first-time readers to Burroughs's novel. His cognitive disorientation (see Hogan 10), then, becomes symbolic of the larger project of *Naked Lunch*. Interestingly, when Carl attempts to leave the room he experiences more hallucinations:

> The door seemed to recede.
>
> "Where can you go, Carl?" The doctor's voice reached him from a great distance.
>
> "Out . . . Away . . . Through the door . . ."
>
> "The Green Door, Carl?"
>
> The doctor's voice was barely audible. The whole room was exploding out into space.
>
> (*Naked Lunch* 165, ellipses in the original)

These words are the last in the section. As readers, we are not afforded a final, non-distorted glimpse at the fictional world. Locked in Carl's consciousness, we are tempted to draw a connection between the explosion and the end of the section, as if the character's hallucinations expanded beyond his skull, warping the fictional space and eventually obliterating everything—including the character himself, who never appears again in the remainder of the novel. "You can't force me to stay," Carl says; but in fact Doctor Benway—and, behind him, Burroughs—can do much more: by giving him hallucinations, they can plunge him into nothingness.

Through these textual strategies, this section addresses what many commentators have identified as the central theme of *Naked Lunch*—social control over the individual, a control that is exercised through drugs, social practices, and language itself. It is no coincidence that Carl's examiner is Doctor Benway, who is introduced at the beginning of the novel as "an expert on all phases of interrogation, brainwashing and control" (*Naked Lunch* 19), and that Carl's first hallucinations are triggered by the doctor's *words*. But *Naked Lunch* does much more than denounce the complicity between language and control systems in a detached, impersonal way; as critics such as Robin Lydenberg and Ron Loewinsohn have argued, Burroughs wants to subject his own readers to the violence of that control in an attempt to free them from it. How this treatment works in this particular passage should be clear enough: having to stick to Carl's hallucinatory perspective, readers empathize with him, only to be dismayed at his strange disappearance from the fictional world. Burroughs once said that it "is precisely [our] automatic reactions to words themselves that enable those who manipulate words to control thought on a mass scale" (*The Job* 59). In this case, the author foregrounds his control over the readers' imaginings through the repressive power of Doctor Benway's words over Carl's consciousness. However, unlike the readers, Carl has no chance to find out that, as Lydenberg puts it, "[o]verexposure to the word [. . .] has a liberating and purgative effect" (43).[5] Such an effect is channeled through, and made more forceful by, the readers' empathetic engagement with the character.

The activation of perceptual and emotional traces makes it possible for Burroughs's novel to challenge readers' conventions at the sociocultural level, exposing the violence of control systems. What's more, the attack on the interpreters' social values is implemented through a systematic violation of their expectations regarding literary form and, in particular, narrative continuity. This kind of distortion, which is abundantly evident in the novel as a whole, manifests itself in this section through the instability of the ending, suspended as it is between the character's hallucinatory perspective and the image of a vanishing fictional world. All in all, by conveying and disrupting the character's perceptual experience and eliciting the reader's confusion as he or she tries to cope with the novel, Burroughs succeeds in advancing the ideological (or, rather, anti-ideological) agenda of *Naked Lunch*.

Playing on Max's Dreams: Max Payne 2

Max Payne 2 represents another striking instance of how distortions in a character's experience can be used to have an effect on the experiential background of story recipients. This case study is made even more interesting by the special features of the video game medium itself, including its multimodality and interactivity; although, as we will see, *Max Payne 2* explicitly thematizes recipients' inability to alter the course of the story. *Max Payne 2* is a story-driven third-person "shooter" with fairly traditional game play. In itself, the plot is "pungently cheesy," as a reviewer puts it (Poole n. pag.). It centers on a conspiracy story heavily influenced by film noir and hard-boiled fiction in which Max Payne, a detective with

Fig. 10.2. Max loses consciousness (a graphic narrative scene from *Max Payne 2*).

a painful past, cracks an evil scheme with the help of Mona Sax, his love interest and herself a hired killer.

Where this game really shines, however, is in how it renders the felt quality of the protagonist's experience and specifically the surreal aspect that leaks from Max's dreams to the game's baseline reality. Before turning to the dream sequences, though, I would like to comment on the first moments of the game in order to briefly examine another technique through which Max's experience is conveyed—namely, the graphic narrative scenes that appear between the chapters. The first comic book page in the game's prologue shows a police car pulling up at an unspecified manor and in juxtaposition, possibly inside the manor, a kiss between Max and Mona. After this initial sequence, the words "the hospital, earlier tonight," alert us to a spatiotemporal leap, and we are transported to the hospital where Max has just been rushed after receiving multiple gunshot wounds. No first-time player is able to understand the causal relationship between the manor and the hospital scene and even less the reasons for Max's hospitalization. Again, the player's disorientation is reflected, at another level, in the character's confusion when he wakes up at the hospital (see figures 10.2 and 10.3).

In both pages the game seems to exploit the expressive potential of comics to provide players with a straightforward access to Max's subjectivity (see Mikkonen), partly making up for the shortcomings of three-dimensional computer graphics. Figure 10.2 shows the character's losing consciousness (in the upper panel) and his regaining his senses (in

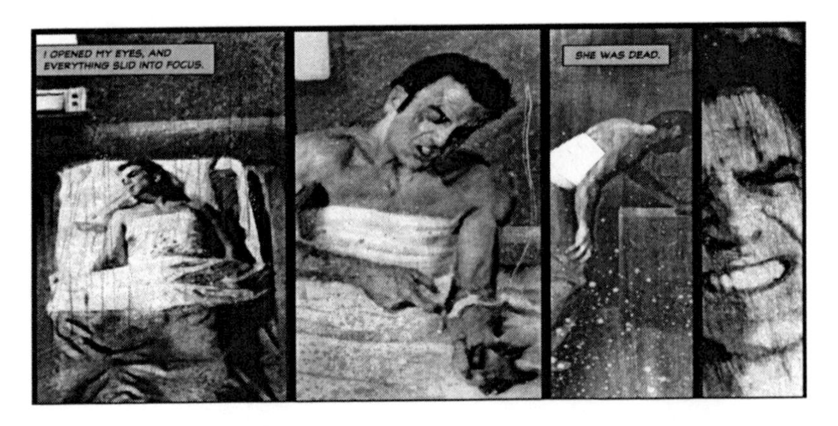

Fig. 10.3. Max wakes up at the hospital (a graphic narrative scene from *Max Payne 2*).

the lower strip). As often in graphic narrative, the character is seen from the outside, but his traumatized state is expressed by stylistic features such as the fuzzy borders of the panels and the visual "noise" that appears more or less everywhere as, most notably, vertical, scar-like lines crossing the panels and white spots that seem to settle on the surface of the drawings. In figure 10.3, by contrast, Max's experience is thrown into sharp relief by his pained facial expressions, which provide players with a "fast track to narrative empathy," in Suzanne Keen's phrase. Both motifs of the character's confusion and of his pain are repeated in the ensuing cinematic sequence, setting the tone for the whole game by placing the character's physical and mental distress center stage.

The three in-game dream sequences that are scattered throughout *Max Payne 2* serve as a powerful reminder of this experiential backdrop, inviting players to align themselves with it by drawing both on their firsthand familiarity with dreams (at the perceptual and emotional levels of the background) and on cultural stereotypes about dreams—for instance, horror film clichés. The underlying narrative structure is identical in all dream sequences: Max runs after a person he cannot catch, makes his way through endless corridors, and encounters some of the game's main characters, usually in absurd but emotionally charged situations. In the first sequence he chases an unknown person, who disappears after knocking on his apartment door and sliding Mona's photograph under it. In the second he runs after Mona, whereas in the third he tries to catch another Max, his alter ego. Indeed, a number of Max's

Fig. 10.4. Max's alter ego (a dream sequence from *Max Payne 2*).

doubles appear in his dreams. In what is probably one of the most bizarre dream scenes, Max walks past a number of holding cells in a police station; in some of the cells another Max mumbles incoherently while signs bearing words such as "mad," "paranoid," and "insane" hang from the walls (see figure 10.4).

Another feature that strikes the player as dream-like is the way many locations and elements from the fictional actual world are injected into Max's dream world in a distorted, incongruous fashion. Consider, for example, the spatial setting. The dreams take place in three game locations: Max's apartment, the hospital, and the police station. These settings are disconnected in the fictional actual world, since the player is instantaneously transported from the one to the other in the transitions between the chapters. In Max's dreams, however, the apartment, the hospital, and the police station are seamlessly—and absurdly—connected by long corridors.

But how does this dream-like quality reflect itself in the players' own experience? To begin with, the distortion filter applied to the "camera" reminds us of the character's altered consciousness by blurring and warping the game world. However, from a game-theoretical viewpoint, the most puzzling aspect of these dream sequences is the fact that while allowing players to directly control Max in the 3-D game world, they foreground their lack of agency. Indeed, the interactivity of these sections is severely limited, and they pose no challenge to the player, who only has to steer the character through a series of interconnected spaces. This design choice poses an interesting paradox. We should not forget that linearity—especially when coupled with a very low difficulty level—is commonly regarded as going against the nature of the video game medium itself. At best, it is associated with the cut-scenes that serve to advance the game's plot. But the dream sequences of *Max Payne 2* neither require the player to succeed in any nontrivial task nor further the story since, of course, what happens in Max's dreams cannot have any effect on the fictional actual world. They are purely atmospheric, serving to convey the felt quality of the protagonist's experience in a way that is innovative and, at the same time, extremely effective. Indeed, by dramatizing the contrast between the apparent interactivity of the dream sequences and their shallow, linear game play, *Max Payne 2* defamiliarizes the players' interaction with the game, thus providing them with a stand-in for the character's unsettling experience. This unnerving aspect of the dream sequences is attested by some forum posts on the Internet, including one that gives its title to this essay (Anonymous, "Insane Dream Sequences"). For example, a forum user writes: "I and every person I know hate the damn dream sequences. They are so twisted, disorienting, and totally do nothing for me in terms of plot development" (Anonymous, "Does Anyone").

Note that these players do much more than express their dislike for the dream sequences; the adjectives they use ("insane," "twisted," "disorienting") signal that players found these sections disturbing because of the way they blur the traditional distinction between online and offline sequences, the actual game and pre-rendered cut-scenes. Similarly to what happens in the Burroughs passage, the distortion in the character's perceptual experience feeds back into recipients' engagement with the story but at a higher, conceptually mediated level. As with the character trapped in his nightmares, the players become aware that they have to follow a linear, pre-scripted trajectory through Max's dreams and, indeed, through the game world; in turn, this realization can strengthen their empathetic bond with Max. The forced linearity of the game is thus blended with the painful lack of agency of the dreamer and, by extension, of Max Payne himself, as announced in an important graphic narrative scene (see figure 10.5).

Fig. 10.5. On linearity and the illusion of free will (a graphic narrative scene from *Max Payne 2*).

Without advancing the story, the dream sequences seem to reveal how narrative causality works in this game: free will is an illusion, an afterthought, and the course of events is deterministically shaped by who you are (for Max) or by which game you play (for the player). Again, this meaning construction would not be possible without a deep resonance between the character's and the player's experience, a resonance that becomes clearly audible in distorted experientiality.

The aim of this chapter was to develop a theory of experientiality that accounts in the same breath for both characters' and story recipients' experiences. Thus, I have argued that a character's experience can only be represented in stories by providing pointers to the experiential background of recipients—that is, to the repertoire that includes all the experiences with which they are acquainted. At the basic level, then, recipients draw on their experiential background in order to attribute experiences to the characters on the basis of textual cues. However, by combining our experiential traces in novel ways, stories can do more than refer recipients to already familiar experiences. Stories can have us undergo full-fledged imaginative experiences that interact with (and leave a mark on) our experiential background, for example, by triggering our emotional reactions or by providing us with cognitive stimulation. This exchange forms the basis for the dynamic relationship between stories and our experiential background that I have investigated in this chapter.

In particular, I have focused on texts in which such a feedback effect is elicited through recipients' empathetic engagement with characters whose consciousness is distorted by hallucinations and dreams. I have found that in these cases the character's experience tends to reflect itself at a higher, culturally mediated level in the recipients' own experiential background by challenging their cultural values and the medium-specific conventions of narrative presentation—the novelistic form, with its demand for narrative coherence and continuity, in *Naked Lunch* and the distinction between in-game sequences and cut-scenes in *Max Payne 2*.

All in all, I have suggested that experientiality manifests itself in the tension between the experiences we attribute to fictional characters and our experiential background. We may therefore hypothesize—although I will not be able to expand on this claim here—that experientiality comes in degrees as a function both of the capacity of a story to have an emotional or cognitive impact on the background of its recipients and of the historical, sociocultural, and individual variations in the background itself. Indeed, it goes without saying that my readings of *Naked Lunch* and *Max Payne 2* reflect my own sensitivity and predispositions. To some extent, the reactions and interpretations of other recipients can be used as an intersubjective touchstone to back up our claims about the effect of a story; thus I've referred to Burroughs critics and to the impressions of other players of *Max Payne 2*. But, of course, the subjectivity of our responses cannot be completely eliminated. What matters, however, is not reaching an agreement on the *content* of our reactions but on the experiential dynamics underlying them. By focusing on such dynamics, my case studies identify a consistent pattern of interaction between the recipients, the experiencing characters, and the storytelling medium itself.

Notes

1. Here and elsewhere in this chapter I use the words "text" and "textual" for any narrative artifact, irrespective of the medium.
2. Compare with Zillmann: empathy through cognitive "role-taking can [. . .] be viewed as mediated through the partial revival of related past experiences" (166).
3. This point does not imply that readers who have never experienced hallucinations won't be able to imagine this passage. Other people's reports are usu-

ally sufficient to form an idea, however imprecise, of experiences we've never undergone in a first-person way. Arguably, though, these readers may be able to empathize with the character less deeply than those readers who do have a greater familiarity with hallucinations.

4. See Caracciolo, "Phenomenological Metaphors."
5. Murphy (*Wising Up*) and Loewinsohn have insisted on the didactic element of *Naked Lunch*.

Works Cited

Alber, Jan. "The 'Moreness' or 'Lessness' of 'Natural' Narratology: Samuel Beckett's 'Lessness' Reconsidered." *Style* 36.1 (2002): 54–75. Print.

Aliaga-Buchenau, Ana-Isabel. "Reading as the Path to Revolt? Emile Zola's Germinal." *Postscript* 20.3 (2003): 14–23. Print.

Anonymous. "Does Anyone Else Hate the Dream Sequences." *Neoseeker Max Payne Forum*. October 10, 2001. Web. October 27, 2003.

———. "Those Insane Dream Sequences (Spoilers Maybe)." *Gamespot Max Payne Forum*. April 8, 2008. Web. October 27, 2003.

Burroughs, William S. *The Job: Interviews with William S. Burroughs*. Ed. Daniel Odier. London: Penguin Books, 1989. Print.

———. *Naked Lunch: The Restored Text*. Ed. James Grauerholz and Barry Miles. London: Fourth Estate, 2010. Print.

Caracciolo, Marco. "Fictional Consciousnesses: A Reader's Manual." *Style* 46.1 (2012): 42–64. Print.

———. "Phenomenological Metaphors in Readers' Engagement with Characters: The Case of Ian McEwan's *Saturday*." *Language and Literature* 22.2 (2013): 60–76. Print.

Colombetti, Giovanna. "Enaction, Sense-Making, and Emotion." *Enaction: Toward a New Paradigm for Cognitive Science*. Ed. John Stewart, Olivier Gapenne, and Ezequiel A. Di Paolo. Cambridge MA: MIT Press, 2010. 145–64. Print.

Coplan, Amy. "Empathic Engagement with Narrative Fictions." *Journal of Aesthetics and Art Criticism* 62.2 (2004): 141–52. Print.

Currie, Gregory, and Ian Ravenscroft. *Recreative Minds: Imagination in Philosophy and Psychology*. Oxford, UK: Oxford University Press, 2002. Print.

Di Paolo, Ezequiel A., Marieke Rohde, and Hanne De Jaegher. "Horizons for the Enactive Mind: Values, Social Interaction, and Play." *Enaction: Toward a New Paradigm for Cognitive Science*. Ed. John Stewart, Olivier Gapenne, and Ezequiel A. Di Paolo. Cambridge MA: MIT Press, 2010. 33–87. Print.

Eder, Jens. "Ways of Being Close to Characters." *Film Studies* 8 (2006): 68–80. Print.

Evans, Vyvyan, and Melanie Green. *Cognitive Linguistics: An Introduction*. Edinburgh: Edinburgh University Press, 2006. Print.

Fludernik, Monika. *Towards a "Natural" Narratology*. London: Routledge, 1996. Print.
Gallagher, Shaun, and Dan Zahavi. *The Phenomenological Mind: An Introduction to Philosophy of Mind and Cognitive Science*. Abingdon, UK: Routledge, 2008. Print.
Gaut, Berys. "Identification and Emotion in Narrative Film." *Passionate Views: Film, Cognition, and Emotion*. Ed. Carl Plantinga and Greg M. Smith. Baltimore MD: Johns Hopkins University Press, 1999. 200–216. Print.
Gibbs, Raymond W., Jr. *Embodiment and Cognitive Science*. Cambridge, UK: Cambridge University Press, 2005. Print.
Heidegger, Martin. *Being and Time*. Trans. Joan Stambaugh. Albany: State University of New York Press, 1996. Print.
Herman, David. *Basic Elements of Narrative*. Oxford, UK: Wiley-Blackwell, 2009. Print.
———. "Cognition, Emotion, and Consciousness." *The Cambridge Companion to Narrative*. Ed. David Herman. Cambridge, UK: Cambridge University Press, 2007. 245–59. Print.
Hogan, Patrick Colm. *Cognitive Science, Literature, and the Arts: A Guide for Humanists*. London: Routledge, 2003. Print.
Jahn, Manfred. "Frames, Preferences, and the Reading of Third-Person Narratives: Towards a Cognitive Narratology." *Poetics Today* 18.4 (1997): 441–68. Print.
John, Eileen. "Art and Knowledge." *The Routledge Companion to Aesthetics*. Ed. Berys Gaut and Dominic McIver Lopes. London: Routledge, 2005. 417–30. Print.
Keen, Suzanne. "Fast Tracks to Narrative Empathy: Anthropomorphism and Dehumanization in Graphic Narratives." *SubStance* 40.1 (2011): 135–55. Print.
Loewinsohn, Ron. "'Gentle Reader, I Fain Would Spare You This, but My Pen Hath Its Will like the Ancient Mariner': Narrator(s) and Audience in William S. Burroughs's *Naked Lunch*." *Contemporary Literature* 39.4 (1998): 560–85. Print.
Lydenberg, Robin. *Word Cultures: Radical Theory and Practice in William S. Burroughs' Fiction*. Chicago: University of Illinois Press, 1987. Print.
McEwan, Ian. *On Chesil Beach*. London: Vintage, 2007. Print.
Mikkonen, Kai. "Presenting Minds in Graphic Narratives." *Partial Answers* 6.2 (2008): 301–21. Print.
Murphy, Timothy S. "Intersection Points: Teaching William Burroughs's *Naked Lunch*." *College Literature* 27.1 (2000): 84–102. Print.
———. *Wising Up the Marks: The Amodern William Burroughs*. Berkeley: University of California Press, 1997. Print.
O'Regan, J. Kevin, and Alva Noë. "A Sensorimotor Account of Vision and Visual Consciousness." *Behavioral and Brain Sciences* 24.5 (2001): 939–1031. Print.
Poole, Steven. "Max Payne 2: The Fall of Max Payne." *Sunday Times* January 18, 2004. Print.
Remedy Entertainment. *Max Payne 2: The Fall of Max Payne*. Rockstar Games, 2003. Windows.

Ryan, Marie-Laure. "On the Theoretical Foundations of Transmedial Narratology." *Narratology beyond Literary Criticism: Mediality, Disciplinarity*. Ed. Jan Christoph Meister. Berlin: De Gruyter, 2005. 1–23. Print.

———. *Possible Worlds, Artificial Intelligence, and Narrative Theory*. Bloomington: Indiana University Press, 1991. Print.

Searle, John. *Intentionality: An Essay in the Philosophy of Mind*. Cambridge, UK: Cambridge University Press, 1983. Print.

Shklovsky, Viktor. "Art as Device." *Theory of Prose*. Trans. Benjamin Sher. Normal IL: Dalkey Archive Press, 1991. 1–14. Print.

Sternberg, Meir. "How Narrativity Makes a Difference." *Narrative* 9.2 (2001): 115–22. Print.

Wolf, Werner. "Narrative and Narrativity: A Narratological Reconceptualization and Its Applicability to the Visual Arts." *Word & Image* 19.3 (2003): 180–97. Print.

Zillmann, Dolf. "Empathy: Affective Reactivity to Others' Emotional Experiences." *The Psychology of Entertainment*. Ed. Jennings Bryant and Peter Vorderer. Mahwah NJ: Lawrence Erlbaum, 2006. 151–81. Print.

Zwaan, Rolf A. "Experiential Traces and Mental Simulations in Language Comprehension." *Symbols and Embodiment: Debates on Meaning and Cognition*. Ed. Manuel de Vega, Arthur M. Glenberg, and Arthur C. Graesser. Oxford, UK: Oxford University Press, 2008. 165–80. Print.

PART 3 *Transmedia Storytelling and Transmedial Worlds*

11 Strategies of Storytelling on Transmedia Television

JASON MITTELL

Few storytelling forms can match serial television for narrative breadth and vastness. A single narrative universe can continue for years, or even decades in the case of daytime serials, with cumulative plotlines and character backstories accruing far beyond what any dedicated fan could reasonably remember. Even a show that fails to find an audience typically airs for a comparatively long time. For instance, the single-season *Terriers* may be seen as a commercial failure, but it still offered thirteen episodes of serial storytelling, with a combined running time of more than nine hours, that eclipses the scope of most novels and nearly every feature film. In short, of all the challenges that the creators of television fiction face, the lack of screen time to tell their stories is hardly an issue.

Given serial television's temporal vastness, it would seem unlikely that producers would want to expand their storytelling scope into other venues, as managing the single-medium realm of a television series is more than enough work for a creative team. However, the 2000s saw the rise of innovative forms of narrative extensions, grouped under the term "transmedia storytelling," that have significantly expanded the scope of a television series into an array of other media from video games to jigsaw puzzles and books to blogs. To understand the phenomenon of transmedia television, we need to look closely at the strategies that various series employ, the motivations behind such narrative extensions, and the tactics that viewers use to make sense of such expanded serialized vastness.[1]

Any thoughtful study of contemporary *transmedia* must start with the vital caveat that transmedia is not a new phenomenon, born of the digital age. Even if the term is new, the strategy of expanding a narrative into other media is as old as media themselves; think of paintings dramatizing biblical scenes or iconic nineteenth-century characters such as Frankenstein or Sherlock Holmes whose narrative scope transcends any single medium. Early television employed transmedia strategies as well, as one of the medium's first hits, *Dragnet*, spanned multiple media. Starting as a radio show, the more popular television series of the 1950s spawned a number of books; a feature film; tie-in toys such as a board game, police badge, and whistle; and even a television reboot in the late 1960s.

Highlighting the history of transmedia is not to suggest that nothing new has happened in recent years; undoubtedly the proliferation of digital forms has led to transmedia techniques that are both greater in degree and different in kind. Certainly technological transformations have helped enable such proliferations, as digital platforms—online video, blogs, computer games, DVD supplements, social networking, and new forms such as alternate reality games (ARGs)—are cost-effective and widely accessible avenues for expanding a narrative universe. Additionally, industrial shifts that have shrunk the relative size of any one program's television audience and expanded ratings competition across numerous cable and broadcast outlets have encouraged producers to experiment with transmedia as a way to get noticed and build viewer loyalty in an increasingly cluttered television schedule. We might characterize this development as a shift in norms; in previous decades, it was exceptional for a program to use a significant transmedia strategy, while today it is more exceptional for a high-profile series not to adopt one.

Despite the growing ubiquity of transmedia, we need to avoid confusing general transmedia extensions with the more particular mode of transmedia storytelling. Nearly every media property today offers some transmedia extensions, such as promotional websites, merchandise, or behind-the-scenes materials. These forms can be usefully categorized as *paratexts* in relation to the core text, whether a feature film, video game, or television series. As Jonathan Gray has argued in his defining work on the topic, we cannot view any text in our media-saturated age in isolation from its paratexts. For instance, films come pre-framed by trailers, DVD covers, and posters, and once any text enters into cultural circulation, it becomes part of a complex intertextual web. However, we can follow Gray's lead by distinguishing between paratexts that function primarily to hype, promote, and introduce a text with those that function as ongoing sites of narrative expansion and that I explore here.

Transmedia storytelling thrives in these ongoing paratexts through a strategy best captured by Henry Jenkins's comprehensive and influential definition of the form: "Transmedia storytelling represents a process where integral elements of a fiction get *dispersed systematically across multiple delivery channels* for the purpose of creating *a unified and coordinated entertainment experience.* Ideally, each medium makes it own *unique contribution* to the unfolding of the story" ("Transmedia 202" n. pag., original emphases). This definition of transmedia storytelling problematizes the hierarchy between text and paratext, for in the most ideally balanced example, all texts would be equally weighted rather than having one being privileged as "text" while others serve as supporting "paratexts." However, in the high-stakes industry of commercial television, the financial realities demand that the core medium of any franchise be identified and privileged, typically emphasizing the more traditional television form over newer modes of online textuality. Thus in understanding transmedia television, we can identify the originating television series as the core text with transmedia extensions serving as paratexts.

This issue of relative emphasis and priority across transmedia is crucial to both the industrial and storytelling logics of serial television. American commercial television's core business model is predicated on attracting viewers to a television program, aggregating them into measurable audience segments, and selling that viewership to advertisers in the currency of Nielsen ratings. Even as television's industrial structures shift toward more flexible measures of audience practice, the emphasis still remains on producing high ratings to generate the majority of revenues used to fund both television and its associated forays into transmedia storytelling. So the industrial edict to protect and strengthen the core business of watching commercial television dictates a creative imperative as well: any television-based transmedia must protect the "mothership," to borrow the term *Lost* producers Damon Lindelof and Carlton Cuse used for the central television series at the heart of their armada of paratextual transmedia extensions. For the industry, transmedia extensions might provide an additional revenue stream, but their primary function is to drive viewers back to the television series; for creators, transmedia storytelling must always support and strengthen the core television narrative experience.

This imperative creates challenges to mesh Jenkins's definitional ideal of distributed transmedia as a "unified and coordinated entertainment experience" with the reality that television storytellers must privilege the mothership by designing experiences that can be consumed by viewers in a wide range of ways without sacrificing coherence or engagement, regardless of how aware they may be of the paratextual extensions. This challenge of differential engagement plays a crucial role in one of this chapter's case studies, as *Lost* embraced a wide range of transmedia strategies that tried both to protect the mothership for television-only viewers and to reward participation for transmedia-savvy fans. But before turning to this detailed example, it is important to chart out some of the earlier established narrative strategies that television has used to extend into other media and clarify precisely what is meant by "storytelling" when discussing transmedia.

Precedents of Transmedia Television

The commonsense notion of *storytelling* assumes the centrality of narrative events, where a story consists of "what happens." Certainly events are crucial ingredients of any story, but a narrative also comprises two additional components that are crucial to transmedia storytelling—characters and settings. A television series works to create a sustained narrative setting, populated by a consistent set of characters who experience a chain of events, with all three factors combining to forge a coherent storyworld. A primary feature of serialized television is that these facets are cumulative and consistent in the storyworld, with everything that happens and everyone we see as a part of this persistent narrative universe. Such cumulative persistence is one of the chief ways that serial storytelling is defined against episodic television. Although an episodic drama or sitcom may have the same characters and storyworld, such characters rarely remember previous events, and there is little sense of continuity between episodes, enabling viewers to watch intermittently and out of chronology.

For fans of serial television, charting the canonical events, characters, and settings featured in a storyworld is a central mode of engagement, with viewers striving for both narrative comprehension and deeper understanding of a fictional universe. The rising prevalence of transmedia television alongside the increase in complex seriality has complicated this question of canon, forcing producers to make difficult choices about how transmedia serial storytelling situates its paratexts in relation to the core television canonical mothership. We can see the important precedents for these issues playing out through older examples of transmedia television in the forms of tie-in books and video games.

Both in conventional prose and comics-based graphic form, books have a long history as paratexts to moving-image media, such as film and television, but their role is typically derided as nonessential add-ons rather than viewed as integrated transmedia. For many film properties, the most common books are novelizations, or direct retellings of the story events, characters, and settings previously seen on-screen, and are typified by cheap mass-market paperback novelizations and their comic book counterparts. Although such novelizations are far from the model of coordinated, dispersed transmedia storytelling as defined by Jenkins, they frequently do add material to the storyworld by filling in gaps in the story left unseen, whether they are events not seen on-screen or internal character thoughts or backstories that are far easier to convey by the written word. Strict novelizations that retell on-screen stories are much rarer for series television, with most examples found in the realm of cult television classics such as the original 1960s-era *Doctor Who* and *Star Trek*, both of which saw many of their episodes adapted to novel format. In these television franchises and others in film, such as *Star Wars*, the novels can become part of the canonical storyworld, with details that are expanded in the novels sometimes appearing in future on-screen installments.

The form of series television encourages another more common form of tie-in novel, with a book functioning similar to a new episode of an ongoing series. This approach makes sense for a highly episodic series, as the established characters and setting can easily host a new set of narrative events without much need for policing canonical boundaries. We see this type of tie-in novel frequently in shows that connect to popular fiction genres, such as police procedurals from *Dragnet* to *Columbo* to *CSI*. In such episodic narratives, the books function mainly to stay true to the characters, tone, and norms of the narrative universe. Their actual plots are frequently irrelevant to larger continuity, and thus questions of canonicity rarely matter. For the cult realm of science fiction, tie-in novels are quite common, but the questions of canon are more fraught. Early cult sci-fi show *Star Trek* featured dozens of new episode-like tie-in novels in addition to novelized retellings. While the franchise's creative team regarded most of them as noncanonical, many fans embraced them, especially in the decades between the original series leaving the air and the emergence of *Star Trek: The Next Generation* in the late 1980s.

Novelistic extensions from more contemporary serialized programs often fall in the awkward realm of semi-canon; that is, they are endorsed by the show's creative team but not fully integrated into the show's complex serial arcs. Examples include *24*, whose novels typically predate the show's continuity by telling tales from character's backstories, and *Buffy the Vampire Slayer*, which features both novelized retellings and new episode novels (in both prose and comic forms) that explore a broad chronology in the franchise's mythology. Such tie-ins are usually written independently from the show's core writers but are based on story outlines that are approved by showrunners and production studios. In some notable instances a show's producer pens his or her own canonical tie-in, as with *Buffy* creator, Joss Whedon, writing an arc of comic books that came to be known as *Season 8* and extended the show's continuity after it left the air. Print extensions of popular series can be quite popular with fans, who often have a love-hate relationship with the books as they try to police boundaries of canon, seek tonal consistencies, and otherwise explore the borders of their favored fictional storyworlds.

While fans typically judge print extensions on how well they capture the tone, setting, and characters of the mothership, the type of integrated transmedia Jenkins explores in his example of *The Matrix* franchise places more emphasis on narrative events, where the plot is distributed across media (*Convergence Culture*). Few television series have attempted to create transmedia extensions that offer such canonic integration, with interwoven story events that must be consumed across media for full comprehension. This reluctance is surely in large part due to the industrial demands of a commercial television system that depends on revenue from "selling eyeballs" to advertisers, and mandatory transmedia might seem to undermine that effort. Additionally, the broad (if erroneous) cultural assumption that television is a low-commitment and passive "lean back" medium would prohibit against experiments that demand more from viewers beyond simply sitting and watching an episode. As complex narratives have demonstrated, viewers will actively engage with challenging television; thus producers have been willing to try more overtly narratively integrated transmedia storytelling, albeit with very mixed results.

One of the first examples of a canonically integrated tie-in book came from complex television pioneer *Twin Peaks*, with the publication of *The Secret Diary of Laura Palmer* in 1990 between the airings of the show's first and second seasons. Written by Jennifer Lynch, series cocreator David Lynch's daughter, *Secret Diary* functions as a distinctive form of transmedia—namely, a *diegetic extension*, where an object from the storyworld gets released in the real world. Most diegetic extensions are objects featured in a series that do not bear much storytelling weight, such as Davy Crockett's coonskin cap, or items bearing the logo of an in-story brand, like a Dunder Mifflin mug from *The Office*. *Secret Diary* was a reproduction of Laura's diary as featured on the series and had pages that were ripped out to obscure crucial narrative revelations still to come, making it both an object from the show and an early experiment in integrated transmedia storytelling. The diary, which sold quite well at the height of *Twin Peaks*' cultural relevance, provided numerous clues about Laura's murder and her hidden dark past. While a viewer need not read the diary to comprehend the show's plotlines—although with *Twin Peaks*, one's comprehension is always a bit vague and muddled—the diary did provide important canonical story information about both events and characters, material that was later explored in the prequel feature film *Twin Peaks: Fire Walk with Me*. The show followed up the diary with two other diegetic tie-in books—an autobiography of Agent Dale Cooper that was "transcribed" from his iconic dictated, tape-recorded notes to "Diane" and a travel guide to the town of Twin Peaks—but neither were particularly popular given the show's deflated ratings and cancellation in its second season.

Although they do not have as long of a history as television-based novels, tie-in video games offer another window into the strategies and challenges of transmedia television. Again, these games are not new phenomena of the contemporary era. *Star Trek* games date back to the 1970s with text-only adventure games and the 1980s with flight simulators, and *Doctor Who* similarly had tie-in games from early on (not to mention even earlier pre-computerized board games). However, we can see a set of strategies emerging in games tied into recent contemporary television serials in terms of how they negotiate the three realms of characters, events, and storyworld and how they tackle the question of canon. While most of these games are not part of larger transmedia narrative campaigns, they do highlight the challenges of extending an ongoing serial across media.

Nearly every tie-in game foregrounds the storyworld of its original television franchise, allowing players to explore the universe that was previously only seen on television. With settings as diverse as the mean streets of *The Shield*'s Los Angeles, the suburban cul-de-sac of *Desperate Housewives*, or the deep space exploration of *Battlestar Galactica*, television tie-ins fulfill Henry Jenkins's suggestion that game narratives function primarily as spatial storytelling; we explore the virtual representations of the storyworlds created in serial television as a way to extend the narrative experience and participate in the fictional universe ("Game Design"). The tie-in games that fans seem to embrace most are those that re-create their television universes with vivid and immersive storyworlds, such as the virtual Springfield found in a number of *The Simpsons* games, with game worlds often surpassing the televisual versions in terms of level of detail and breadth. While such games need not relay vital narrative information through their spatial reconstructions, one key criterion that fans use to judge the merits of such games is the accuracy with which they re-create the storyworld and make them feel consistent with the fictional spaces they have come to know over the course of years of a television series.

The treatment of characters within tie-in games has proven to be trickier to navigate. While the digital animation of games enables developers to re-create television settings with depth and fidelity, the creation of robust and engaging people is still a technical challenge where games clearly lag behind television production. Adding to the challenge is the frequent problem of games not featuring the original actors voicing their parts, widening the gap between a television character and its game avatar for viewers. Arguably, the most intense bond that fans of a television serial have with the show is their affection for and connection with the characters; thus a game that fails to re-create a beloved, well-known character often alienates fans. Even when original actors are used, players often bristle at how limited a game's versions of beloved characters become, often reducing complex character depth into a set of quirks or a limited menu of actions. For instance, the game *Buffy the Vampire Slayer:*

Chaos Bleeds allows you to play many different characters from the series (some with original voices and others with soundalikes), but it limits what you can do as each character when navigating a level, fighting monsters, and spouting wisecracks. The ability to try on the skin of a favorite television character is certainly a major appeal for licensed games, but seemingly no television tie-in game has been able to re-create the core pleasure of spending time with fully realized characters in a television serial, an issue that will become pertinent in discussing more wide-ranging transmedia franchises.

One common strategy to overcome this gap between television and game characterizations is to focus a tie-in game on a new protagonist placed within an already established storyworld. For example, in the *Sopranos* game *Road to Respect*, you play as Joey LaRocca, the never-before-mentioned son of late gangster Big Pussy Bonpensiero. Joey explores fictionalized New Jersey locales such as the Bada Bing and Satriale's and interacts with core characters such as Tony Soprano, Christopher Moltisanti, and Paulie "Walnuts" Gualtieri. Even though Joey is a new character unburdened by the need to accurately re-create a television version, the action of the game reduces the storytelling scope to focus solely on the violent life of a mobster and thus eliminates the interplay between Tony's dual "families" that helped define the series as a television landmark. Similar tie-in games, including *The X-Files Game*, *Prison Break: The Conspiracy*, and *Lost: Via Domus*, use new characters as a way to navigate an existing storyworld and interact with established television characters. Thus whether they are exploring established or new characters, tie-in games are marked by a narrowing and simplification of characters, contrasting how they frequently expand upon the original show in creating an immersive and expanded storyworld.

The problems with tie-in characters often stem from a lack of depth and a fidelity to the original, but the third facet of story events suffers more from issues of confounded coordination with its serialized source material. Following the patterns outlined for novels, tie-in games typically choose one of two options for what narrative events will be told. The first is to retell events from the source material, allowing players to participate in an original core narrative. This strategy is common for film tie-ins, as most games from franchises such as *The Lord of the Rings* and *Toy Story* vary little from the original narrative events, although I've yet to find a television-based game using a retelling strategy comparable to those in novelizations. More commonly, television tie-ins treat the game as a new episode in the series, depicting events that could feasibly function as an episode from the series but have not. Thus the *24* and *Alias* games both place their heroes in situations very similar to an arc from the original series and have them interacting with core characters in familiar locales, but the plots are essentially stand-alone stories amid highly serialized narratives. At their worst, such "new episode" tie-in games are merely conventional formulaic games in a typical genre, like espionage or action, with a thin veneer of another diegetic world and a cast of characters ported from a television series. They are not fully realized games that capture the tone or spirit of the original narrative.

Even when they are enjoyable gaming experiences, most television tie-ins fail to provide a transmedia resonance that delivers on the pleasures from the original series. Sometimes such games are peppered with mythological information, allowing a die-hard fan to recognize a reference to the show's backstory or ongoing mystery, but I have yet to find a tie-in game that delivers an integrated narrative payoff that feels tied to a serial canon in a significant rather than superficial way, aside from creating a navigable storyworld. I do not attribute this lack of integrated transmedia storytelling to any deficiency in video games as a medium, as many games do create compelling narrative experiences, deep and nuanced characters, and engaging plotlines. And Jenkins's example of *The Matrix* franchise shows that it is possible for a video game to offer canonical integration into a series narrative, even though most saw *Enter the Matrix* itself as a less-than-satisfying gameplay experience. This lack of an effective television-based integrated game speaks to a creative challenge that plagues the entire transmedia enterprise: how do you create narrative extensions from an ongoing core franchise that reward fans seeking out canon but do not become essential consumption for single-medium fans, especially when the core narrative experience is serialized over time and requires a sustained investment in time and attention? In other words, the constraints of the television industry and norms of television consumption insist that *transmedia extensions from a serial franchise must reward those who partake in them but cannot punish those who do not.*

Lost in Transmedia Television

While individual transmedia extensions such as novels or video games can exemplify some general strategies storytellers use to expand their narrative horizons, it is useful to look at how a particular show mounts an extensive transmedia campaign to get a sense of the scope that a television serial might embrace. Exploring transmedia storytelling poses significant research challenges, as many paratexts are hard to access after their initial release, whether they are online sites that are pulled from the web, ephemeral objects that disappear from circulation, or emergent practices that change over time. In many cases, such as that of ARGs, the paratext itself is experiential more than textual, making it impossible to re-create the narrative moment of participating in the game. Thus, as researchers, we must rely either on our own experiences or secondhand accounts of transmedia consumption rather than being able to revisit a story for analytical purposes.

A number of expansive transmedia television landmarks, including *Heroes*, *24*, and *The Office*, might prove effective as a primary case study, but I have chosen to focus on *Lost* for two main reasons. First, it is undoubtedly one of the most extensive and expansive examples of both complex television narrative and transmedia storytelling, with extensions sprawled across nearly every medium throughout the show's six-season run.[2] Second, I approach the show's transmedia as a participant observer, having been highly involved in following and documenting the first ARG and having consumed most of the other paratexts in real time as they were released. Many of these texts no longer exist in accessible form, so I hope to use my personal consumption as a source for critical reflection on how the show used transmedia storytelling within the context of an ongoing serial narrative.[3]

Lost's approach to transmedia storytelling is expansionist, working to extend the narrative universe across media and introducing many new characters, settings, plotlines, time periods, and mythological elements. While few viewers would accuse *Lost*'s television mothership of being too simplistic in its narrative scope, the show used transmedia to extend itself into tales that surpassed the wide scope of the series itself. This expansionism led *Lost* to add to its six seasons of television with four alternate reality games, four novels, a console/PC video game, multiple tie-in websites and online videos, DVD extras, and an array of collectible merchandise. Owing to both its fantasy genre and its storytelling commitments to create a rich mythological universe, *Lost* is suited to this expansionist approach to transmedia, using paratexts to extend the narrative outward into new locales and arenas through an approach we might term "centrifugal storytelling."

One important aspect of *Lost* that makes it ripe for transmedia extensions is its unique locale in a mysterious place with a rich history. The unnamed island has been inhabited by various factions of people since ancient Egyptian times and offers a deep well of backstory to be exploited. Showrunners Lindelof and Cuse have used the metaphor of an iceberg to represent the storyworld: the material appearing on the show is what is visible above the waterline, but underwater depths and layers exist that are never directly addressed on television. As with other deep mythologies, such as J. R. R. Tolkien's Middle Earth or the *Star Wars* universe, *Lost*'s producers tapped into a wide range of styles, characters, and eras to extend the narrative universe to other media. And such transmedia extensions helped encourage viewers to engage with the show and its paratexts as forensic fans, drilling into texts to crack their hidden meanings and discover secrets, and to collaborate on building extensive databases of story information such as Lostpedia, the vast fan wiki detailing the *Lost* universe.

One strategy that *Lost* took advantage of throughout its run was creating openings within the television show to invite viewers to explore the storyworld in more depth. Such invitations, sometimes called "Easter eggs" if they are seen as throwaway bonus features or "trailheads" if they lead to larger narrative pathways, rarely were central to *Lost*'s core narrative, but typically they provided a bit of backstory, cultural references, or deep history of the island. Lindelof and Cuse have discussed in interviews and podcasts that they had a specific litmus test for what mythology to reveal and explore on the show itself versus in the transmedia extensions: it would only appear on the show if the main characters cared about it. While we can quibble as to how precisely they followed their own edict, it is instructive in establishing the show's orientation as a character-centered drama rather than as a mythological fantasy.

Lost, in large part due to its centrifugal use of transmedia, offered a wide range of genres, styles, and appeals simultaneously: a puzzling science fiction mystery, a dimension-spanning romance, a rip-roaring outdoors adventure, and a religious parable about letting go of the past and finding fellowship. In the end, the television series downplayed the puzzle box of trailheads it had left throughout its journey and, in doing so, betrayed the expectations of many of its most hard-core fans. One of *Lost*'s biggest challenges was always in managing the rabid fan base's divergent expectations. Fans were invested in a wide range of the show's narrative facets, from the complex mythology to romantic relationships and heady time-traveling sci-fi to adventure-driven action sequences. While at times fans split on the relative merits of particular plotlines, episodes, or characters, as a whole the show did an admirable job of servicing such a broad array of appeals and fan bases. A key strategy for accomplishing this storytelling breadth was to center the core television show around its characters, particularly their adventures and dramas, and how they encountered the mythology, allowing the more in-depth mythological explorations and explanations to flower both in fan-created extensions and transmedia properties.

The majority of *Lost*'s transmedia extensions prioritized storyworld expansion and exploration instead of building on the show's emotional arcs and character relationships, with some narrative events posited in an awkward relationship to the narrative canon. Two high-profile paratexts—the video game *Lost: Via Domus* and the novel *Bad Twin*, which was posited as a diegetic extension authored by deceased Oceanic 815 passenger Gary Troup—were initially framed as canonical extensions, but later the showrunners partially recanted and claimed they were not fully connected to the core story. In both cases, Lindelof and Cuse highlighted that the outsourced creators of these extensions took the plotlines they outlined in new directions that contradicted the core canon from the television show; instead, both fell into familiar traditions of "new episode" storytelling outside the core canonical arc. One of the chief challenges for creating canonically integrated transmedia for an ongoing serial is that the demands of running such a complex show as *Lost* already tax the energies of producers; thus paratexts are left in the hands of outsourced writers who frequently fail to meet the expectations of both creators and producers. Creating coherent complex narratives requires a degree of storytelling control that the current systems of transmedia production seem unable to meet.

Aside from the video minisodes that appeared online and on DVDs (which were produced by the standard television production personnel), the transmedia paratext over which the core writers had the most control was arguably its most innovative—namely, the first ARG, *The Lost Experience* (TLE). Running in the summer of 2006, TLE was the first extensive ARG to emerge during an ongoing mainstream hit television series, and it filled the hiatus between seasons 2 and 3 of the television series. Lasting four months and spanning an array of media across the world, including websites, podcasts, television appearances, voice mail, live events, and merchandise, it is also arguably the most ambitious and extensive ARG yet attempted for a television series. It thus established many of the industry's assumptions about the form and its possibilities and limitations. TLE was conceived by *Lost* showrunners Lindelof and Cuse, with leadership from staff writer Javier Grillo-Marxuach, making the ARG an integrated aspect of the show's narrative canon and core production team.

Lost's producers have suggested that TLE had three main goals: to offer narrative revelations for hard-core fans that would not be addressed in the show itself, to experiment with innovative forms of storytelling, and to keep the show active in press coverage and the public consciousness during its summer hiatus (Cuse and Lindelof). The last objective was clearly successful as the experiments of TLE generated a good deal of press coverage, including a June *Entertainment Weekly* story teased on the magazine's cover; effectively avoided a summer slump of waning enthusiasm; and placed ARGs in the mainstream consciousness like never before. As an innovative form of narrative, the lessons learned from storytelling mistakes and problems outweighed any compelling formal innovations. TLE consistently had to balance the desires of ARG players wanting to be challenged with innovative puzzles and the television fans clamoring for more direct narrative payoffs. The in-game story of Rachel Blake investigating the Hanso Foundation rarely resonated as much more than a skeleton upon which to hang clues, and the game's narrative does not stand alone from the storyworld established in the television series. The gameplay and immersive experience were too erratic in quality and sophistication for hard-core ARG players, driving many of them away after the first few weeks and leaving less experienced players to try to work through subsequent puzzles. Additionally, the integrated marketing with sponsors such as Jeep, Verizon, and Sprite struck many players as crass and intrusive, violating the playful spirit that ARGs aim to capture (Mittell, "Lost").

As to the goal of revealing narrative mythology for the ongoing television series, the ARG proved to be more frustrating than rewarding. The canonical narrative content was not sufficiently integrated into the television series as a whole, making some players feel as if they had wasted their time on "trivia" rather than getting a head start on what was to come during *Lost*'s season 3. The biggest revelations in *TLE* came from the so-called Sri Lanka Video, which included an orientation film featuring Danish industrialist Alvar Hanso, explaining the origins and mission of the research project known as the Department of Heuristics and Research on Material Applications (DHARMA) Initiative, the meaning of the "numbers" (a central mystery from the show's first two seasons) as being part of an equation predicting the end of the world, and the numerous other clues that connected directly with the television canon. The video received more than a million views on YouTube, but that number is still a small fraction of the show's global television audience. Moreover, its revelations never appeared in the show itself, and the numbers were given a different (but not contradictory) explanation in the show's final season. For the fans who had participated in the ARG and already had solved the mystery of the numbers, they felt the show's new explanation was a slap in the face that undermined fan engagement by placing the narrative events uncovered in the ARG into an ambiguous para-canonical status. In contrast, some of the revelations from *TLE* were considered "unanswered questions" by television fans, who were left unsatisfied with the mythological ambiguity of the show's final season. That the numbers and DHARMA were only explained in the ARG increased these fans' frustration over the television show's narrative, as they wanted to be able to comprehend the show fully without doing "online research." Even for *TLE* players who learned the secrets of the Sri Lanka Video, that these revelations were never addressed, or subsequently contradicted or displaced, on the television show made the gameplay more frustrating. In retrospect it was more of a waste of time rather than a storytelling bonus.

The scaled-down efforts to use ARGs in the *Lost* franchise in subsequent years suggest that many of these lessons were in fact learned as the producers reduced their ambitions to create transmedia experiences that were less robust and complex but ultimately less disappointing to their target audiences. Lindelof and Cuse told me that they found the challenges of running an integrated ARG within the already complicated television production process too daunting to try again; thus they scaled back the subsequent ARGs to be less integral to the show's canon. No matter how enjoyable such games and extensions were to fans, they often fell short in rewarding the core edict of adding to the franchise's storytelling without taking away from the main television experience. One of the great contradictions of *Lost* is that the series built as robust a mythological universe as was ever devised for television but then undermined the importance of its own mythology by relegating many of its mysteries to transmedia extensions, or "bonus content," rather than to core storytelling. The show was unmatched in its ability to posit mysteries and encourage fans to immerse themselves expansively into clunky alternate reality games and poorly paced video games and novels with the hope of uncovering answers. Yet by the final season, while the show offered emotional character resolutions and thrilling adventure storytelling, it left many mythological questions unaddressed in the television series itself or was ambiguously vague in its answers. On its own, I found the show's emotional payoffs and sweeping character arcs sufficiently engaging and entertaining; however, its use of transmedia and cultivation of a forensic fandom encouraged us to expect more, leading many fans to revolt against the show in its final hours for not delivering its answers in a clearly marked package.

This dichotomy between forensic fans watching (and playing) for coherence and emotional viewers getting swept up in the adventurous melodrama mirrors one of the show's main thematic structures—the contrast between rational and supernatural outlooks as embodied by the battle between Jack Shephard's "man of science" and John Locke's "man of faith." Even though neither character survives the narrative, it is clear by the show's conclusion that faith trumps science, with Jack sacrificing himself to the island's mystical forces and endorsing John's vision of fate and spiritual meaning. In choosing faith over science and in turn privileging the genre of fantasy adventure over science fiction, *Lost* was willing to let many of the show's dangling mysteries go unexplained as it offered instead a spiritual celebration of Jack's (and by extension, our) "letting go" the need for rational understanding in the show's closing moments. And yet, the show's transmedia strategy still sided with the rational exploration of the island's mythology, despite its frequently frustrating incoherence. The final DVD released contained a bonus twelve-minute "epilogue" video that provided a flood of answers to dangling questions about the island, DHARMA, the unresolved fate of Walt, and various other mythological mysteries. The playful video winks at viewers as a DHARMA worker chastises the character Ben and says, "Wait. You can't just walk out of here. We deserve answers!" And even though the answers resolve some ambiguity, it becomes clear that this additional content is canonical but considered nonessential, relegated to a paratext simply to appease those hard-core forensic fans who would not follow the finale's message to let go.

Thus *Lost*'s transmedia seems to follow some clear parameters: use paratexts to expand access to the storyworld and island mythology, but keep character arcs and dramas centered on the television mothership. While this strategy might reward hard-core fans who are willing to expand their narrative consumption across media, it frustrates both transmedia consumers who are underwhelmed by the payoffs and television fans who do not want to have to do "homework" to understand their favorite shows. Although I would not claim that most *Lost* fans who were left frustrated by the finale had been transmedia consumers, the show's reliance on transmedia to parcel out answers did set up expectations that the finale would offer answers based on forensic rationality rather than spiritual acceptance. *Lost*'s commercial and creative successes have established the show as a model for transmedia television and have inspired numerous clones in both television and paratextual formats, including *Heroes*, *FlashForward*, and *The Event*. But another case study suggests a very different approach to television transmedia that seems more modest but ultimately more successful.

Breaking Bad as Character-Driven Transmedia

Mixing riveting suspense and pitch-black comedy, AMC's *Breaking Bad* is an intense character study of a chemistry teacher who gradually turns into a drug kingpin. The show most closely resembles a television serial that the Coen brothers would produce. While *Lost* used transmedia to expand its narrative universe outward to the breaking point, *Breaking*

Bad demonstrates the alternate vector, creating transmedia to fold in on itself in a centripetal fashion. Most television shows that have embraced transmedia aggressively are in fantasy or comedic genres, like *Heroes* and *The Office*. Fantasy and science fiction shows can use transmedia to create more expansive and detailed versions of their storyworlds, which typically are a core appeal within the genre. The emphasis on world building through paratexts is a time-honored strategy for narratives set in universes with their own scientific or magical properties that beg further investigation and exploration. For comedies, transmedia can be a site to develop additional gags or highlight throwaway plotlines for secondary characters without disrupting the plot and character arcs of the television mothership.

While *Breaking Bad* has not been as aggressive in its use of transmedia, its modest strategies offer an interesting contrast. If *Lost*'s expansive transmedia offered new narrative events and broadened the storyworld, *Breaking Bad*'s focus has been primarily on character. Its use of character-based transmedia makes sense given *Breaking Bad*'s genre and narrative strategies; as the show has no underlying mythology or complex mystery to parse, the transmedia extensions offer virtually no narrative events that seem particularly relevant to the story as a whole. Likewise, *Breaking Bad*'s storyworld is a fairly realistic version of Albuquerque, New Mexico, so its transmedia offers almost no attention to the setting itself. This deemphasis on storyworld and plot arcs in its transmedia is partly tied to the show's genre of serious drama, but even the similarly dramatic *Mad Men* grounds its small excursions into transmedia, such as its online Cocktail Guide and Fashion Show sites, within its periodized world.

Instead, *Breaking Bad*'s transmedia extensions focus on character over setting or plot, providing additional depth to a show that already features highly realized characters. Most of this transmedia character development focuses on secondary figures from the show rather than on the main protagonist, Walter White, and highlights the show's comedic rather than dramatic tone. It offers additional videos and websites illuminating the amusing backgrounds of Hank and Marie Schrader, Brandon "Badger" Mayhew, and Saul Goodman, some of the least serious characters in the show (especially in early seasons). The most enjoyable is the diegetic extension promotional website for Goodman's law firm, serving as a dual parody of both ambulance-chasing lawyers and cheesy website design. Even when Walter is featured in a minisode, it paints the dark main character in a more comedic light, with the shorts showing him listening to the pre-wedding sexual hijinks of his future brother-in-law, Hank, or carrying out a bungled breaking and entering with a drugged-out Badger. These minisodes do not contradict the show's plot arcs and offer a different but compatible comedic tone that tends to be downplayed on the darker mothership.

Although *Breaking Bad* lacks the mythological expanses that tend to encourage tie-in games to explore the storyworlds, the show has spawned two online mini games that point to another direction for game-based transmedia. Both were created for AMC's website with direct coordination from the show's producers and feature motion comic–style graphics with an interactive narrative design. The first, "The Interrogation," was launched during the show's third season in the spring of 2010, while the follow-up, "The Cost of Doing Business," was released for both the web and mobile devices prior to season 4 in the summer of 2011. "The Interrogation" places us in the shoes of Drug Enforcement Agency (DEA) agent Hank Schrader as he interrogates a suspected member of a drug-smuggling organization; in "The Cost of Doing Business," we play as Jesse Pinkman, trying to get paid what he is owed from a drug customer. Neither plotline is canonic to the show, but both feel as if they are plausible moments for the characters in the new episode model common to tie-in games. Gordon Smith, a writer's assistant for the show, scripted the games and suggests that each game "hopefully is true to the characters as they are on the show, but it's not stories that literally take place in the timetable of the series. We feel like they're part of the show that somebody could have experienced at some point, [with events that] had the same *feel* of something on the show" (Dixon and Gilligan, n. pag., original emphasis). This emphasis on creating extensions that coordinate characters' identities and a consistent tone with the show points to a strength of *Breaking Bad*'s transmedia: by downplaying the plot, the extensions work by allowing viewers to spend time with the characters without encouraging the forensic attention to the story that most canonic extensions require.

The minisodes featuring Jesse are indicative of this approach. His story lines on the show can frequently be quite dark and serious, but his minisodes focus comedically on his fledgling band and artistic creations rather than on his struggles with addiction or his quest for self-discovery as Walt's surrogate son. Most interesting, one video features a hypothetical animated series, *Team S.C.I.E.N.C.E.*, featuring superhero versions of the characters as created by Jesse, who transformed them into a crime-fighting team rather than a burgeoning criminal enterprise. Not only does this video offer an amusing take on the show's characters for die-hard fans, but it also provides a compelling look into Jesse's psychology, exploring how he narrativizes and rationalizes his own experiences, and positions his impressive artistic skills in relation to his criminal actions. Nothing that happens in this video is canonical, as it is clearly outside the storyworld. Perhaps it could be read as a diegetic extension of something Jesse would make, but more likely it is a hypothetical game of speculation, playing with genre, tone, and production mode while retaining a consistency of character. As with most of *Breaking Bad*'s transmedia, such videos draw you into the core television series and offer some additional depth rather than expanding the storyworld's scope and breadth. All of the show's extensions seem as though they could easily be canonical, if only because their modest scope rarely intersects with the main thrust of the television story, but they do not invite the type of intense dissection of plotlines typical of *Lost*'s transmedia.

None of *Breaking Bad*'s transmedia extensions reward viewers with trailheads into deeper narrative experiences, flesh out the fictional universe, or relay any seemingly vital story events. Instead, they allow us to spend more time with characters to whom we've grown close over the course of the television serial. While they may not seem as innovative or immersive as *Lost*'s paratexts, *Breaking Bad*'s transmedia may even work better as extensions to the core narrative by playing to the strengths of serial television and establishing connections to the characters. Nobody exploring *Breaking Bad*'s transmedia would have their expectations of the show transformed or misdirected as they are clearly positioned as supporting, nonessential "extras" rather than as true transmedia plotting. But in their modest success, I think they more effectively accomplish the goal of rewarding viewers who consume them and not punishing those who do not. And as we see further experimentation and innovation with transmedia storytelling, *Breaking Bad* and *Lost* both offer valuable lessons in how to balance viewer expectations, canonical concerns, and the relative importance of events, storyworld, and characters.

"What Is" versus "What If?" Transmedia

In the contrast between *Lost* and *Breaking Bad*'s paratextual strategies, we can see two larger tendencies that typify the practices of transmedia storytelling, dueling approaches that we might label "What Is" versus "What If?" The former is embodied on television by *Lost* and fits with Jenkins's definition of the form as exemplified by *The Matrix*. "What Is" transmedia seeks to extend the fiction canonically, explaining the universe with coordinated precision and hopefully expanding viewers' understanding and appreciation of the storyworld. This narrative model encourages forensic fandom with the promise of eventual revelations once all the pieces are put together. The emblematic example of a "What Is" paratext might be *Lost*'s jigsaw puzzles, which literally require assembling all the pieces of four separate puzzles to reveal extra narrative information hidden within a glow-in-the-dark map. If one goal of consuming a story is mastery of its fictional universe, then "What Is" transmedia scatters narrative understanding across a variety of extensions so that a collective team of die-hard fans can piece together the elaborate puzzle.

The majority of official storytelling extensions seem designed to fulfill the goals of "What Is" transmedia, and the measuring stick critics and fans use to assess those paratexts typically revolves around canonical coordination and narrative integration. However, an opposite mode of transmedia points to different narrative goals and markers of success—namely, the "What If?" extension as suggested by *Breaking Bad*'s *Team S.C.I.E.N.C.E.* This approach to transmedia poses hypothetical possibilities rather than canonical certainties, inviting viewers to imagine alternative stories and approaches to storytelling that are distinctly not to be treated as potential canon. The goal for "What If?" transmedia is to launch off the mothership into parallel dimensions, with connections foregrounding issues of tone, mood, character, or style more than continuing with canonical plots and storyworlds. We are never meant to believe that Jesse really created a comic and animated series fictionalizing his friends into a superhero team, but we are presented with the possibility that he could have and invited to imagine what would happen if he did. This style of hypothetical narrative paratext highlights the fictionality of all narrative: there is nothing more "real" in the characterization of Walter White as an accidental drug dealer than in Jesse's reinterpretation of him as Doctor Chemistry, fighting off zombies "for the right to be awesome," for both representations are works of fiction, albeit with one subsidiary to the other. Just as we embrace serial narrative for its creation of compelling storyworlds in which we can immerse ourselves, "What If?" transmedia multiplies the possibilities of those fictions into the realm of hypothetical variations and transmutations.[4]

Both "What Is" and "What If?" transmedia can best be seen as vectors or tendencies rather than as distinct categories, with fluidity and blur between the dual approaches. For instance, we might think of the *Lost* tie-in novel *Bad Twin* as conceived as a "What Is" diegetic extension that transformed through its troubled production process into a "What If?" hypothetical paratext. Many tie-in novels and games function as non-canonical "What If?" paratexts but lack the playful variation and imagination of *Team S.C.I.E.N.C.E.*; instead, they often function as failed "What Is" extensions, setting up viewers to search futilely for narrative continuities and canon but forcing them to come up empty. Both transmedia tendencies embrace a ludic narrative quality, but they draw upon different style of play: "What Is" transmedia work in the same way as puzzles, with proper solutions and final revelations, while "What If?" extensions feature more of a sense of dressing up or performative role-playing, spinning off scenarios with no real outcome or canonical narrative function.

We can see important precedents for both of these transmedia modes in the realm of fan productions and consumption practices. Some fan cultures produce paratexts that are clearly in the "What Is" realm. One example is what Bob Rehak terms "blueprint culture," as typified by the detailed schematics of the technology found in the *Star Trek* universe. This strategy of mapping and cataloguing the canonical universe has boomed with the rise of wikis, such as Lostpedia or *Star Trek*'s Memory Alpha, with fans collaborating in creating encyclopedic documentation of a storyworld. Such modes of affirmative fan engagement prioritize canonical authenticity, seek narrative mastery, and search for connections and theories to fill narrative gaps—all facets prioritized by "What Is" transmedia.

The more well-known models of fan productivity follow the "What If?" paradigm, with fan fiction, remix videos, and other forms of fan creativity making no claims to canonical authenticity but playfully positing a range of hypothetical narrative possibilities. Such paratexts are valued for their transformational expansiveness, thinking beyond the terrain of canon by proposing possibilities that clearly could not be "real" within the fictional universe—whether building on subtexts that could never be explicitly represented or offering intertextual crossovers to other franchises or real life. Some "What If?" fan creations do offer stories that strive to seamlessly fit within the canonical mothership or offer alternate interpretations that fans may view as more in keeping with their vision of a series than the ongoing narrative does. However, such fan creativity nearly always positions itself as outside the core canon and embraces its hypothetical possibilities, even when they might be regarded as more satisfying than the official narrative canon. This tension speaks to the urge for some fans to create their own stories that mimic the canonical, regardless of authorial endorsement or in-show confirmation, and that at times even masquerade as official licensed transmedia (Örnebring).

If fans step in to create pseudo-canonical "What Is" transmedia, there is potential tension in the opposite direction as well. As fans primarily have occupied the terrain of "What If?" transmedia, there is legitimate concern that the industry producing such extensions could work to co-opt fannish creativity and close down the realm of the hypothetical to fan producers. For instance, Sci-Fi Network (now called SyFy channel) offered an online video site for *Battlestar Galactica* fans to create their own remixes but only within the channel's chosen clips and usage policies, thus effectively constraining the free play of "What If?" creativity (see Russo). But I'd contend that the official production of a video such as *Team S.C.I.E.N.C.E.* celebrates the fannish "What If?" impulse without closing down possibilities and validates it by using the official talent of the show's cast members to make the hypothetical feel more authentic and fully realized. While fans cannot get Aaron Paul to record voice-over for their creative work, the short does open up new raw materials and hypothetical directions for future fan transmedia without enforcing a hierarchy between licensed and unlicensed material around the question of canon.

Jenkins's model of "What Is" coordinated transmedia, where plot coherence is distributed across media, is an exciting possibility for storytellers and deserves the attention it has gotten. But for transmedia properties with a clear mothership in serialized television, it may be an untenable model as the commercial system cannot effectively sustain a franchise that risks eroding television ratings points for viewers who are uninterested in straying beyond a single medium, not to mention the storytelling challenges of crafting complex plots that can function both over time and across media. I would point to the comparatively unexplored realm of "What If?" transmedia television as a potentially more productive avenue for serial television to develop, building on its strengths of character and mood over plotting and mythology, as well as tapping into the clear fan interest in imagining non-canonical possibilities. Potentially, the proliferation of hypothetical transmedia narrative offers another dimension of complexity that has yet to be discovered.

Notes

1. See Evans for an in-depth account of transmedia television.
2. See Askwith; Rose; and Smith for detailed accounts of *Lost*'s transmedia strategies.
3. For more on my role within *Lost* fandom, see Mittell, "Sites of Participation."
4. See Sconce for a discussion of the "What If?" impulse within television serials.

Works Cited

Askwith, Ivan. *Television 2.0: Reconceptualizing Television as an Engagement Medium*. Master's thesis MIT, 2007. PDF file. May 1, 2012.

Cuse, Carlton, and Damon Lindelof. Personal interview. March 23, 2010.

Dixon, Kelley, and Vince Gilligan. "*Breaking Bad* Insider Podcast for Episode 409." Sony Pictures Television. September 13, 2011. Web. May 1, 2012.

Evans, Elizabeth. *Transmedia Television: Audiences, New Media, and Daily Life*. London: Routledge, 2011. Print.

Gray, Jonathan. *Show Sold Separately: Promos, Spoilers, and Other Media Paratexts*. New York: New York University Press, 2010. Print.

Jenkins, Henry. *Convergence Culture: Where Old and New Media Collide*. New York: New York University Press, 2006. Print.

———. "Game Design as Narrative Architecture." *FirstPerson: New Media as Story, Performance, and Game*. Ed. Noah Wardrip-Fruin and Pat Harrigan. Cambridge MA: MIT Press, 2004. 118–30. Print.

———. "Transmedia 202: Further Reflections." *Confessions of an Aca-Fan*. August 1, 2011. Web. May 1, 2012.

Mittell, Jason. "Lost in an Alternate Reality." *Flow*. June 16, 2006. Web. May 1, 2012.

———. "Sites of Participation: Wiki Fandom and the Case of Lostpedia." *Transformative Works and Cultures* 3 (Fall 2009). Web. May 1, 2012.

Örnebring, Henrik. "Alternate Reality Gaming and Convergence Culture." *International Journal of Cultural Studies* 10.4 (December 1, 2007): 445–62. Print.

Rehak, Bob. "Franz Joseph and *Star Trek*'s Blueprint Culture." *Graphic Engine* (blog). Web. March 11, 2012.

Rose, Frank. *The Art of Immersion: How the Digital Generation Is Remaking Hollywood, Madison Avenue, and the Way We Tell Stories.* New York: W. W. Norton, 2011. Print.

Russo, Julie Levin. "User-Penetrated Content: Fan Video in the Age of Convergence." *Cinema Journal* 48.4 (2009): 125–30. Print.

Sconce, Jeffrey. "What If? Charting Television's New Textual Boundaries." *Television after TV: Essays on a Medium in Transition*. Ed. Lynn Spigel and Jan Olsson. Durham NC: Duke University Press, 2004. 93–112. Print.

Smith, Aaron. *Transmedia Storytelling in Television 2.0*. Honors thesis, Middlebury College, 2009. Web. May 1, 2012.

12 A Taxonomy of Transmedia Storytelling

COLIN B. HARVEY

Transmedia storytelling refers to the endeavor of conveying connected stories using a variety of media platforms. These stories can either be understood in isolation or viewed contingently with regard to those other stories that share the same storyworld but are conveyed using different media. Such media might include novels, films, video games, comic books, websites, alternate reality games (ARGS), and, increasingly, user-driven content (UDC) of various kinds.

Henry Jenkins explicitly differentiates transmedia storytelling from licensed cross-media storytelling but allows for pre-digital precedents. Stephen Dinehart echoes this viewpoint in his belief that "[t]ransmedia storytelling is not marketing and merchandising based extensions into an existing franchise" (n. pag.), suggesting instead that the term should be used to refer to franchises envisaged as cross-media from the outset. Dinehart contends that true transmedia storytelling "enable[s] the imagination via story-driven extensions in a 'world' in which a player seeks to be further immersed" (n. pag.).

In this chapter I argue that transmedia storytelling is more fruitfully understood as a broad category to describe instances of convergent storytelling but also varieties of pre-digital, licensed tie-in production that anticipate convergence, as well as contemporary cross-media production that incorporates elements of the analogue and the digital. I contend that there are significant parallels between these kinds of narrativizing—with regard to production, organization, and reception—to make grouping them into the same genus a logical course of action. At the same time, I propound a method for differentiating kinds of transmedia storytelling from one another rooted in the idea of what I term "legally proscribed memory."

I argue that varieties of cross-media storytelling are linked by their reliance on memory not only in terms of what a creator asks the audience to remember but also in terms of what a creator requires the audience to forget. In all cases of professional transmedia production, the use of memory is circumscribed by legally binding documents that dictate what elements of a franchise can and cannot be used and in what context. This idea is not new. In 1950 the renowned sociologist Maurice Halbwachs went some way in articulating the interrelationship between the law and remembering (140, 161–62, 164).

In the course of this chapter, I use this concept of legally proscribed memory as a way of differentiating kinds of transmedia storytelling in the form of a taxonomy, drawing on theoretical positions from the diverse field of memory studies as appropriate. I use theorist and practitioner Christy Dena's categories for transmedia writing as a starting point before going on to utilize my own insights as a writer of officially licensed spin-off material for the *Doctor Who* and *Highlander* franchises, produced by the British company Big Finish under license from the British Broadcasting Corporation (BBC), Metro-Goldwyn-Mayer Studios (MGM), and Davis-Panzer Productions, respectively. I also discuss how the entries within a franchise such as *Tron* might be classified according to the taxonomy I propose.

Transmedia Storytelling and the Importance of Memory

Central to transmedia storytelling is consistency—perhaps of scenario, of plot, of character—expressed through narrative and iconography. What differentiates varieties of transmedia storytelling from one another is the extent to which such consistency is managed by the owners of the property in question and by other active agents in the transmedial process. Crucial to these processes are the relative power of the various active agents involved in the transmedia storytelling process to deploy, erase, or otherwise alter existing world-internal elements of the franchise in question.

Understood in these terms, the role of memory is central to the transmedia storytelling process. Does the mythology of the urtext allow for a character to behave in a particular way? At what point did a specific battle occur in the spin-off comic's plotline? In transmedia storytelling, what is remembered is crucial—and so is what is forgotten. Furthermore elements that are subject to "non-memory" (Reading 383) are also vital.

The varieties of transmedia storytelling that exist emerge from transactions between owners of intellectual property (IP) rights, in-house operatives, licensees, and, of course, consumers. These legally framed interactions produce different kinds of "collective" or "fan" memory and enable us to differentiate one kind of transmedial storytelling from another. As Joachim J. Savelsberg and Ryan D. King suggest, "Law affects collective memory indirectly by regulating the production, accessibility, and dissemination of information about the past" (189). This assessment is evident from the verdicts of trials and the subsequent reportage of such cases, in government statutes, and in licensing agreements that determine the nature of storyworld franchises and their various transmedia extensions. Barbara Misztal similarly observes the extent to which collective memory is shaped by the legal system (20–21).

Christy Dena's Categories of Transmedia Writing

Christy Dena is an academic and practitioner working actively with industry to explore ideas of transmedia storytelling and producing her own transmedia work. In her overview of transmedia writing for *if:book*, the weblog of the Institute for the Future of the Book, Dena makes the point that "[t]ransmedia is not synonymous with digital media, as it often involves *both* digital and non-digital media" (n. pag., original emphasis).

This observation recalls the early work on transmediality undertaken by Marsha Kinder in which she explores the interplay between the digital and the analogue in children's consumption of media and provides the basis for much contemporary discussion of transmediality (39–86). Indeed, while some aspects of contemporary digitally based storytelling afford experiences unique to digitality, anyone who grew up in the 1970s and 1980s reading spin-off novels and comics or playing with action figures will recognize many techniques from today's more formally identified transmedia storytelling. Such techniques find their antecedence in an era when digital technology was far less prevalent and indeed date from a still earlier era.

Dena then proceeds to outline four key methods to have emerged in the area of transmedia writing as the field currently stands. Dena identifies one approach as a "collection of mono-medium stories." Typically in this approach individual components produced in different media—a film, a book, or a game, for instance—contribute distinct but related stories that add up to the wider storyworld. Dena observes that this phenomenon is different from the "pre-transmedia paradigm" in which a dominant story in a single medium spins off into other media, often in the form of adaptations rather than continuations. Certainly this distinction, which numerous commentators have made, does seem important. Transmedia storytelling cannot refer to the process of adaptation, as we already have a complex lexicon to describe that particular process, and the often connected but distinct process of dramatization.[1]

Dena's second category is "a collection of media that tells one story" and refers to a narrative spread across multiple media forms. To understand the totality of the story, the user needs to engage with all parts of the story, and it is distinct from the first category, where each element is capable of standing alone. Dena suggests that for creators working with this second category an understanding of *interactivity*—that is, the dynamic means by which consumers engage with the various aspects of the storyworld—is paramount.

Dena's third and fourth categories of transmedia writer skills are both concerned with timing rather than form and focus on the point at which the transmedia world is initiated. She identifies *expansion analysis* as the process through which an existing mono-media property is expanded into a transmedial property. According to Dena, it involves fixing the world-internal history of the characters and settings as already established, identifying essential aspects of the storyworld, and pinpointing any areas yet to be explored. This process then results in the creation of a transmedia "bible," ensuring continuity in terms of any transmedia expansion. Importantly, expansion analysis would seem to directly contradict Dinehart's suggestion that transmedia storytelling is not descriptive of the enlargement of an extant franchise.

The fourth category Dena specifies are those projects "designed to be transmedia from the beginning." Dena poses a series of questions that the writer in this situation will need to address: which characters operate in which media, which characters and settings suit sequential media or interactive platforms, the issues concerning moving audiences between media, and which elements are essential and which ones are tertiary. Again, a bible results from this process.

As a developmental tool for transmedia storytellers, Dena's categories supply a useful foundation for thinking about the broad categories of transmedia storytelling that can occur. As I show, a number of existing transmedia enterprises simultaneously incorporate a variety of approaches accounted for by Dena's categories. At a fundamental level, however, all are dictated by the degree of control afforded by the IP holder to the licensee and/or the consumers of the transmedia artifact in question. From the perspective of the transmedia storyteller, such legally framed relationships are central to the question of what can and cannot be remembered.

Transmedia Categories

The multiplicity of media types and the diverse ways in which they can be used in transmedia storytelling would make any attempt at a medium-led taxonomy hopelessly unwieldy. The taxonomy I propose instead uses legal relationships as its basis. It comprises six categories, with the first identifying the *intellectual property* in question. The second category, *directed transmedia storytelling*, refers to those transmedial extensions over which the IP holder exercises close control. It might refer equally to material produced by the IP holders themselves or to licensed material produced under close supervision by a third party. Remembering, in this instance, is tightly controlled by the IP holder. The third category, *devolved transmedia storytelling*, suggests more of a degree of flexibility on the part of the IP holder's relationship to the material being produced. In this instance, while core ideas and themes might be maintained, certain aspects of the established continuity can be forgotten or otherwise misremembered or reimagined within the terms of the licensing agreement.

The fourth category, *detached transmedia storytelling*, refers to those works inspired by a storyworld but that are not licensed by the IP holder and over which the IP holder does not therefore exercise legal control. The lack of legal sanction means that some elements, such as names of characters or places used within the storyworld, might be deliberately misremembered in order to avoid infringement of copyright. However, archetypes, plot developments, or events within the storyworld's continuity could be covertly referred to using these replacement names and terms.

The fifth category, *directed transmedia storytelling with user participation*, is used to describe content produced by consumers of the franchise that is circumscribed by the owners of the IP or the license holders. This material might take the form of resources provided by the producer from which the user can then generate their own stories, as is the case with The Official Star Wars Fan Film Awards.[2] Licensed toys, a material manifestation of such resources, might be equally understood as falling under this category. Again, in this instance memory is strictly controlled, at least in terms of the available iconography if not of the stories that might be told.

Directed transmedia storytelling with user participation is distinct from the final category, *emergent user-generated transmedia storytelling*, which is used to describe varieties of "unofficial" transmedia storytelling that are not licensed. Such fan fiction might occur across media. In some cases characters, places, and events from the storyworld continuity might be remembered with fidelity, but there is not necessarily any requirement on the part of the fan-creator to abide by these rules because the work is not officially sanctioned. Content appearing on the websites fanfiction.net, *Twisting the Hellmouth*, and *The Unknowable Room* would all fall under this category.

Doctor Who

The science fiction and fantasy series *Doctor Who* began in 1963 and ran until 1989 (BBC). A coproduction between the BBC and Universal aired in 1996 in the shape of a television movie, but the anticipated series did not appear because of lackluster U.S. viewing figures. In 2005, the BBC successfully relaunched the series, which is now produced by BBC Cardiff. In its new iteration, *Doctor Who* is now in its seventh series and has spawned two successful BBC-produced shows—the adult-oriented *Torchwood* (BBC) and *The Sarah Jane Adventures* (BBC), which is aimed at children. A further television spin-off titled *K9* appeared in 2009 but with no involvement from the BBC (Disney Europe, Park Entertainment, Stewart & Wall Entertainment, and Screen Australia producers).

Meanwhile, the *Doctor Who* television program has always spun off merchandise, running the gamut from ice lollies (popsicles) to comic strips to novelizations of television episodes to the so-called Dalekmania of the 1960s. The *Doctor Who Annuals* produced by World Distributors ran from 1966 to 1986 and were resurrected when the 2005 series began. Two *Doctor Who* feature films, both starring Peter Cushing as the lead character, appeared in 1965 and 1966 and were based on stories from the television series (see Richards 380–81). However, many of these spin-off stories bore only fleeting fidelity to the urtext of the television series, contradicting such "facts" as the design of the Doctor's Tardis or the origin of the eponymous hero.

In 1991, Virgin Publishing Books purchased W. H. Allen, the company responsible for producing officially licensed novel versions of *Doctor Who* stories. Since the license still existed but no more stories were available to adapt, Virgin was able to produce original *Doctor Who* novels (Richards 379). These books in the New Adventures series were seen as the official continuation of the series and featured contributions from such writers as Paul Cornell and Mark Gatiss, both of whom went on to write for the revived television series (and in Gatiss's case, to appear in it). Russell T Davies, showrunner for the first four series of the new *Doctor Who* and creator of both *Torchwood* and *The Sarah Jane Adventures*, also wrote for the Virgin series of novels. That the novel *Human Nature* should subsequently be adapted into an episode of the revived *Doctor Who* series is suggestive of the extent to which "spin-offery" can inform the wider universe of the storyworld in question (see Cornell). It also suggests that the increasingly porous relationship between merchandising and urtext is important in terms of both production and consumption.

The BBC has effectively split *Doctor Who* into two related brands. One strand is allied to the post-2005 television program and manifested as original novels produced by BBC Books, original audio stories produced by AudioGO, a toy range manufactured by Character Options, and recently video games for the Nintendo Wii and DS platforms, with a further video game, *The Eternity Clock*, released for the PlayStation 3, PlayStation Vita, and personal computer (PC) in 2012. A key feature of this strand of *Doctor Who* is a series of fictional tie-in websites that are timed to go live at crucial points during the run of the program. As such, *Doctor Who* has come to constitute a paradigmatic example of transmedia storytelling for the BBC (see Perryman 22). This observation is borne out by the fact that other high-profile BBC shows, such as *Merlin* and *Sherlock*, have sought to emulate *Doctor Who*'s approach in their attitude to transmediality; although, as Evans has observed, the BBC's spy series *Spooks* pioneered transmedial expansion via fiction-based websites (see Evans 9–10).

The "other" *Doctor Who* brand is constituted by the license that the British company Big Finish possesses. In 1998, Big Finish won the rights to produce officially licensed *Doctor Who* audio stories (see Cook 11).

These dramas would go on to feature five of the actors to have played the role of the Doctor, as well as other actors reprising roles from the television series. In common with the Virgin series, a number of Big Finish writers—including Paul Cornell, Mark Gatiss, and Joseph Lidster—have gone on to work on the revived *Doctor Who* and its stable mates *Torchwood* and *The Sarah Jane Adventures*. Big Finish has also produced an additional range of spin-off audios and books set in the *Doctor Who* universe, as well as licensed material for other franchises such as *Stargate* and *Dark Shadows*.

In terms of *Doctor Who*, what the various layers of spin-off media have created is—arguably—a very complex example of transmedia storytelling, spanning some fifty years of continuity and canonicity. This complexity derives precisely from the nature of *Doctor Who*'s fantasy content. Because the fundamental conceit of *Doctor Who* is that of time travel—and on occasion visits to alternate realities—it is entirely possible within these broad boundaries to include all iterations of the *Doctor Who* franchise, no matter how seemingly contradictory. In fact, some spin-off material actively engages in this process of "suturing" together transmedial aspects of the *Doctor Who* franchise, deploying explanations rooted in the fantasy of the series where appropriate (see Harvey, "Canon" 35).

The post-2005 version of the program itself offers a further degree of flexibility in the form of the "Time War," an epochal event in which proceedings from the program's past episodes may or may not have occurred or have been otherwise altered. The Time War not only provided Russell T Davies with a useful means of introducing the program to a new audience after a nine-year absence from television but also acts as another mechanism by which both the fan base and authors of spin-off material can negotiate "past" events (31).

The restrictions on writers working on Big Finish's *Doctor Who* license depend on the nature of the arrangement between Big Finish and the BBC and on the specific nature of the commission. The license from the BBC to Big Finish stipulates that nothing from the post-2005 iteration of the series can be referred to in the Big Finish stories. The implicit intention is that the Big Finish stories should exist in a state of "non-memory" in relation to the contemporary television series—that is, the *other Doctor Who* brand. For Reading, *non-memory* is descriptive of events that occur outside of the record; these events have not been forgotten because there is no trace of them (383). In other words, the Big Finish stories have not "forgotten" the new series; instead, the new series, as well as what occurs in the "past" of the new television series, simply has not *happened* yet. (At least that is the official intention; but in actual fact subtle and not-so-subtle references creep into the Big Finish stories. For instance, the Daleks' ability to "elevate," variously hinted at throughout the show's classic run but exploited to spectacular effect during the Russell T Davies era, becomes a recurring aspect of Big Finish's later audio stories, while the format of the Paul McGann audio stories owes much to the pacey approach of its television counterpart. So traces are evident.) Non-remembering also extends to the BBC's giving the go-ahead to Big Finish on story ideas in order to prevent the latter from compromising the television production.

A writer on Big Finish's *Doctor Who* is allowed to "remember" certain aspects of the classic show's past but not others (see Harvey, "Canon" 31–35). Remembering is circumscribed by the nature of copyright arrangements appertaining to specific elements of the show's past, particularly with regard to characters and monsters from the classic show. However, certain Big Finish commissions will be founded on the basis that permission to use a specific element has been sought and granted. Beyond this stipulation, writers must remain true to characterization established in the urtext of the classic iteration of the program. Within these limitations, however, Big Finish writers and producers are awarded considerable flexibility regarding the kinds of stories they can tell using the resources of the classic iteration of the *Doctor Who* franchise.

In building a taxonomy of transmedia storytelling, the *Doctor Who* franchise in its division into two distinct brands offers a useful point of comparison. We can characterize the post-2005 material over which the BBC exercises close control as directed transmedia storytelling. The Big Finish material—and preceding spin-off material from the 1960s onward, including the *Annuals* (World) and Virgin Books from the 1990s—is perhaps better described as devolved transmedia storytelling, whereby the BBC lays down parameters but largely leaves the licensee company to pursue its own narrative agenda. In terms of remembering, directed transmedia storytelling requires of the writer and production team greater fidelity to the memory of the urtext; devolved transmedia sto-

Intellectual property	Direct transmedia storytelling	Devolved transmedia storytelling	Detached transmedia storytelling	Directed transmedia storytelling with user participation	Emergent user-generated transmedia storytelling
Doctor Who	Spinoff novels from BBC Books; audio books; video games	*Doctor Who* audio plays and prose fiction licensed to Big Finish; *Doctor Who Annuals* published by World	*Faction Paradox* novels, graphic novels, and audio plays; *K9* television series	*Doctor Who Comic Maker* on official website; *Doctor Who* toys produced by Character Options; licensed role-playing game	Fan fiction as both films and prose; modded role-playing game

Fig. 12.1. The *Doctor Who* franchise.

rytelling demands specific remembering but allows flexibility of recall with regard to areas of world-internal ambiguity in the urtext. It should be noted that the terms refer not to the position of third-party producers in the creation of transmedial storytelling but to the degree of control exercised by the IP holders.

Doctor Who would seem to fulfill Dena's concept of an "expansion analysis" form of transmedia storytelling, whereby the urtext of the television program has been expanded over time into numerous other media. While it is predominantly true, the longevity of the franchise means other kinds of transmedia narrativizing also occur. The *Faction Paradox* stories are a transmedial spin-off from a *Doctor Who* spin-off novel that legally cannot refer to BBC-owned characters or scenarios, although the stories do allude to very similar characters and stories (Tardis Data Core). As such, *Faction Paradox* represents an intriguing deliberate *misremembering* of the *Doctor Who* urtext and can be situated as detached transmedia storytelling in our taxonomy.

Highlander

By comparison, the development of the *Highlander* franchise, though considerably newer than that of *Doctor Who*, is also complex. The first *Highlander* film appeared in 1986 to a mixed critical response (Walker 380). A poorly received sequel titled *Highlander II: The Quickening*, which contradicted events from the first movie, appeared in 1990. Another sequel, called *Highlander III: The Sorcerer*, was released in 1994. This second sequel contradicted the events of both the original film and the first sequel. A further level of complexity was added in a director's cut of *Highlander II* that is considered canon by a section of *Highlander* fandom (*There Can Only Be One*). A television series ignored all the sequels but incorporated some—but not all—elements of the original film and spawned its own short-lived televisual spin-off (*There Can Only Be the One*). Another series of films spun off from the television series and attempted to "retcon" the events of the first film.[3]

Additional spin-offs included a well-received feature-length anime, an animated television series for children, a comic book series from Dynamite, a Flash-based online series, and video games for the ZX Spectrum and Atari Jaguar. A role-playing game intended for PS3, Xbox 360, and Windows was canceled in December 2010.

Big Finish's permission to produce *Highlander* audio stories is one of a number of more recent American licenses awarded to the company. In this case, the long-running television series constitutes the urtext from which the audio spin-offs must draw their identity in terms of both characters and continuity. However, because the television series incorporated elements from the original 1986 film, practitioners working on the Big Finish audios were able to tap into this resource. Different writers chose to remember different aspects of the mythology, some explicit and some more discreet. For instance, for the fourth episode of the first audio series titled *Highlander: Kurgan Rising*, the writers Cavan Scott and Mark Wright chose to bring back the Kurgan character, who was the chief enemy—the "Big Bad"—from the original motion picture. For my story, the second episode in Big Finish's audio series titled *Highlander: Love and Hate*, I brought back the antique shop owned by Duncan MacLeod, the central character played by Adrian Paul in the television series, subsequent feature films, and audio productions.

The audio stories had to remain consistent with not only the preceding television series but also the feature films that came afterward in the continuity. Big Finish's contract with MGM and Davis-Panzer is more restrictive because in the case of *Highlander*, despite the multiple iterations of the franchise, the television version has become the dominant brand identity and the version to be remembered. In this case, then, Big

Intellectual property	Directed transmedia storytelling	Devolved transmedia storytelling	Detached transmedia storytelling	Directed transmedia storytelling with user participation	Emergent user-generated transmedia storytelling
Highlander	*Highlander* television series; *Highlander* television movies; Highlander audio plays produced by Big Finish; *Highlander* novels; *Highlander The Game* (cancelled); *Highlander* comic licensed to Dynamite	*Highlander the Animated Series*; *Highlander: The Last of MacLeods* video game		*Highlander* massively multiplayer online role-playing game (cancelled)	Fan fiction

Fig. 12.2. The *Highlander* franchise.

Finish's *Highlander* output might be understood much more as directed transmedia storytelling in contrast to the devolved transmedia storytelling of Big Finish's *Doctor Who* output across audio and prose. Arguably, devolved transmedia storytelling in the early history of the *Highlander* franchise led to multiple, continuity-contradicting iterations; thus directed transmedia storytelling has become the dominant mode in relation to the contemporary control of the *Highlander* franchise. The animated television series from 1994 and the video game based upon it constitute examples of devolved transmedia storytelling in relationship to the *Highlander* franchise.

Tron

Tron would seem to constitute a paradigmatic example of contemporary transmedia storytelling, specifically of the kind Jenkins refers to when he circumscribes transmedia storytelling as "*a process where integral elements of a fiction get* dispersed systematically across multiple delivery channels *for the purpose of creating a* unified and coordinated entertainment experience" (n. pag., original emphases).

The original *Tron* movie was a fantasy adventure featuring pioneering special effects. The film tells the story of Kevin Flynn, played by Jeff Bridges, a brilliant programmer who is sucked into the video game of his own devising in what Farah Mendlesohn would term a "portal fantasy" (1–58). Here, the Flynn character must band together with the ace warrior Tron to help defeat the Master Computer Program. In 2003, an official sequel was launched in the form of a game for PC, *Tron 2.0* (Monolith Productions), and a comic book, *Tron: Ghost in the Machine* (Walker, Jones and De Martinis). A range of tie-in action figures was also released. The game and comic book told the story of Jethro (Jet) Bradley, son of the original character, who returns to the realm of the Tron video game.

In 2010, Disney launched the high-profile film *Tron: Legacy*, a further transmedial sequel to the original movie that again starred Jeff Bridges as Kevin Flynn. The video game *Tron: Evolution* (Propaganda Games) and the comic book *Tron: Betrayal* (Nitz, Matsuda, and Tong) were also launched, along with a range of tie-in toys. An animated television series called *Tron: Uprising* aired from May 2012 to January 2013. The 2010 *Tron* continuation erases the memory of the 2003 video game sequel, associated comic book, and toy range. The 2003 material is effectively "non-remembered," at least by the producers if not a portion of the fan base.

The *Tron* films and tie-ins are not only an example of Dena's expansion analysis, in that the approach draws on an existing premise, characters, and events established in the 1982 film, but also something that has been designed as a transmedia approach from the beginning, at least in terms of the 2010 material. Darren Hedges, the game's director, makes abundantly clear that the "filmmakers and the game team wanted to have a trans-media experience and have the film and game narrative tie together" rather than retelling the game's story in the video game medium (McCabe 52). Even with a close level of integration between the development of the film, game, and comic book, some fans have identified contradictions between the comic book and film (TRON Wiki).

Clearly those involved in the creation of the 2010 *Tron* material considered themselves to be working on a transmedial project. This perspective further problematizes Dinehart's view that existing products cannot be transformed into transmedial stories but that they must be designed in that fashion from the outset. Arguably, *Tron: Legacy*, *Tron: Evolution*, and *Tron: Betrayal* can be conceived of as a new transmedia endeavor, yet

Intellectual property	**Directed transmedia storytelling**	**Devolved transmedia storytelling**	**Detached transmedia storytelling**	**Directed transmedia storytelling with user participation**	**Emergent user-generated transmedia storytelling**
Tron; *Tron: Legacy*	*Tron: Evolution* video game; *Tron: Betrayal* comic; *Tron: Uprising* TV show			*Tron* toys; *Tron* alternate reality game	Fan fiction

Fig. 12.3. The *Tron* franchise.

this view neglects the memory of the original *Tron* that has been handed down and informs the newer iterations of the brand, from the world-internal of the new material displayed in the film, video game, and comic book through to associated marketing.

Equally, according to Dinehart's position, the post-2005 *Doctor Who* material constitutes transmedia storytelling, but the other "side" of the license does not, even though both examples aim to enable "the imagination via story-driven extensions in a 'world' in which a player seeks to be further immersed" (n. pag.). Again, the movement of some writers working on both kinds of spin-off product between the two varieties, as well as the movement of writers from spin-off material to urtext, is worth noting at this point. We can presume commonalities of process on this basis and commonalities in terms of the skill sets of those involved in the production of these different kinds of material.

Transmedia storytelling is, by its very nature, dependent upon the interactions between manifold types of media. As Dena has observed, it often involves both the digital and the analogue; I would further argue that just as there are examples that are exclusively digital, so in the past there existed exclusively analogue examples of transmedia storytelling. The multiplicity of media forms involved and the sheer number of resulting interactions that can occur render attempts at adumbrating a medium-led taxonomy impossible, necessitating another approach.

As I have demonstrated, the role of memory is central to the activity of transmedia storytelling. The legal owner(s) of the franchise in question control the extent to which their in-house operatives, licensees, and ultimately the consumer base are afforded access to these memories. Legally binding contracts circumscribe what can and cannot be done in terms of remembering, forgetting, non-remembering, and misremembering the plot events, characters, and settings that writers and producers can deploy and that can link one entry in a transmedial franchise to another. These restrictions are consistent with Halbwachs's belief that the law supplies a framework through which groups' collective memories are discursively constructed (see Reading 385).

In the case of transmedia storytelling, the law's impact on collective memory is more explicit than Savelsberg and King observe (189). Licensing agreements offer up legally sanctioned memories that can be used to determine one kind of transmedia storytelling from another and that reflect approaches being pursued by industry in a number of contexts, even if the individuals and organizations in question do not necessarily articulate these processes in these terms. Conceiving of transmedia storytelling in terms of legally proscribed memory affords a way of understanding how legal directives affect the stories that are told and the ways in which they are understood by those purchasing and engaging with such material. This conception in turn enables the creation of the taxonomy I have outlined, one that is formulated around the relationships between the various agents directly involved in the creation of transmedia stories: IP holders, in-house operatives, licensees, and, in some instances, the audience themselves. These relationships, rather than the particular medium being deployed at any specific point, can help illuminate the particular character of transmedia storytelling in all its manifold forms.

Notes

1. It is worth observing that the International Association of Media Tie-In Writers is home to many individuals who work on licensed material that are sometimes adaptations and sometimes continuations.
2. The Official Star Wars Fan Film Awards were authorized by Lucasfilm and undertaken by AtomFilms from 2002 until their discontinuation in 2012 (StarWarsFanpedia).
3. The term "retcon" is a shortened version of "retroactive continuity" and origi-

nally derives from Tupper. Both creators and fan circles of pulp fiction in various media widely use it to describe the process by which the existing continuity of a fictional world is modified, perhaps to enable the inclusion of sequels or the privileging of a specific plot point.

Works Cited

BBC. *"Doctor Who" Comic Maker*. 2011. Web. December 30, 2011.

BBC Worldwide. "*Doctor Who: The Eternity Clock* Teaser Trailer." December 9, 2011. Web. December 12, 2011.

Cook, Benjamin. *"Doctor Who": The New Audio Adventures*. London: Big Finish, 2003. Print.

Cornell, Paul. *Human Nature*. London: Virgin, 1995. Print.

Dena, Christy. "Do You Have a Big Stick?" *if:book Australia*. February 7, 2011. Web. December 17, 2011.

Dinehart, Stephen. "Transmedia Storytelling Defined." *The Narrative Design Explorer*. January 6, 2011. Web. December 10, 2011.

Doctor Who. Dir. Various. BBC. 1963–. Television.

Doctor Who: Human Nature/Family of Blood. Dir. Charles Palmer. BBC Cardiff. 2007. Film.

ESM Trailers HD. "*Tron: Uprising* Official Trailer." March 7, 2011. Web. December 30, 2011.

Evans, Elizabeth. *Transmedia Television: Audiences, New Media, and Daily Life*. London: Routledge, 2011. Print.

fanfiction.net. n.d. Web. December 30, 2011.

Halbwachs, Maurice. *On Collective Memory*. Chicago: University of Chicago Press, 1992. Print.

Harvey, Colin B. "Canon, Myth, and Memory in *Doctor Who*." *The Mythological Dimensions of "Doctor Who."* Ed. Anthony S. Burdge, Jessica Burke, and Kristine Larsen. Crawfordville FL: Kitsune Books, 2010. N. pag. Print.

———. *Highlander: Love and Hate*. London, 2009. CD.

Highlander. Dir. Russell Mulcahy. 1986. Film.

Highlander—the Series. Dir. Various. 1992–1998. Television.

Highlander II: Renegade Version. Dir. Russell Mulcahy. 1995. Film.

Highlander II: The Quickening. Dir. Russell Mulcahy. 1990. Film.

Highlander III: The Sorcerer. Dir. Andrew Morahan. 1994. Film.

Jenkins, Henry. "Transmedia 202: Further Reflections." *Confessions of an Aca-Fan*. August 1, 2011. Web. December 10, 2011.

Kinder, Marsha. *Playing with Power in Movies, Television, and Video Games: From Muppet Babies to Teenage Mutant Ninja Turtles*. Berkeley: University of California Press, 1993. Print.

K9. Dir. Various. Disney Europe; Park Entertainment; Stewart & Wall Entertainment; Screen Australia. 2009–. Television.
McCabe, Joseph. "Game Changing." *SFX*, January 2011. 46–52. Print.
Mendlesohn, Farah. *Rhetorics of Fantasy.* London: Wesleyan Press, 2008. Print.
Misztal, Barbara A. *Theories of Social Remembering.* Maidenhead, UK: Open University Press, 2003. Print.
Monolith Productions. *Tron 2.0*. Buena Vista Interactive, 2003. Windows.
Nitz, Jai, Jeff Matsuda, and Andie Tong. *Tron: Betrayal.* New York: Marvel, 2010. Print.
Perryman, Neil. "*Doctor Who* and the Convergence of Media: A Case Study in Transmedia Storytelling." *Convergence* 1 (2008): 21–39. Print.
Propaganda Games. *Tron: Evolution.* Disney Interactive, 2010. Windows.
Reading, Anna. "Identity, Memory and Cosmopolitanism: The Otherness of the Past and a Right to Memory?" *European Journal of Cultural Studies* 14.4 (2011): 379–94. Print.
Richards, Justin. *Doctor Who: The Legend Continues.* London: BBC Books, 2005. Print.
The Sarah Jane Adventures. Dir. Various. BBC. 2007–2011. Television.
Savelsberg, Joachim J., and Ryan D. King. "Law and Collective Memory." *Annual Review of Law and Social Science* 3 (2007): 189–211. Print.
Scott, Cavan, and Mark Wright. *Highlander: Kurgan Rising.* London, 2009. CD.
Star Wars Fanpedia. "The Official *Star Wars* Fan Film Awards." 2011. Web. December 30, 2011.
Tardis Data Core (Doctor Who Wiki). "Faction Paradox." n.d. Web. December 30, 2011.
There Can Only Be the One: The Highlander Continuity Guide! March 2, 2008. Web. December 29, 2011.
Torchwood. Dir. Various. BBC. 2006–. Television.
Tron. Dir. Steven Lisberger. 1982. Film.
Tron: Legacy. Dir. Joseph Kosinski. 2010. Film.
TRON Wiki. "Tron: Betrayal." N.d. Web. February 23, 2012.
Tupper, Elgin F. *The Theology of Wolfhart Pannenberg.* London: SCM Publishing, 1974. Print.
Twisting the Hellmouth. n.d. Web. February 22, 2012.
The Unknowable Room. n.d. Web. February 22, 2012.
Walker, John, ed. *Halliwell's Film and Video Guide, 2000.* London: Harper Collins, 1999. Print.
Walker, Landry, Eric Jones, and Louie De Martinis. *Tron: The Ghost in the Machine.* San Jose: Slave Labor Graphics, 2006–2008. Print.

13 *Game of Thrones*

Transmedial Worlds, Fandom, and Social Gaming

LISBETH KLASTRUP AND SUSANA TOSCA

In recent years, we have seen a growing body of scholarship on transmediality from different perspectives: storytelling, world building, industry practices, and studies that look at both "old" media formats, such as film and television and "new" media formats such as websites, digital games, and mobile phones (see, e.g., Dena; Bechmann Pedersen; Evans). This development indicates that the study of cross- or transmediality might slowly be maturing into a field of study in its own right. However, research into transmedial structures and products is constantly challenged by the fact that new digital communication formats and practices continue to emerge, providing new opportunities for transmedial content production. These new formats and new production modes force us to revise how we analytically approach transmedial works. This revision includes considering the many ways fans can now be involved with a transmedial world, not the least through social media, an area of user-involvement that has so far not been examined in this context.

In this chapter, we revisit our previous work on transmedial worlds (TMW) by looking at a recent example of a transmedial world campaign that included the use of social media and micro-gaming and involved fans in a variety of ways. The marketing agency Campfire developed a campaign during the spring of 2011 to create awareness and hype around the American channel HBO's launch of the new TV series *Game of Thrones* (GOT), which is based on the fantasy novel series *A Song of Ice and Fire* written by George R. R. Martin. The books, set in a medieval-style universe, are extremely popular beyond the genre niche and have generated a dedicated fan following despite the long time gaps between one novel and the next. The first season of the TV series is based on the first of the books, *A Game of Thrones*, and its first ten episodes aired from

April to June 2011. The fan community of the TMW was very active during preproduction of the series, with countless websites, forums, and social network activity related to casting, shooting, and other production topics.

The campaign itself sought to reach out to both existing fans of the books and to a potential new audience of TV viewers mainly through an episodic puzzle game called *The Maester's Path*, which included both online and off-line components and ran from February 2011 to April 2011. The campaign is interesting as a case because it included elements from both the known book and the still-unknown TV series and because it encouraged its users to spread the word about the game through Facebook, Twitter, and GetGlue. It therefore included a complex interweaving of world actualizations and the integration of social media as a means to create world awareness.

While it is obvious to approach a campaign such as this one from an industry practice perspective (which Dena argues should be an integral part of the way we approach transmedial products in general), we want here to combine perspectives on practice and theory. That is, we want to discuss how the game practices and the fan reception we can observe in relation to the GOT campaign can inform and perhaps change the theory of transmedial worlds that we have previously introduced with a main interest in online game world use.[1] Our focus has always been on worlds as abstract content systems and not as particular instantiations, or products. This approach is more appropriate for large, unified, and detailed worlds (such as *The Lord of the Rings* and *Game of Thrones*) rather than for more loosely defined creations that grow overtime (such as *Doctor Who* or the Ramasjang Danish TV universe).

Transmedial World Theory

Here we build upon our previous work on transmedial worlds, where we introduced our theoretical framework and applied it to the analysis of various cyberworlds and online computer games. The first paper focused on the design and success criteria of online TMWs, and the second and third addressed reception processes, dissecting the aesthetic experience of fan players.

Transmedial worlds are abstract content systems from which a repertoire of fictional stories can be actualized or derived across a variety of media forms (see Klastrup and Tosca, "Transmedial Worlds" 409). That is, TMWs are mental constructs shared by both the designers/creators of the world and the audience/participants. The TMW is not defined by the material entity of any particular instantiation (the media platform) but by the shared idea of the world, a sort of platonic approach that situates the ontological status of the TMW in a disembodied plane. We call this mental image "worldness," and a number of distinguishing and recognizable features of the TMW originate from the first version, or *instantiation*, of the world but can be elaborated and changed over time. For example, the world of Middle Earth has its origin in the writings of J. R. R. Tolkien, but it has been reinterpreted by Peter Jackson's films or the designers of the *Lord of the Rings Online* (LOTRO) multiplayer game. TMWs often have dedicated fans invested in both expanding the world (for example, by writing fan fiction) and keeping watch over new instantiations, making sure they respect the original spirit of the urtext's actualization.

The experience of worldness is informed by three different dimensions:

- **Mythos**—the establishing story, legend, or narration of the world, with the defining struggles. It is the backstory that gives meaning to the current situation of the world, and it includes creational myths and legendary characters and gods.
- **Topos**—the setting of the world in both space (geography) and time (history). It shows how places have changed and events have unfolded.
- **Ethos**—the explicit and implicit ethics, or the moral codex of behavior for characters. It can be considered generally, as valid for the whole world (e.g., nobody performs or even talks about sex in *Lord of the Rings*), or locally, as appropriate to a determined group of inhabitants of that world (e.g., elves would never burn a tree).

Any story set in a TMW has to comply with its particular definition of worldness and belong within the three dimensions. Audiences will react negatively if any of these categories is subverted. A factual error about an important element of the mythos, the invention of a new place that disrupts the original topos, or a character not conforming to the particular ethos defined in the urtext's actualization will cause a bitter uproar in the fan community.[2]

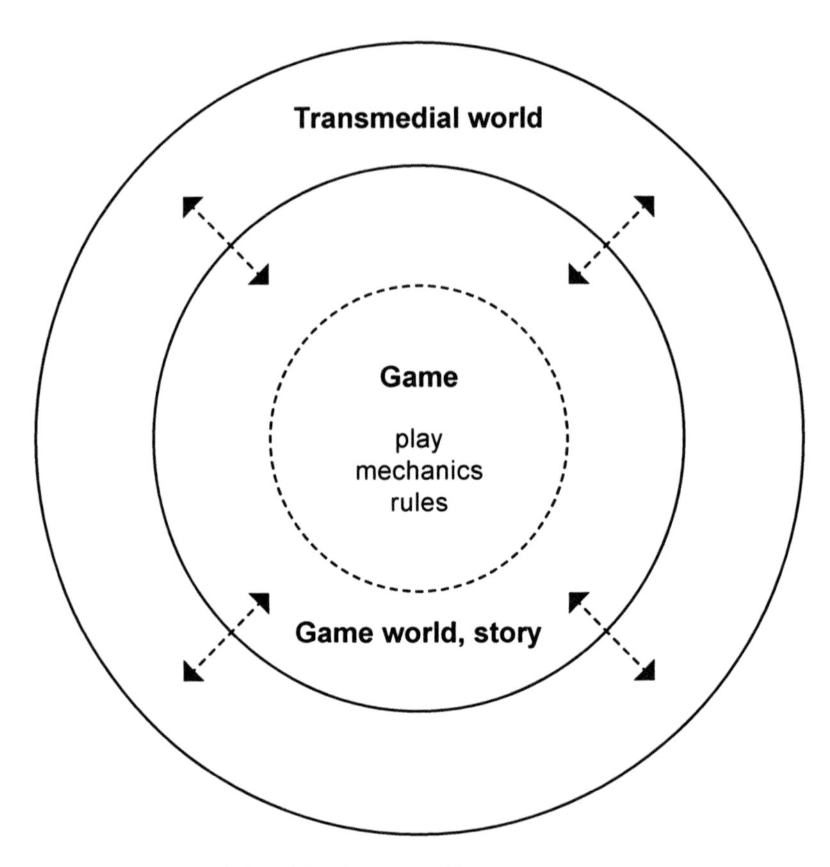

Fig. 13.1. Transmedial world and game world.

In our previous research we have found that users or participants perceived the possibility of interacting directly with the TMW they love as the strongest advantage of cyberworlds over other kinds of instantiations. Online game worlds call forth the extensive repertoire of knowledge that fans already possess and allow them to be cocreators of personal stories within the cherished frame of the TMW. Digital instantiations encourage a special kind of performance that takes participants out of their "receiving" position and give even more value to the TMW memories they already treasure (Klastrup and Tosca, "When Fans").

Our model of player interaction with a TMW game world explicitly illustrates the circulation of meaning across the different layers that relate the interpretation of a particular instantiation to the general ecology of the TMW (see figure 13.1). Non-TMW fans would stay at the inner circle, or the pure game, but TMW fans have access to extra layers of meaning. Being able to relate the different levels to each other results in added emotional value for the recipients of the texts (Klastrup and Tosca, "When Fans"), a process that, we venture, might explain the attachment and enthusiasm of the fans of TMWs.

The Case

The TMW of *A Song of Ice and Fire* is a raw medieval world similar to the European Middle Ages. It is realistic in its depiction of power struggles, violence, and sex, but it also has a few magical elements such as dragons, undead warriors, and spells. The world is extremely well fleshed out: nature, weather, cities, places, people, religions, clothes, and food are described in meticulous detail; the writing style is generally polished and vivid; the characters multidimensional and memorable; and the multithreaded plots rather complex. The overaching story is the fight among various noble houses for the right to rule all of the kingdom of Westeros, the continent on which the main part of the novels are set, and this struggle, referred to as "the game of thrones," continues through all the books.

Our case is *The Maester's Path*, an online game experience that Campfire developed as part of its marketing campaign to promote HBO's new series *Game of Thrones*. The game was launched in February 2011, a month and a half before the airing of the series, and a new puzzle would open every week up to the series premiere to ensure renewed fan visits. The game site is unfortunately no longer available online, but features from it can be experienced in a promotional video by Campfire.[3]

The Maester's Path was designed to create hype and expectation before the TV show's opening. The riddles could be solved without previous knowledge of the books, but the game's design and its exploitation of detailed symbolism from the TMW talked directly to fans, who were the only ones with a strong enough motivation to engage with the interactive experience, as our questionnaire results indicate. The game is an interesting media product in that it remediates both the novels and the television series, but its content—for example, the amount of portrayed characters, plot details, and so on—is not identical. The game's title, *The Maester's Path,* is inspired by the class of the maesters, a sort of priesthood of wise men, who receive training in such different arts as healing, alchemy, and so forth. They forge links in a chain they wear

Puzzle	Sense	How to	Clip
Symbol wheel	Smell	15 scents, 15 symbols	Jon gives Arya her sword
Inn sound, heraldry	Hearing	Hear gossip at inn, place sigils right	Tyrion is seized by Catelyn in inn
Blast the horn at the wall	Sight	Give alarm when wildlings approach	Tyrion and Maester Aemon: Winter is coming
Reassemble a book	Touch	Weather app, could be done by translating text	Daenerys and Ser Jorah talk about Viserys
Find the secret password	Taste	Fold the menus and print	Ned and Robert, country scene
Final reward	The Social	Making 5 friends register (apprendices)	George Martin thanks you! + social media pics

Fig. 13.2. A summary of the five senses puzzles.

around their neck, and each link represents a particular area of knowledge that they have learned and mastered. Players were invited to forge five links of such a chain by solving five riddles, with one appearing at weekly intervals. The prize each time was an "exclusive" preview video clip from the unaired series. Each riddle was related to one of the five senses and had a pendant in the real world, where Campfire also ran a marketing campaign (Westeros Revealed) with different events and activities (see figure 13.2). For example, the digital puzzle about smell was accompanied by a chest of different smells from the TMW land of Westeros that was sent to different journalists and bloggers, who posted about their "gift" online. They documented its appearance and the clues it contained so that players who had not seen it also could solve the riddle. When the taste puzzle had to be solved, food wagons appeared in Los Angeles and New York City, where people could taste food from Westeros for free.

The Maester's Path website maintained a design in dark colors and evocative sounds, introducing participants into the mysteries of Westeros with a good re-creation of its atmosphere. The language was semi-archaic, and interaction instructions were given in ways that tried to respect the medieval world as much as possible. The invitation to the third puzzle, for example, was inspired by sight: "The Men of the Night's Watch stand guard here, looking over the forests of the North for possible attacks. If you choose now to take the black, you must stand guard here and alert your brothers at the first sign of trouble" (Campfire).

If the player clicked on "yes" and this way "took the black," he or she then entered a three-dimensional (3-D) rendering of one of the legendary scenarios of the TMW—namely, the wall of ice that is the frontier between the civilized Westeros and the wild lands of the North. The player had to walk around, look over the edge, and blast an alarm horn as soon as he or she saw some wildlings attacking. The charm of this puzzle was the sense of the player's immersion in the 3-D world, which players appreciated.[4]

Once the mission was completed, the game prompted the player to share any progress this way: "Send out a Raven. That others should learn of your quest." In the TMW, distance communication is performed by sending out ravens, not pigeons. To send the raven, the player had the option of clicking on a Facebook or a Twitter button, which automatically posted a message in the respective social network that told of the accomplished mission. The player's friends would see this message, and this way could be recruited to try the game as well. The recruiting of other players was an integral part of the campaign, as the idea was that each player should attract five other "apprentices" in order to claim the final prize, an "exclusive" final video of the book's author, Martin himself, congratulating the player for his or her progress.

Methodology

Our approach included both quantitative and qualitative explorations of the development and reception of the campaign, which ran from February 2011 to April 2011. One of us took part in the campaign by solving the puzzles on *The Maester's Path* as they were released and keeping track of fan discussions of it, while the other explored the game and the puzzles after the TV series was launched and everything was still available online. We both watched the TV series as the episodes were released, as the ordinary fan would, and followed fan discussions on the content of the TV episodes on various fan forums. The day after the last episode of the first season of the TV series aired, June 20, we launched an online survey that was spread through Twitter primarily. Both Steve Coulson of Campfire and the administrator behind the very popular WinterIsComing.net and Twitter profile retweeted our survey; thus we were able to attract quite a few responses from online fans in a very short time.[5] Obviously, these fans are active on social media, so a certain bias in the use of social media should be expected in their answers. Nevertheless, as our findings reveal, that these respondents use social media to keep updated about developments in the *Game of Thrones* universe does not mean that they unequivocally used social media when they participated in the campaign.

In total, 192 fans started, and 166 respondents completed the general questions about their world and game involvement in our survey. Of them, 100 had not played the game (that is, the puzzles on themaesters path.com), and 66 had.[6] In the non-gamer group, the gender distribution was 67 percent men and 33 percent women. In the gamer group, the gender distribution was 54.5 percent men and 45.5 percent women. The average age of the respondents in total was around thirty years old. When we refer to answers from the survey, we refer to the gender, age, and nationality of the respondent; for example, a twenty-six-year-old female from France is represented as "F, 26, France."

After we looked at the initial responses to the survey, we used the answers as a starting point for two e-mail interviews: one with Steve Coulson at Campfire who is situated in New York, and one with a thirty-eight-year old female Spanish fan, who had also played the game. In the interview with Coulson, we asked about the background and goal of the campaign and Campfire's thoughts on how to reach out to both fans and potential newcomers to the universe and its sharing incentives. In the interview with the fan, we asked about her experiences with the campaign and the game and about her thoughts on the use of social media as part of playing the game.

The main objective of our *Game of Thrones* study has been to discover how TMW fans embrace and respond to the combination of online game elements and social media features as part of the launch of a new TWM instantiation. In the following section, we present some of the findings from the survey and our interviews, revealing how fans and users have in fact experienced the campaign.

Transmedial World Knowledge

Inspired by our previous study "When Fans Become Players: LOTRO in a Transmedial World Perspective," we asked respondents how they first learned about the world. Of the gamers, 97 percent knew the *Game of Thrones* universe from the books, 1.5 percent from the TV series, and, judging from the free-text answers, 1.5 percent from other instantiations such as the Fantasy Flight Living Card Game or the Fantasy Flight board game. After reading the books, 71 percent of the gamers played the game and then (72 percent) went on to watch the TV series.

In the non-gamer group, the pattern is evidently different: 82 percent of them first learned about the universe through the books, 16 percent though the TV series, and 2 percent through "nonapplicable" ways (again, we suspect, through card or board games). Then 70 percent went on to watch the TV series and 15 percent also read the books. After that 18 percent of the readers went on to watch the TV series and 3 percent of those who watched the series went on to read the books, but most of them had yet to engage with a third instantiation.

These numbers are interesting in that they indicate, albeit only slightly, that those respondents who chose to play the game are more hard-core fans than those who did not play it, since almost all gamers had read the books before they started playing the game, and most of them (75 percent) watched the TV series, too. Getting to know the TV series, however, also inspired people to read the books: of the 17 non-gamer respondents who first saw the TV series, 14 of them then went on to read the books.

In the survey, we also asked people how they got to know the world in the first place—that is, what motivated them to start reading the books, watching the TV series, and so on. To this optional question, folks provided a free-text answer, and 163 people (both gamers and non-gamers) responded to it. Judging from the answers, recommendations from friends or peers play an important role in disseminating knowledge about a TMW such as the *Game of Thrones* universe, since 72 out of the 163 people said some form of word of mouth led them to pick up the book or to watch the TV series. Typical examples of the ways people describe how they were introduced to the TMW of *Game of Thrones* are: "Friends gave me the book." "Back in 2004, people were talking about it in a metal music forum." "Was reading a thread in a forum about the fantasy series *The Wheel of Time* and someone in the thread said that *A Song of Ice and Fire* was better so I bought the first book." This finding is not surprising since research indicates that both children and grown-ups hear about new books and other media through friends, peers, or "experts" (such as librarians) and that reading habits and practices are fundamentally socially conditioned (see, for instance, Train; Lund; Knoester). It reminds us that the sharing of worlds, such as the *Game of Thrones* universe, is fundamentally a social practice. Thus tapping into or extending the knowledge of the TMW universe by encouraging existing fans to share their enthusiasm proactively in a social media context, reaching out to not just one but many friends at the same time, is an obvious goal for producers and marketers.

Fan Reception and Sharing Practices

If we look at how the campaign was received, it does indeed appear that Campfire's strategy of attracting fans to the game through transmedial marketing efforts was successful. According to an interview by Mitch Wagner with Mike Monello, executive director of Campfire, the company expected 3,000 fans to register on the website but in fact logged 40,000 users. Campfire expected 100,000 unique monthly visitors and ended up with 200,000. And *The Maester's Path* website had more than 2 million page views, with an "average time spent on the Website of 10 minutes," which is a long time by web standards. Perhaps even more interesting, Campfire estimates in the same interview that all together the campaign had more than 120 million "social impressions"—that is, the total number of people who had seen a status update, a blog post, or similar reference relating to *Game of Thrones* on social media sites such as Facebook, GetGlue, Twitter, and blogs (n. pag.).

In order to supplement Campfire's numbers on social media use, we decided to look more closely at YouTube, which also played a central role regarding the game in the period leading up to the TV series. We quickly discovered that the videos that players were able to watch as a reward for solving *The Maester's Path* puzzles were posted on YouTube on the same day as or soon after the puzzle had been launched. Thus players who either did not want to spend time solving the puzzles or became stuck could skip the sometimes time-consuming work solving the puzzle and instead simply watch the YouTube videos. Based on the videos we were able to find on the website, as of June 24, 2011, the game reward videos had a total of 165,208 views, which is a fairly impressive number. One should remember that it does not represent unique viewers; indeed, the number might very well reflect that some interested fans have

	Name of Poster				Total Views	Comments
	Arithine	Rumpelr	BalerionsWatch	StevePirate		
1st reward	28,941	10,986	13,855		53782	70
2nd reward	6,944	18,326	19,072		44,342	53
3rd reward		12,604	14,754		27,358	24
4th reward			11,654	9,673	21,327	27
5th reward			1,409	16,990	18,399	27

Fig. 13.3. The life of game puzzle videos on YouTube.

watched all five videos or that the same person watched the same video repeatedly. It is noticeable that only a handful of people posted the videos and that the number of video viewers and comments to the videos seems to decline steadily as time passes. It might indicate that it was the first video that gave the first insight into what the universe would look like on TV, and thus attracted the most interest, while the following videos saw increasing competition from other official trailer videos from HBO to appease fans' thirst for new glimpses of the world. It might also indicate that people lost interest in the puzzles over time and therefore did not bother to look for the video rewards. Figure 13.3 documents the variation in number of views from the first to the last (fifth) video posted.

Clearly, the low number of comments, or less than 1 percent of the views, indicates that fans and players did not use YouTube to interact and discuss. Thus, a study of the comments show that very few comments (around 14 out of 201) relate to the puzzles and the game, as most of them are comments on the choice of an actor for a particular character or similar issues relating to the depiction of the universe. It appears that fans simply also checked YouTube for videos related to the TV series, and some came across these videos, knowing nothing about the game, as this comment and response show: "I imagine Jorah as older, but I'm happy with the choice. Why are these named as they are?" [MalLionheart]. "@MalLionheart: They're from a promotional website HBO set up. You answer some riddles and solve some puzzles, and receive a clip from the show as a reward."[7]

Meanwhile, sharing the videos on YouTube seems to be done in the spirit of service to the fan community, which also appreciates the effort. One person commented: "Thank you so much! I have no patience for puzzles :) ." Arithine, one of the video posters, wrote: "Sorry about

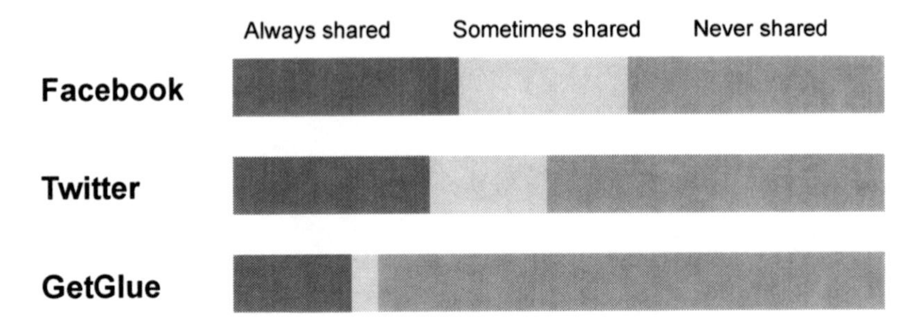

Fig. 13.4. Sharing practices on Facebook, Twitter, and GetGlue.

the quality on this one. HBO had it locked down more then last time. I needed to do a screen capture to get it, watch in HD [high definition] to help get rid of some artifacts." Thus she showed that she really has cared about what to present to the viewing audience.

In our survey, we explicitly asked the gamer respondents about their sharing practices in relation to the social media websites that the game producers promoted through the game (e.g., Facebook, Twitter, and GetGlue). We asked them whether they always, sometimes, or never shared material from the game on these sites and accordingly filtered the following questions to find out which channel was most used for sharing. In practice, the filtering proved to be a bit confusing, so answers are not always representative; nevertheless we believe that they are a good indication of what was most common.

As we can see in figure 13.4, Facebook is the most popular channel, with more than 50 percent of the people sharing, while Twitter and GetGlue are less popular. Still, it seems that a big number of participants never or very rarely shared. We therefore included a free text question about this issue in our survey and received some interesting answers regarding why they had not shared.

- "None of my friends or family have read the series. They probably knew I was excited about the TV series coming, but giving them details like this would have just bugged them" (F, 28, US).
- "I don't spam my friends on social media. I hate it when people do it to me" (M, 47, US).

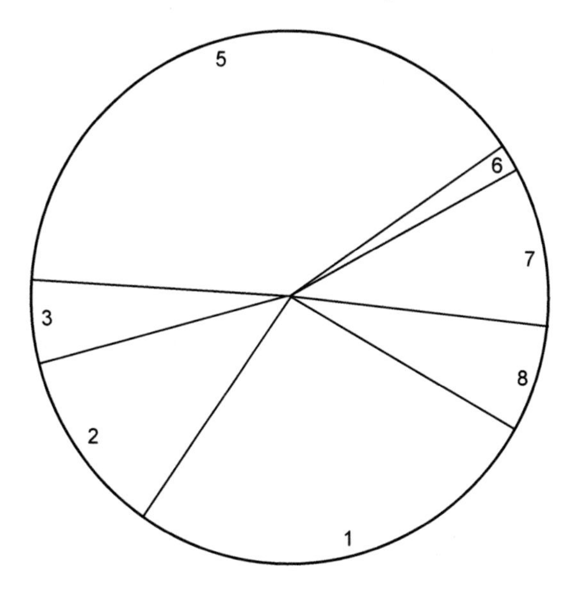

Fig. 13.5. Reactions to the "recruiting option."

- "I didn't want to spam my Twitter account because that is my most heavily trafficked social media channel and a number of people would have been annoyed" (F, 24, US).

The same pattern can be observed in the responses regarding the recruitment of apprentices required in order to complete the game (see figure 13.5). Of the sixty-one people who answered this question, a bit fewer than half of them tried to recruit friends, but most chose friends who knew the universe. Thirty-one would not recruit for various reasons, and four were not aware of the option. Ten supplemented with free text answers such as this one: "I don't like games that rely on 'forcing' friends to play to in order to unlock rewards. So I used made-up email accounts for my 'novices' instead, as a way to protest this system" (F, 26, France). Another wrote:

> And ended up HATING the people at HBO who decided to force me to Spam my friends or to not complete the path. I chose the latter. I've

been an evangelist for this series for ten years. I have purchased and given away over a dozen copies of the first novel. But I will NOT spam my friends. I will berate those who spam me and be disinclined to anything that is forwarded by a spammer site like that stupid game was. Of course, with my history with ASOIAF [the book], nothing was going to keep me from watching GoT. (M, 47, US)

Core Findings

When we started this research, we had two major research questions in mind: how would a transmedial campaign such as this fit into our previous TMW theoretical model, and how does a TMW fan community respond to social media marketing practices (a theoretically under-explored area)?

In regard to the first question, reception of the transmedial campaign followed the same pattern as any other TMW instantiation that we have observed for novels, films, computer games, and other products, with the same worries about the integrity of the mythos, ethos, and topos reflected in the fan discussions and with the fans' expressing the same satisfaction about exploring their favorite TMW from a different angle. Two-thirds of our respondents were enthusiastic about the campaign.[8] Some comments we received were: "It's great to see a book come alive onscreen" (F, 27, Switzerland). "It was great that some of the books' symbolism found its way into the game. The riddles were a challenge" (M, 41 US). And even most of the fans who were critical appreciated the effort that had been put into giving flesh to the TMW. Ultimately, the fan experience of "visiting" the TMW, interacting with and sharing the investigation process with others, was the biggest reward, and the video clips curiously lost their appeal as prizes as the premiere day approached.[9]

As for our general reception model, we can say that in contrast to computer game worlds, where playing the game can be a self-contained activity separated from any TMW actualizations, *The Maester's Path* campaign only made sense in the context of the TMW. It was true that players who did not know the universe could play the game—that is, they could figure out the puzzles—and for those who could not, help was available on blogs and forums. But the point is that people who had not read the books would not play the game, as our empirical material supports, be-

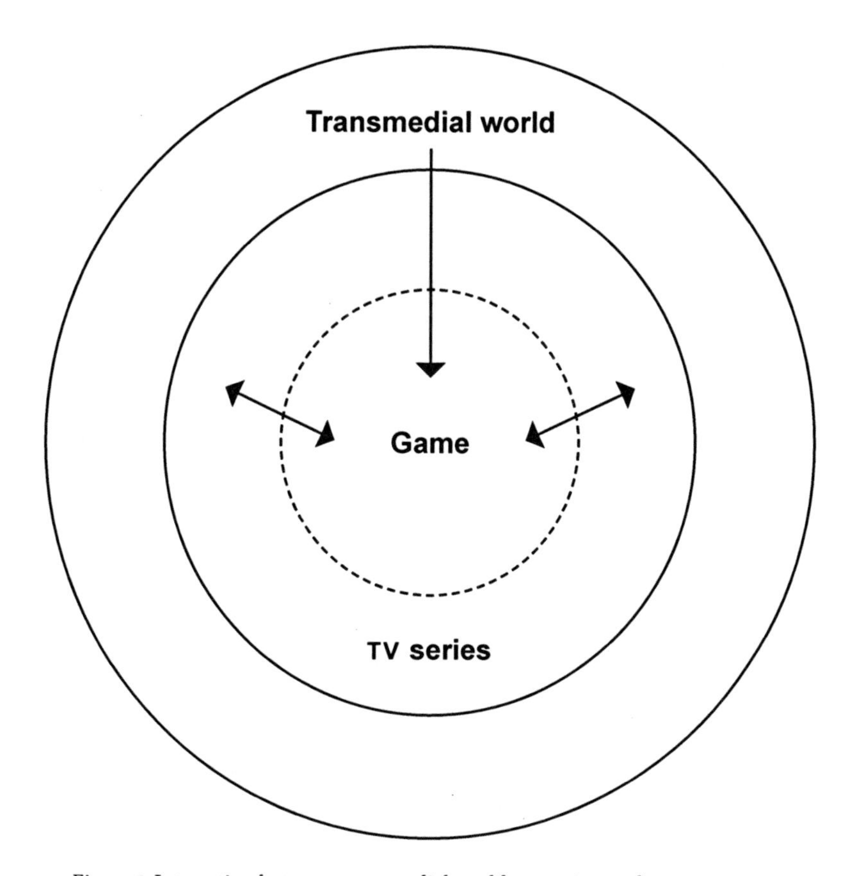

Fig. 13.6. Interaction between transmedial world, TV series, and game.

cause they had no motivation to engage with it. This finding suggests that the publicity benefits are generated not by the content of the game per se but by the evangelist zeal of fans who would tell others about the upcoming TV series and spread the news of their interaction with the game through their social networks.[10] It also means that a transmedial marketing product is a much less independent entity than another TMW instantiation, such as a book or film, and that we might be able to distinguish between degrees of independence of the products of a transmedial media ecology (see figure 13.6).

Our second interest area, the use of social media in relation to fan practice, also reveals some interesting findings, mostly through analyzing the fans' dilemma about sharing or not sharing their progress in the game or recruiting apprentices in their social networks—the key to the success of this kind of campaign. When trying to understand why fans were bothered by the game's asking them to share, it is worthwhile noting a point Green and Jenkins (2001) made concerning spreadable media: "Choosing to spread media involves a series of socially embedded decisions: that the content is worth watching; that it is worth sharing with others; that the content might interest specific people we know; that the best way to spread that content is through a specific channel of communication; and, often, that the content should be circulated with a particular message attached. However, even if no message is attached at all, just receiving a piece of media content from someone we know gives the text a range of new potential meanings" (113–14).

In other words, sharing content is not an easy decision, as it has many dimensions. Cultural content, such as a message about a transmedial game you are playing, is always loaded. As Green and Jenkins point out, fans do not live in a social vacuum where they assume that something they like is automatically worthy of being noted by the people who know them. It might seem that an easy recommendation (simply push a button and have it directly published into the social media of your choice) is not a high price to pay to be able to enjoy content about your favorite TMW, but fans do not want to mix them. They love their TMW, but they also appreciate the social capital they have built and refuse to spread content as it puts them in a vulnerable social situation. As fan Bronn Stone puts it:

> This particular style of social marketing will most likely kill social marketing as an effective tool for creating a buzz for a new product. I don't spam my friends. My friends know this about me. They know that when I do say something, it is because I am genuinely interested in it. Not because I am getting a Space Turnip in FarmVille or 10,000 free chips in WPT [World Poker Tour] Poker. I am not going to break that rule just to get extra preview commercials for GoT. When I know that someone linking ME to a site did it for some cheesy reward, I am strongly disinclined toward the linked object even if it might have interested me otherwise. (N. pag.)

Not all fans are as belligerent, but our respondents also pointed to the problematic nature of the sharing scheme: the reward obtained by sharing robs the recommendation of its authenticity. For the majority of our

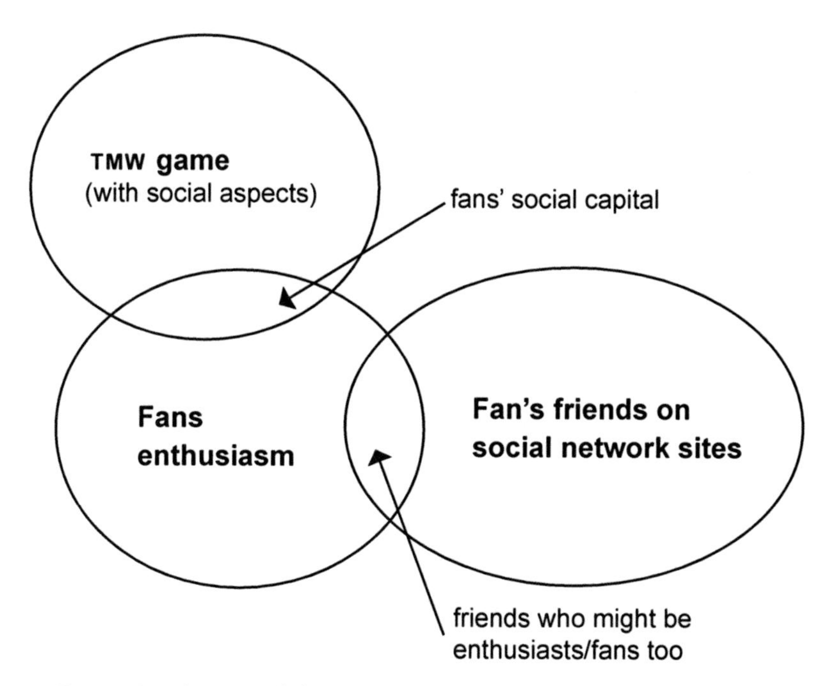

Fig. 13.7. Social aspects of *The Maester's Path*.

respondents, social media sharing should be free of any gain that turns what should be a gift (a recommendation about something the sender thinks his or her friends will enjoy) into a transaction. A marketing scheme that turns shares into currency is perceived as somehow corrupted. For some people, this antipathy extends to the "announced" product so that the whole marketing scheme would backfire, and most would be much more amenable to sharing (as they normally do with any kind of online content they like) *if it was not a requirement*.

The problem is aggravated by the *collapsed contexts* dynamics described by Joshua Meyrowitz in relation to broadcast media and applied by Danah Boyd to the study of networked publics. Social media sites (at the time of the game) made it mostly impossible for users to maintain distinct social contexts so that one share goes to all the acquaintances and relations (of a very different nature) that the person maintains artificially united online (see figure 13.7).

A portion of the user's friends might also be fans of the particular promoted product (in this case *A Song of Ice and Fire* and its TV adaptation), but for most, to share it would be perceived as irrelevant and/or strange. A campaign such as the one studied in this chapter wants to exploit the fans' social capital and reach people who might otherwise not have heard of the product. Paradoxically, that very group represents the people whom the players we talked to want to "protect," and it is in this light that the sharing is perceived as an aggression in the form of spam. This finding indicates that a great deal of underlying meanings and perceptions cluster around the act of sharing and that it is never a straightforward recommendation. Our research shows that even when the shared content is perceived as valuable (when we asked, many of the fans would like the people they like to be acquainted with the series), it is problematic that the sharing is part of a marketing scheme and not initiated by the user as a private expression of interest or emotion. In this sense, the explicit persuasive intention of the apprentice-recruiting scheme is a problem for its effective spreading, and one can only wonder if the success of the *Game of Thrones* campaign would have been even bigger had the persuasion remained implicit. It would also be interesting to research if fans are more wary of sharing information in social networks about their favorite TMW than about other things (like a funny YouTube video)—that is, if increased protectiveness is one of the feelings related to TMW fandom. But this question will have to be explored in the next instantiation of our ongoing research on transmedial worlds.

Notes

1. See Klastrup and Tosca, "Transmedial Worlds"; Klastrup and Tosca, "MMOGs"; Klastrup and Tosca, "When Fans."
2. We found some examples of this reaction both in our previous studies and in the fan activity surrounding the launch of the *Game of Thrones* series. In fact, one of the main points that fans who had played *The Maester's Path* reported to us in the questionnaire was that, in the words of one of the respondents: "It did a very good job of settling my fears that HBO might not do the series justice. The game made it pretty clear that HBO understood what made the world so interesting" (M, 28, US).
3. The Campfire video can be found at http://campfirenyc.com/work/hbo-game-of-thrones/.
4. Several of our interviewees mentioned this puzzle as a satisfying example. One said, "I really liked the mini-game on the wall, it was cool to play the part of

a brother of the Night's Watch! That was my favorite part of the game" (M, 19, US).

5. WinterIsComing.net is a fan-driven website that shares news of all things related to the TV series. As far as we can establish, it also cooperates with HBO and is considered one of the main news sources among GOT fans.
6. The final question in the survey focused on the experience of the TV series compared to the book, and 159 respondents, or 8 fewer than for the previous questions, replied to this question. As the experience of the game has been our main interest, the statistics presented in the discussion are based on the 166 respondents.
7. From the comments to *The Maester's Path*, fourth reward, at http://www.youtube.com/watch?v=AKPqafP-dEE.
8. Of those who had played the game.
9. As confirmed by our interview subject as well.
10. We borrow the use of the term "evangelism" in this sense from our interview with Coulson.

Works Cited

Bechmann Pedersen, Anja. *Crossmedia: Innovationsnetværk for traditionelle medieorganisationer.* Diss. Aarhus University, 2009. Print.

Boyd, Danah Michelle. *Taken Out of Context: American Teen Sociality in Networked Publics.* Diss. University of California, Berkeley, 2008. Print.

Campfire. "*The Maester's Path*: Project Trailer for HBO's *Game of Thrones*." 2011. Web.

Dena, Christy. *Transmedia Practice: Theorising the Practice of Expressing a Fictional World across Distinct Media and Environments.* Diss. University of Sidney, 2009. Print.

Evans, Elizabeth. *Transmedia Television: Audiences, New Media, and Daily Life.* New York: Routledge, 2011. Print.

Green, Joshua, and Henry Jenkins. "Spreadable Media: How Audiences Create Value and Meaning in a Networked Economy." *The Handbook of Media Audiences.* Ed. Virginia Nightingale. Oxford, UK: Wiley-Blackwell, 2011. 109–27. Print.

Klastrup, Lisbeth, and Susana Tosca. "MMOGs and the Ecology of Fiction: Understanding LOTRO as a Transmedial World." *DIGRA 2009 Proceedings.* DIGRA, London, 2009. Web. May 1, 2012.

———. "Transmedial Worlds—Rethinking Cyberworld Design." *Proceedings of the 2004 International Conference on Cyberworlds.* Los Alamitos CA: IEEEE Computer Society, 2004. N. pag. PDF file. June 1, 2012.

———. "When Fans Become Players: LOTRO in a Transmedial World Perspective." *Ringbearers: "The Lord of the Rings Online" as Intertextual Narrative.* Ed. Tanya Krzywinska, Esther MacCallum-Stewart, and Justin Parsler. Manchester, UK: Manchester University Press, 2011. 46–69. Print.

Knoester, Matthew. "Inquiry into Urban Adolescent Independent Reading Habits: Can Gee's Theory of Discourses Provide Insight?" *Journal of Adolescent & Adult Literacy* 52.8 (May 2009): n. pag. Print.

The Lord of the Rings: The Fellowship of the Ring. Dir. Peter Jackson. New Line Cinema, 2001. Film.

The Lord of the Rings: The Return of the King. Dir. Peter Jackson. New Line Cinema, 2003. Film.

The Lord of the Rings: The Two Towers. Dir. Peter Jackson. New Line Cinema, 2002. Film.

Lund, Henriette Romme. "Hvad skaber en lystlæser? En undersøgelse gennemført i et samarbejde mellem Gentofte Bibliotekerne og Center for Børnelitteratur." Gentofte: Center for Børnelitteratur, Danmarks Pædagogiske Bibliotek, 2007. Web. September 2, 2011.

Meyrowitz, Joshua. *No Sense of Place: The Impact of Electronic Media on Social Behavior*. New York: Oxford University Press, 1985. Print.

Stone, Bronn. "A Forum of Ice and Fire." March 21, 2011. Web. June 1, 2011.

Tolkien, J. R. R. *The Fellowship of the Ring: Being the First Part of The Lord of the Rings*. London: George Allen & Unwin, 1954. Print.

———. *The Return of the King: Being the Third Part of The Lord of the Rings*. London: George Allen & Unwin, 1955. Print.

———. *The Two Towers: Being the Second Part of The Lord of the Rings*. London: George Allen & Unwin, 1954. Print.

Train, Briony. "What Do You Like to Read? An Evaluation Report." Centre for the Public Library in the Information Society, Department of Information Studies, University of Sheffield, 2003. PDF file. May 1, 2012.

Wagner, Mitch. "Marketing *The Game of Thrones*." The CMO site. June 2011. Web. June 1, 2011.

14 Transmedial Narration and Fan Fiction

The Storyworld of The Vampire Diaries

MARIA LINDGREN LEAVENWORTH

An ever-increasing number of Internet-published fan fictions (fanfic) based on the transmedial storyworld of *The Vampire Diaries* (TVD) evidences a desire to present alternatives to the narrative or to fill in perceived gaps. In their stories, fanfic authors in subtle or profound ways change conditions, plotlines, or characterizations, and in these ways they contribute new associations and interpretations to the extended storyworld. Despite increased academic interest in fan activities, there are still tendencies to see the relation between production and consumption as hierarchical. While the sanctioned products, in fanfic vernacular referred to as "canon," inspires a desire for interaction, the resulting fan products are not necessarily perceived as on par with the "original" or incorporated into processes of meaning making. The term "canon" works in relation to "fanon," or the fan-produced, unsanctioned developments of plot and character that over time acquire legitimacy within the fan community even though they may contest or be incompatible with canon elements. In what follows, it is argued that the concept of storyworld holds great potential for allowing a leveling of hierarchies between sanctioned and unsanctioned products. To rethink different contributions, especially in light of the contemporary stress on audience participation, is productive when seeing fan fiction as part of a larger archive.

Rather than presenting logically consistent, essentially compatible narratives along the lines of a traditionally defined storyworld, TVD illustrates alternative narrative developments and characterizations in its transmedial instantiations, the novels written by L. J. Smith and the TV series produced by Kevin Williamson and Julie Plec, that in some ways may seem to complicate the notion of TVD as one cohesive storyworld.[1] Adding the variations, alternatives, and sometimes critical commentary found in fan fiction further suggests the possibility of a collapse of any inherent logical narrative consistency. However, both the openness of TVD in terms of fan investment and general tendencies in global convergence culture that encourage audience participation would seem to point at the necessity of a more encompassing notion of *storyworld*. As Bronwen Thomas argues, "storyworlds are generated and experienced within specific social and cultural environments that are subject to constant change" (6). Considering the specificities of TVD in terms of origin and fan participation, contradictions and incompatibilities are bound to surface and rise to the point where they become intrinsic to the storyworld itself.

Although the storyworld is in a state of flux, on a concrete level fan fiction is still a fairly static text form, which in this case is based on likewise fairly static text forms such as written novels and a TV series. Interest thus further lies in what affordances and limitations the concepts of interactivity have and in what aspects specific to TVD need to be taken into account to better understand what goes on between authorized, sanctioned products and fan responses. Finally, four fan fictions are analyzed; two of which are connected to the storyworld's written instantiations, and two of which take the TV series as their starting point (all published in 2011). At focus are the ways in which the fanfic authors negotiate assignations and portrayals of good and evil and how they criticize cultural norms influencing contemporary romance, all adding new interpretations and new associations to an ever-expanding storyworld archive.

The Transmedial TVD Storyworld

TVD is designated as *transmedial* here in accordance with the simplest possible definition: the narrative is dispersed across different media forms. However, it is not a cohesive storyworld in which each instantiation contributes pieces to the overall puzzle, contains exactly the same characters, or presents identical ontologies. In Henry Jenkins's definition of an "ideal" storyworld, the Wachowski siblings' *The Matrix* trilogy is used as an example of how, in addition to "multiple media platforms [. . .] each new text [should make] a distinctive and valuable contribution to the whole" and how "[r]eading across media" theoretically can result in a full understanding (*Convergence* 95–96). The instantiations in TVD, rather than contributing to the whole, veer off in different directions.

Viewers of the CW Television Network's TV series cannot turn to L. J. Smith's novels to find answers to all questions (although they can get answers to some) and vice versa.[2] Differences are, however, likely the result of a conscious transmedial strategy to present a story evolving in different directions rather than merely offering the TV series as an adaptation.

The transmedial strategy is also visible in encouraged early fan involvement, which illustrates a particular kind of accessibility. Kimberley McMahon-Coleman notes that fans were invited to take part in the creation of the storyworld via the website Vampire-diaries.net, which "predate[s] the existence of the actual show," and to offer commentary and suggestions via social media (170). The initial posts on the website concern Smith's novels and establish that the TV series does take its inspiration from them, but it is progressively made clear that the visual text will take a slightly different route. McMahon-Coleman envisions the result as three locations, sprawling in different directions: Fell's Church (the fictional setting in the novels), Mystic Falls (the setting in the TV series), and "cyberspace [which becomes] a third and intermediated location [and which] has facilitated direct conversations between writers, producers, actors and fans" (170). The possibilities for communication and influence suggest that there was no desire on the part of the TV producers to maintain a narratively cohesive storyworld. Instead, alternative paths were imagined, encouraged, and finally realized. The creativity of many individuals thus influences the directions the narrative takes. These sometimes conflicting paths result in a number of differences between written and visual instantiations, some of which have no real bearing on the narrative itself, such as characters' names and physical appearance, and some of which are more profound, with connections to ontologies and the main characters' functions.

The novels feature a vast host of supernatural creatures and depict different fantastical realms between which the characters move, and the main protagonist, Elena, undergoes multiple transformations. At the end of *The Struggle* she drowns but, having previously ingested vampire blood, comes back as undead in the next novel, *The Fury*. This novel too ends with Elena's death as she sacrifices herself in order to kill the evil vampire Katherine, but again she makes a comeback, this time as a ghost or angelic presence. These transformations, the vampires, the other supernatural creatures, and the different realms are kept hidden from the citizens of Fell's Church, and Elena herself has to remain hidden from her immediate family (an aunt and a baby sister) since they believe she is dead. Elena provides an initial possibility for audience identification, and the use of the diary format gives the reader ample opportunity to gradually come to terms with the changing circumstances. Elena is initially unwilling to accept anything unnatural until her meeting with her soul mate, the vampire Stefan, forces her to do otherwise, but she is then progressively made "other" not only to the readers but also to her human friends. The destabilization of the initially realistic premise is furthered in *The Return* trilogy, where not only Elena is superhuman but also her hitherto human friend Meredith is revealed to be a hunter-slayer. The threats directed at the community of Fell's Church are unrelated to the main vampire characters—Stefan and his brother, Damon—and seem to amass because of specificities of the town's geographical location.

Where Elena is concerned, the TV series initially represented more stability, keeping Elena human. The fourth season, however, revolves around her struggle in accepting that she has involuntarily been turned into a vampire. As in the novels, Elena is orphaned, but her guardian, Aunt Jenna, who only tenuously represents parental authority (until she is killed toward the end of the second season), is significantly younger than her novel counterpart, and baby Margaret has been replaced with a brooding and drug-abusing brother named Jeremy. The change in familial relationships means increased opportunities for romantic subplots and might be read as a strategy to attract a slightly different and slightly older audience than the novels did. Although family members and friends are for a long time kept in the dark regarding vampire activity, the community has a secret society that is aware of vampires and has quite a few gadgets to assist in their destruction. As opposed to the novels, where Damon Salvatore and Stefan Salvatore are made vampires in late fifteenth-century Italy, in the TV series they are local boys who were turned in Civil War times. They have periodically returned to Mystic Falls and are vaguely familiar to the townsfolk. In contrast to the novels, then, where Elena needs to stay hidden because the town presumes she is dead, it is the vampires who might be objects of suspicion and need to keep a low profile. The main threats of each season are in various ways connected to Elena and the Salvatore brothers rather than to geography. The antagonists in the main story lines invariably are also variations on the vampire trope, making issues of good and evil vampirism more central to the TV series than to the novels.

So far, differences may seem to point at two separate storyworlds rather than one, but two central themes unite the written novels and the TV series—the romantic love between Stefan and Elena and the animosity between the Salvatore brothers. These themes underpin each major narrative event and are intertwined since Damon's advances toward Elena feed into the sibling feud. Another motif in both the novels and the show is the question of what constitutes evil where vampires are concerned, and Damon, the initially evil vampire, becomes progressively more humanized and vulnerable as the motif is woven with the romantic theme. The romantic love, the sibling rivalry, and the questions about good and evil are also chief aspects in TVD fanfic, thus working toward the argument that despite differences, TVD can be conceived of as one (albeit not cohesive) storyworld.

Interactivity and Archontic Texts

Interactivity is a key term in many discussions about digital or "new" media, but the written novels and the TV series cannot always be equated with the types of storyworlds that are most often mentioned—that is, interactive fictions, databases, games, and hypertexts—as they do not respond to physical interaction. Both text forms, however, elicit interactive responses from fans. In a discussion about television fandom, Sara Gwenllian Jones notes that "[t]he television text itself [. . .] has no facility for material intervention [however] the fiction that it generates, and which vastly exceeds containment by any discrete text, is a different matter" ("Web Wars" 167). Fan fiction, as one expression, illustrates the authors' desire to interact with the canon texts, and it is not the material affordances of the medium that enable interaction but the excess of meaning. As Gwenllian Jones puts it: "Interactivity here occurs not as a material process involving physical interventions but as an imaginative one" ("Web Wars" 167). However, fan fiction can still be seen in relation to more overarching discussions about interactivity—for example, as in Marie-Laure Ryan's refinement of the concept. She makes two main distinctions, which are divided into dichotomous pairs: "internal versus external involvement and exploratory versus ontological involvement" (339). The ontological aspect of the second binary is of particular relevance to fan fiction. Ryan maintains that in this kind of involvement "the decisions of the user send the history of the virtual world on different forking paths. These decisions are ontological in the sense that they determine which possible world, and consequently which story, will develop from the situation in which the choice presents itself" (339).

The fanfic category AU (Alternate Universe) represents these kinds of ontological alterations as AU fanfics answer the "What If?" question (see also chapter 11, Mittell's contribution in this volume). The canon texts in the storyworld do not provide links to possible other worlds in any manifest way, but gaps and discrepancies do. Situations that are not explored fully, characters who are not developed, and tensions that are unsatisfactorily resolved provide the fanfic author with possibilities to take the story imaginatively in another direction and subtly or profoundly destabilize the ontology of the storyworld.

Say that a fanfic author asks, what if Elena was never attracted to Stefan in the first place? The love story between Elena and Stefan guides virtually every plot and character development in TVD, and upsetting or canceling it would radically change the storyworld's ontology. The question may stem from the fanfic author's sense that the characters' attraction to each other is not sufficiently explained in the canon, leaving an imaginative gap. It may be based on the author's detection of a discrepancy: a century-old vampire and a seventeen-year-old girl are incompatible on several levels. It may simply come from the author's individual opinion that Elena would be better off paired with someone else. The resulting hypothetical fanfic in which Elena meets Stefan, says thanks but no thanks, resumes the relationship with her high school sweetheart, Matt, and has no further run-ins with vampires and other supernatural creatures would contribute new associations and create a new possible world.

Fan fiction, and then particularly the category AU, thus shares traits with forms of interactivity in which clicking on a particular link or choosing a specific pathway evidence material media affordances. Lisbeth Klastrup and Susana Tosca identify three core features of the interactive transmedial storyworld: *mythos*, *topos*, and *ethos*. Put simply, the terms signify, respectively, the backstory, or "the central knowledge one needs to have in order *to interact with or interpret events in the world* accordingly"; the setting and with it "knowing *what is to be expected from the physics and navigation in the world*"; and the ethics of the storyworld, or "the knowledge required in order to know *how to behave* in the world" (Klastrup and Tosca n. pag., original emphases). "Interaction," "navigation," and "behavior" are all terms that draw attention both to active, physical choices made when transversing the storyworld and to the fact that the interface has to allow these choices to be made and have consequences.

In a discussion about fan activity in the Xenaverse, Gwenllian Jones lists "'stages' of knowledge and interpretation" that in various ways coincide with Klastrup and Tosca's terms but also allow for a focus on less material interactions ("Starring" 17). Sharing affinities with mythos, "Background Hard Data" signifies the "'facts' about [Xena's] background, family, relationships and experiences" emerging through the extended diegesis of the show, whereas "Real-Time Hard Data" is constituted by the accumulation of information in each episode ("Starring" 18). A certain amount of fidelity to the canon's hard data is necessary in fan fiction as readers of the story otherwise would not know how to interpret it. In TVD, as indicated, the differences between instantiations means that the author needs to specify what mythos, or hard data, he or she has in mind. The easiest way to signal this data is to file the fanfic according to the instantiation on which it is based.[3] In stories relying on real-time data, and then particularly in those connected to the TV series, it is common for fanfic authors to specify precisely where in the narrative arc the stories are placed (e.g., "set after 1.14").

Gwenllian Jones's next stage is "Competencies," which "determine [the characters'] range of possible actions and reactions" ("Starring" 18). Competencies are based on individual characters' "personalities," or their weaknesses and strengths; and to depict actions and reactions too far removed from what is plausible, given the canon competencies, may result in fan fiction with Out of Character (OOC) characters.[4] "Themes and Motifs," Gwenllian Jones further claims, "extend far beyond the limits of the diegesis; they are reiterated and explored" in different forms of fan expressions ("Starring" 18). In the case of TVD, the central romance is an example of such a theme, which is visible in stories about characters who are not romantically linked in the canon, and the good versus evil motif is similarly reiterated in ways that move beyond events in the canon and put a different spin on things.

"Behaviour, Ethics, and Psychology" also have strong affinities with Klastrup and Tosca's ethos, and "[i]t is in this area," Gwenllian Jones maintains, "that fan engagement and speculation is at its most intense" ("Starring" 18). The psychological gaps in the diegetic story can be filled in in fanfics that develop the perspective of minor characters or offer alternative readings of major characters. Fanfic authors may also profoundly destabilize the storyworld's ethics by removing aspects that are arguably essential to the very ontology. Fanfics based on vampire storyworlds and categorized as "All Human" or "AU-human" do away with the vampire element altogether and are examples of such destabilization. The pre-formed knowledge of how characters (and readers) are to react to and imaginatively behave in this type of story is canceled along with the supernatural element.[5]

The final item of Gwenllian Jones's list is "Erotics" ("Starring" 19). Whereas the storyworld at the center of her analysis consciously plays with the characters' sexual identities and desires, TVD is fairly heteronormative. However, fan responses to the erotics of a storyworld can take a number of forms, and the fanfic category "slash," denoting a same-sex pairing between characters who are not a couple in the canon, is by no means nonexistent because of the lack of homoeroticism in the storyworld.

In contemporary popular culture where storyworlds are not confined to isolated media and where audiences are asked to participate in the meaning-making process, interaction thus occurs on both literal and figurative levels. When regarding fan fiction as one form of interaction, it is profitable to see the storyworld comprising not only sanctioned instantiations but also the fans' interpretations. Abigail Derecho's suggestion is to designate this type of text world as "archontic literature," and she argues that the "archontic text's archive is not identical to the text but is a virtual construct surrounding the text, including it and all the texts related to it" (65). Thus each addition to the archive influences it and supplies new associations and interpretations that subsequent authors then can be inspired by or relate to. To view a storyworld along these archontic lines can be liberating because fan-deposited material is put on par with sanctioned products rather than being regarded in terms of lineage and derivation.

The excess of meaning concomitant with complex transmedial storyworlds illustrates the creators' "encyclopedic ambitions" (Jenkins, "Transmedia" sec. 19) but also triggers an encyclopedic drive in fans. As Jenkins notes: "None of us can know everything; each of us knows something; and we can put the pieces together if we pool our resources and combine our skills" (*Convergence* 4). Derecho notes a similar drive, but in line with her aim to equalize creators and fans, she ascribes it to the archive itself: the "drive within an archive that seeks to produce more archive, to enlarge itself" (64). When viewed as a site of interaction, then, each fanfic story deposited in the TVD archontic text enlarges it by suggesting slight or profound differences.

Good, Evil, and Romance in the TVD Archive

Vampire storyworlds commonly hinge on a tension between good and evil with the vampire figured as some kind of threat to humans or symbolizing aspects of human fears. As Nina Auerbach has famously claimed, "[e]very age embraces the vampire it needs" (145), and each age has its own fears and desires. Whereas what Milly Williamson has termed "the sympathetic vampire" is not exclusive to contemporary narratives but rather has ties to the Romantic vampire figures in the works of Lord Byron and John Polidori, it is nevertheless the case that the vampire "is no longer predominantly a figure of fear in Western popular culture" (29). Rather, the "otherness" of contemporary vampires enable them to elide normative constructions and give rise to new possible forms of positive identification, and they constitute a particular attraction. TVD's Stefan is no exception. He is figured as a romantic outsider, in close contact with his emotions, and as offering Elena a companionship her human peers cannot. His goodness is periodically offset in contrast to the evil of other vampires and more consistently in relation to his brother's wicked ways. Both the novels and the TV series suggest that it is not simply vampirism that is evil but the extent to which human emotions are repressed, and when outside threats are introduced, Stefan's good and Damon's evil roles become relative, often with Damon stepping up to offer protection for the humans. Good and evil are further relativized in the TV series when it is revealed that Stefan originally embraced his turning and forced a reluctant Damon to join him in the undead state. Discussing his past with Elena, she reflects that "it sounds like you were Damon," to which Stefan answers, "I was worse" ("The Dinner Party"). The backstory and these admissions progressively shift associations to Stefan being good and make Damon's actions in terms of vengeance more understandable and his evil more nuanced.[6]

If turning off human emotion is one element that signals evil and otherness, the most common sign of monstrosity in vampire storyworlds is unquestionably the sucking of human blood. The vampire's invasion of another's bodily space through the bite has traditionally been figured as particularly evil since it carries with it the threat of transforming the human victim into a monster. When the vampire text falls into the romance genre, this transformation is not always constructed as negative, however, since it also ensures everlasting togetherness. In the novels, Damon repeatedly asks Elena to allow this transformation. She never willingly accepts the offer to be turned, but the central issue of blood taking is consistently figured as an intimate encounter rather than as evil behavior. Even when Elena first learns the truth about Stefan's real nature, the initial shock gives way to an embrace, and the kiss turns to a bite. The initial pain is "replaced by a feeling of pleasure that made her tremble" (Smith, *The Awakening* 186). It is not only Stefan who feeds off Elena but Damon too, and this act exacerbates the ongoing feud between the brothers and heightens Elena's attraction to them both.

In the TV series, Stefan, in accordance with human morals, abstains from human blood for a long time. Damon, meanwhile, initially embraces his status as superior: he sees humans as a food source, "lives" without regard for moral consequences, and continuously taunts Stefan, arguing that his little brother does not "feed properly"("The Night of the Comet"). As a sign of his own increasing humanity, however, Damon progressively abandons his hunting practices and subsists on a basement stash of supplies pilfered from a blood bank. In scenes depicting the taking of human blood, there is no mutual pleasure or signs of minds meeting through the intermingling of blood; instead, most situations are visualized along traditional lines with the vampire as predator and the human as prey.

The question is, of course, if the taking of human blood really is evil, where vampires are concerned, or if it is merely natural behavior, barely repressed by the veneer of humanity in good and emotional vampires. Several of the studied fanfic authors question a vampire's true nature, and blood is a crucial ingredient in bogwitch's "Blood, the Tooth and the Claw." The story warns that it contains plot spoilers for the last episode in the second season of the TV series and adds an internal view of the hunger for blood to the TVD archive. In the fanfic the evil Klaus has captured

Stefan and forced him to drink human blood. When Stefan wakes up, he has a "*screaming*" hunger inside him and a "desperate *need* to rend, to rip and to kill" (n. pag., original emphases). Stefan has repressed these invading primal emotions and demands, it is suggested, for a long time as he has maintained his human morals. "He's been starving for decades and he's never even known," bogwitch writes, and he has lived "a half life of shadow" (n. pag.). In the canon TV episode we see only Stefan's struggle and his self-loathing, but the fanfic rather suggests that his dietary choices have caused him to starve, if not physically then on the level of his nature. Stefan's punishment at the hands of Klaus here is used as a wake-up call and as a reminder of Stefan's true nature, one with which he is not comfortable. Repeatedly, he tries to convince himself of his other, human side, thus creating ties to the canon episode, but the story represents the struggle from an inside perspective. The craving for blood is stronger than his desperate negotiations, however, and the short story ends with Stefan giving into it again and forever.

Blood fills another and more symbolically nurturing function in MimiRose113's "A Bit of Give and Too Much Take," which is set during the final installment of the novel series. In *Midnight*, the human characters take turns feeding a famished Stefan, who has been rescued after a long period of imprisonment and starvation. At the end of the previous novel, *Shadow Souls*, Damon has unexpectedly been re-turned (made human), and MimiRose113 uses this canon element for Stefan to feed on his brother. Damon has agreed to this sacrifice since his basic view of humans as having value only as a food source still holds true. The intimate nature of bloodsucking establishes close ties to the way it is figured as mutually pleasurable in the canon and is intensified as the brothers can sense each other's thoughts. In the fanfic, Stefan reflects, "[O]ur emotions flow[ed] into one another [and] he received my intense pleasure and appreciation of the blood I was guzzling from him, with the subtle undertones of feelings of nurture and being cared for" (n. pag.). While the long animosity between the brothers in the canon has not prevented them from periodically protecting each other, the vulnerability that surfaces in "A Bit of Give and Too Much Take" lifts this protection, care, and nurturing to another level. Damon tastes different than the humans do, Stefan notices, because he carries in his blood the blood of individuals he has killed in the past. The taking of blood means another chance to be reacquainted with "the brother [Stefan] hadn't been this close to in years" (n. pag.), with all that entails of both past sins and present redemption.

The motif of two feuding brothers is doubled in the TVD TV series through the depiction of the ancient vampires Elijah and Klaus. In contrast to Stefan and Damon they do not slide as easily into antithetical roles as they both present major threats to the protagonists and their evil is a matter of degree rather than kind. Elijah and Klaus are featured in Sandrine Shaw's fanfic "Barefoot on Broken Glass (One Step at a Time)," which also reiterates a suggestion brought up in many fanfics: Elena could have a relationship with two brothers at once. Whereas the majority of fanfics depicting this motif have Damon and Stefan as central characters and thus start from a relatively benign position where Elena is desired and adored, "Barefoot on Broken Glass" starts with Klaus piercing Elena's heart with a dagger. Waking up as a vampire, hunger drives her to kill a woman brought in as prey. As do many fanfic authors, Sandrine Shaw uses an inside perspective to elicit sympathy for the monster through Elena's repeated references to her own weakness and her struggle with bloodlust. Her humanity is still close, and she judges her actions against it, deeply aware that she has turned monstrous. She also recognizes the irony in being "once again caught between two warring brothers, too much in love with one of them and too attracted, however unhealthily, to the other to step away" (n. pag.). But whereas human morals in the canon seem to prevent Elena from acting on her desire for both brothers, her vampire existence in the fanfic gives her new freedom. Embraced by both Elijah and Klaus, "for the first time since she woke up a vampire, [she] feels that it's going to be okay" (n. pag.). This fanfic, which was published in 2011, adds alternative depictions of the three characters to the TVD archive, with the foremost, naturally, being a "new" Elena since her existence as a vampire had not yet been explored in the TV series. On the thematic level and connected to the previous theme of feuding brothers and the three-way attraction, the fanfic importantly also shifts associations, suggesting that many of the tensions in the canon triggered by human jealousy and stress on exclusive relationships can be resolved in a less normative construction.

As suggested, the main contemporary attraction of the popular culture vampire lies in the realms of romance, and in the TVD storyworld, any threats to the seemingly fated love between Elena and Stefan can be perceived as evil.[7] In fan fiction, changing the conditions or substituting one member of the fated pair is not always viewed as a sign of evil directed at the central romance. Rather fanfics of this type demonstrate a desire to play with the given conditions and to see what happens if Stefan or Elena is paired with someone else. But authors also demonstrate an awareness of the unhealthy focus in contemporary romance on sacrifice and unequal relationships. In the story notes preceding the fanfic "The Most Impulsive Thing," author Piper writes that the "story is born out of my kind of intense hate for something that's running rampant in the Vampire fandom given the rise of the Twilight series: the female who's willing to give up everything for her vampire boyfriend" (n. pag.).[8] Like Elena, the human protagonist Bella in Stephenie Meyer's *Twilight* novels is a teenager who is immediately drawn to the handsome vampire Edward. Similar to Stefan, Edward has experiences and strengths that render the relationship with Bella unequal. Discussions of Meyer's novels have emphasized Bella's restricted agency and Edward's monitoring of her actions and have criticized the portrayal of the sacrifices Bella makes to be with the vampire she loves (see, e.g., Isaksson and Lindgren Leavenworth 2011).

"The Most Impulsive Thing" is based on the TVD novels in which Elena has a rather different function than being merely a submissive girlfriend, but which *do* repeatedly stress that she and Stefan are fated to be together and that she will (literally) go to hell and back to save him. Piper sets her story almost a decade after the novels' story arc and uses Bonnie, one of Elena's friends, as a thoughtful and critical protagonist. Here, Bonnie is in a relationship with Damon, who wants to turn her into a vampire but is patient and considerate of her wishes. Damon is depicted as also loving Bonnie for being human. Thinking back on the years after high school, she has made a life for herself while "Elena left for Europe with Stefan, bypassing college completely, not to mention life altogether" (n. pag.). Thus the fated love has not only made Elena give up pretentions of a life of her own but has also made her consent to being turned. Bonnie, meanwhile, has great plans for her life—to see the sights of the world and be alive when she does. Although in love with Damon, she says, "This isn't some romance novel, you know? I'm not going to swoon into your incredibly handsome arms and present my pale, virgin neck to you. Those girls apparently don't have anything to do with their lives" (n. pag.).

This in-text nod to romance novels stresses the inhumanity of expecting a young woman to put her life on hold (or canceling it altogether) in favor of abiding by her lover's wishes. Whereas it may be unfair to expect supernatural vampire storyworlds to be realistic, the criticism is directed toward the unreasonable choices made by those who arguably *could* represent realism—namely, the humans. Piper's depiction of Bonnie relies on years having passed between canon and fanfic so that a mature woman rather than a teenager says to her loved one, "I love you. I'm not ready to change everything I am for you. I'm not ready to die for you." The addition of an older, less naive protagonist to the TVD archive makes possible readings of the canon material that are at least open for a more critical view of unquestioning sacrifices and the stress on exclusive, all-consuming romantic relationships.

The links between storyworld and fan fiction go in both directions, and when seen as parts of the archive, each text holds the possibility of influencing how others are interpreted. Derecho argues that "[t]he prior text is available and remains in the mind even as one reads the new version. The two texts resonate together in both the new text and the old one" (73). The TVD canon is a prerequisite for TVD fan fiction in the first place, and authors are careful about signaling from what specific point in the canon's narrative arc their stories should be approached. That is, the canon is ever present, resonating in the fan fictions. But fanfic additions to the TVD archive may similarly complement the canon and supply shifting associations to elements in it. Alternative depictions of characters, romance, good and evil, and human and vampire nature are deposited into the archive and hold the possibility of influencing each reader's and viewer's reading of the canon material. In a contemporary media climate that encourages audience participation in meaning-making processes, it seems worthwhile to stress the importance of seeing texts on par with each other rather than in hierarchical terms of original and copy, derivation and influence. While terms such as "canon" and "storyworld" are useful to denote the material that invites such interaction in the first place, the meaning of the latter term can profitably be enlarged, especially if we want to include fan expressions as contributing to its mythos, topos, and ethos.

Notes

1. A fully expanded definition of *storyworld* naturally encompasses expressions such as production details, interviews and merchandise, and, in the case of TVD, computer games and webisodes, which contribute more straightforwardly narrative details. However, the vast majority of TVD fanfic (based on the initial survey it can be argued all of it) is based on either the novels or the TV series, and the analyses here center on the narrative as it develops in these media forms.
2. There is a temporal lag between Smith's original novel quartet, published in 1991, and the trilogy with the series title *The Return* that roughly coincided with the airing of the first two seasons of the TV series (2009 and 2011). The TV series in October 2013 moved into its fifth season. The fan fictions analyzed later in this chapter are based on either Smith's novels or the first two seasons of the series.
3. The stories analyzed here are taken from sites that provide the fanfic author with the option of filing either under TVD the book series or TVD the show.
4. It should be noted that the creation of an OOC character may at times be a fanfic author's expressed desire. This type of character may, however, give rise to deriding comments from readers who do not wish to see a removal too far from canon behavior.
5. All Human or AU-human fanfics have not yet gained popularity in the TVD storyworld, but as an example from another fandom, the *Twilight*-specific website Twilighted.net has a filing option labeled "AU-human," containing, at present, close to twenty-seven hundred fanfics, more than in any other section at the site (see "Categories").
6. The backstory is fleshed out in *Stefan's Diaries*, the ghost-authored novel spin-offs of the TV series.
7. It should be noted that the notion of Elena's fated love for Stefan is radically undermined in the fourth season of the TV series, as she (as vampire) is instead romantically paired with Damon.
8. See Isaksson and Lindgren Leavenworth (56–67) for a longer discussion about Piper's fanfic.

Works Cited

Auerbach, Nina. *Our Vampires, Ourselves*. Chicago: University of Chicago Press, 1995. Print.

bogwitch. "Blood, the Tooth and the Claw." *Archive of Our Own*. May 31, 2011. Web. June 17, 2011.

"Categories." *Twilighted*. Web. June 17, 2011.

"The Dinner Party." *The Vampire Diaries*. Season 2, episode 15. Warner Home Video, 2011. DVD.

Derecho, Abigail. "Archontic Literature: A Definition, a History, and Several Theories of Fan Fiction." *Fan Fiction and Fan Communities in the Age of the Internet*. Ed. Karen Hellekson and Kristina Busse. Jefferson NC: McFarland, 2006. 61–78. Print.

Gwenllian Jones, Sara. "Starring Lucy Lawless?" *Continuum: Journal of Media & Cultural Studies* 14:1 (2000): 9–22. Print.

———. "Web Wars: Resistance, Online Fandom and Studio Censorship." *Quality Popular Television*. Ed. Mark Jancovich and James Lyons. London: British Film Institute, 2003. 163–77. Print.

Isaksson, Malin, and Maria Lindgren Leavenworth. "Gazing, Initiating, Desiring: Alternative Constructions of Agency and Sex in Twifics." *Interdisciplinary Approaches to "Twilight": Studies in Fiction, Media, and a Contemporary Cultural Experience*. Ed. Mariah Larsson and Ann Steiner. Lund, Sweden: Nordic Academic Press, 2011. 127–42. Print.

Jenkins, Henry. *Convergence Culture: Where Old and New Media Collide*. New York: New York University Press, 2006. Print.

———. "Transmedia Storytelling 101." *Confessions of an Aca-Fan*. March 22, 2007. Web. June 17, 2011.

Klastrup, Lisbeth, and Susana Tosca. "Transmedial Worlds—Rethinking Cyberworld Design." *Proceedings of the 2004 International Conference on Cyberworlds*. Los Alamitos CA: IEEEE Computer Society, 2004. N. pag. PDF file. June 1, 2012.

Lindgren Leavenworth, Maria, and Malin Isaksson. *Fanged Fan Fiction: Variations on "Twilight," "True Blood," and "The Vampire Diaries."* Jefferson NC: McFarland, 2013.

McMahon-Coleman, Kimberley. "Mystic Falls Meets the World Wide Web: Where Is *The Vampire Diaries* Located?" *Fanpires: Audience Consumption of the Modern Vampire*. Ed. Gareth Schott and Kirstine Moffat. Washington DC: New Academia Publishing, 2011. 169–86. Print.

MimiRose113. "A Bit of Give and Too Much Take." *FanFiction.net*. May 4, 2011. Web. June 17, 2011.

"The Night of the Comet." *The Vampire Diaries*. Season 1, episode 2. Warner Home Video, 2011. DVD.

Piper. "The Most Impulsive Thing." *Archive of Our Own*. January 1, 2011. Web. June 17, 2011.

Ryan, Marie-Laure. "Will New Media Produce New Narratives?" *Narrative across Media: The Languages of Storytelling*. Ed. Marie-Laure Ryan. Lincoln: University of Nebraska Press, 2004. 337–59. Print.

Sandrine Shaw. "Barefoot on Broken Glass (One Step at a Time)." *Archive of Our Own*. May 21, 2011. Web. June 17, 2011.

Smith, L. J. *The Awakening & The Struggle*. 1991. London: Hodder Children's Books, 2009. Print.
———. *The Fury & The Reunion*. 1991. London: Hodder Children's Books, 2009. Print.
———. *The Return: Midnight*. London: Hodder Children's Books, 2011. Print.
———. *The Return: Nightfall*. 2009. London: Hodder Children's Books, 2010. Print.
———. *The Return: Shadow Souls*. 2009. London: Hodder Children's Books, 2010. Print.
Thomas, Bronwen. "What Is Fanfiction and Why Are People Saying Such Nice Things about It?" *Storyworlds* 3 (2011): 1–24. Print.
The Vampire Diaries. Season 1. Warner Home Video, 2010. DVD.
The Vampire Diaries. Season 2. Warner Home Video, 2011. DVD.
The Vampire Diaries. Season 3. Warner Home Video, 2012. DVD.
The Vampire Diaries. Season 4. Warner Home Video, 2013. DVD.
Williamson, Milly. *The Lure of the Vampire: Gender, Fiction and Fandom from Bram Stoker to Buffy*. London: Wallflower Press, 2005. Print.

15 The Developing Storyworld of H. P. Lovecraft

VAN LEAVENWORTH

This chapter investigates the storyworld that has developed out of terror tropes presented in the fiction of American Gothic writer H. P. Lovecraft (1890–1937). The Lovecraft storyworld is elicited by textual fiction, interactive fiction, short and feature-length films, fan art, comics, music, board games, role-playing games, computer games, and interactive environments in *Second Life*, to name a few examples. Specifically, I explore the poetics of the Lovecraft storyworld's development, its transmedial adaptability, and its cultural significance for both contemporary audiences and Lovecraft's legacy.

The Lovecraft storyworld is different from other storyworlds in that it is not unified by a specific story or stories. Although there is no accepted definition across disciplinary boundaries, in narrative theory *storyworlds* are frequently defined as "worlds evoked by narratives," which means that narratives act "as blueprints for world-creation" (Herman vii). For example, a reader's mental construction of the environment, characters, and actions presented in Margaret Atwood's *A Handmaid's Tale* is a storyworld, as is the more comprehensive "world" of characters and events fostered by reading J. R. R. Tolkien's *The Lord of the Rings* trilogy. In this definition, the logical consistency of a story or interrelated stories is central; Offred always experiences painful subjugation in the *Handmaid's Tale* storyworld and Frodo always bears the ring in the *Lord of the Rings* storyworld. But fictional practice is not always narratively consistent, particularly when several different authors and producers engage with a storyworld's original "blueprint" narrative(s) over a long period of time. In such a case, the storyworld may develop contradictions or lose narrative consistency altogether. However, such alterations do not discount the possibility of a storyworld, as is demonstrated by the "multiverse" of parallel storyworlds used to logically account for narrative contradictions in long-running superhero comics (Kukkonen

40). The Lovecraft storyworld provides a further example of how narrative inconsistencies may be accommodated. Rather than rely on story, the Lovecraft storyworld is logically consistent due to factors that derive from the original blueprint narrative(s) but are not dependent upon their presence.

The Lovecraft storyworld is a shared mental model of an indistinct world that is unified by a specific thematic focus. Conceiving of this denarrativized storyworld involves imagining the fuzzy idea of a "world" created when audiences collectively share their experiences of it.[1] Lisbeth Klastrup and Susana Tosca's notion of transmedial worlds, although used primarily to discuss authorized cyberworld design, provides a helpful lens for examining the Lovecraft storyworld. "Transmedial worlds are abstract content systems from which a repertoire of fictional stories and characters can be actualized or derived across a variety of media forms. What characterises a transmedial world is that audience and designers share a mental image of the 'worldness' (a number of distinguishing features of its universe). The idea of a specific world's worldness mostly originates from the first version of the world presented, but can be elaborated and changed over time" (n. pag.). This definition helpfully avoids the comprehensive uniformity and narrative consistency that the term "world" might suggest. Audiences and creators share an idea of "worldness," of things that contribute to a sense of a world, rather than a distinct image of a world, and this world-like image has the potential to develop with each new aesthetic work that evokes it. In the Lovecraft storyworld, recurring scenarios feature human characters in realistic settings who discover coexisting cosmic realities and the unspeakably scary beings that inhabit them. These realities appear to rupture natural laws and cannot be conceived of by human minds, and so the encounters produce terror, eternal unease, and/or mental instability in the protagonists. The characters are left with a sense of the insignificance of humanity in the cosmos. These unifying elements provide the thematic foundation of the Lovecraft storyworld's worldness—namely, its logical consistency.

Although the theme of humanity's hopeless encounter with an indifferent cosmic reality is the cornerstone of the Lovecraft storyworld, recurring beings, locations, and occult tomes may help to conjure it. Examples include not only minor creatures such as Byakhees and Migos but also inconceivable, masterful, alien entities such as Cthulhu, Hastur, or Azathoth; such locations as decaying towns or settlements in New England; and the *Necronomicon*, the most famous occult tome.[2] However, works that feature these well-known elements without employing the unifying themes do not evoke the storyworld but merely allude to details in Lovecraft's fictional legacy. For example, Cthulhu has been depicted as a cute, childish figure and is even a hero in the 2010 Xbox Live independent game *Cthulhu Saves the World*. Such re-envisionings of Cthulhu are parodies of but do not develop the Lovecraft storyworld. Klastrup and Tosca's concept of transmedial worlds helps explain the potential but not required use of certain elements in Lovecraft storyworld works. They claim that three core features define a transmedial world's worldness: the *topos* represents the setting and physical laws of the world, the *ethos* includes character ethics and codes of behavior, and the *mythos* is the implied underlying understanding of how things should play out or, as they put it, the "central knowledge one needs to have in order *to interact with or interpret events in the world*" (n. pag., original emphasis). Within this schema, works that contribute to the Lovecraft storyworld may or may not employ commonly used settings (topos) and follow the few rules of character conduct that exist (ethos), but they always engage with the theme of humanity's troubling contact with a cosmic reality (mythos).[3]

The development of the Lovecraft storyworld prompts several questions. What is alluring about it and why has it developed so extensively? As the Lovecraft storyworld's growth is supported by a variety of art forms in different media, how do works engage with its mythos in familiar yet media-specific ways? Finally, how has the Lovecraft storyworld contributed to "pulp" writer Lovecraft's elevation into the American literary canon? In the first section of this chapter, I argue that its allure is attributable to the spiritual appeal of mythos themes, the satisfaction derived from hunting for knowledge, and the desire for aesthetic fulfillment. In the second section, I demonstrate how media-specific limitations engender central mythos themes. Last, I explore how the circle of influence between popular and critical developments has changed Lovecraft's status. The scope and influence of the unique Lovecraft storyworld suggest that it exemplifies the powerful position that storyworlds may occupy in our contemporary media ecology.

Allure

The allure of the Lovecraft storyworld derives from the valued but unsettled nature of knowledge at its mythic core. Many people are spiritually and intellectually drawn to the epistemological rupture produced by human contact with a cosmic reality, some to the extent that Lovecraftian concepts are employed religiously. In a more secular fashion, many find cosmic elements intriguing enough to hunt for more information about them in successive works. The majority of the Lovecraft storyworld audience is likely to appreciate the number and diversity of works available, as each has the potential to provide a fulfilling aesthetic experience.

A fundamental appeal of the Lovecraft storyworld is the nearly religious sense of what Lovecraft referred to as "cosmic fear." In his essay "Supernatural Horror in Literature," he presents cosmic fear as a mixture of terror, wonder, and curiosity. To create this effect in a story, "[a] certain atmosphere of breathless and unexplainable dread of outer, unknown forces must be present; and there must be a hint, expressed with a seriousness and portentousness becoming its subject, of that most terrible conception of the human brain—a malign and particular suspension or defeat of those fixed laws of Nature which are our only safeguard against the assaults of chaos and the daemons of unplumbed space" (426). Cosmic fear derives from suspicion or evidence of "unknown forces," such as so-called Old Ones, including Cthulhu, whose very existence ruptures the systems of knowledge that humanity uses to make sense of the world. Noël Carroll aligns cosmic fear with religious belief, describing it as responding to a "primordial or instinctual human intuition about the world," including a "visionary dimension which is said to be keenly felt and vital" (163). In other words, cosmic fear has a transcendent element, a quality the majority of Lovecraft storyworld works strive to achieve for "explorers."[4] At the same time, the insignificance of humanity within the trope of cosmic fear suggests a humility that is also akin to religious belief as it provides a "healthy" perspective on humanity's actions. Humanity cannot afford to be arrogant, selfish, and shortsighted when more powerful beings in the universe regard it as irrelevant. The Lovecraft storyworld is thus appealing for the quasi-religious mixture of transcendent knowledge and humility that it espouses through the theme of cosmic fear.

An extreme example of the spiritual appeal of cosmic fear is found in contemporary occult practice. In "The Influence of H. P. Lovecraft on Occultism," K. R. Bolton examines several cults that have incorporated Lovecraft's ideas into their beliefs and rituals in similar ways.[5] Lovecraft is considered to have gained "genuine occult knowledge" in his dreams and unwittingly conveyed it through his fiction, which may be contextualized into an occult tradition dating back to Sumerian writings (n. pag.). The cults also share the attitude that the Old Ones, such as Cthulhu, are real and should be brought back to Earth. However, while some occult practitioners view them as morally ambiguous or even evil, Kenneth Grant of the Typhonian Cultus, Michael Aquino of the Church of Satan, and others feel that Lovecraft's interpretation of these beings was faulty; the Old Ones are not evil and may even be regarded as benevolent. Significantly, despite the cults' focus on Lovecraft as an unwitting prophet, Bolton demonstrates that they draw from the Lovecraft storyworld mythos generally and so mistakenly attribute to him details, such as the Old One Gnoph-Hek or the star-shaped Elder Sign, that come from other authors.[6] The inclusion of aspects of the cosmic reality in alternative religious practices emphasizes the intellectual and spiritual allure of ideas in the storyworld.

Another reason for the appeal of the Lovecraft storyworld is the fulfillment derived from hunting for knowledge about specific elements of the cosmic reality. For example, Hastur is commonly regarded as an Old One, but he only receives a vague mention in Lovecraft's tale "The Whisperer in Darkness" (215). Looking for more information about Hastur may lead an explorer to find references in the board game *Arkham Horror* (where the Old One is linked to Byakhees), in an Ambrose Bierce story (where Hastur is a god of shepherds), in Robert W. Chambers's short story collection *The King in Yellow* (where Hastur seems to be both a character and a place), and the trail continues. Henry Jenkins notes that hunting for information is a common practice for communities built around collective consumption and shared knowledge (95, 98–99). Klastrup and Tosca hints at the benefits of this activity when they claim that "by encountering one of the world's actualizations [. . .], the imaginary construct of the world is evoked in the participant's imagination, and each simple act gains a much wider meaning" (n. pag.). This assertion suggests that subsequent encounters with a storyworld enrich the participant's imaginary construct, creating an increasing sense of investment and expertise. In the Lovecraft storyworld, this behavior places the explorer in the same position as human characters in many narratives who attempt to piece together details about the cosmic reality. Like such characters, what begins as a curiosity-driven endeavor may develop into an addictive need to "know," justified by a growing sense of authority and understanding.[7]

As the hunt for Hastur example demonstrates, the knowledge gaps and unfulfilled expectations in many Lovecraft storyworld works encourage further exploration. Lovecraft laid the foundations for these traits with incomplete and inconsistent hints at cosmic elements in his tales (see Joshi 144, Price 239). Recurring clues and details pepper his fiction and the fiction of several of his contemporaries, all of whom borrowed from each other as a means of creating verisimilitude (see Dziemianowicz 21). Narrative gaps are, of course, inherent effects of the difference between events in a story and how they are narrated, as Wolfgang Iser and Meir Sternberg have demonstrated (see Abbott 44), but the gaps in Lovecraft's fiction and the work by others that he has inspired by others also function as the Gothic conventions of fragmentation at key revelatory moments and story-within-a-story layering. These puzzle-like gaps are likely to encourage what Marie-Laure Ryan calls "epistemic immersion" or "the desire to know," which is one of the pleasures incumbent to imaginative engagement with a mystery narrative or narrative-generating work (55).

Ironically, the explorer's quest to learn things about the Lovecraft storyworld may also derive from a lack of storytelling skill in many works. Lovecraft's occasionally monotonous narration may keep readers from fully appreciating the intriguing ideas in his stories, creating a motivation to read more in search of a better experience. To paraphrase Iser, Lovecraft's writing style sometimes hinders "the coming together of text and imagination" so that there is only a limited "fulfillment of the potential, unexpressed reality of the text" (279). For example, consider the following passage: "Out of the unimaginable blackness beyond the gangrenous glare of that cold flame, out of the Tartarean leagues through which that oily river rolled uncanny, unheard, and unsuspected, there flopped rhythmically a horde of tame, trained, hybrid winged things that no sound eye could ever wholly grasp, or sound brain ever wholly remember" ("The Festival" 116). This sentence indicates Lovecraft's penchant for description, drama-dampening phrasing, and inclination to tell (rather than show) the reader about subverted natural laws. In homage to Lovecraft or not, many works evoking the storyworld are of similar questionable quality and so encourage further exploration. Creatively minded individuals, of course, may address this concern through their own artistic production. As testament to this effort, one need only look at the Internet Movie Database, which lists nearly eighty titles based on or inspired by Lovecraft in the last two decades ("H. P. Lovecraft").

Taken together, the quasi-religious character of the Lovecraft storyworld themes, the gap-filling quest for knowledge, and the desire for a satisfying aesthetic experience lead to a cycle of increasing consumption and production.

Thematic Media Specificity

Creative efforts in many different media forms demonstrate the Lovecraft storyworld's transmedial adaptability. Surprisingly, the limitations of the media forms are often used to enable mythos concepts. This enabling limitation is evident in the silent film *The Call of Cthulhu: The Celebrated Story by H. P. Lovecraft* (2005) from the H. P. Lovecraft Historical Society (HPLHS); Chaosium's role-playing game *Call of Cthulhu: Horror Roleplaying in the Worlds of H. P. Lovecraft* (1981–present), authored by Sandy Petersen and Lynn Willis; and Michael S. Gentry's text-based interactive fiction *Anchorhead: An Interactive Gothic* (1998). These works use two Lovecraft storyworld mythos concepts uniquely—the loss of control that occurs when human characters encounter knowledge of the cosmic reality and the inability of any human communication to express this knowledge. These themes are exemplified in Lovecraft's short story "The Call of Cthulhu" when a group of sailors encounter Cthulhu on R'lyeh, a strange island newly risen from the sea. Immediately upon spying the Old One, two sailors perish "of pure fright" and the remaining sailors frantically try to escape (167). Cthulhu is not comprehensively portrayed because the "Thing cannot be described—there is no language for such abysms of shrieking and immemorial lunacy, such eldritch contradictions of all matter, force, and cosmic order" (165). Cthulhu's indescribability symbolizes not only that the narrative format breaks down or fragments in a suitably Gothic manner but also that language is ineffectual, and by extension the cognitive processes that have produced language are insufficient, when it comes to understanding the cosmic reality (see Leavenworth 97, 98).

As previously noted, one expression of the allure of the Lovecraft storyworld is the desire to produce aesthetically fulfilling works. The black-and-white silent film *The Call of Cthulhu*, released directly to DVD, is a result of this motivation. Coproducer and writer Sean Branney explains that "we wanted to make a movie that was a real, serious, sincere [. . .] truthful adaptation of one of Lovecraft's works"; thus he implies his belief that few such adaptations exist ("Hearing 'The Call'"). The film is faithful in a number of ways. Shot using techniques available in the 1920s—the decade that saw the original publication of "The Call of Cthulhu" and concluded major silent film production in America—it uses no color, no synchronized sound, no audible dialogue, and no computer animation (see HPLHS, "The Call of Cthulhu"). Such fidelity is logical and stylistically in keeping with Lovecraft's old-fashioned writing style, and the choice to render the story as a silent film in the twenty-first century foregrounds the viewer's loss of "control" and the narrative's inability to express cosmic knowledge. In our contemporary media ecology where color images, advanced sound technologies, and computer-generated effects are ubiquitous, the black-and-white silent film is a curio of limited expression. The viewer does not encounter the common cinematic features that drive a narrative and so most likely experiences a loss of cognitive control in the sense that he or she must interpret more from less.

The already constrained expressiveness of the film is reduced even further when the sailors find Cthulhu's home on R'lyeh. The techniques used in this sequence foster a loss of cognitive control for the viewer and symbolize a failure to communicate cosmic knowledge. While title cards that display dialogue or narration appear at regular intervals throughout the forty-seven-minute film before and after the climactic scenes on R'lyeh, they are absent throughout the approximately eight minutes it takes to depict the horrifying events on the island, despite several instances of character dialogue or exclamation. Removing the title cards in the most crucial sequence simulates a loss of control for the viewer, particularly as some of the words that the sailors shout are not easily deciphered by lip reading.

Alongside this loss of control, the film is unable to portray the full significance of the cosmic reality with its representation of Cthulhu. While Cthulhu's mountainous size, frightening form, and devastating effects on the crew are apparent, the viewer is not likely to have a fearful reaction to the Old One, as Cthulhu is rendered in clay and animated via

Fig. 15.1. Photo of Cthulhu. Courtesy H. P. Lovecraft Historical Society, ©HPLHS, Inc., 2005.

stop-motion filming techniques. This old-fashioned method creates a naive, token image of the Old One and all it represents, demonstrating the film's inability to show the "unshowable."

The tabletop role-playing game *Call of Cthulhu* (*CoC*) engages with Lovecraft's writing and other elements in the Lovecraft storyworld via a ludic, narrative-generating framework that prioritizes the hunt for cosmic knowledge. Gameplay involves social interaction between players who act to resolve a mysterious situation, usually one in which strange things occur as a prelude to encountering a supernatural phenomenon or entity, such as an Old One. Although the scenarios or adventures vary widely, the conceptual, rule-governing foundations of the game emphasize the quest for information. The characters most players control are called "investigators" because that label reflects what they spend their time doing, a practice cemented by the standardized mystery format of most published scenarios (Petersen and Willis 24, Hite 32). One player acts as the "Keeper of Arcane Lore" and leads the investigators through a scenario by describing scenes, portraying characters whom the investigators meet, and ensuring the rules are followed (Petersen and Willis 24–25). Accumulating information is such a major pastime for investigators that the rulebook provides a surprising number of recommendations for how to do it, beginning with the advice of "going to the library," continuing with the importance of visiting historical and municipal organizations, and ending, four paragraphs of further suggestions later, with a recommendation to interview relevant individuals (26). This focus on research remediates both the characters' actions in Lovecraft storyworld narratives and the explorers' hunt for knowledge.

CoC ensures that over the course of several scenarios players will eventually lose control over their characters and, as a consequence, their ability to play strategically. Scenario designer Keith Herber explains that while other role-playing games offer "tangible rewards" to encourage player participation, *CoC* play is driven by curiosity about the cosmic reality, so "[i]nvestigators usually finish adventures in worse shape than they began, with less money, less sanity, and possibly a lowered social standing" (41). As this downward spiral is most often continued in each successive adventure, investigators move toward unavoidable destruction (Hite 35). Through their failing investigators, players experience an increasing loss of control, which simulates the most common situation for characters in stories that evoke the Lovecraft storyworld.

The *CoC* rules assert the danger of cosmic knowledge through a game mechanic that, as in Lovecraft's short story, fails to communicate such knowledge. The threat to humanity's worldview is addressed by the sanity rules. Sanity represents an investigator's "flexibility and resilience to emotional trauma," and so a high number of sanity points allow an investigator to cognitively deal with horrific events whereas a low sanity level makes the investigator unreliable in threatening situations (Petersen and Willis 75). While any personal shock can cause sanity loss, several things guarantee it, and a significant drop in sanity points in a short amount of game time makes an investigator insane (76, 83). Serious shocks then produce permanent sanity loss. An extremely insane investigator illustrates the role-playing game's inability to express the ramifications of the cosmic reality. *Role-playing* is a combination of playing and acting. A player with a permanently insane investigator is very limited in terms of play (i.e., his or her investigator is strategically ineffective as a game agent) but may act out the investigator's instabilities. Unlike other situations in which the keeper may provide narrative support for an investigator's personal experience, the rulebook makes it clear that players are to interpret madness as they see fit (84–86). In this sense, the player occupies a similar position to that of the Lovecraft reader who must creatively imagine the indescribable Cthulhu. But in role-playing such individual interpretation is part of the process; so only if a player becomes too authentic in his or her performance does the game break down. If a player tries "to act out too many elements of his investigator's insanity," it may disturb the other players, and the keeper is encouraged to "quash the interruption" (86). In other words, a player who tries to fully express the effects of cosmic knowledge has the potential to disrupt the game. Like Lovecraft's narrative, *CoC* is symbolically unable to communicate the ramifications of contact with the cosmic reality.

The interactive fiction (IF) *Anchorhead* encapsulates many Lovecraft storyworld themes and has been praised for being "consistently both scary and playable" (Stevens n. pag.).[8] As with most contemporary IFs, *Anchorhead* is wholly text based and proceeds in alternating steps of textual output from the software (describing a location, event, character, and so forth) and short commands input by the player (such as "take key," "examine book," "talk to Michael"). The player's commands govern the player character, a focalizing agent that the player uses to investigate the town of Anchorhead. A typical exchange follows, with the player character addressed via the second person "you" in descriptions and with player commands written in capitals after the prompt (>):

> Study
>
> This smaller room adjoining the library seems comfortable enough, although it is dusty and cluttered from having not been lived in for the better part of a year. Aside from the desk and the chair and the empty shelves, the only real feature of the room is the large, ornate fireplace in the southern wall. [. . .]
>
> `>LOOK AT FIREPLACE`
>
> The fireplace is carved from beautiful, dark-veined marble, a strange shade that is not quite a deep, forest green and not quite a murky, dusty red. The mantelpiece is flanked by a pair of polished brass spheres.

>EXAMINE SPHERE

You see the room behind you in distorted miniature, and your own face swelling and stretching comically as you peer into the sphere's reflective surface.

Looking closely, you notice some smudges on the otherwise immaculately polished brass.

>TURN SPHERE

The sphere twists clockwise a few degrees, there is a barely audible "click", and the sphere snaps back into its original position. Suddenly, the entire fireplace slides about eighteen inches to the left with a hollow grinding sound, revealing a narrow corridor in the southwest wall.[9]

As this progression demonstrates, play involves reading textual output carefully for clues as to what to interact with, and as there is no time limit for inputting commands, the player may spend time considering the details both within the context of an exchange and in the wider context of other elements encountered in the IF. In *Anchorhead*, the female player character has recently moved to the New England town of Anchorhead with her husband, Michael, in order to inherit the estate of a distant, mysterious branch of Michael's family. While exploring the town, the player learns of and must deal with many strange and sinister clues, revelations, and events involving Michael's family and the citizenry.

In situations where the player character is indirectly threatened by some aspect of the cosmic reality, her depicted loss of control is simulated for the player. For example, at one point the character discovers an old slaughterhouse. The ground inside the slaughterhouse is covered in strange footprints, a child's drawing is found depicting what is described as "[a]n octopus on human legs, maybe," and the dried-up well next to the slaughterhouse is found to be knee-deep in children's bones (Crumbled Ruin, In the Well).[10] When the player directs the player character to leave this gruesome area by backtracking the way she came, this action prompts the following: "You are about to step back through the eastern wall when a noise makes you stop. In the woods outside, to the east—something is there. Something breathing. Something huge. [. . .] A branch cracks sharply; and another. It's coming this way" (Crumbled

Ruin). With each successive command the software produces a more frantic description of the thing's approach. Since the player does not know how quickly the creature will arrive, each command suddenly takes on immense importance as an integral step in keeping the player character from harm.[11] As this scenario occurs late in the IF and the player has not previously experienced a direct correlation between individual commands and timed events in the game, the surprise and stress of the player character's situation are simulated for the player.

The player's loss of control is even greater when the player character directly encounters an unspeakable being. The way this confrontation is enacted also indicates the IF's inability to convey the epistemological rupture of cosmic knowledge. In the previous scenario, the player may hide the player character under the pile of children's bones in the well. Once the player enters the final allowable command, something unusual happens to the software interface. The typical procedure is that commands are input and text is output at the bottom of the screen, creating a script of the player character's actions that scrolls up the screen. When the creature reaches the well, however, the player's final command unexpectedly shoots to the top of the interface, producing an empty screen, absent of the record of events. Without this record the brief output text below the player's last command becomes the only event that matters, particularly as it describes the player character's encounter with an unspeakable being: "[T]he circle of light above you is blotted out by a shape so utterly, blasphemously hideous that it is all you can do to remain conscious. Two grotesquely blue and childlike eyes blink down into the darkness of the well, searching . . ." (In the Well). At this point the player cannot enter a command but may only press a key to move on to the next screen, a reduction in agency from player to reader. Pressing a key produces a new blank screen, but the output text is once again down at the bottom and followed by the command prompt, signaling a return to normal operating procedure. The player character has "lost consciousness" for a while, and the creature is gone (In the Well). These blank screens reflect the player character's unconscious state, and this loss of agency is simulated for the player via the loss of text and an inability to enter a command. Blank screens also gesture toward the media form's inability to portray an interaction with a cosmic horror beyond human understanding.

I have previously argued that affecting the player's illusion of control is central to the development of Gothic effects in interactive fictions such as *Anchorhead* (see Leavenworth 183–85). While this claim is arguably generalizable when it comes to horror games, the works investigated here demonstrate the broad adaptability of this conceit.[12] Together, the illusion of control and the failure to express cosmic knowledge in these Lovecraft storyworld works indicate the value of media limitations, rather than allowances, when bringing together mythos content and form for explorers.

Canonization

The most explicit indication of Lovecraft's changed status from xenophobic pulp writer to literary author are the recently published scholarly editions of his writings. Examples of these include 2000's *Tales of H. P. Lovecraft*, with an introduction by Joyce Carol Oates; three Penguin Classics anthologies of his prose fiction, edited by S. T. Joshi (1999, 2001, 2004); and a 2005 Library of America volume that establishes the author as a peer to Gothic writers such as Edgar Allan Poe and Shirley Jackson. The extent to which Lovecraft's reputation has changed among scholars, the general public, and publishers begs the question: what has happened to bring about this change? In providing a plausible answer to this question, I illuminate the potential cultural impact of storyworlds in the twenty-first century. The author's canonization is owing to an interplay between trends in contemporary scholarship and the cultural capital generated by the Lovecraft storyworld.

In the last few decades a number of shifts have occurred in literary studies and related analytical fields that have enabled fresh perspectives on Lovecraft's fiction. Cultural studies, media studies, and several sociopolitical critical perspectives have led to a revaluing of popular culture artifacts (i.e., texts, games, films, and such). One result, visible at the level of genre, is that the Gothic has now been established as a significant space for the interplay of cultural meanings. The formulaic, essentialist analyses carried out on Gothic fiction several decades ago have given way to criticism sensitive to "how the idea of the human is constituted historically and ideologically" and how the portrayal of figures excluded from "dominant cultural discourses" allows for a reconsideration of the institutions that support prevailing values (Botting and

Townshend 15–16). Freed from previous critical disdain, Lovecraft's fiction may now be examined in sophisticated ways as part of the American Gothic tradition. He is seen to have evolved the grotesque, hybrid beings of fin de siècle British Gothic in a new pulp form (see Hurley 137–39, 142; Luckhurst xv, xxxi). His conception of cosmic fear has been linked to Julia Kristeva's notion of self-abjection (see Ralickas 388–91) and to Edmund Burke's and Immanuel Kant's conceptions of the sublime (see Nelson; Will; Leavenworth 82–83). His writing has also been employed as a means of exploring Gilles Deleuze and Félix Guattari's philosophy of becoming (see MacCormack). These examples suggest that Lovecraft studies are on the rise and helping to cement his place in the canon.

At the same time, the author's legacy is gaining popular cultural value via the Lovecraft storyworld. Works that evoke it typically reference Lovecraft's name, so that it functions similar to a brand name and initiates in the knowledgeable "customer" a set of expectations and associations that influence a desire for the product. This familiar stamp signals the promise of fulfilling what Oates refers to as the "tacit contract" between consumers of genre fiction and the producer, a contract where consumers expect familiar formulas but appreciate experiencing them in new and unique ways (xiii). In short, Lovecraft's name takes on what Pierre Bourdieu describes as "cultural capital" (243). In his investigation of the circulation of cultural value surrounding prize-winning literature, James F. English notes that for Bourdieu, capital "is not merely understood in its narrow economic sense [. . .] but rather is used to designate anything that registers as an asset, and can be put profitably to work, in one or another domain of human endeavor" (9). An object's capital (its value and meaning) is specific to particular groups and changes in accordance with the fluctuating "terms of valuation and exchange" generated by the interaction of group members (9; see Bourdieu 247). Thus, among Lovecraft storyworld explorers the name "Lovecraft" on a work signals the promise of familiar enjoyment and investment, among occult practitioners the name is linked to spiritual enlightenment, and among fans of the historical romance the name may not signal any capital at all. However, the growth of the Lovecraft storyworld ensures that the Lovecraft brand is increasingly likely to represent some form of capital for the general public because ubiquity is linked to the creation of cultural meaning. According to Stefan Dziemianowicz, the Lovecraft legacy will become evident to "a younger generation raised on graphic novels, manga, computer games, YouTube clips, and Twitter feeds" because they will encounter mythos ideas there that may foster a lasting interest (20). Lovecraft's canonization may explicitly be due to his significant literary achievements, both as an author and as an influence on countless other authors, but the Lovecraft storyworld has undoubtedly played a part in this process by demonstrating the lasting popular relevance of his ideas.

In a contemporary media ecology where authorized transmedial production is increasingly becoming the creative (and marketable) norm, the Lovecraft storyworld stands out as a culturally important example of unauthorized, denarrativized storyworld development. Evoked by a variety of different media forms, the Lovecraft storyworld embodies a model of the shared participatory wisdom implicit in contemporary paradigms of information flow, knowledge use, and convergence. The Lovecraft storyworld's allure, transmedial adaptability, and cultural impact assert the value of organic and thematic storyworld growth for contemporary audiences and producers.

Notes

1. The collective consumption and shared knowledge inherent to storyworld development is emphasized in Jenkins's conception of how audiences respond to transmedia storytelling (3–4), a phenomenon that is distinct from storyworld engagement but shares certain aspects with it.
2. Although a few returning human characters exist, most are forgettable and merely symbolize humanity.
3. Throughout this chapter I use the term "mythos" in this manner and not to refer to the "Cthulhu Mythos," a problematic term that may be defined in several ways. For an overview of debates surrounding the Cthulhu Mythos, see Joshi (129). Alternate conceptions of the term have been suggested by Smith (25–26) and Lowell (47).
4. To avoid privileging any one media form I use the term "explorer" to denote the player, reader, viewer, participant, user, audience member, and others who engage with any work that evokes the storyworld.
5. Evans also considers Lovecraft's influence on occult thinking in *The History of British Magic after Crowley*.
6. Both details are the creations of August Derleth, Lovecraft's literary executor.
7. This endeavor is not unique to storyworlds. Thorne and Bruner describe the

investment-expertise development as typical of devoted fans in many knowledge spheres: fiction, sports, music, and so on (58).

8. My arguments pertaining to *Anchorhead* derive partly from the second chapter of my doctoral dissertation, *The Gothic in Contemporary Interactive Fictions*.
9. Since there is no fixed sequence of events in much of the interactive fiction, rooms where particular exchanges occur are the primary means of referencing play. Room names, like the Study, will thus be used to provide specific information in *Anchorhead*.
10. Rooms may be indoor or outdoor locations.
11. Replaying the scene indicates that four commands are allowed before the creature finds the player character.
12. See Krzywinska's similar arguments about visual computer games in the horror genre (216–17) or Ryan's discussion of how "taking control away from the user" may be used to create suspense in a game that provides narrative immersion (55).

Works Cited

Abbott, H. Porter. "Story, Plot and Narration." *The Cambridge Companion to Narrative*. Ed. David Herman. Cambridge, UK: Cambridge University Press, 2007. 39–51. Print.

Bolton, K. R. "The Influence of H. P. Lovecraft on Occultism." *The Irish Journal of Gothic and Horror Studies* 9 (2011): n. pag. Web. January 4, 2012.

Botting, Fred, and Dale Townshend. General Introduction. *Gothic: Critical Concepts in Literary and Cultural Studies*. Ed. Fred Botting and Dale Townshend. Vol. 1. London: Routledge, 2004. 1–18. Print.

Bourdieu, Pierre. "The Forms of Capital." *Handbook of Theory and Research for the Sociology of Education*. Ed. J. G. Richardson, trans. Richard Nice. Westport CT: Greenwood Press, 1986. 241–58. Print.

The Call of Cthulhu: The Celebrated Story by H. P. Lovecraft. Screenplay by Sean Branney. Dir. Andrew Leman. HPLHS, Inc., 2005. DVD.

Carroll, Noël. *The Philosophy of Horror or Paradoxes of the Heart*. London: Routledge, 1990. Print.

Dziemianowicz, Stefan. "Terror Eternal: The Enduring Popularity of H. P. Lovecraft." *Publishers Weekly* July 12, 2010: 19–22. Print.

English, James F. *The Economy of Prestige: Prizes, Awards, and the Circulation of Cultural Value*. London: Harvard University Press, 2005. Print.

Evans, Dave. *The History of British Magic after Crowley: Kenneth Grant, Amado Crowley, Chaos Magic, Satanism, Lovecraft, the Left Hand Path, Blasphemy and Magical Morality*. Hertfordshire, UK: Hidden Publishing, 2007. Print.

Gentry, Michael S. *Anchorhead: An Interactive Gothic*. Vers. 5. 1998. *The Interactive Fiction Archive*. N.p., May 2011. Web. January 4, 2012.

"Hearing 'The Call.'" *The Call of Cthulhu: The Celebrated Story by H. P. Lovecraft*. Screenplay by Sean Branney. Dir. Andrew Leman. HPLHS, Inc., 2005. DVD.

Herber, Keith. "On 'The Haunted House.'" *Second Person: Role-Playing and Story in Games and Playable Media*. Ed. Pat Harrigan and Noah Wardrip-Fruin. Cambridge MA: MIT Press, 2007. 41–43. Print.

Herman, David. "The Scope and Aims of *Storyworlds*." *Storyworlds: A Journal of Narrative Studies* 1 (2009): vii–x. Print.

Hite, Kenneth. "Narrative Structure and Creative Tension in *Call of Cthulhu*." *Second Person: Role-Playing and Story in Games and Playable Media*. Ed. Pat Harrigan and Noah Wardrip-Fruin. Cambridge MA: MIT Press, 2007. 31–40. Print.

The H. P. Lovecraft Historical Society (HPLHS). "The Call of Cthulhu—an HPLHS Motion Picture." *The H. P. Lovecraft Historical Society*. HPLHS, Inc., June 2011. Web. January 4, 2012.

"H. P. Lovecraft (1890–1937): Writer." *The Internet Movie Database*. *IMDb.com*, n. d. Web. January 4, 2012.

Hurley, Kelly. "Abject and Grotesque." *The Routledge Companion to Gothic*. Ed. Catherine Spooner and Emma McEvoy. London: Routledge, 2007. 137–46. Print.

Iser, Wolfgang. *The Implied Reader: Patterns of Communication in Prose Fiction from Bunyan to Beckett*. Baltimore MD: Johns Hopkins University Press, 1974. Print.

Jenkins, Henry. *Convergence Culture: Where Old and New Media Collide*. New York: New York University Press, 2006. Print.

Joshi, S. T. *A Subtler Magick: The Writings and Philosophy of H. P. Lovecraft*. Berkeley Heights NJ: Wildside, 1999. Print.

Klastrup, Lisbeth, and Susana Tosca. "Transmedial Worlds—Rethinking Cyberworld Design." *Proceedings of the 2004 International Conference on Cyberworlds*. Los Alamitos CA: IEEEE Computer Society, 2004. N. pag. PDF file. June 1, 2012.

Krzywinska, Tanya. "Hands-on Horror." *ScreenPlay: Cinema/Videogames/Interfaces*. Ed. Geoff King and Tanya Kryzwinska. London: Wallflower Press, 2002. 206–23. Print.

Kukkonen, Karin. "Navigating Infinite Earths: Readers, Mental Models, and the Multiverse of Superhero Comics." *Storyworlds* 2 (2010): 39–58. Print.

Leavenworth, Van. *The Gothic in Contemporary Interactive Fictions*. Diss. Umeå University, 2010. Umeå, Sweden: Print & Media, 2010. Print.

Lovecraft, H. P. "The Call of Cthulhu." *The Call of Cthulhu and Other Weird Stories*. Ed. S. T. Joshi. London: Penguin, 1999. 139–69. Print.

———. *The Dreams in the Witch House and Other Weird Stories*. Ed. S. T. Joshi. London: Penguin, 2004. Print.

———. "The Festival." *The Call of Cthulhu and Other Weird Stories*. Ed. S. T. Joshi. London: Penguin, 1999. 109–18. Print.

———. *H. P. Lovecraft: Tales.* Ed. Peter Straub. New York: Library of America, 2005. Print.
———. "Supernatural Horror in Literature." *H. P. Lovecraft Omnibus 2: Dagon and Other Macabre Tales.* London: Voyager, 2000. 421–512. Print.
———. *The Thing on the Doorstep and Other Weird Stories.* Ed. S. T. Joshi. London: Penguin, 2001. Print.
———. "The Whisperer in Darkness." *The Call of Cthulhu and Other Weird Stories.* Ed. S. T. Joshi. London: Penguin, 1999. 200–267. Print.
Lowell, Mark. "Lovecraft's CTHULHU MYTHOS." *Explicator* 63.1 (2004): 47–50. Print.
Luckhurst, Roger. Introduction. *Late Victorian Gothic Tales.* Ed. Roger Luckhurst. Oxford, UK: Oxford University Press, 2009. ix–xxxi. Print.
MacCormack, Patricia. "Lovecraft through Deleuzio-Guattarian Gates." *Postmodern Culture* 20.2 (2010): n. pag. Web. January 4, 2012.
Nelson, Dale J. "Lovecraft and the Burkean Sublime." *Lovecraft Studies* 24 (1991): 2–5. Print.
Oates, Joyce Carol. Introduction. *Tales of H. P. Lovecraft.* By H. P. Lovecraft. Ed. Joyce Carol Oates. New York: Harper Collins, 2000. vii–xvi. Print.
Petersen, Sandy, and Lynn Willis. *Call of Cthulhu: Horror Roleplaying in the Worlds of H. P. Lovecraft.* 6th ed. Haywood CA: Chaosium, 2005. Print.
Price, Robert M. "With Strange Aeons: H. P. Lovecraft's Cthulhu Mythos as One Vast Narrative." *Third Person: Authoring and Exploring Vast Narratives.* Ed. Pat Harrigan and Noah Wardrip-Fruin. Cambridge MA: MIT Press, 2009. 225–42. Print.
Ralickas, Vivian. "'Cosmic Horror' and the Question of the Sublime in Lovecraft." *Journal of the Fantastic in the Arts* 18.3 (2007): 364–98. Print.
Ryan, Marie-Laure. "From Narrative Games to Playable Stories: Toward a Poetics of Interactive Narrative." *Storyworlds* 1 (2009): 43–59. Print.
Smith, Don G. *H. P. Lovecraft in Popular Culture: The Works and Their Adaptations in Film, Television, Comics, Music and Games.* Jefferson NC: McFarland, 2006. Print.
Stevens, Duncan. Rev. of *Anchorhead,* by Michael S. Gentry. SPAG: *The Society for the Promotion of Adventure Games.* September 1999. N. pag. Web. January 4, 2012.
Thorne, Scott, and Gordon C. Bruner. "An Exploratory Investigation of the Characteristics of Consumer Fanaticism." *Qualitative Market Research: An International Journal* 9.1 (2006): 51–72. Print.
Will, Bradley A. "H. P. Lovecraft and the Semiotic Kantian Sublime." *Extrapolation* 43.1 (2002): 9–21. Print.

Contributors

Marco Caracciolo is a postdoctoral researcher at the Arts, Culture, and Media Department of the University of Groningen in the Netherlands. While working on his dissertation in comparative literature at the University of Bologna, he was also a visiting scholar at the Ohio State University (Project Narrative) and at the University of Hamburg (Interdisciplinary Center for Narratology). He is mainly interested in cognitive approaches to literature and in literary aesthetics. His work has been published in journals such as *Poetics Today*, *Storyworlds*, *Phenomenology and the Cognitive Sciences*, and *Partial Answers*. He has also coauthored (with Marco Bernini) an introduction to cognitive literary studies in Italian (Carocci, 2013). Caracciolo's book-length study of how literary texts figure the quality or texture of conscious experience is currently under review for De Gruyter.

Jared Gardner is a professor of English and film at the Ohio State University, where he also directs the Popular Culture Studies Program. He is the author most recently of *Projections: Comics and the History of Twenty-First-Century Storytelling* (Stanford University Press, 2011) and *The Rise and Fall of Early American Magazine Culture* (University of Illinois Press, 2012), and is coeditor of the ongoing complete collection of Percy Crosby's *Skippy* for the Library of American Comics.

Wolfgang Hallet is a professor for teaching English as a foreign language, a member of the executive board of the International Graduate Centre for the Study of Culture (GCSC), and head of its Teaching Centre at Justus Liebig University, Giessen, Germany. He is coeditor of a series of handbooks on teaching literature and culture: the Giessen Contributions to Foreign Language Research (Narr), the Giessen Contributions to the Study of Culture (WVT), and Concepts for the Study of Culture (De Gruyter). His research and publications, including several monographs, cover studies of culture-based theories of teaching literature and culture, cognition and literature, the methodology of the contextualization of literary texts, contemporary novels, and narratology.

Colin B. Harvey is a fiction writer, narrative designer, and academic specializing in shared storyworlds, licensed fiction, and transmedia storytelling. Harvey is the author of *Dead Kelly*, set in the Afterblight shared world and published by Abaddon Books (forthcoming). He also wrote *Love and Hate*, a *Highlander* audio book starring Adrian Paul and produced by the British company Big Finish under license from MGM and Davis-Panzer. He contributed to Big Finish's official *Doctor Who* line, published under license from the BBC, and won the inaugural Pulp Idol award, jointly conferred by *SFX* magazine and Gollancz Publishing. He has written numerous video game story design documents for Sony. His academic writing uses memory theory to analyze his own creative writing, Neil Gaiman's comics, the BBC's *Sherlock*, *The Green Hornet* comic, *Doctor Who*, and *Battlestar Galactica*. Harvey authored *Grand Theft Auto: Motion-Emotion* (Ludologica, 2005) and is currently writing *Understanding Transmedia Storytelling: Fantasy, Memory, Play* for Palgrave Macmillan. He is an adjunct associate professor at the University of Western Sydney but is based in London.

Patrick Colm Hogan is a professor of English in the Department of English at the University of Connecticut, where he is also on the faculties of the Program in Cognitive Science, the Program in Comparative Literature and Cultural Studies, and the Program in India Studies. He is the author of sixteen books, including *How Authors' Minds Make Stories* (Cambridge University Press, 2013) and *Ulysses and the Poetics of Cognition* (Routledge, forthcoming). *Conversations on Cognitive Cultural Studies*, a series of discussions between Hogan and Frederick Aldama, is also forthcoming in 2014 (Ohio State University Press).

Jesper Juul has been working with the development of video game theory since the late 1990s. He is an associate professor at the Danish Design School but has previously worked at the New York University Game Center, the Singapore–Massachusetts Institute of Technology (MIT) GAMBIT Lab at MIT, and at the IT-University in Copenhagen. His books include *Half-Real: Video Games between Real Rules and Fictional Worlds* on video game theory (MIT Press, 2005) and *The Art of Failure: An Essay on the Pain of Playing Video Games* (MIT Press, 2013). He maintains the blog *The Ludologist* on "game research and other important things." For more information, see his webpage, http://www.jesperjuul.net.

Lisbeth Klastrup is an associate professor at the IT-University in Copenhagen and leader of the Digital Culture Research Group there. Klastrup studies the interplay between design, sociality, and content production online and the mundane and professional uses of social media formats such as Facebook, Twitter, YouTube, and weblogs, including looking at the relation between these media forms and other media platforms. Her research interests also encompass digital storytelling and the study of game worlds as worlds. She has published several articles and papers on all these subjects and is coeditor of the *International Handbook of Internet Research* (Springer, 2010). She is currently working on a book on social network sites.

Maria Lindgren Leavenworth is a senior lecturer at the Department of Language Studies, Umeå University, Sweden. Her previous research focused on travel literature, particularly on contemporary works utilizing nineteenth-century travelogues as maps, and on images of Scandinavia in travel texts by Selina Bunbury, S. H. Kent, and Bayard Taylor. Previous publications also include articles on the intermediated moves between Virginia Woolf's *Mrs Dalloway* and Michael Cunningham's novel and Stephen Daldry's film *The Hours*, as well as on novels in the horror and science fiction genres—Dan Simmons's *The Terror* and Ursula K. Le Guin's *The Left Hand of Darkness*, respectively. Lindgren Leavenworth is currently working with fan practices, with an emphasis on fan fiction. Work in the project *FAN(G)S: Fan Fiction and the Vampire Trope*, funded by the Swedish Research Council, has resulted in numerous articles and anthology chapters, and in the monograph *Fanged Fan Fiction: Variations on "Twilight," "True Blood," and "The Vampire Diaries"* (McFarland, 2013).

Van Leavenworth is an assistant professor of English literature at the Department of Language Studies, Umeå University, Sweden. He teaches contemporary literature, cultural studies, and composition. His doctoral dissertation, *The Gothic in Contemporary Interactive Fictions* (Umeå University, 2010), explores digital mediations of literary Gothic conventions. He has published articles on science fiction, the Gothic (in diverse media forms), and conceptions of otherness in narrative storyworlds.

Jason Mittell is a professor of film and media culture and American studies at Middlebury College in Vermont. He is the author of *Genre and Television: From Cop Shows to Cartoons in American Culture* (Routledge, 2004), *Television and American Culture* (Oxford University Press, 2009), and *Complex Television: The Poetics of Contemporary Television Storytelling* (New York University Press, forthcoming), and is the coeditor of *How to Watch Television* (New York University Press, 2013). He writes the blog *Just TV*.

Marie-Laure Ryan is an independent scholar. In 2010–11 she was a Johannes Gutenberg Fellow at the Johannes Gutenberg-University of Mainz, Germany, where she researched the phenomenon of narrative distributed across various media. She is the author of *Possible Worlds, Artificial Intelligence, and Narrative Theory* (University of Indiana Press, 1991); *Narrative as Virtual Reality: Immersion and Interactivity in Literature and Electronic Media* (Johns Hopkins University Press, 2001); and *Avatars of Story* (University of Minnesota Press, 2006), and more than a hundred articles on narratology and digital media. She has also edited a number of books, among them the *Routledge Encyclopedia of Narrative Theory* (2005), together with David Herman and Manfred Jahn, and the *Johns Hopkins Guide to Digital Media* (2014) with Lori Emerson and Benjamin Robertson. Her scholarly work has earned her the Prize for Independent Scholars and the Aldo and Jeanne Scaglione Prize for Comparative Literature, both from the Modern Language Association, and she has been the recipient of Guggenheim and National Endowment for the Humanities followships.

Jan-Noël Thon is a research associate at the Department of Media Studies of the University of Tübingen, Germany. His current research interests include transmedial narratology, comics studies, film theory, game studies, sound studies, transmedial characters, and convergent media culture. He has published widely in these areas and has coedited *Computer/Spiel/Räume: Materialien zur Einführung in die Computer Game Studies* (*Computer/Game/Spaces: Introduction to Computer Game Studies* [IMK, 2007, with Klaus Bartels]); *Probleme filmischen Erzählens* (*Problems of Film Narration* [LIT, 2009, with Hannah Birr and Maike Sarah Reinerth]); *Poetik der Oberfläche: Die deutschsprachige Popliteratur der 1990er Jahre* (*Poetics of the Surface: German Pop Literature of the 1990s* [De Gruyter, 2011, with Olaf Grabienski and Till Huber]); and *From Comic Strips to Graphic Novels: Contributions to the Theory and History of Graphic Narrative* (De Gruyter, 2013, with Daniel Stein).

Jeff Thoss teaches English at the Free University of Berlin. He wrote his PhD thesis on metalepsis in popular fiction, film, and comics at the University of Graz and has given talks and published papers on topics relating to narrative theory, intermediality, popular culture, and comics studies. In addition, he collaborated with Werner Wolf and Katharina Bantleon on two collections of essays—*Metareference across Media: Theory and Case Studies* (Rodopi, 2009) and *The Metareferential Turn in Contemporary Arts and Media: Forms, Functions, Attempts at Explanation* (Rodopi, 2011). Currently, Jeff is working on his habilitation thesis, which traces media rivalry in English literary history.

Susana Tosca is an associate professor at the IT-University of Copenhagen. Her PhD thesis, a poetics of hypertext literature, was awarded the summa cum laude distinction. She has worked for many years on electronic literature, the storytelling potential of computer games, and complex reception processes, with a side interest in fan activity and the distributed aesthetic formats of the Web 2 era. Her last book is the second edition of *Understanding Videogames: The Essential Introduction* with Simon Egenfeldt-Nielsen and Jonas Heide Smith (Routledge, 2013).

Werner Wolf is a professor and chair of English and general literature at the University of Graz in Austria. His main areas of research are literary theory (aesthetic illusion, narratology, and metafiction/metareference in particular), functions of literature, eighteenth- to twenty-first-century English fiction, and intermediality studies (relations and comparisons between literature and other media, notably music and the visual arts). Besides numerous essays, reviews, and contributions to literary encyclopedias, his publications include the monographs *Ästhetische Illusion und Illusionsdurchbrechung in der Erzählkunst* (*Aesthetic Illusion and the Breaking of Illusion in Fiction* [Niemeyer, 1993]) and *The Musicalization of Fiction: A Study in the Theory and History of Intermediality* (Rodopi, 1999). Furthermore, he is the editor of *Metareference across Media: Theory and Case Studies* (Rodopi, 2009) and *The Metareferential Turn in Contemporary Arts and Media: Forms, Functions, Attempts at Explanation* (Rodopi, 2011), as well as the coeditor of various volumes in the book series Studies in Intermediality and Word and Music Studies (both published by Rodopi).

Frank Zipfel is a senior lecturer (*Akademischer Oberrat*) at the Department of Comparative Literature (Institut für Allgemeine und Vergleichende Literaturwissenschaft) of the Johannes Gutenberg-University of Mainz. His main research topics include theory of fiction, narratology, genre theory, European drama, intercultural studies, and intermedial studies. Publications include *Fiktion, Fiktivität, Fiktionalität: Analysen zur Fiktion in der Literatur und zum Fiktionsbegriff in der Literaturwissenschaft* (*Fiction, Fictivity, Fictionality: Analyses Regarding Fiction in Literature and the Concept of Fiction in Literary Criticism* [Erich Schmidt, 2001]); *Literatur@Internet* (*Literature@Internet* [Aisthesis, 2006, coedited with Axel Dunker]); *Ecriture Migrante/Migrant Writing* (Georg Olms, 2008, coedited with Danielle Dumontet); and *Tragikomödien: Kombinationsformen von Tragik und Komik im europäischen Drama des 19. und 20. Jahrhunderts* (*Tragicomedies: Combinations of the Tragic and the Comic in 19th and 20th Century European Drama* [forthcoming]). He also published numerous articles on literary theory, German modern literature, literature and digital media, and intercultural studies.

Index

IN THE FRONTIERS OF NARRATIVE SERIES:

Useful Fictions: Evolution, Anxiety, and the Origins of Literature
by Michael Austin

Stories and Minds: Cognitive Approaches to Literary Narrative
edited by Lars Bernaerts, Dirk De Geest, Luc Herman, and Bart Vervaeck

Telling Children's Stories: Narrative Theory and Children's Literature
edited by Mike Cadden

Coincidence and Counterfactuality: Plotting Time and Space in Narrative Fiction
by Hilary P. Dannenberg

The Emergence of Mind: Representations of Consciousness in Narrative Discourse in English
edited by David Herman

Story Logic: Problems and Possibilities of Narrative
by David Herman

Handbook of Narrative Analysis
by Luc Herman and Bart Vervaeck

Affective Narratology: The Emotional Structure of Stories
by Patrick Colm Hogan

Spaces of the Mind: Narrative and Community in the American West
by Elaine A. Jahner

Talk Fiction: Literature and the Talk Explosion
by Irene Kacandes

Ethos and Narrative Interpretation: The Negotiation of Values in Fiction
by Liesbeth Korthals Altes

Contemporary Comics Storytelling
by Karin Kukkonen

The Imagined Moment: Time, Narrative, and Computation
by Inderjeet Mani

Storying Domestic Violence: Constructions and Stereotypes of Abuse in the Discourse of General Practitioners
by Jarmila Mildorf

New Narratives: Stories and Storytelling in the Digital Age
edited by Ruth Page and Bronwen Thomas

Fictional Minds
by Alan Palmer

Writing at the Limit: The Novel in the New Media Ecology
by Daniel Punday

Storyworlds across Media:
Toward a Media-Conscious Narratology
edited by Marie-Laure Ryan
and Jan-Noël Thon

Narrative Beginnings:
Theories and Practices
edited by Brian Richardson

Narrative across Media:
The Languages of Storytelling
edited by Marie-Laure Ryan

Fictional Dialogue:
Speech and Conversation in the Modern and Postmodern Novel
by Bronwen Thomas